子連れ狼

LONE WOLF AND CUB

子連れ狼

story
KAZUO KOIKE

art
GOSEKI KOJIMA

DARK HORSE MANGA™

translation
DANA LEWIS

lettering & retouch
DIGITAL CHAMELEON

cover artwork
FRANK MILLER with **LYNN VARLEY**

publisher
MIKE RICHARDSON

editor
MIKE HANSEN

assistant editor
TIM ERVIN-GORE

consulting editor
TOREN SMITH for **STUDIO PROTEUS**

book design
DARIN FABRICK

art director
MARK COX

Published by Dark Horse Manga, a division of Dark Horse Comics, Inc.,
in association with MegaHouse and Koike Shoin Publishing Company., Ltd.

Dark Horse Comics, Inc.
10956 SE Main Street, Milwaukie, OR 97222
www.darkhorse.com

First edition: June 2001
ISBN: 1-56971-511-4

3 5 7 9 10 8 6 4 2

Printed in Canada

To find a comics shop in your area, call the
Comic Shop Locator Service toll-free at 1-888-266-4226

HOSTAGE
CHILD

子連れ狼

By **KAZUO KOIKE**
& GOSEKI KOJIMA

VOLUME
10

A NOTE TO READERS

Lone Wolf and Cub is famous for its carefully researched re-creation of Edo-Period Japan. To preserve the flavor of the work, we have chosen to retain many Edo-Period terms that have no direct equivalents in English. Japanese is written in a mix of Chinese ideograms and a syllabic writing system, resulting in numerous synonyms. In the glossary, you may encounter words with multiple meanings. These are words written with Chinese ideograms that are pronounced the same but carry different meanings. A Japanese reader seeing the different ideograms would know instantly which meaning it is, but these synonyms can cause confusion when Japanese is spelled out in our alphabet. *O-yurushi o* (please forgive us)!

LONE WOLF AND CUB

TABLE OF CONTENTS

the fiftieth

The Yagyū Letter

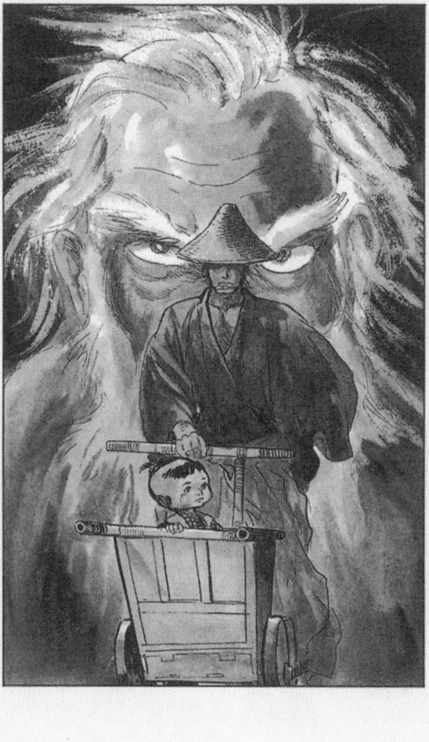

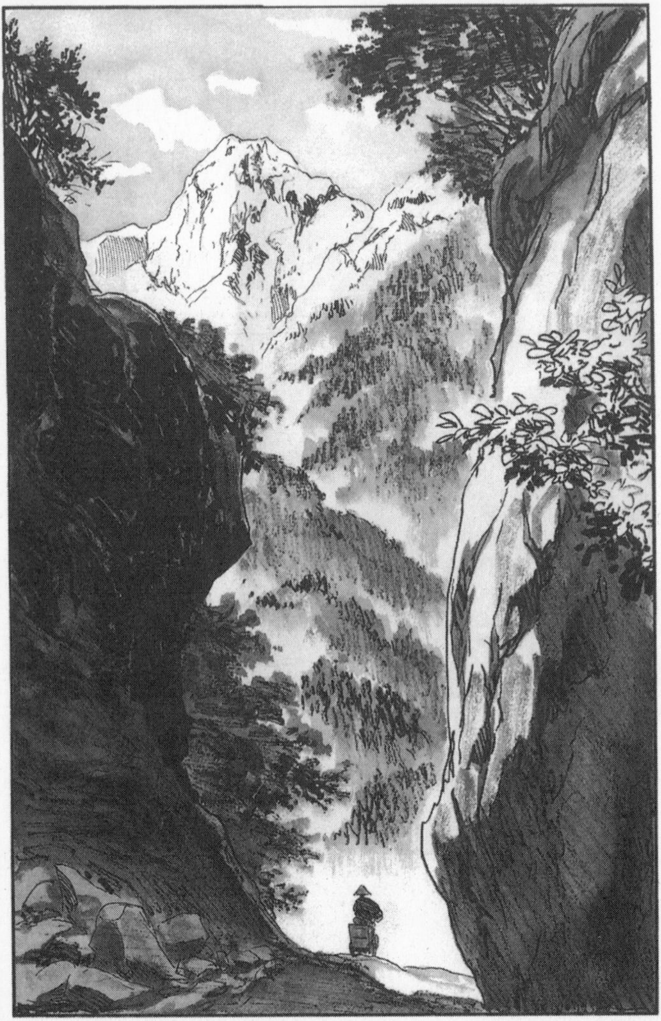

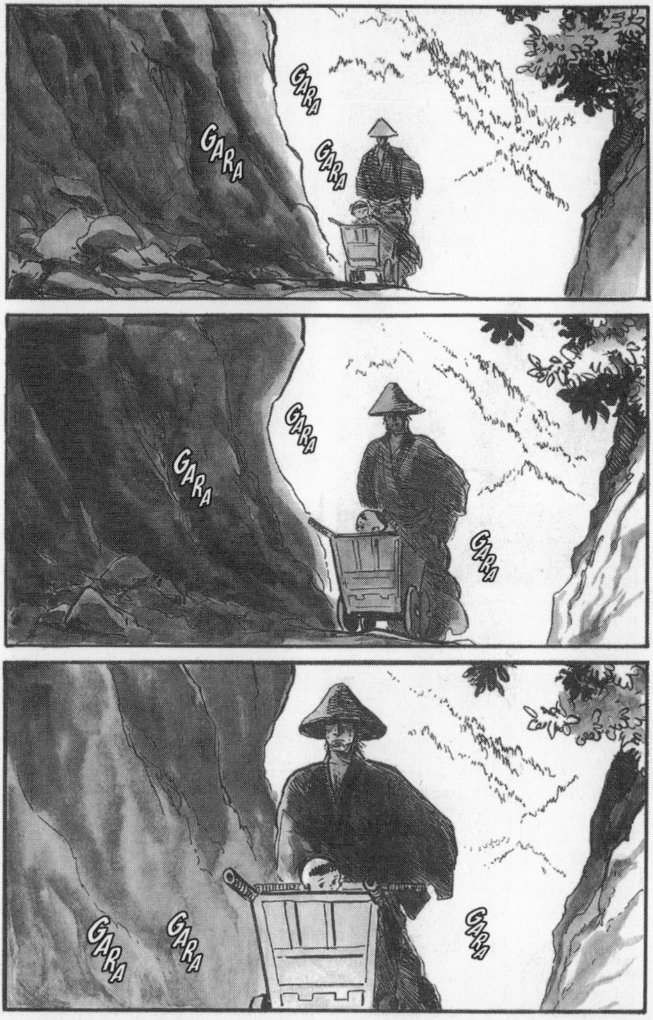
GARA
GARA
GARA
GARA
GARA
GARA
GARA
GARA
GARA

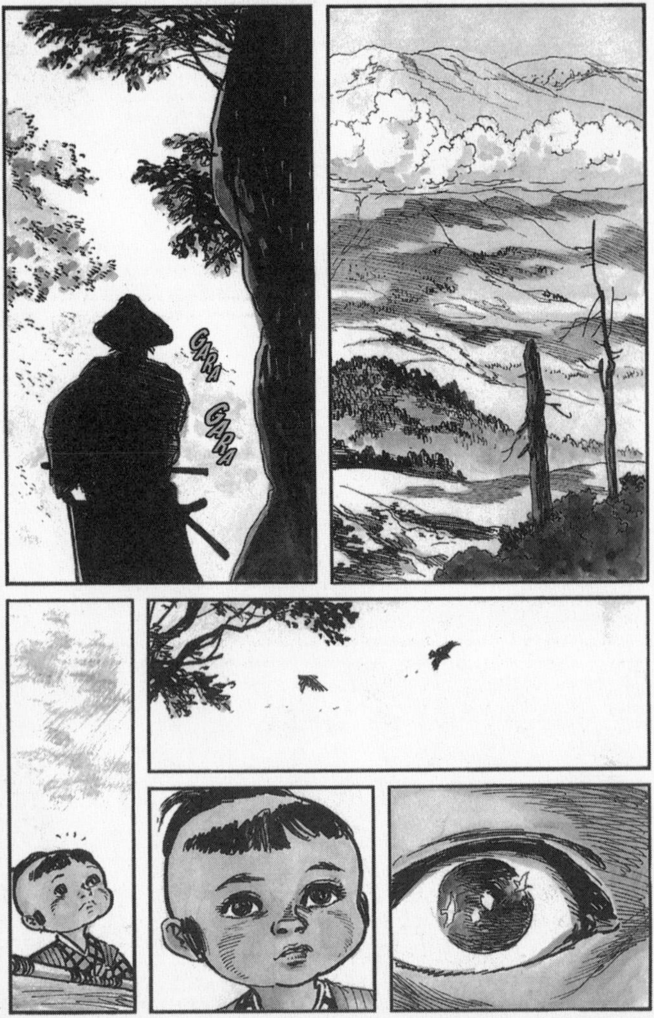
GARA
GARA

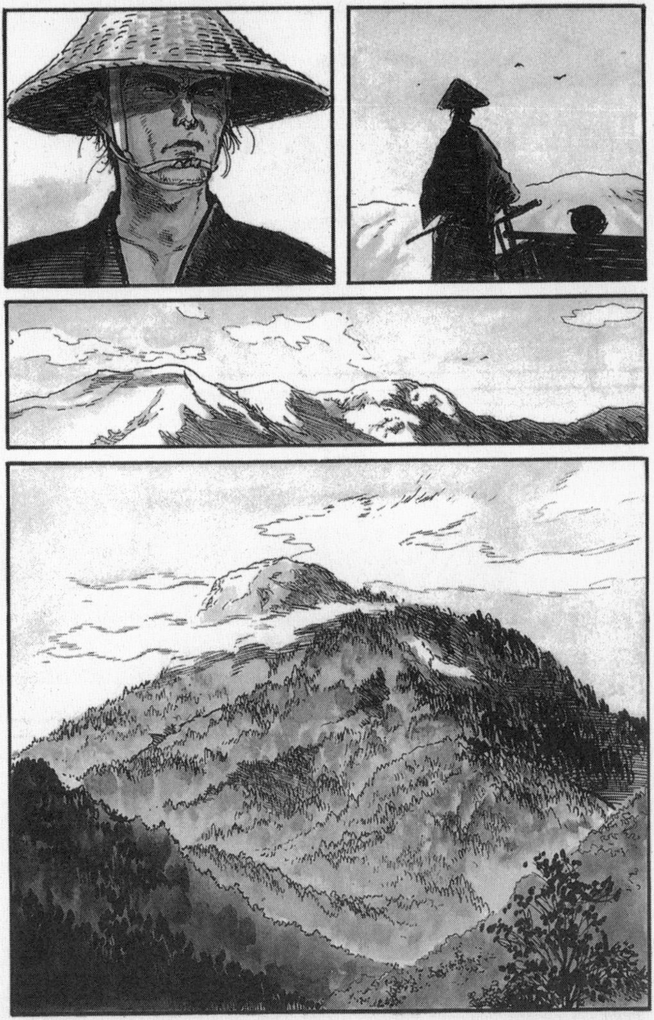

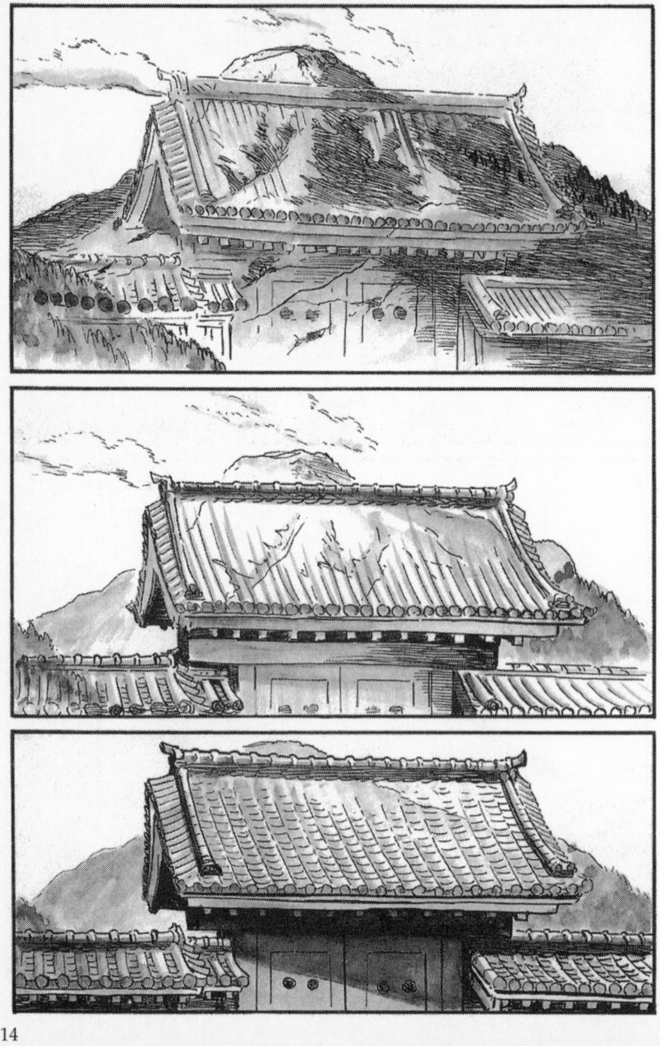

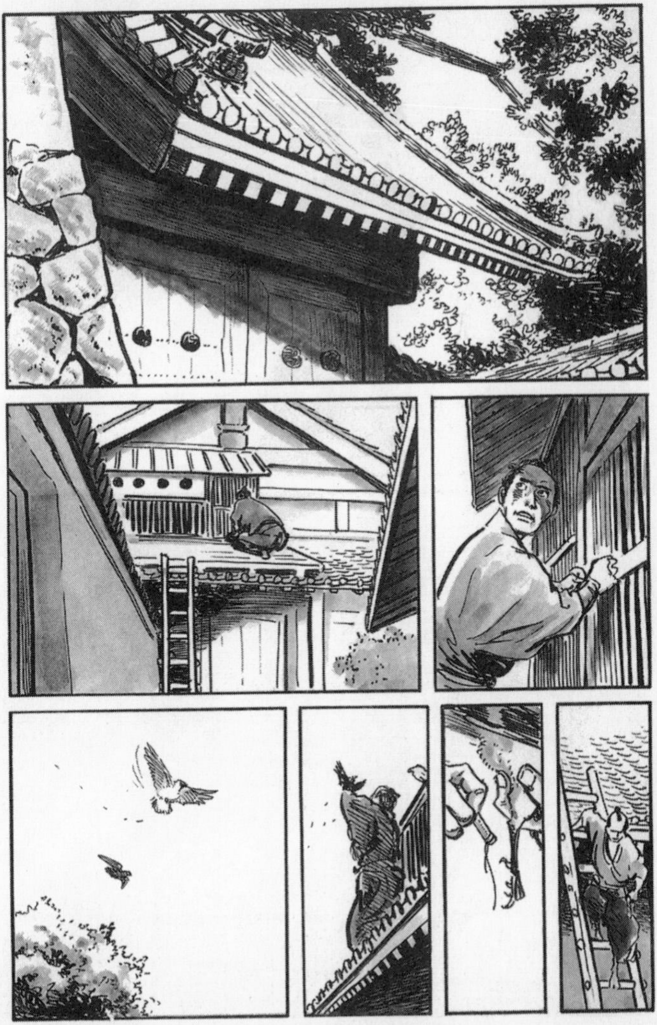

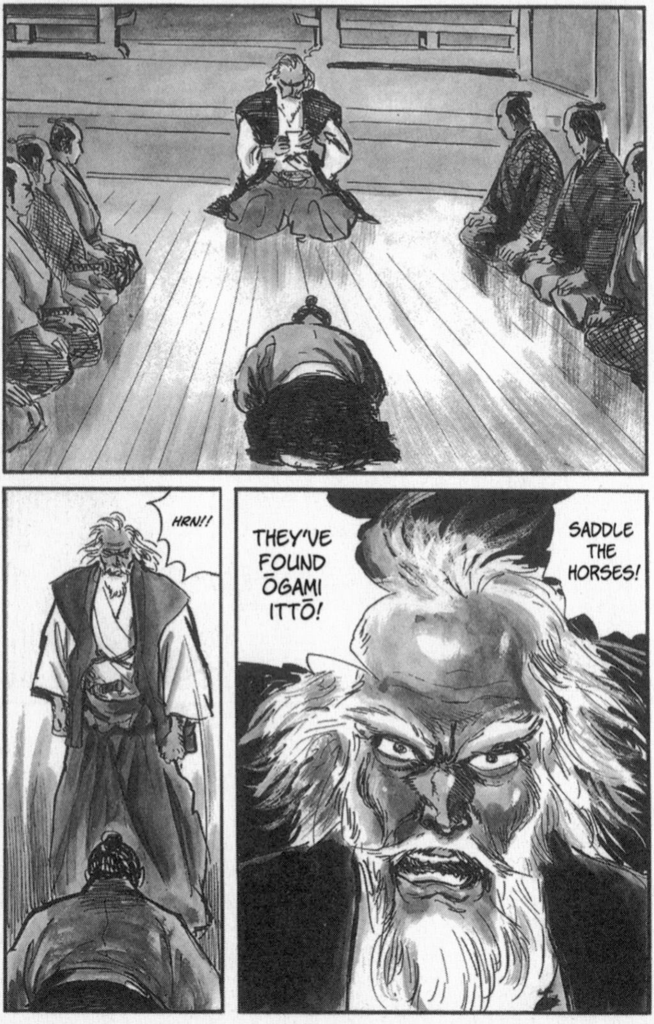
HRN!!
THEY'VE FOUND ŌGAMI ITTŌ!
SADDLE THE HORSES!

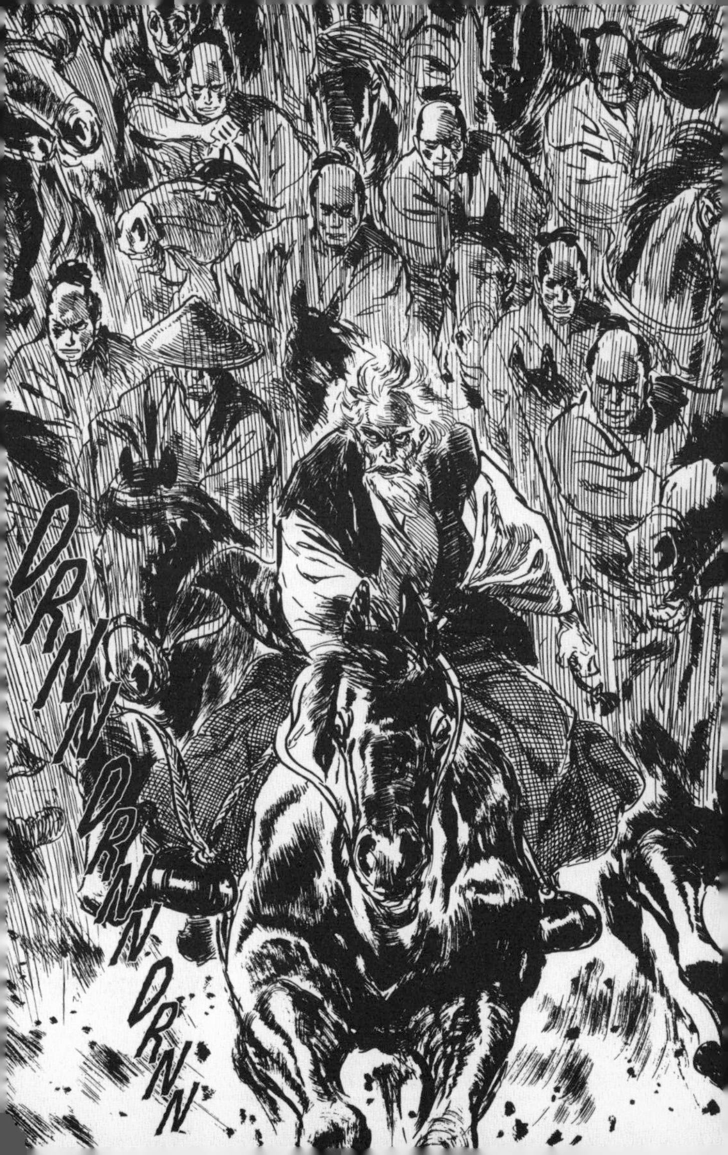
DRNN
DRNN
DRNN

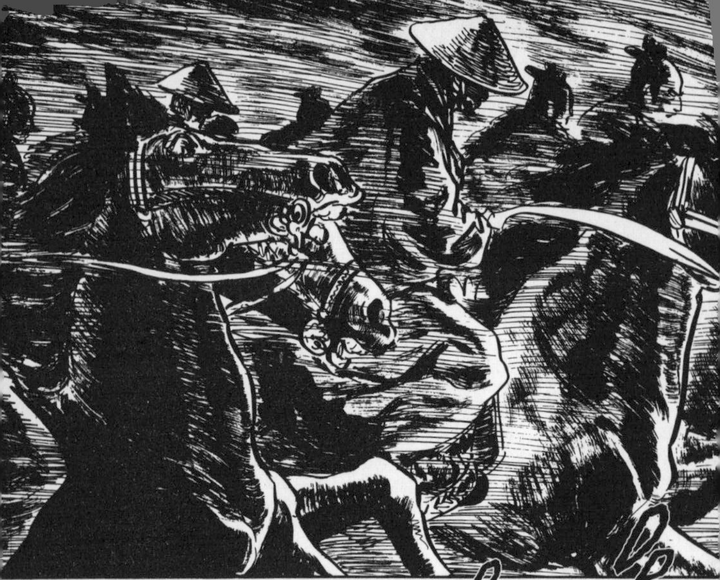
DRNN
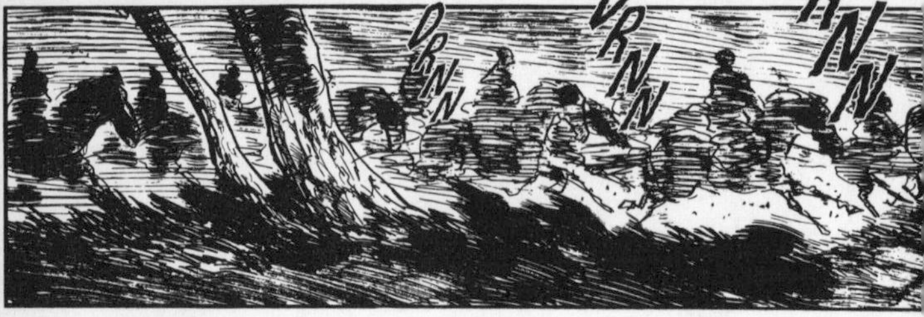
DRNN
DRNN
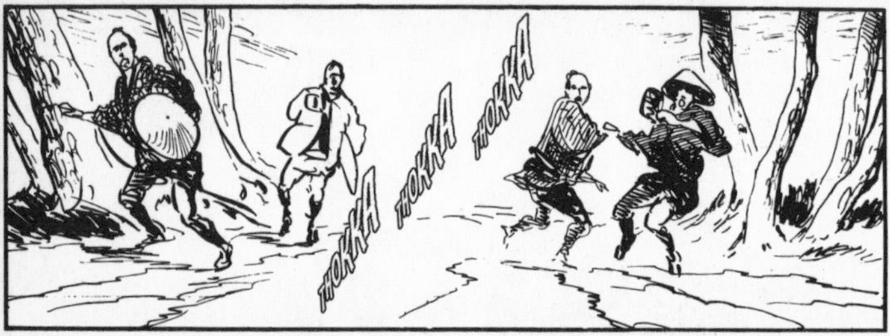
THOKKA
THOKKA
THOKKA

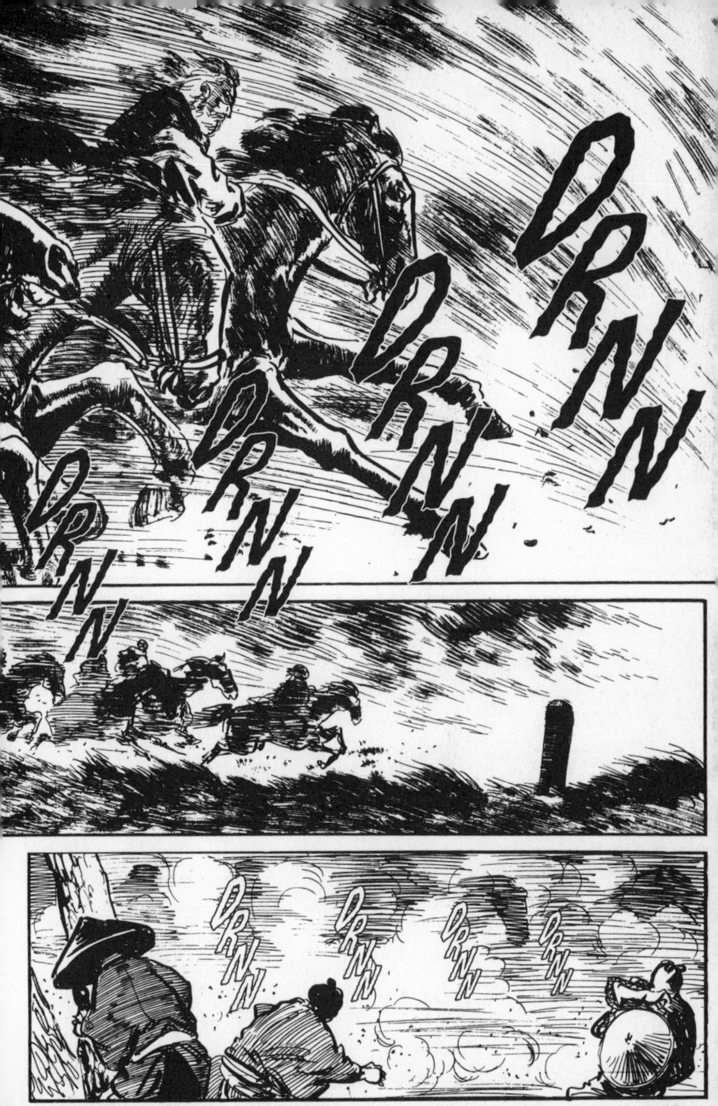
DRNN
DRNN
DRNN
DRNN
DRNN
DRNN
DRNN
DRNN

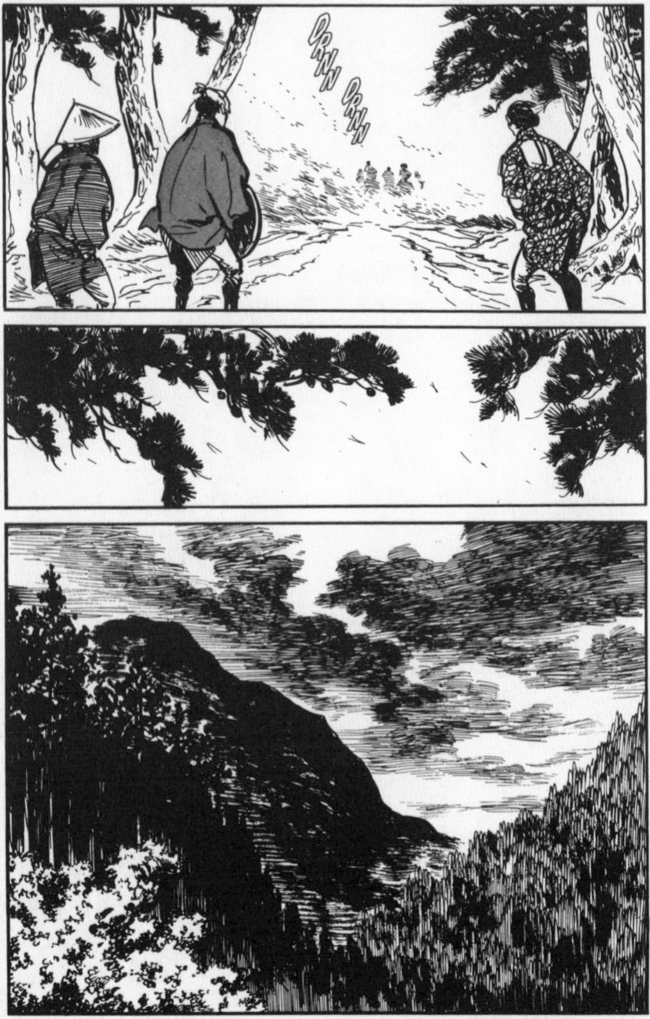
DRNN DRNN

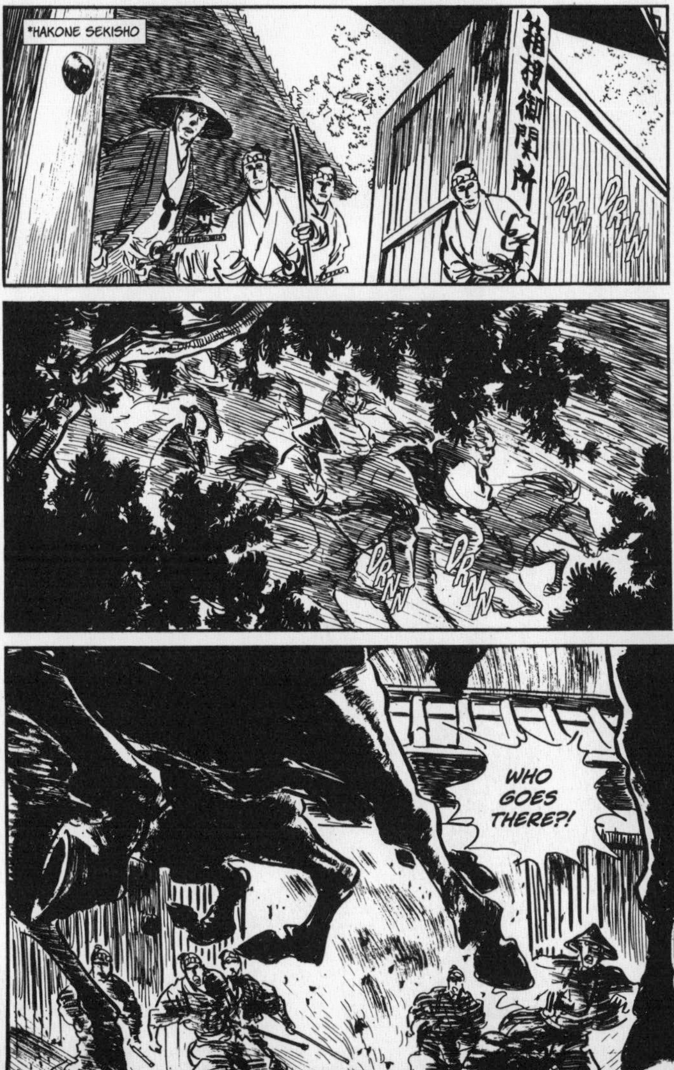
*HAKONE SEKISHO
箱根御関所
DRNN
DRNN
DRNN
DRNN
WHO GOES THERE?!

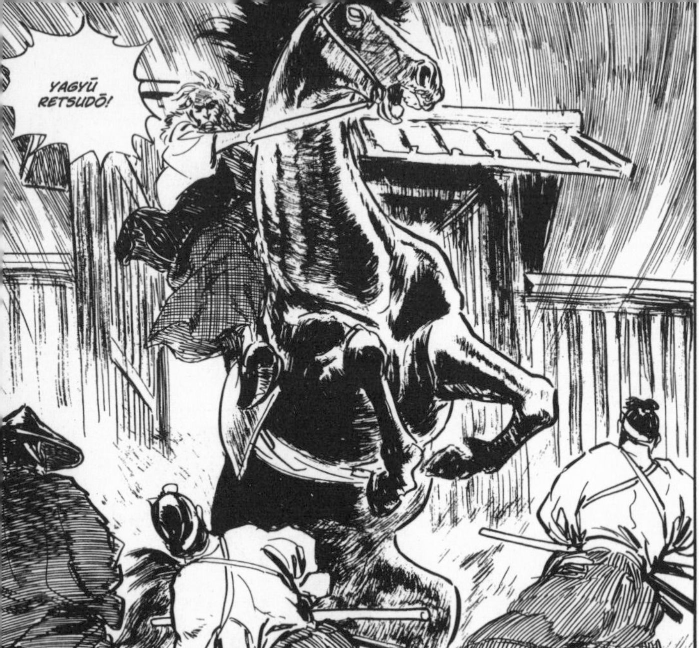
YAGYŪ RETSUDŌ!
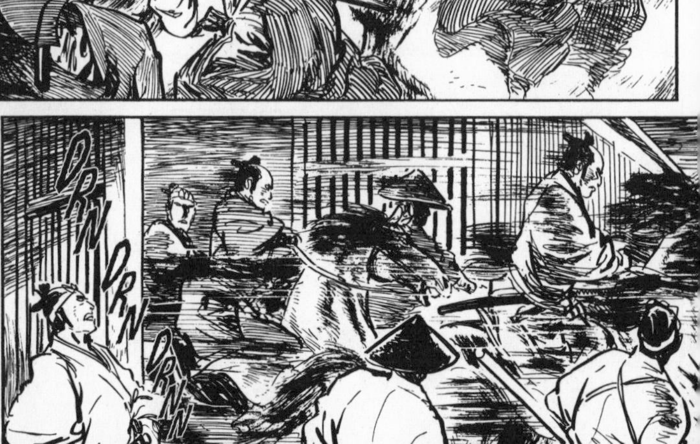
DRN DRN DRN DRNN

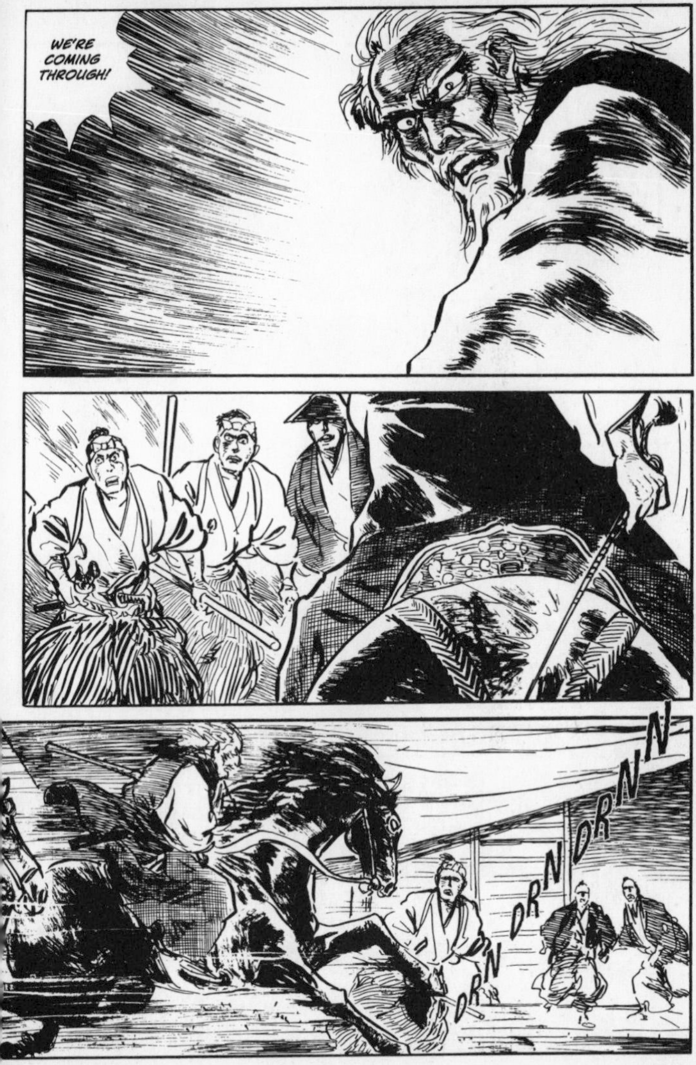
WE'RE COMING THROUGH!
DRN DRN DRN DRNNN

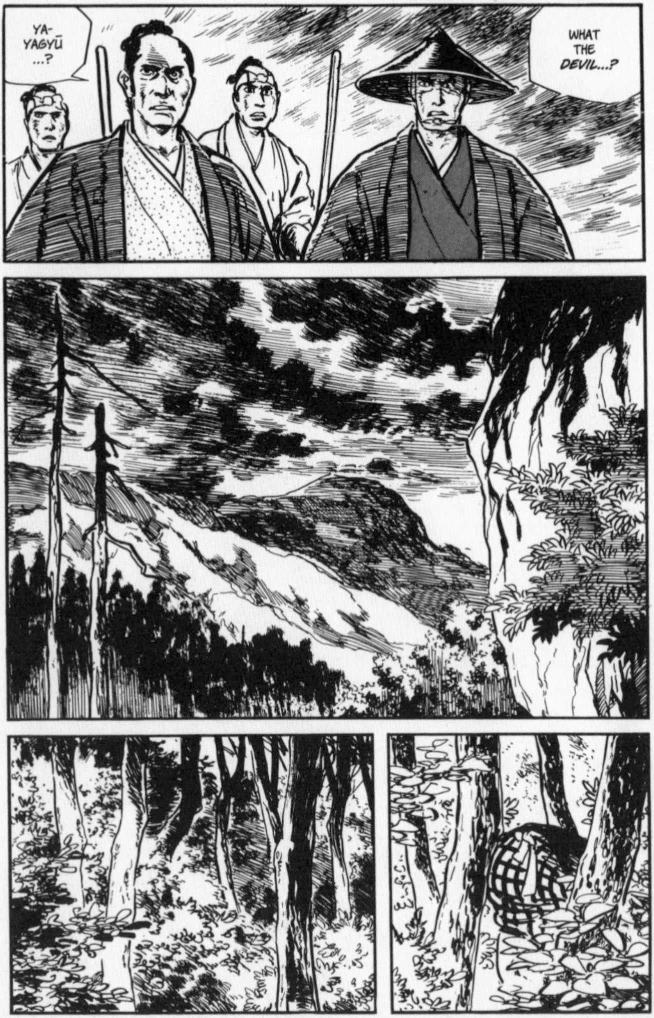
YA-YAGYŪ ...?
WHAT THE DEVIL...?

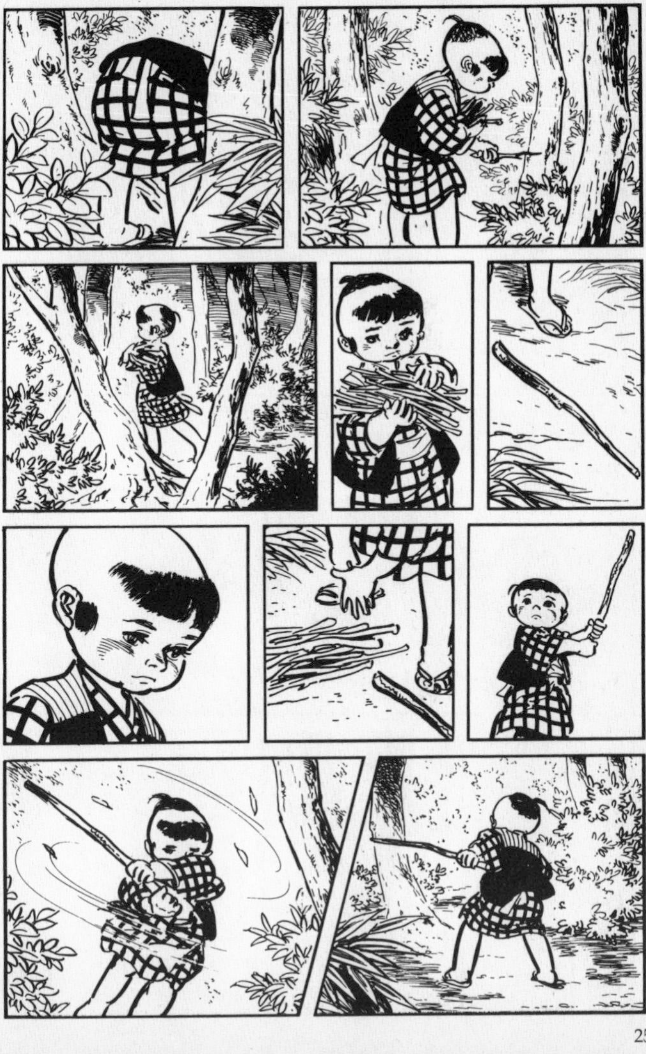

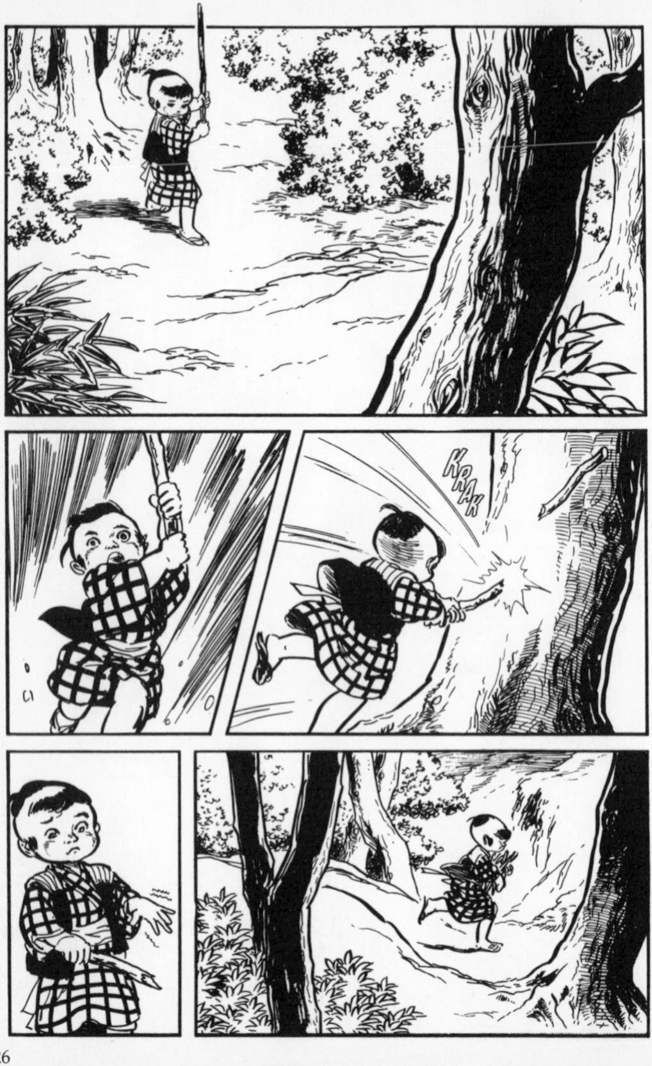
KRAK

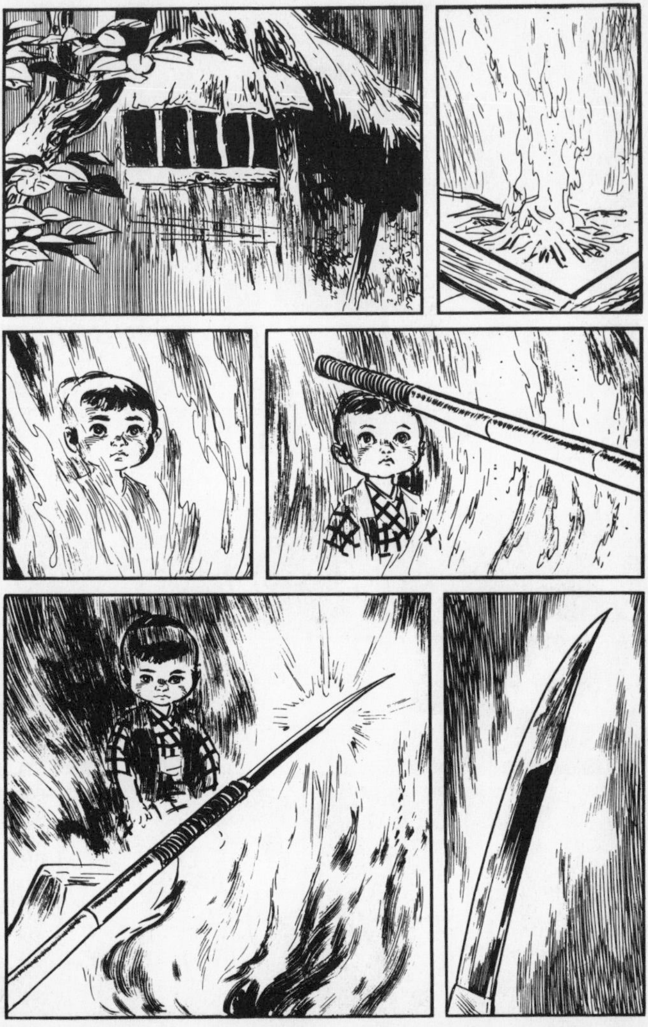

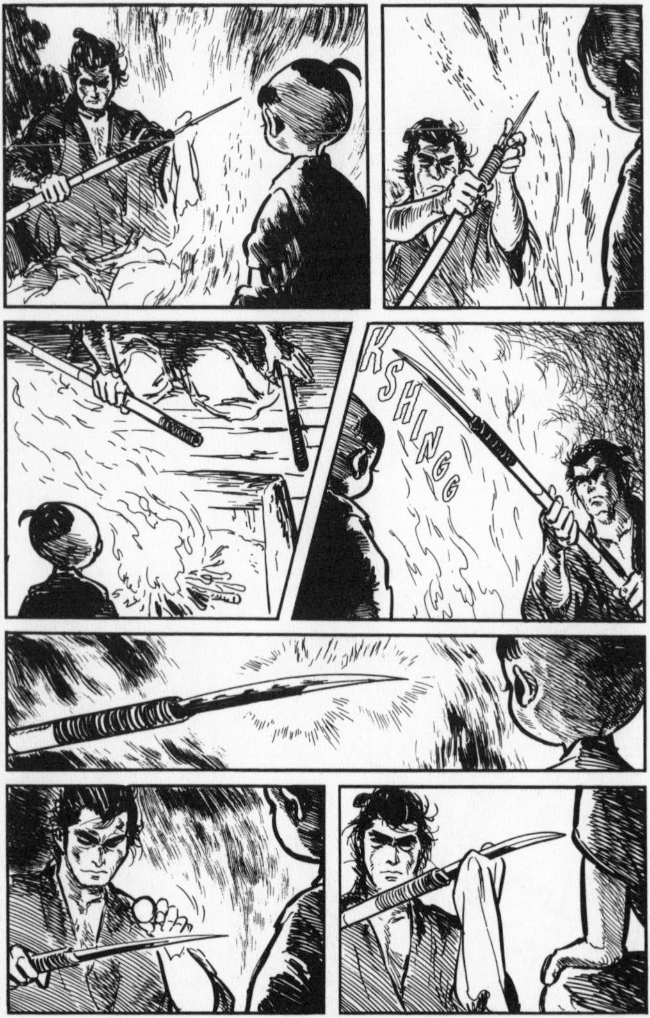
KSHINGG

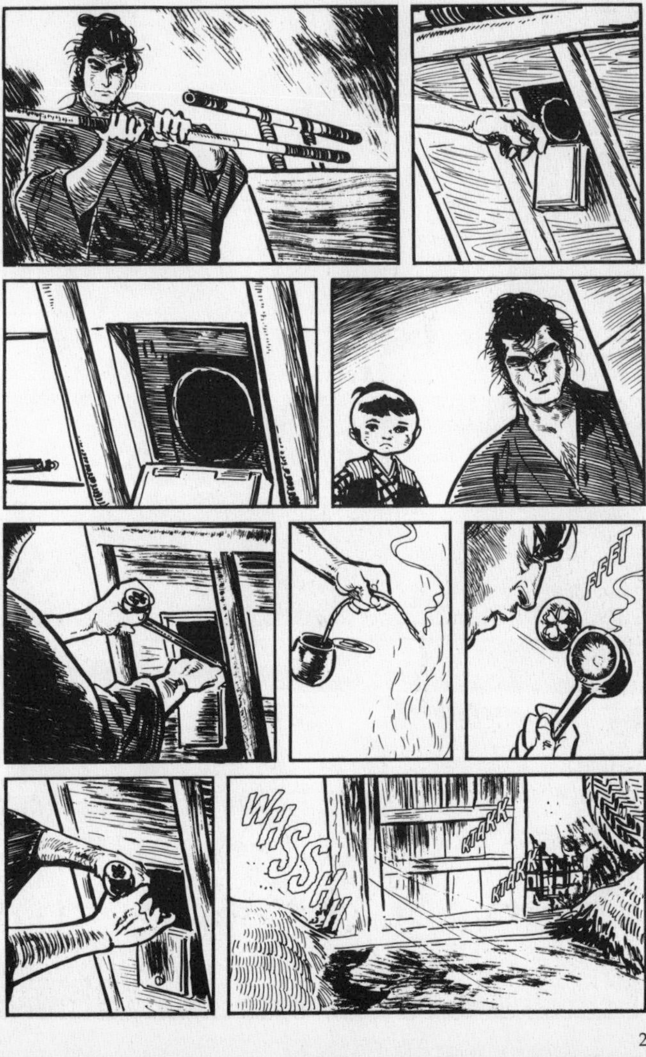

FFFT
WHSSHH
KTAKK
KTAKK

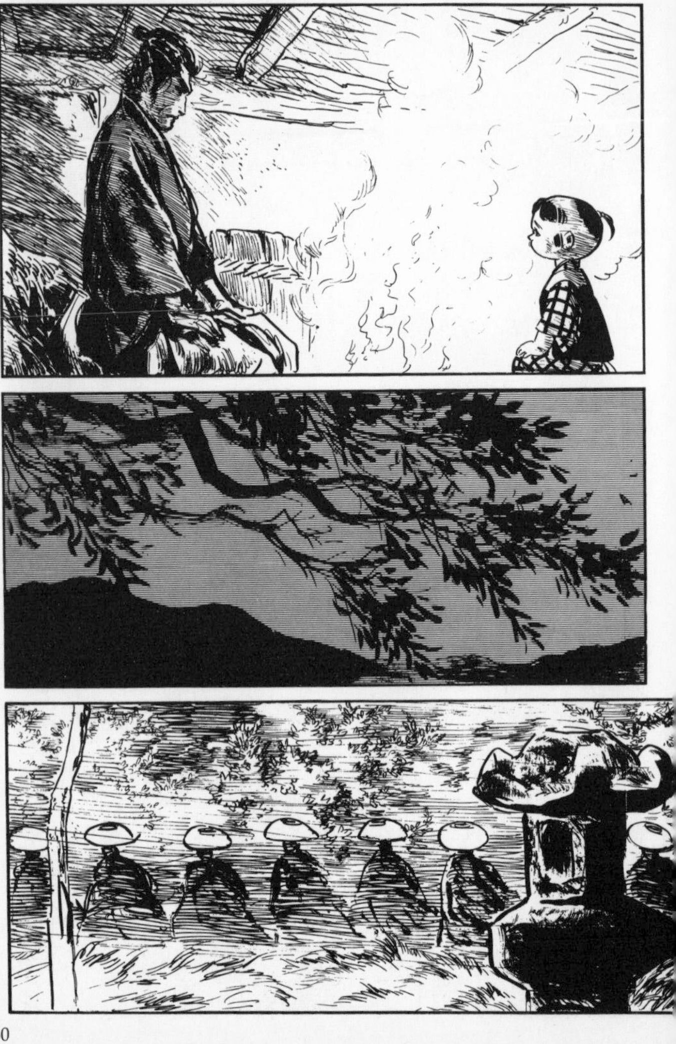

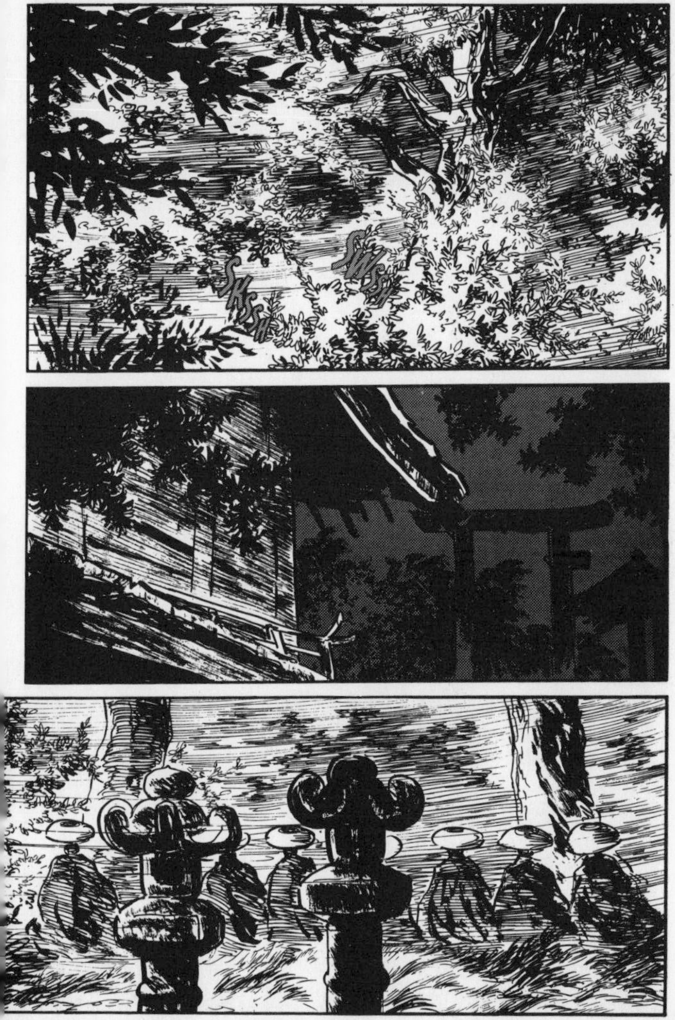
SKSSH
SWSSH

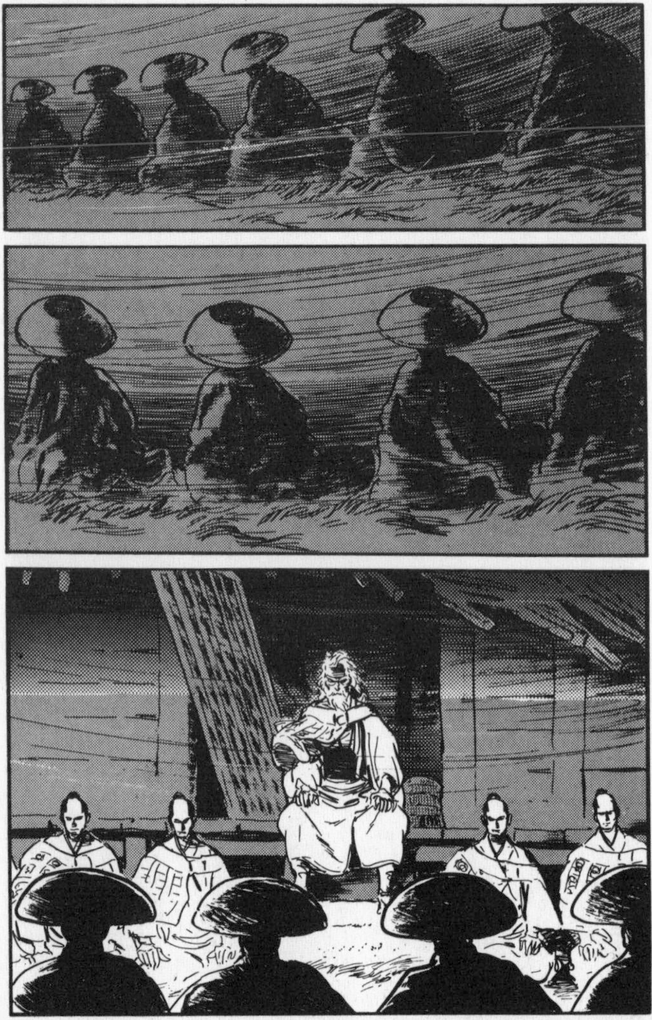

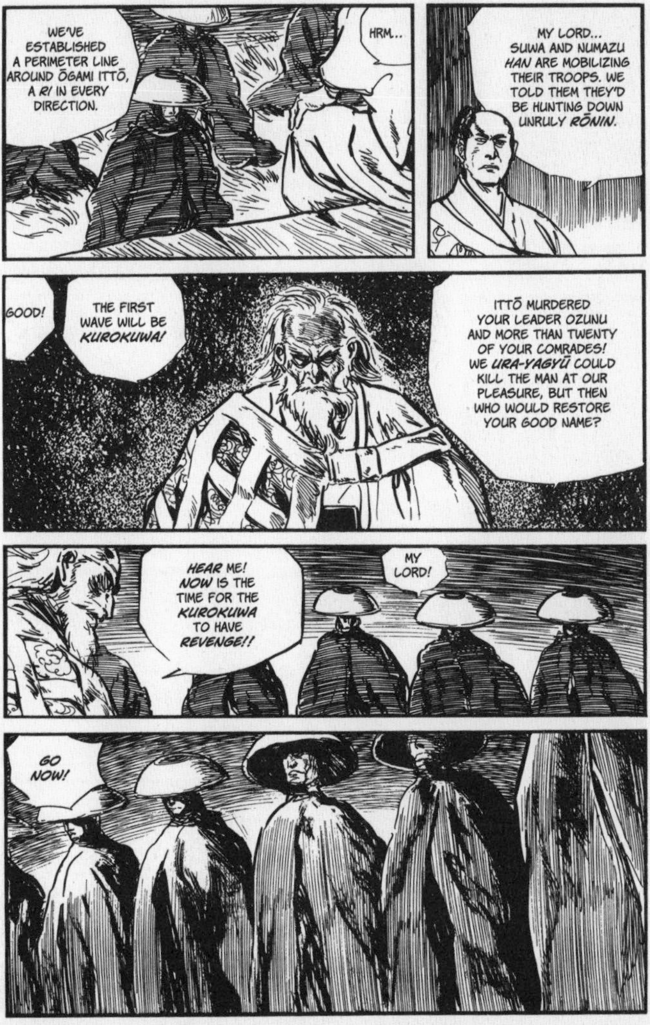
WE'VE ESTABLISHED A PERIMETER LINE AROUND ŌGAMI ITTŌ, A *RI* IN EVERY DIRECTION.
HRM...
MY LORD... SUWA AND NUMAZU *HAN* ARE MOBILIZING THEIR TROOPS. WE TOLD THEM THEY'D BE HUNTING DOWN UNRULY *RŌNIN*.
GOOD!
THE FIRST WAVE WILL BE *KUROKUWA!*
ITTŌ MURDERED YOUR LEADER OZUNU AND MORE THAN TWENTY OF YOUR COMRADES! WE *URA-YAGYŪ* COULD KILL THE MAN AT OUR PLEASURE, BUT THEN WHO WOULD RESTORE YOUR GOOD NAME?
HEAR ME! *NOW* IS THE TIME FOR THE *KUROKUWA* TO HAVE *REVENGE!!*
MY LORD!
GO NOW!

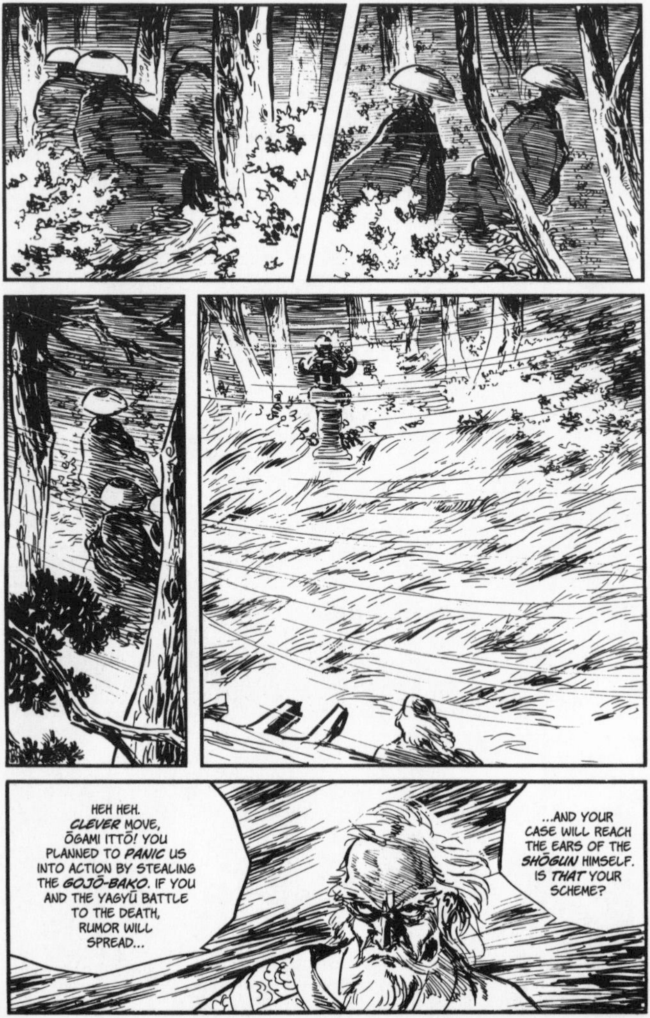
HEH HEH. CLEVER MOVE, ŌGAMI ITTŌ! YOU PLANNED TO PANIC US INTO ACTION BY STEALING THE GOJŌ-BAKO. IF YOU AND THE YAGYŪ BATTLE TO THE DEATH, RUMOR WILL SPREAD...
...AND YOUR CASE WILL REACH THE EARS OF THE SHŌGUN HIMSELF. IS THAT YOUR SCHEME?

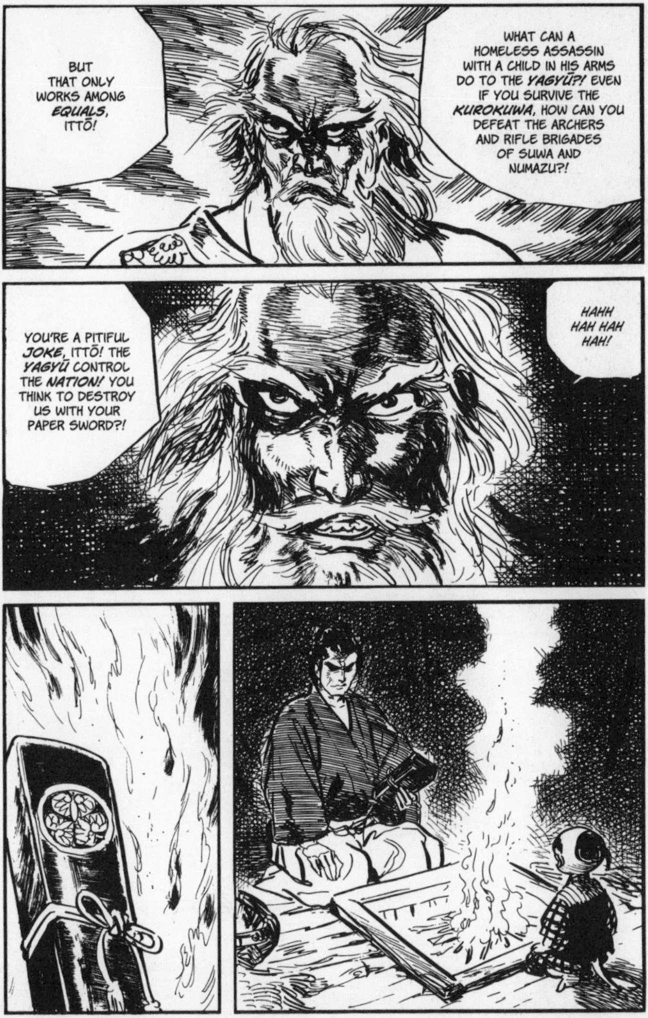
BUT THAT ONLY WORKS AMONG EQUALS, ITTŌ!
WHAT CAN A HOMELESS ASSASSIN WITH A CHILD IN HIS ARMS DO TO THE YAGYŪ?! EVEN IF YOU SURVIVE THE KUROKUWA, HOW CAN YOU DEFEAT THE ARCHERS AND RIFLE BRIGADES OF SUWA AND NUMAZU?!
YOU'RE A PITIFUL JOKE, ITTŌ! THE YAGYŪ CONTROL THE NATION! YOU THINK TO DESTROY US WITH YOUR PAPER SWORD?!
HAHH HAH HAH HAH!

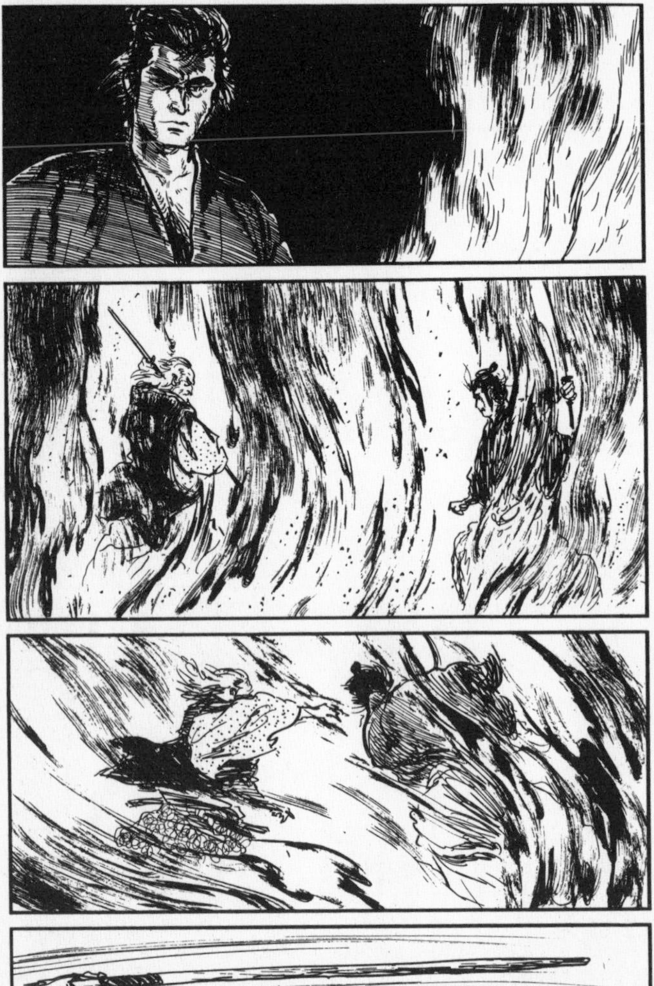

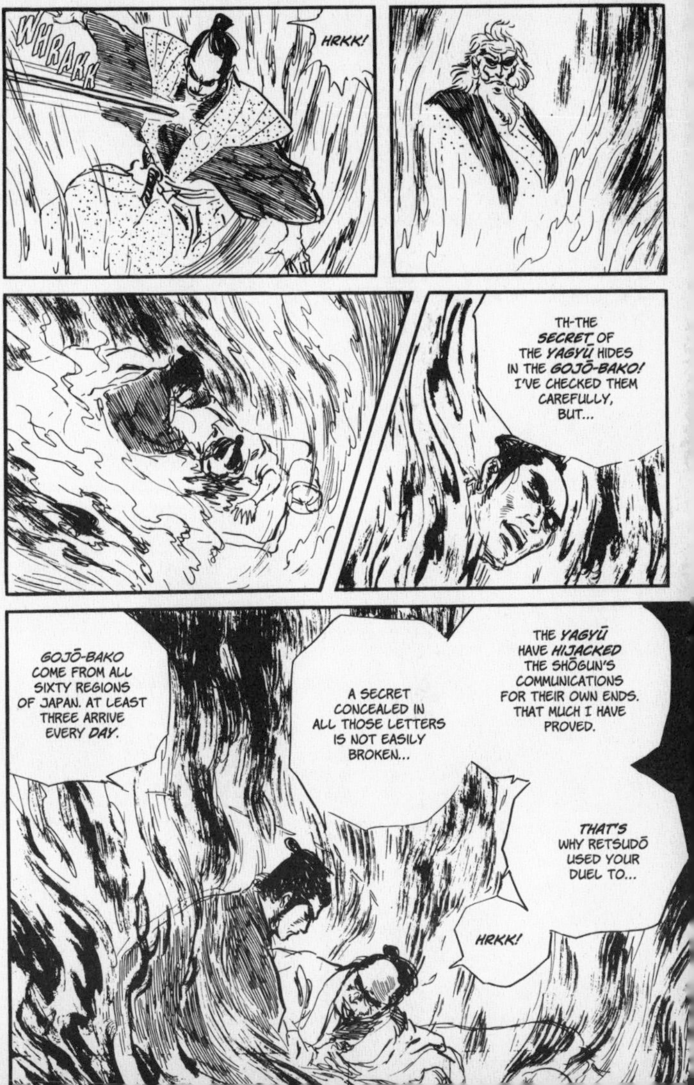
WHRAKK
HRKK!
TH-THE SECRET OF THE YAGYŪ HIDES IN THE GOJŌ-BAKO! I'VE CHECKED THEM CAREFULLY, BUT...
GOJŌ-BAKO COME FROM ALL SIXTY REGIONS OF JAPAN. AT LEAST THREE ARRIVE EVERY DAY.
A SECRET CONCEALED IN ALL THOSE LETTERS IS NOT EASILY BROKEN...
THE YAGYŪ HAVE HIJACKED THE SHŌGUN'S COMMUNICATIONS FOR THEIR OWN ENDS. THAT MUCH I HAVE PROVED.
THAT'S WHY RETSUDŌ USED YOUR DUEL TO...
HRKK!

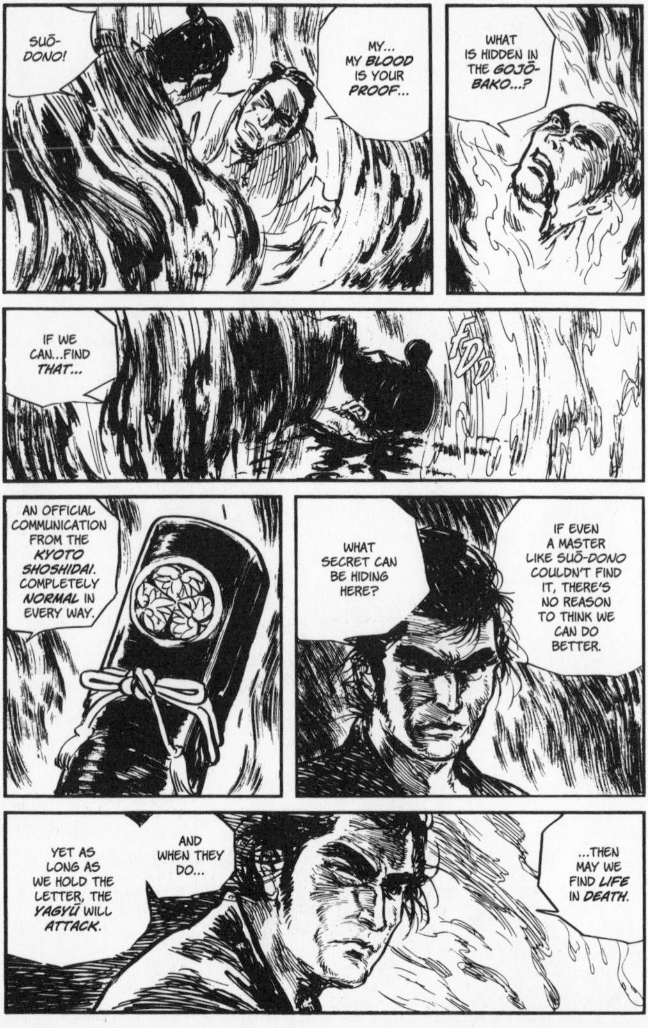
SUŌ-DONO!
MY... MY BLOOD IS YOUR PROOF...
WHAT IS HIDDEN IN THE GOJŌ-BAKO...?
IF WE CAN...FIND THAT...
FDD
AN OFFICIAL COMMUNICATION FROM THE KYOTO SHOSHIDAI. COMPLETELY NORMAL IN EVERY WAY.
WHAT SECRET CAN BE HIDING HERE?
IF EVEN A MASTER LIKE SUŌ-DONO COULDN'T FIND IT, THERE'S NO REASON TO THINK WE CAN DO BETTER.
YET AS LONG AS WE HOLD THE LETTER, THE YAGYŪ WILL ATTACK.
AND WHEN THEY DO...
...THEN MAY WE FIND LIFE IN DEATH.

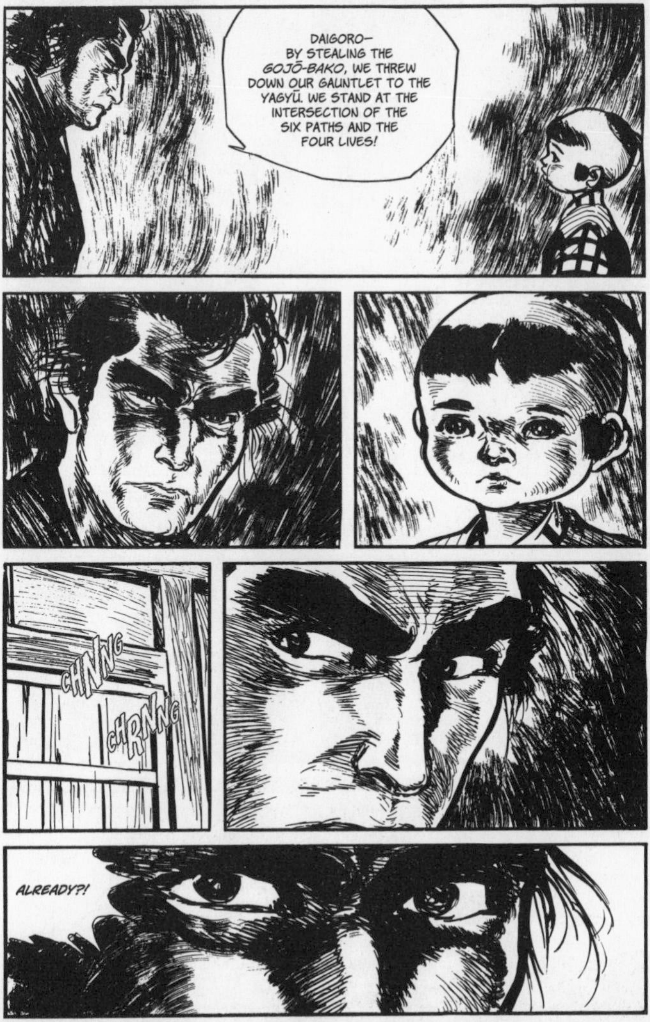
DAIGORO— BY STEALING THE GOJŌ-BAKO, WE THREW DOWN OUR GAUNTLET TO THE YAGYŪ. WE STAND AT THE INTERSECTION OF THE SIX PATHS AND THE FOUR LIVES!
CHNNG
CHRNNG
ALREADY?!

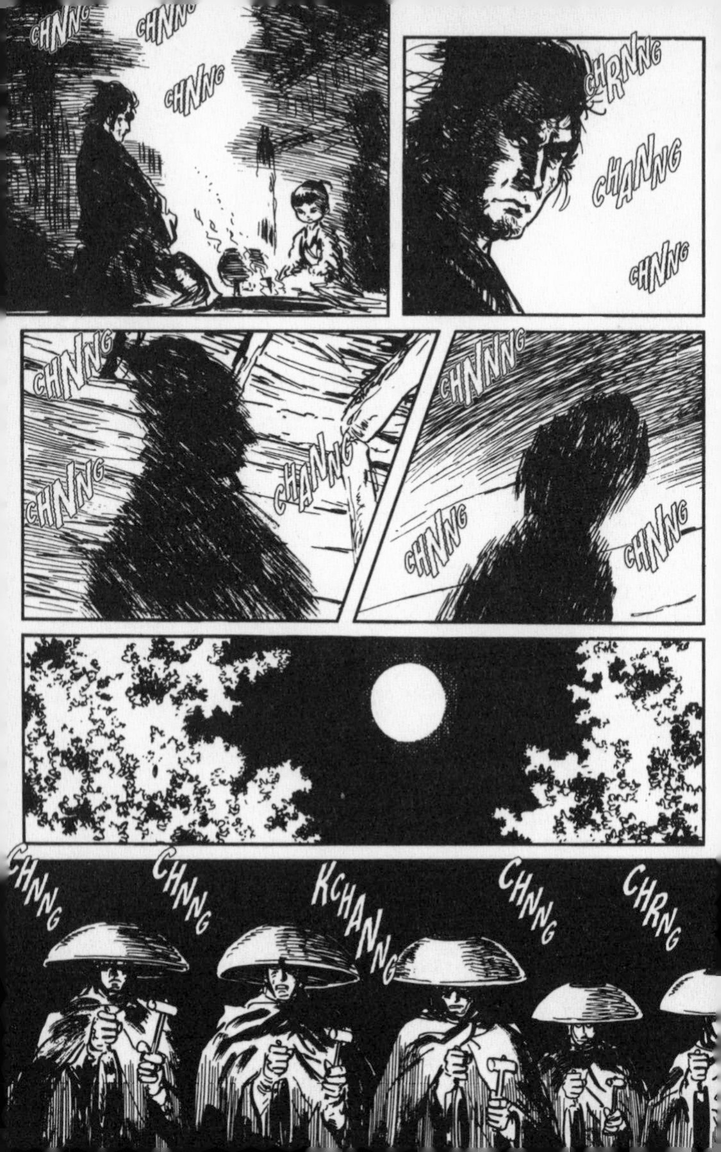
CHNNG
CHNNG
CHNNG
CHRNNG
CHANNG
CHNNG
CHNNG
CHNNG
CHANNG
CHNNNG
CHNNG
CHNNG
CHNNG
CHNNG
KCHANNG
CHNNG
CHRNG

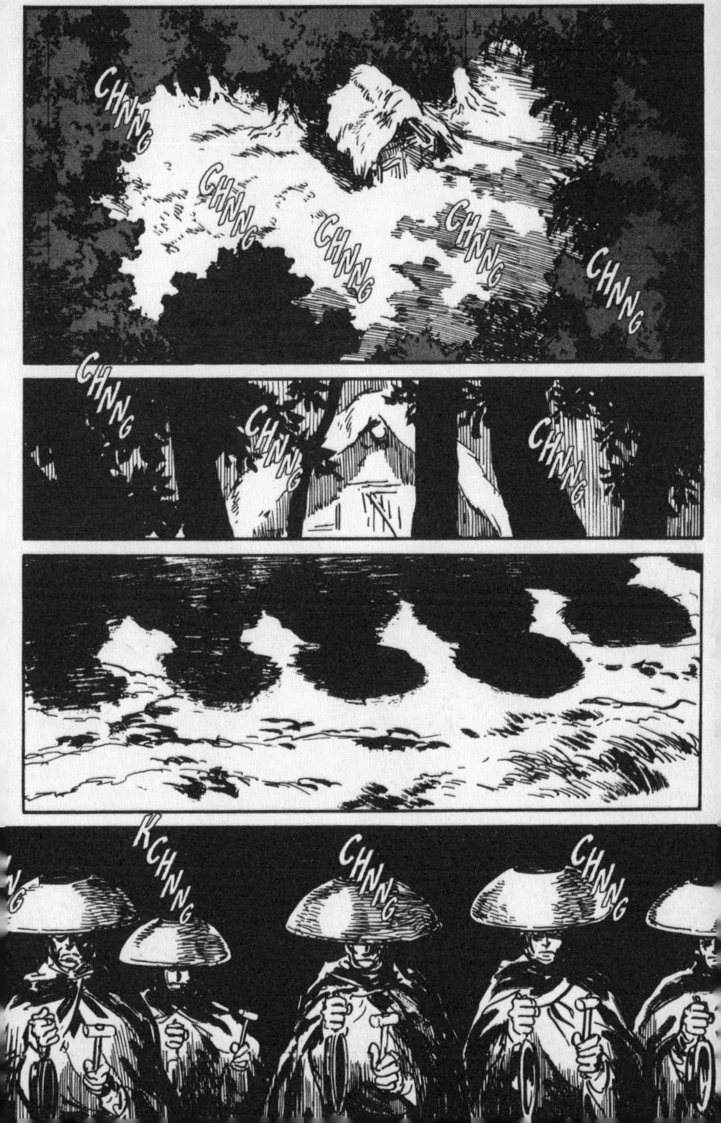
CHNNG
CHNNG
CHNNG
CHNNG
CHNNG
CHNNG
CHNNG
CHNNG
KCHNNG
CHNNG
CHNNG

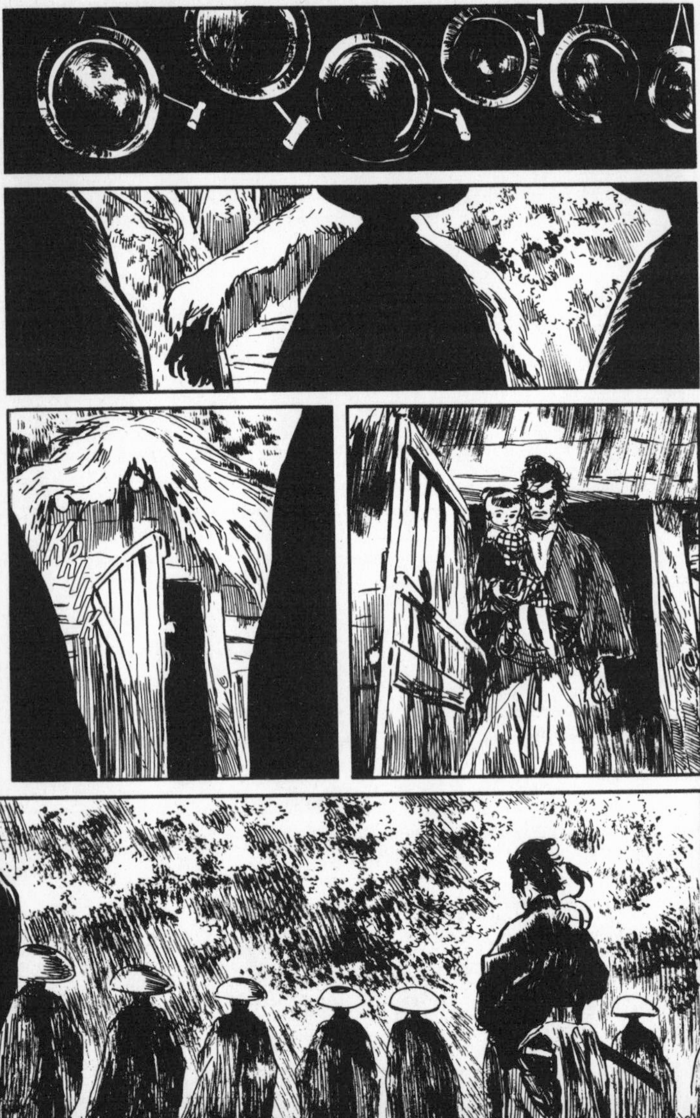
KRIIIK

THE *KUROKUWA* SERVE THE *SHŌGUN*!

YET NOW YOU RUN ERRANDS FOR THE *YAGYŪ*? PATHETIC.

A *SHINOBI* IS VERSED IN SPYCRAFT AND DEFENSE. A *SHINOBI* NEVER ATTACKS.

EASY TO WEAVE OUR STRATAGEMS AND KILL YOU FROM THE *SHADOWS*...BUT THIS WOULD BRING US NO *HONOR*.

WE ARE HERE TO AVENGE OZUNU AND OUR SLAIN CLANMEN!

AND THUS WE *REVEAL* OURSELVES, AND MEET YOU IN *FAIR COMBAT*!

FIGHT, ŌGAMI ITTŌ! TASTE THE *HATRED* OF THE *KUROKUWA*!

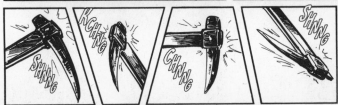

SHINNG

KCHING

CHINNG

SHINNG

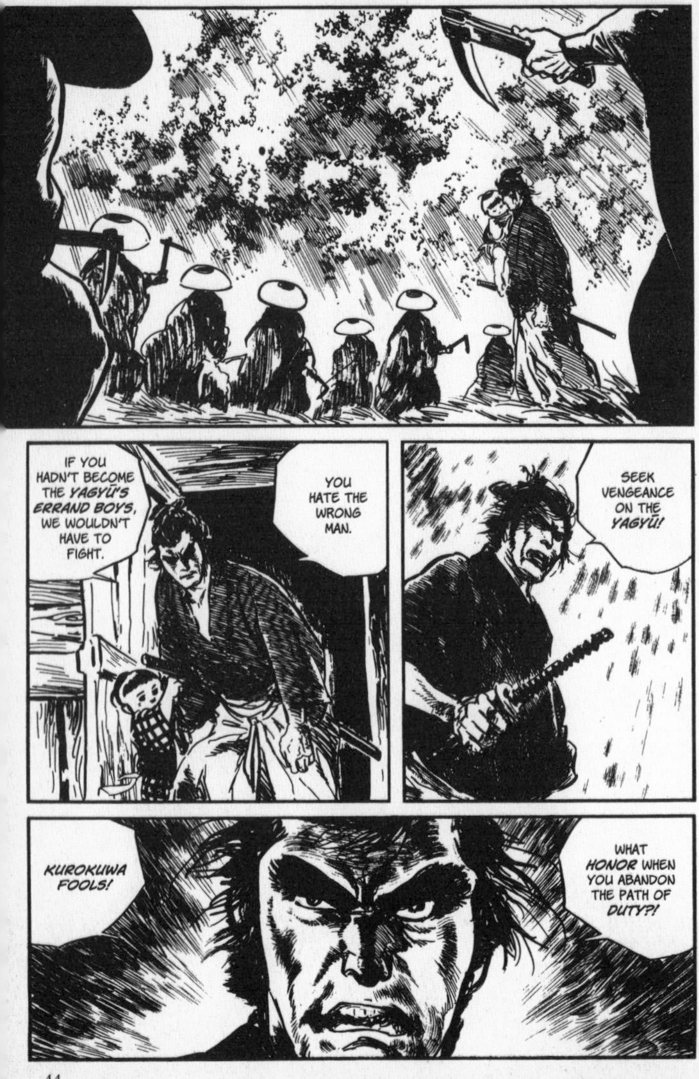
IF YOU HADN'T BECOME THE *YAGYŪ'S ERRAND BOYS*, WE WOULDN'T HAVE TO FIGHT.
YOU HATE THE WRONG MAN.
SEEK VENGEANCE ON THE *YAGYŪ!*
KUROKUWA FOOLS!
WHAT *HONOR* WHEN YOU ABANDON THE PATH OF *DUTY?!*

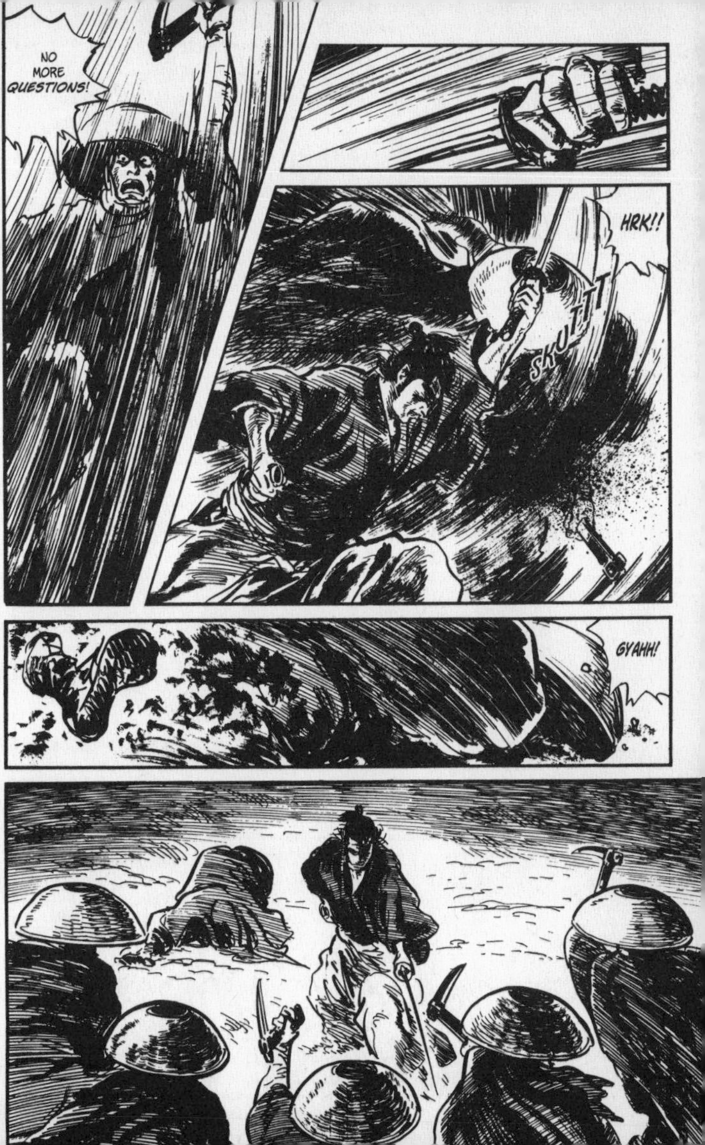
NO MORE QUESTIONS!
HRK!!
SKUTTT
GYAHH!

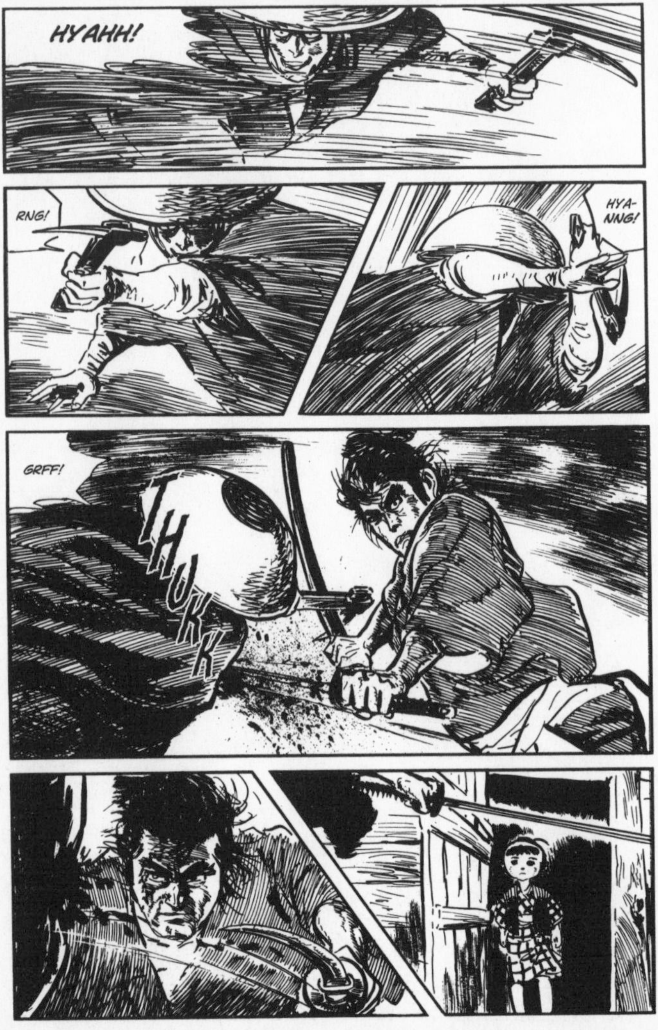
HYAHH!
RNG!
HYA-NNG!
GRFF!
THUKK

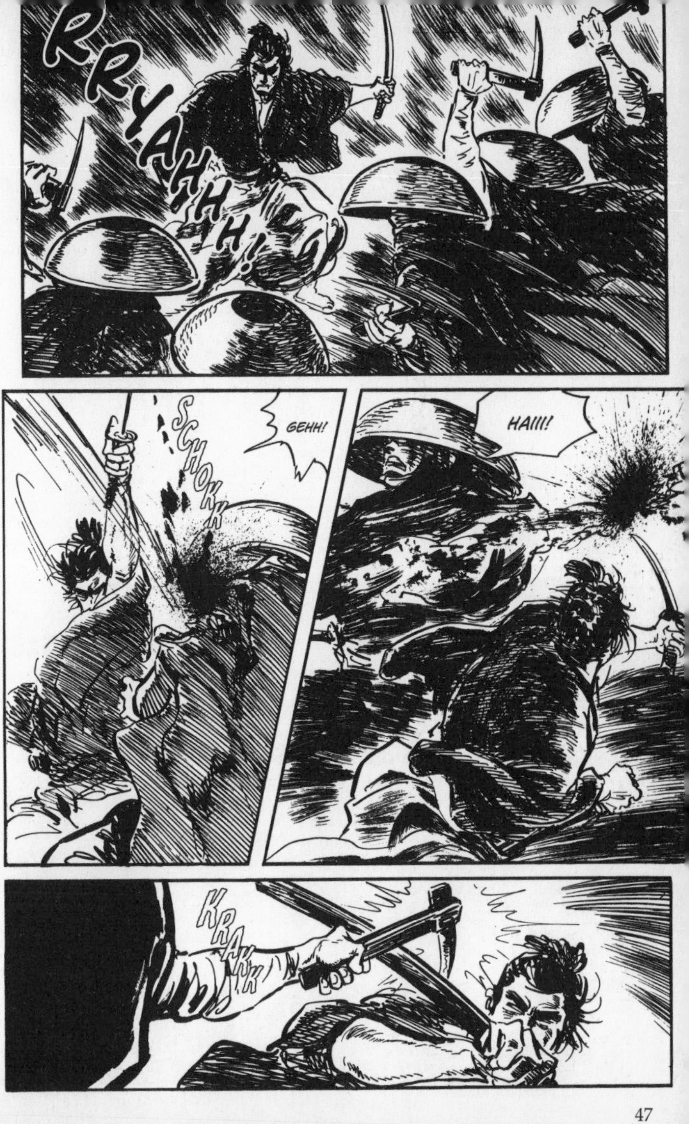
RRYAHHH!
SCHOKK
GEHH!
HAIII!
KRAKK

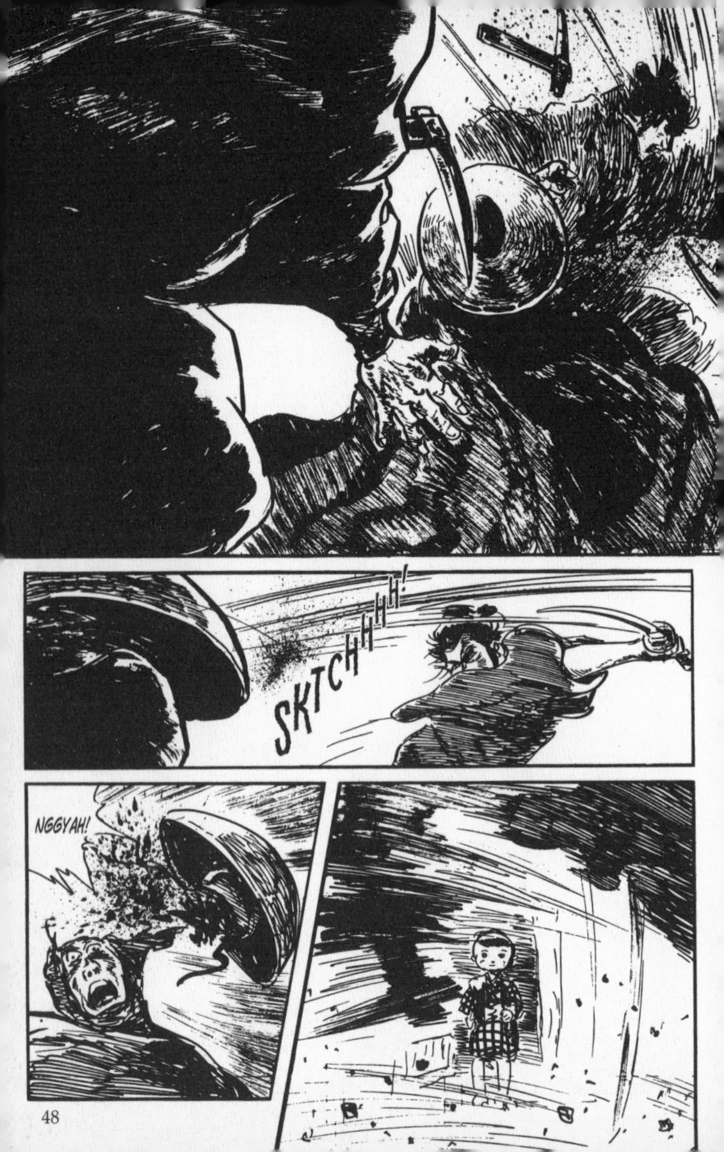
SKTCHHHH!
NGGYAH!

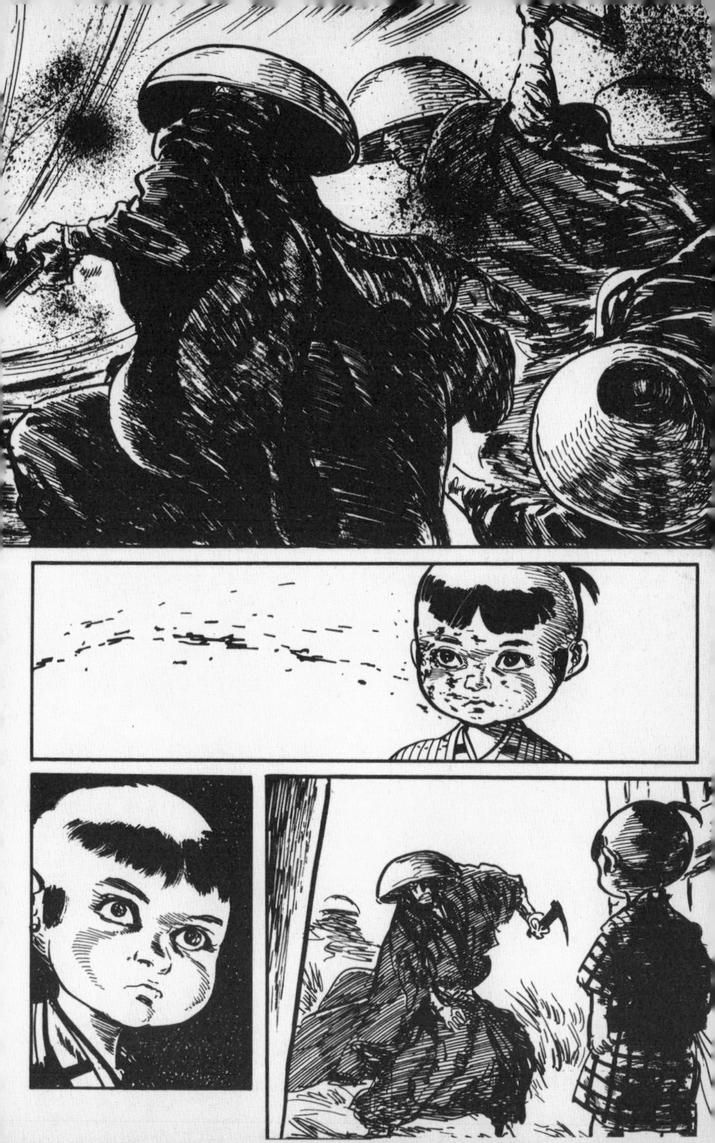

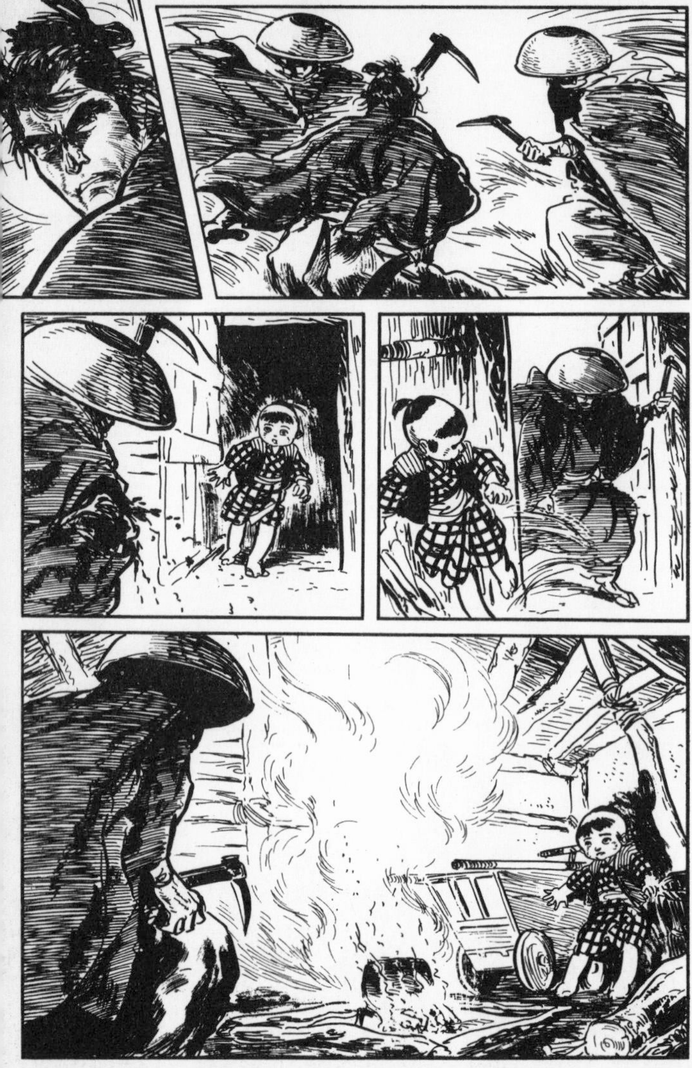

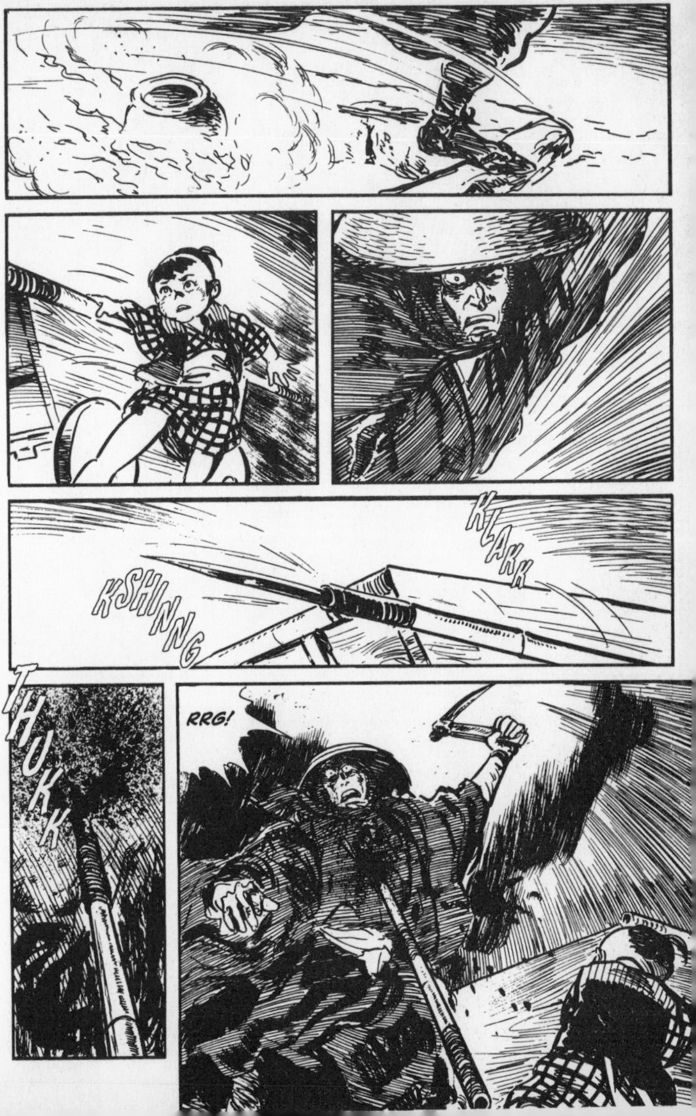
KLAKK
KSHINNG
THUKK
RRG!

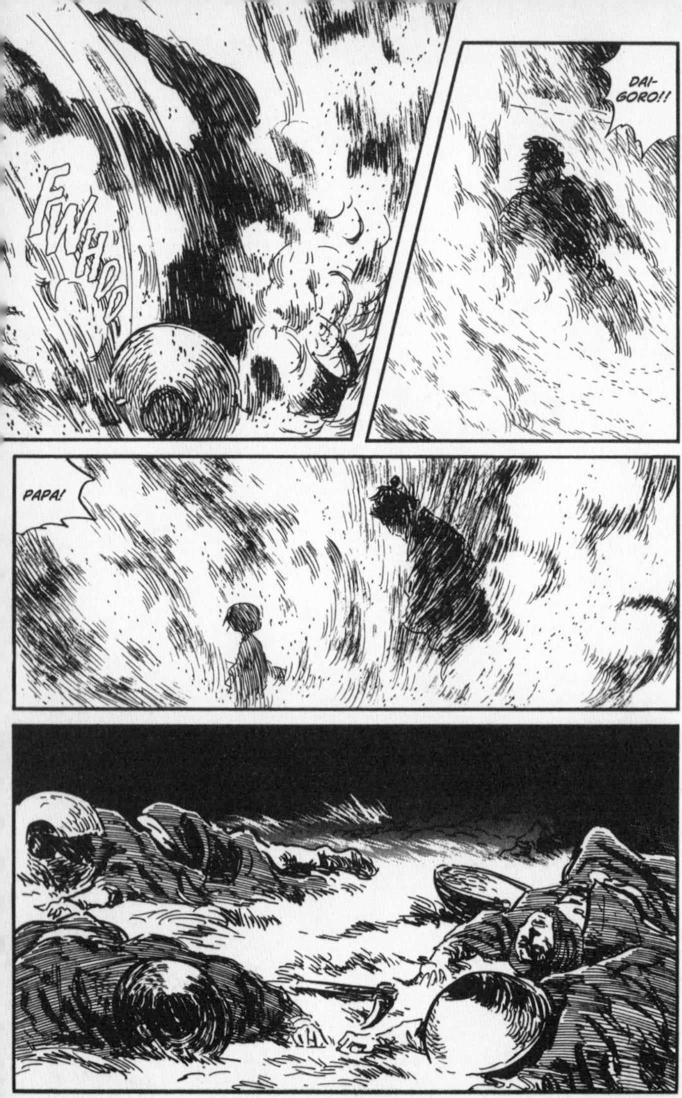
FWHOO
DAI-GORO!!
PAPA!

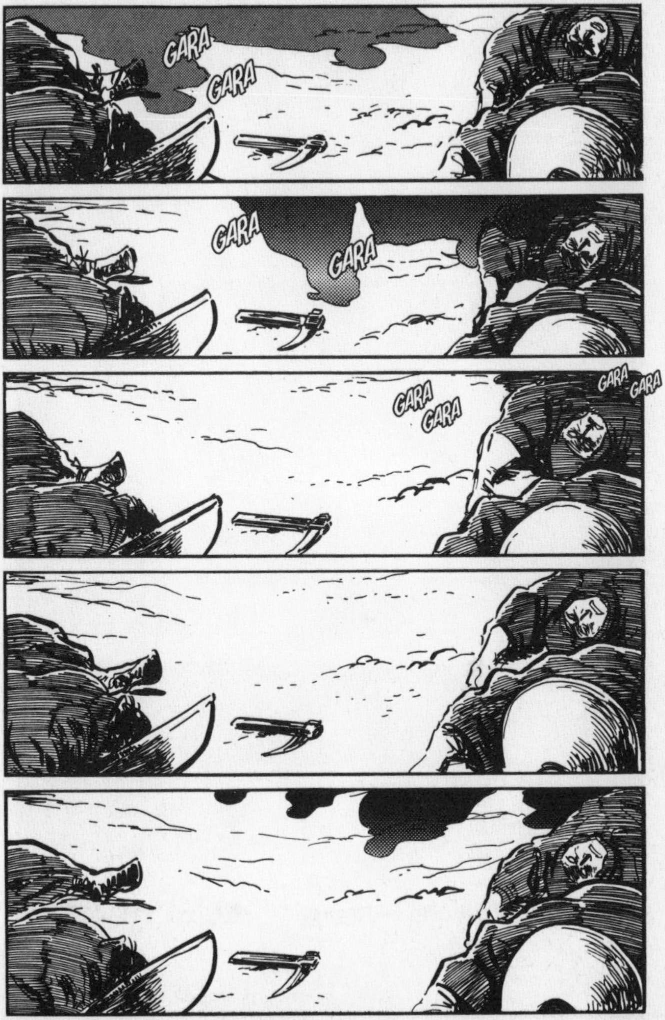
GARA
GARA
GARA
GARA
GARA
GARA
GARA
GARA

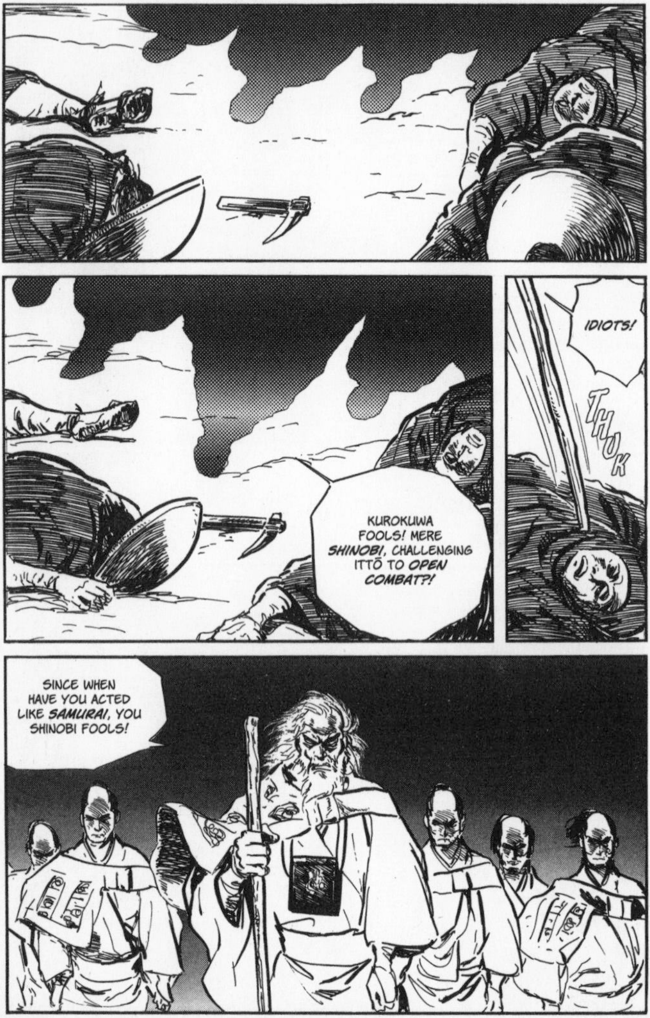
KUROKUWA FOOLS! MERE SHINOBI, CHALLENGING ITTŌ TO OPEN COMBAT?!
IDIOTS!
THOK
SINCE WHEN HAVE YOU ACTED LIKE SAMURAI, YOU SHINOBI FOOLS!

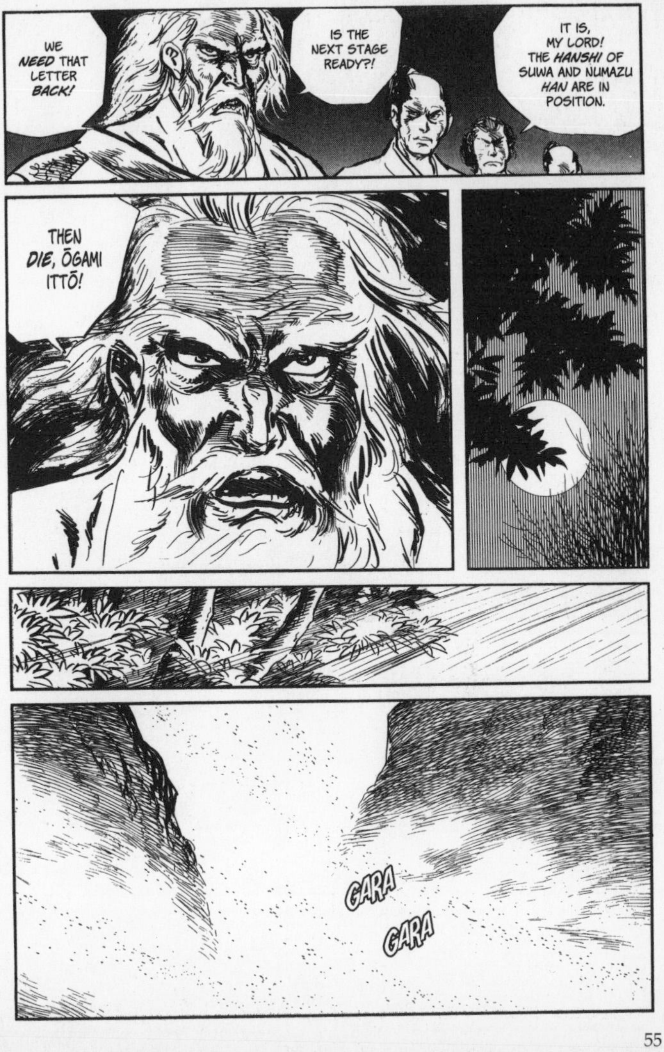
WE *NEED* THAT LETTER *BACK!*
IS THE NEXT STAGE READY?!
IT IS, MY LORD! THE *HANSHI* OF SUWA AND NUMAZU *HAN* ARE IN POSITION.
THEN *DIE*, ŌGAMI ITTŌ!
GARA
GARA

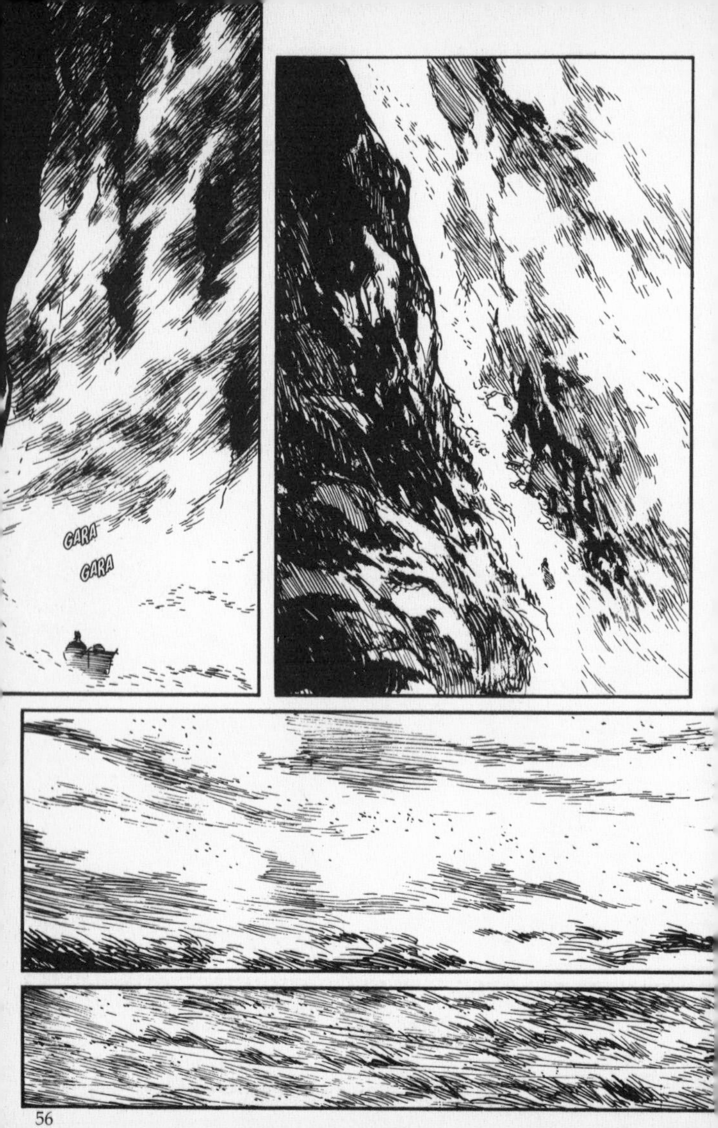
GARA
GARA

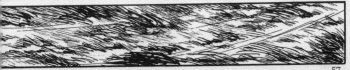

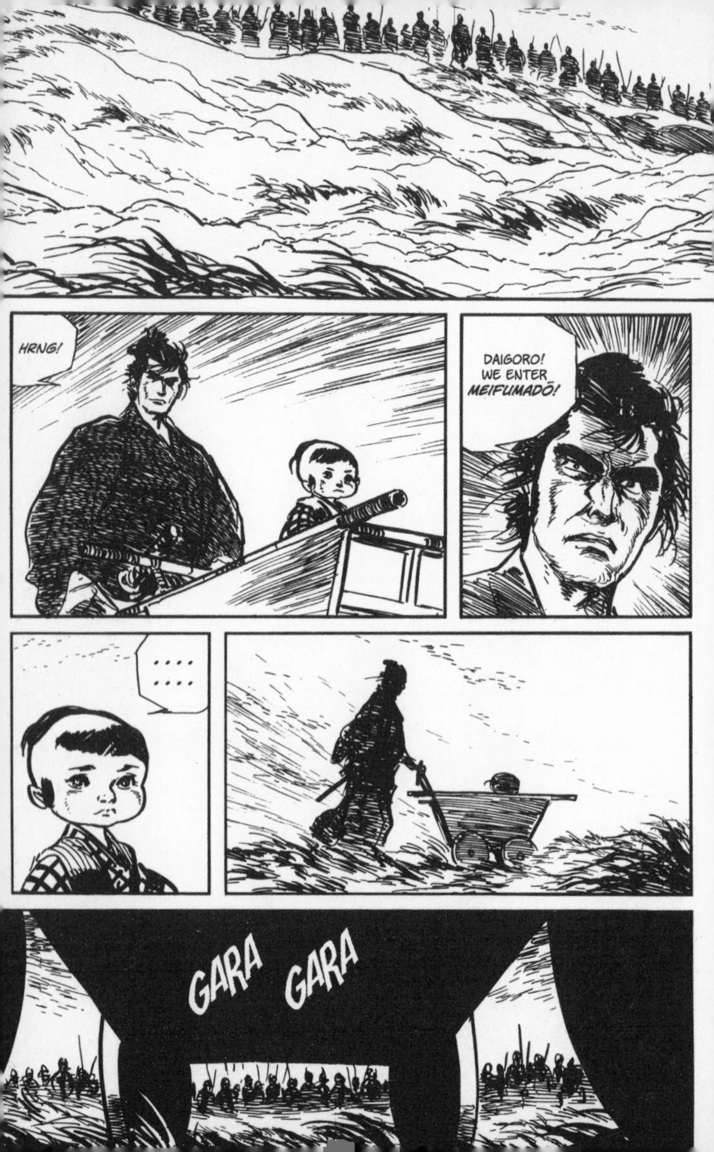
HRNG!
DAIGORO! WE ENTER MEIFUMADŌ!
....
....
GARA GARA

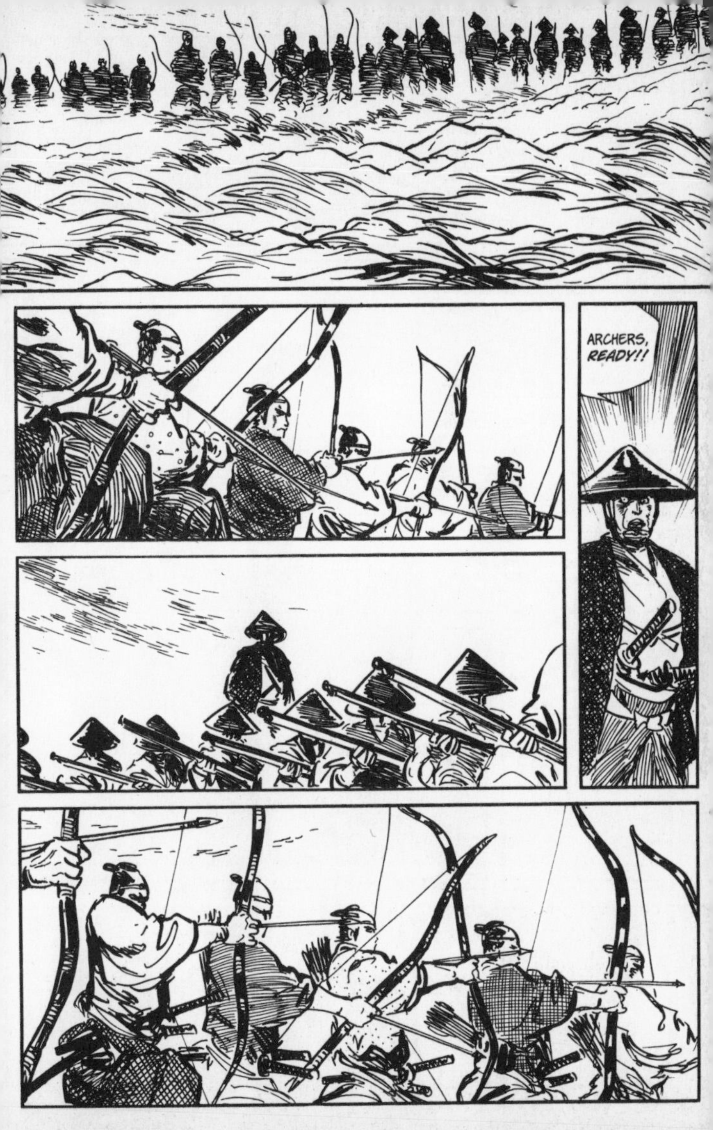
ARCHERS, READY!!

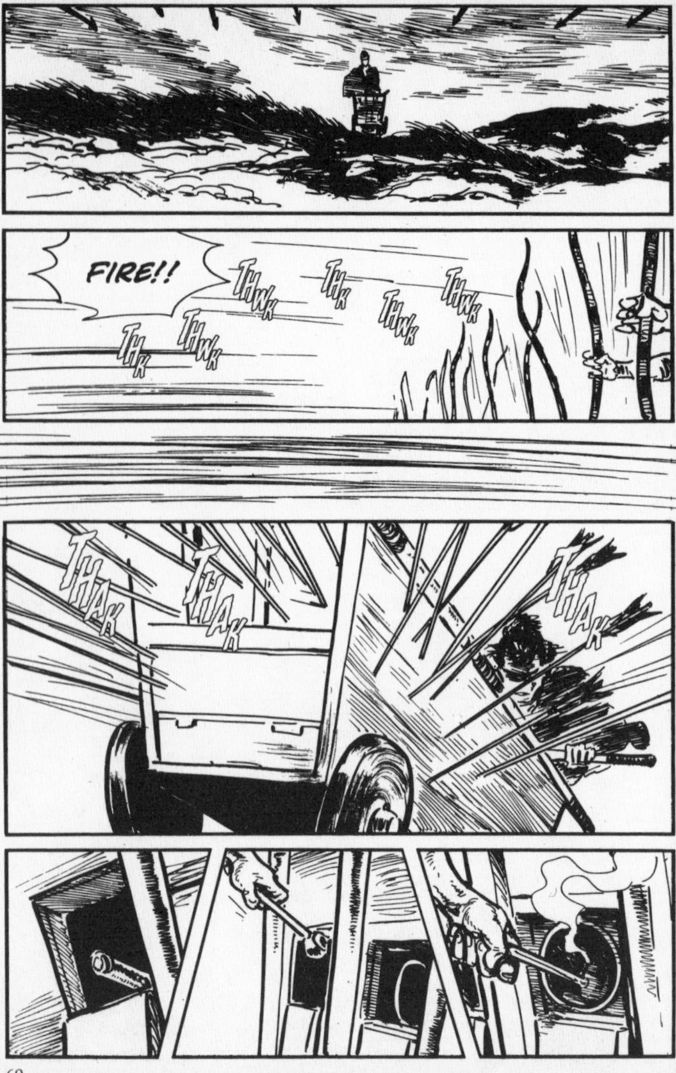
FIRE!!
THWK
THK
THWK
THWK
THK
THWK
THAK
THAK
THAK

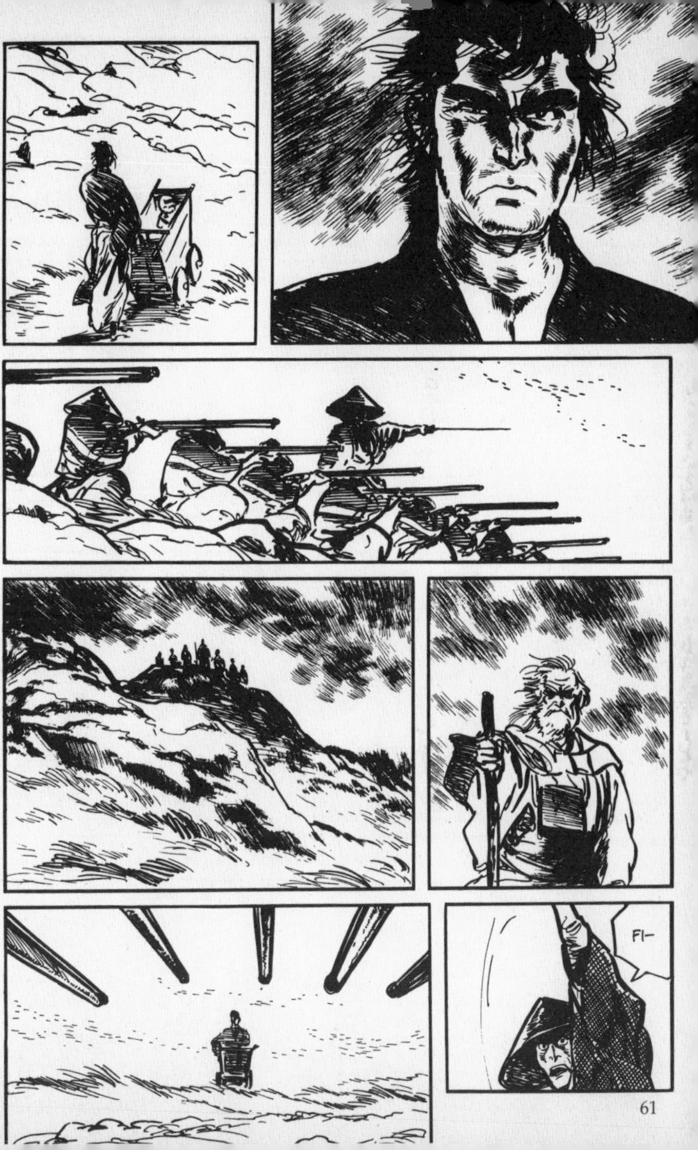
FI–

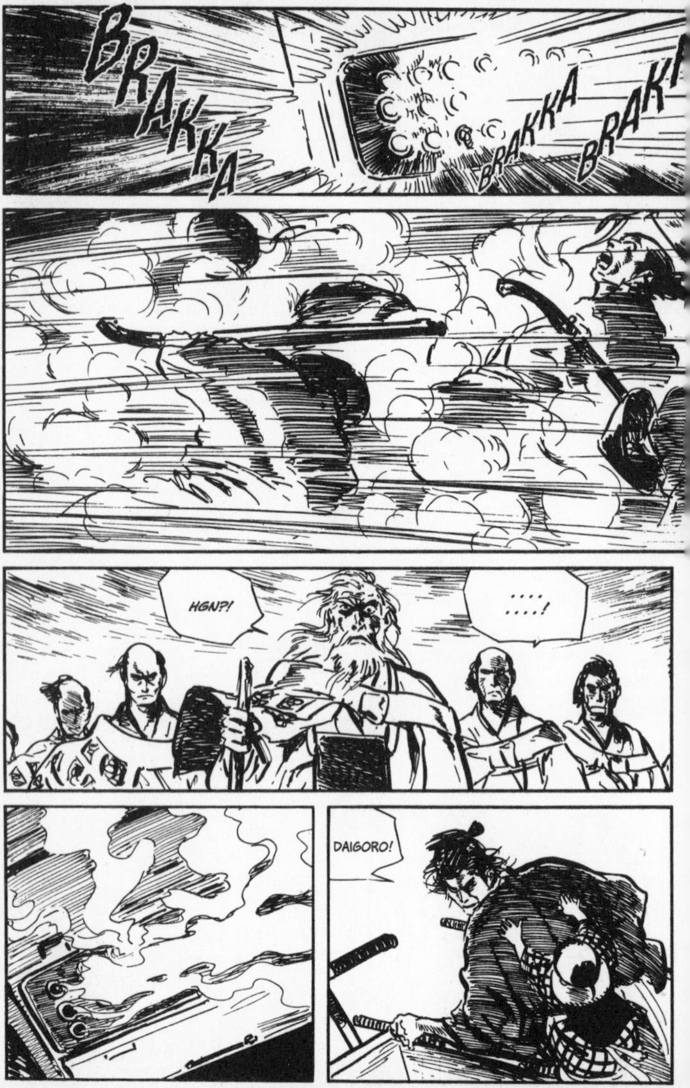
BRAKKA
BRAKKA
BRAKK
HGN?!
....
....!
DAIGORO!

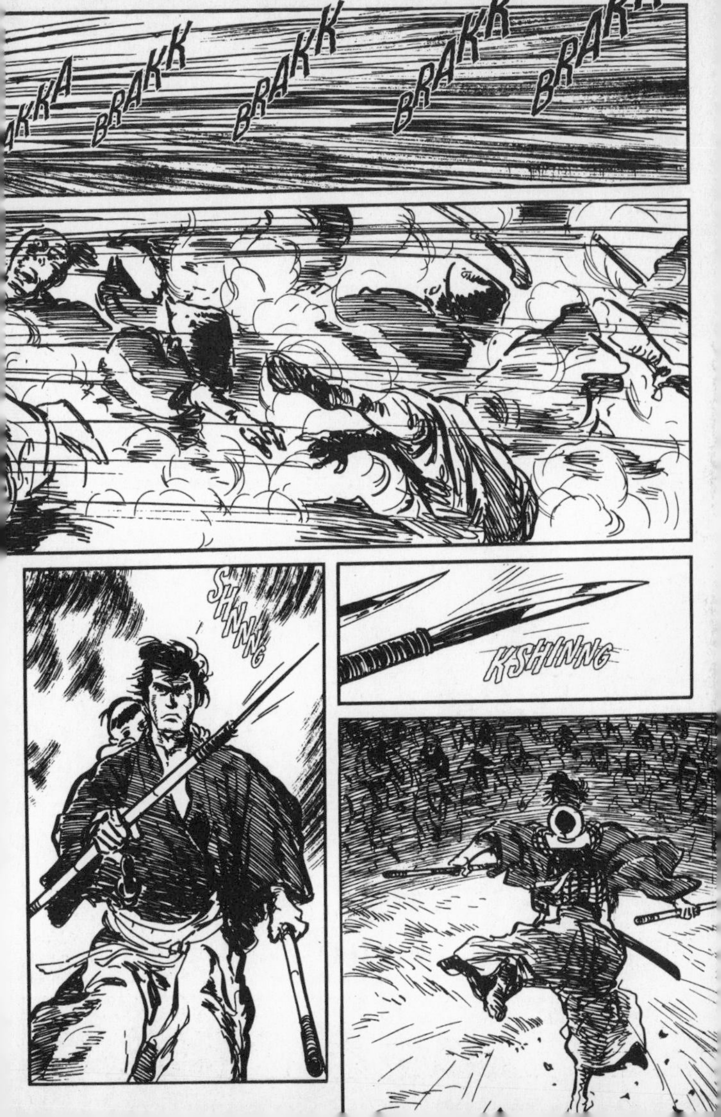
AKKA
BRAKK
BRAKK
BRAKK
BRAKK
SHINNNG
KSHINNG

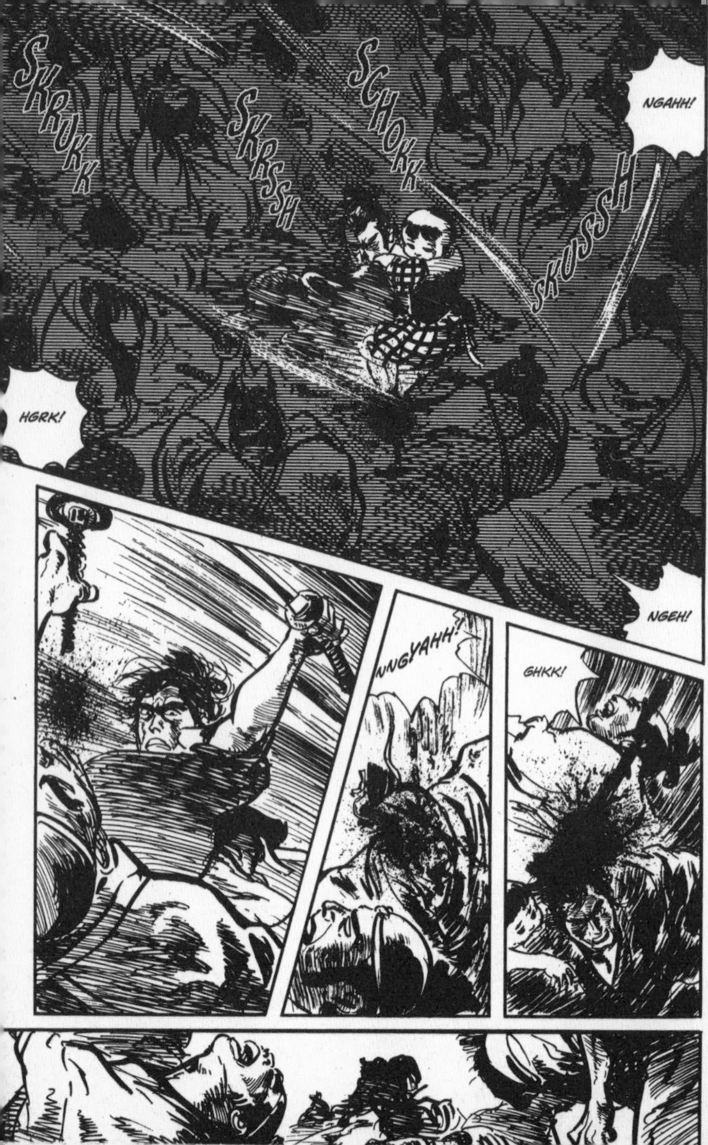
SKRUKK
SKRSSH
SCHOKK
NGAHH!
SKUSSSH
HGRK!
NGEH!
NNGYAHH!
GHKK!

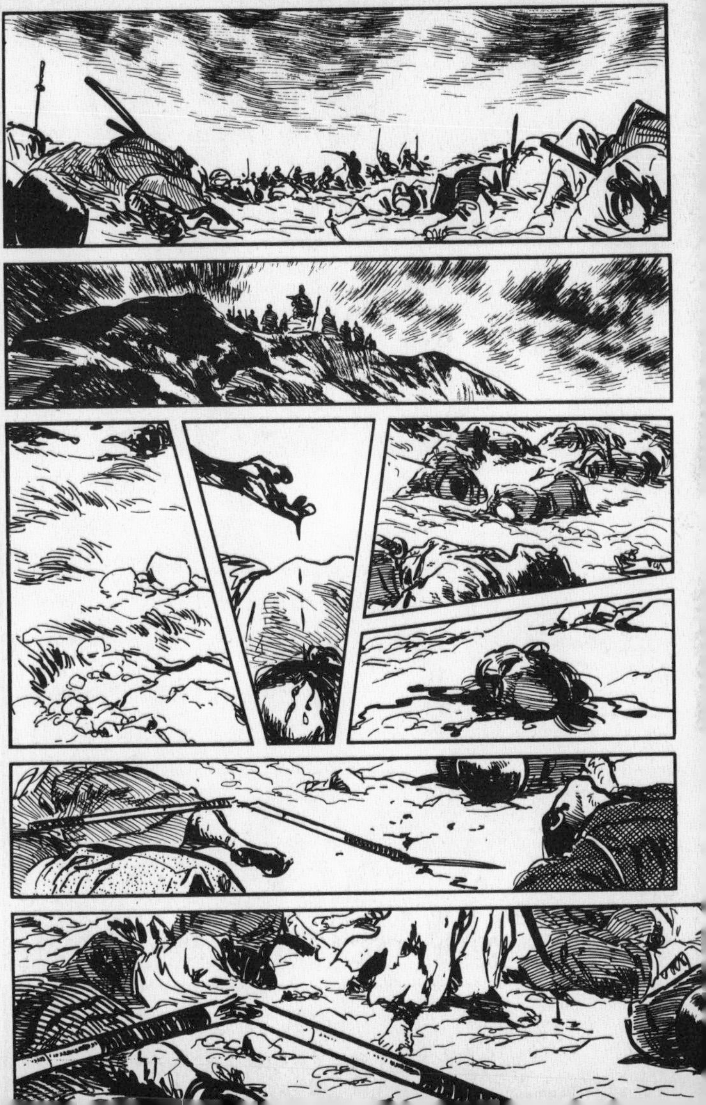

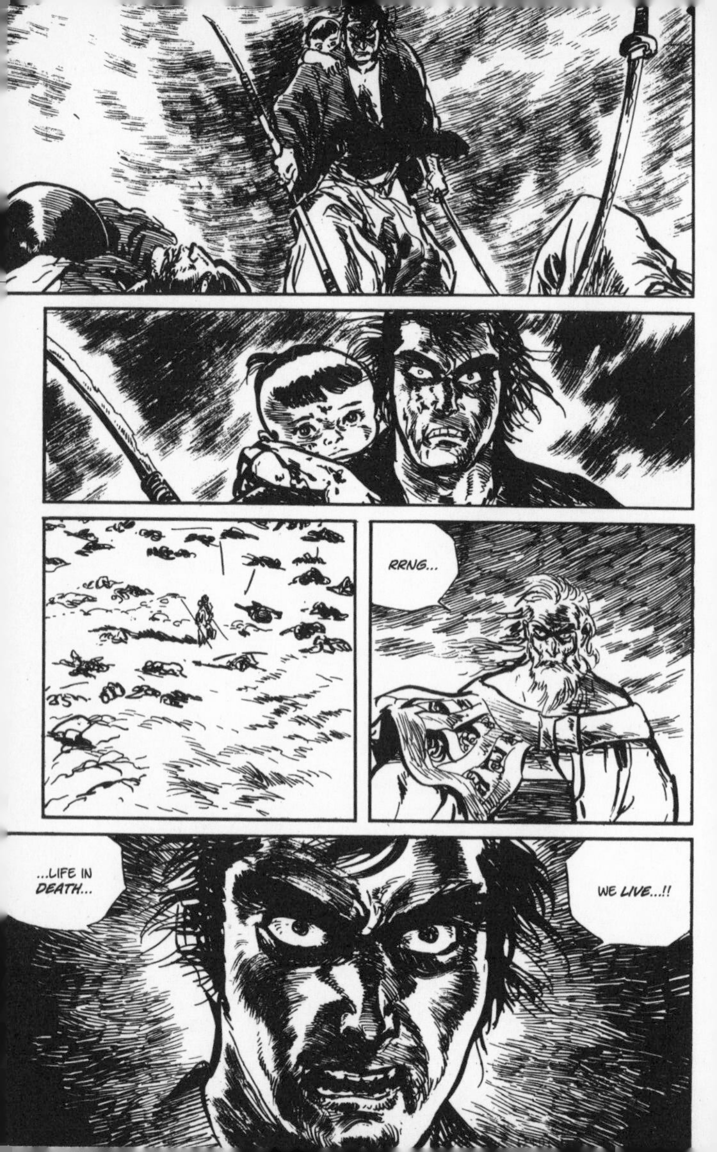
RRNG...
...LIFE IN DEATH...
WE LIVE...!!

the fifty-first

The Tears of Daigoro

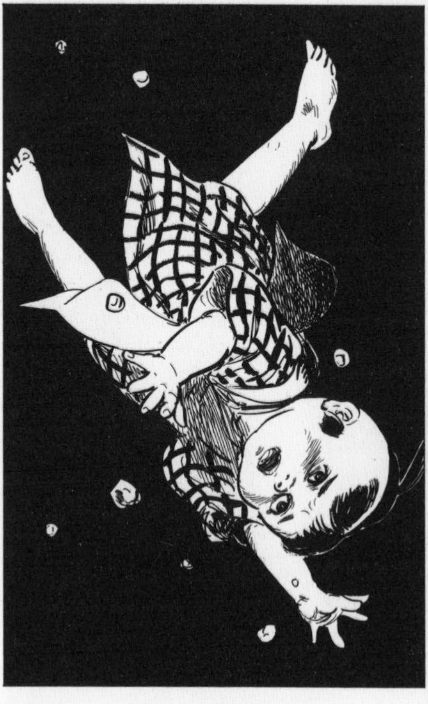

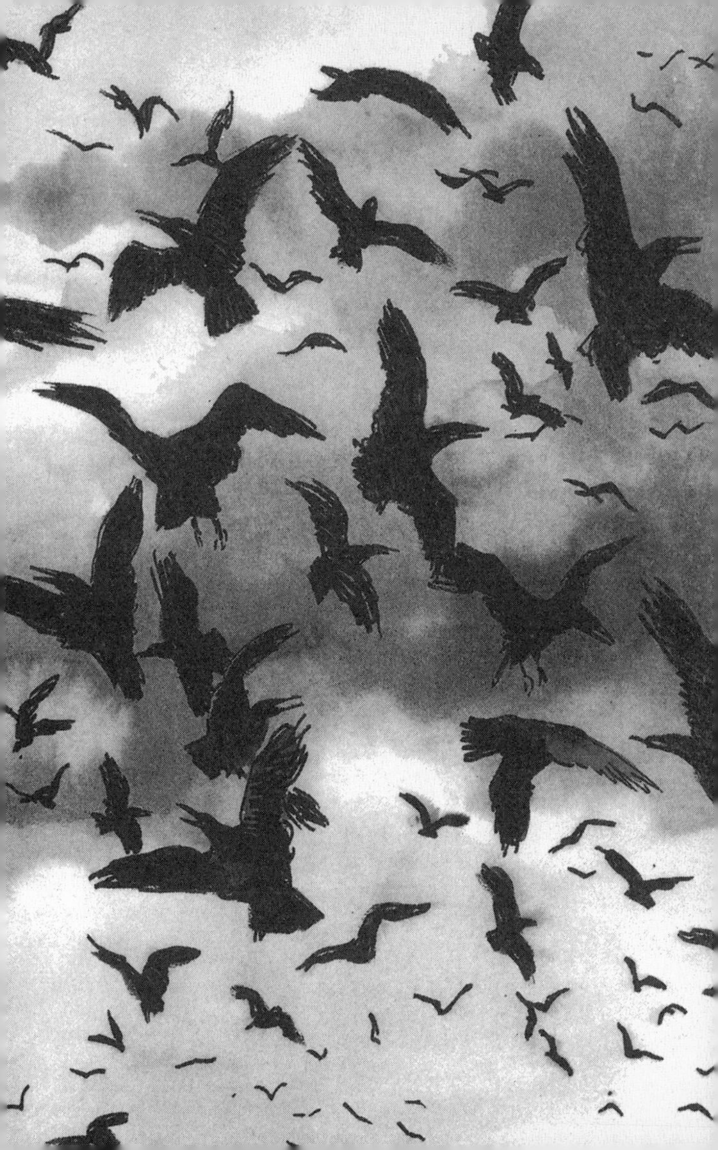

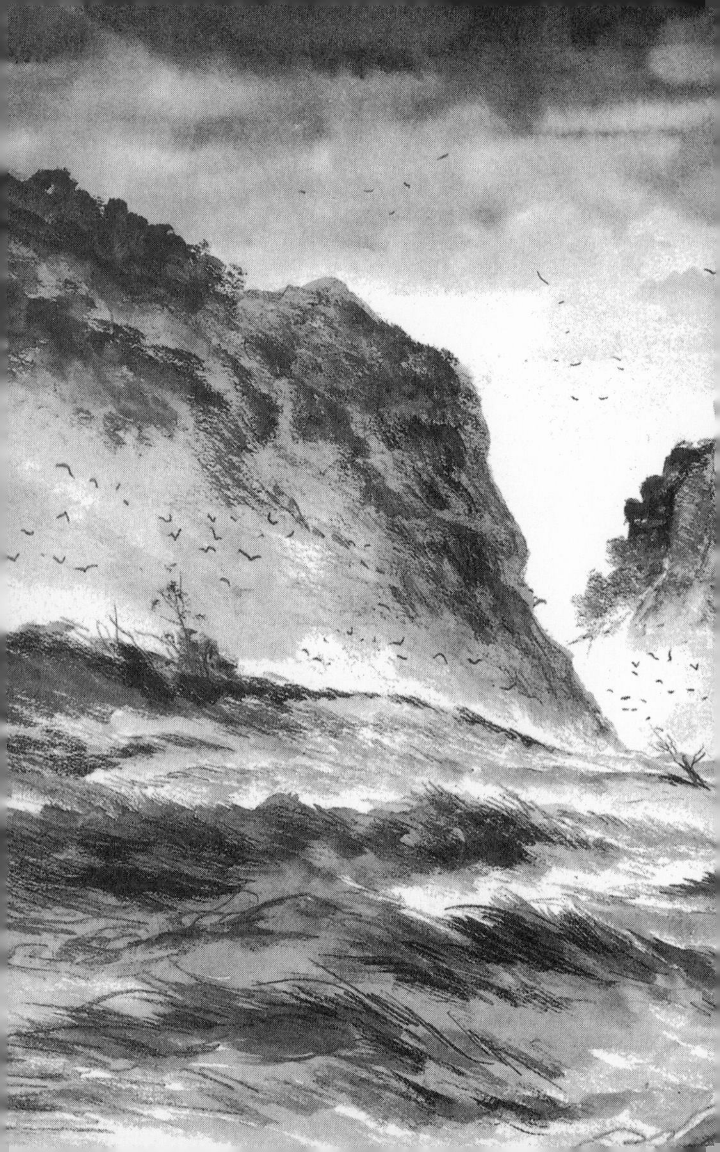

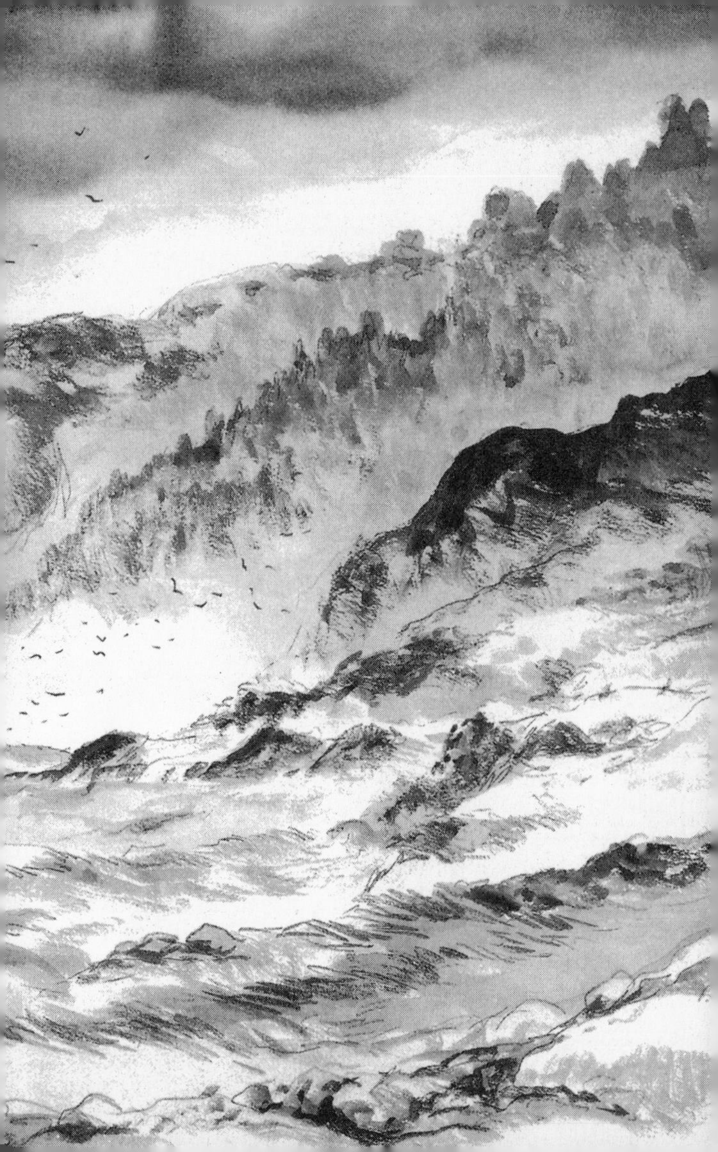

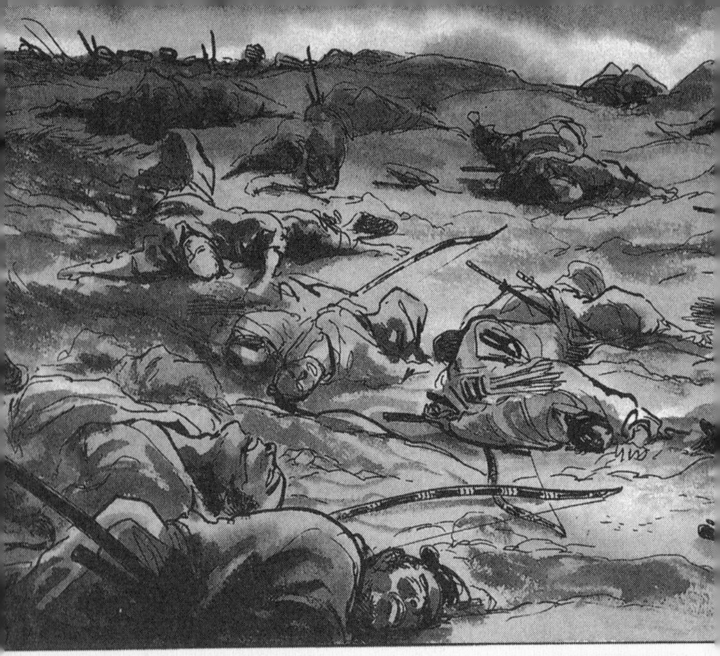
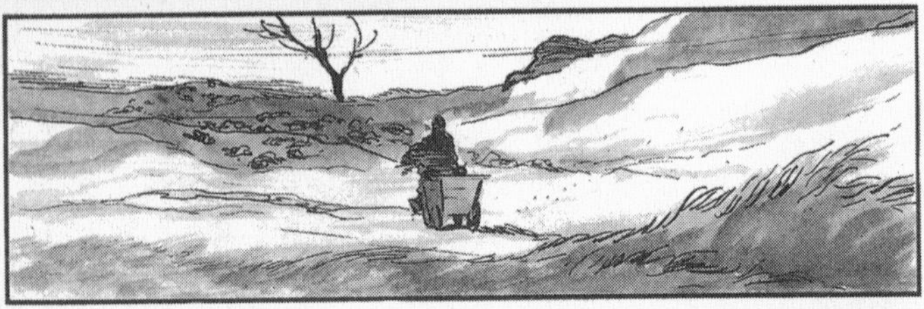
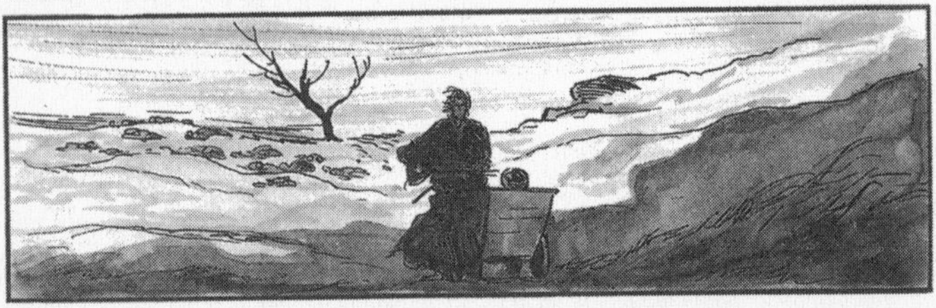

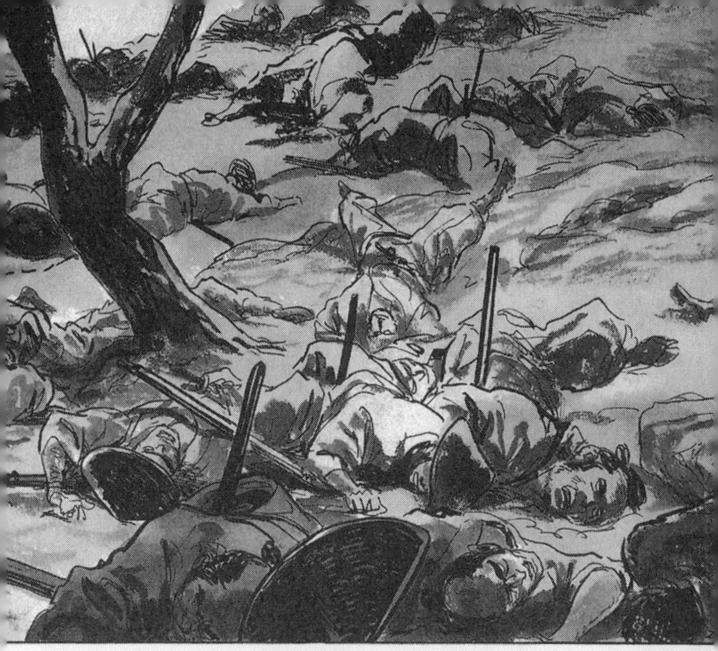

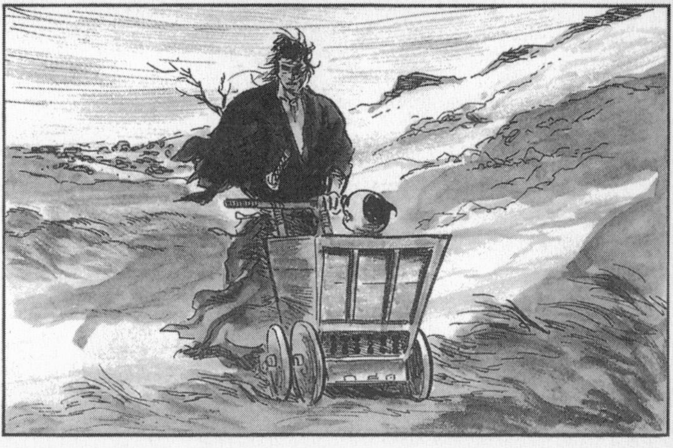

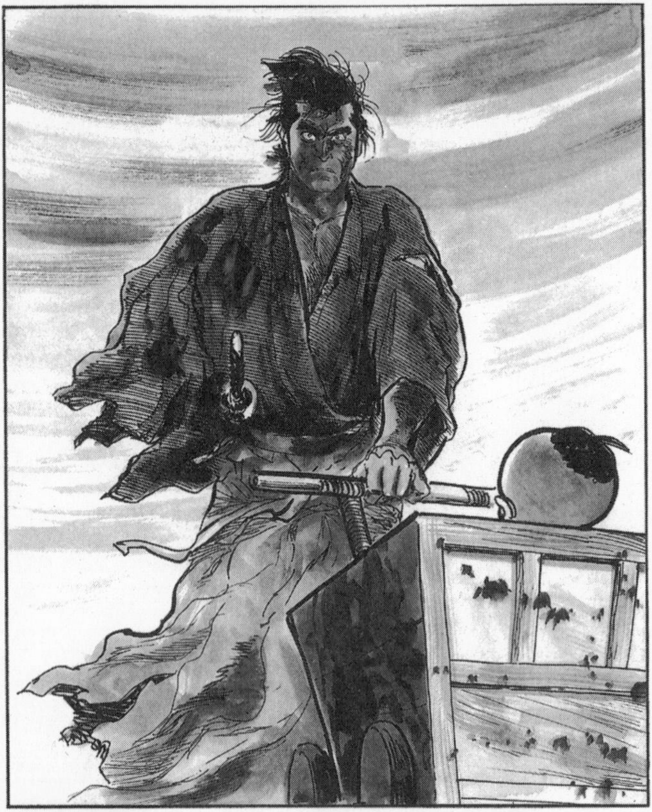

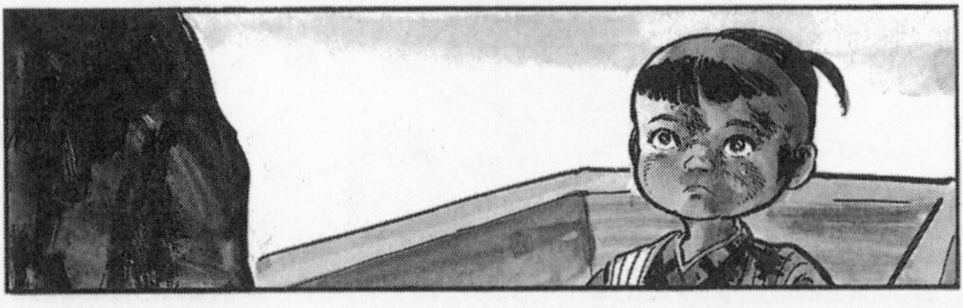

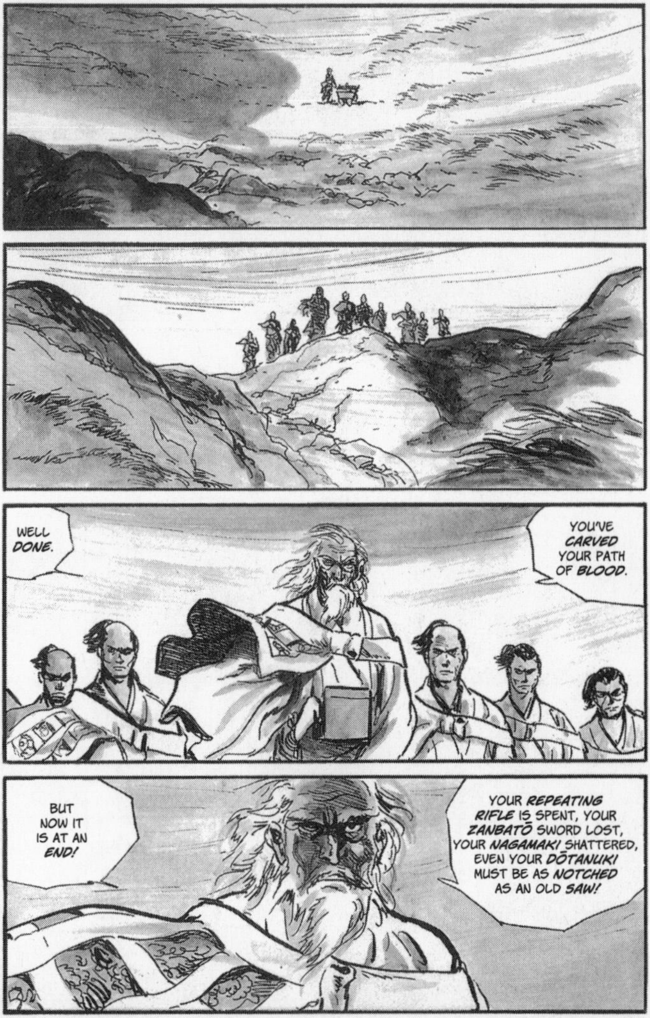

WELL DONE.
YOU'VE CARVED YOUR PATH OF BLOOD.
BUT NOW IT IS AT AN END!
YOUR REPEATING RIFLE IS SPENT, YOUR ZANBATŌ SWORD LOST, YOUR NAGAMAKI SHATTERED, EVEN YOUR DŌTANUKI MUST BE AS NOTCHED AS AN OLD SAW!

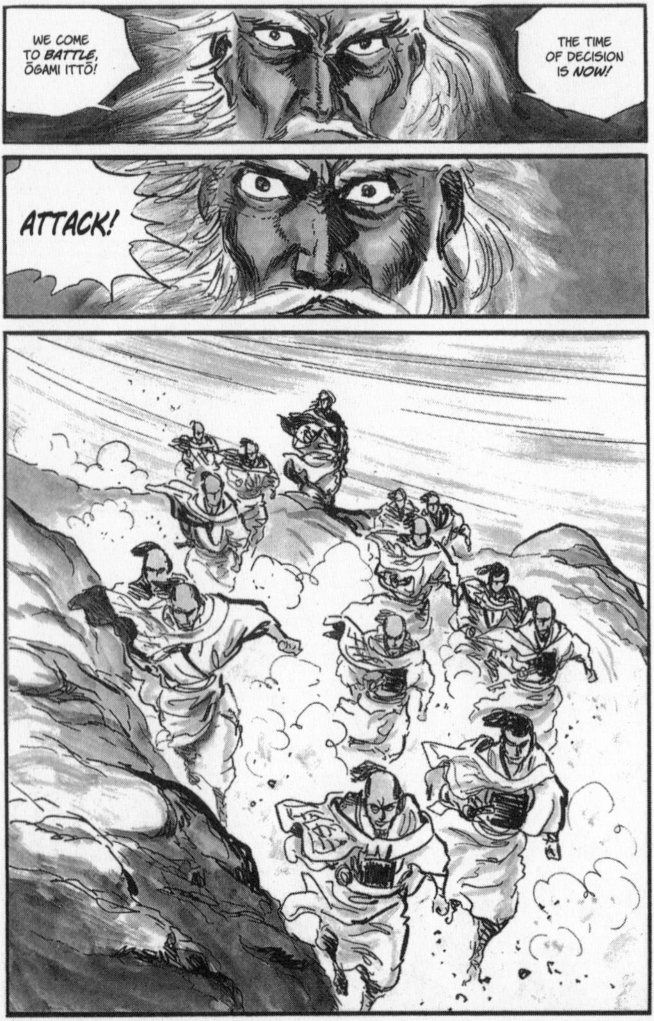
WE COME TO BATTLE, ŌGAMI ITTŌ!
THE TIME OF DECISION IS NOW!
ATTACK!

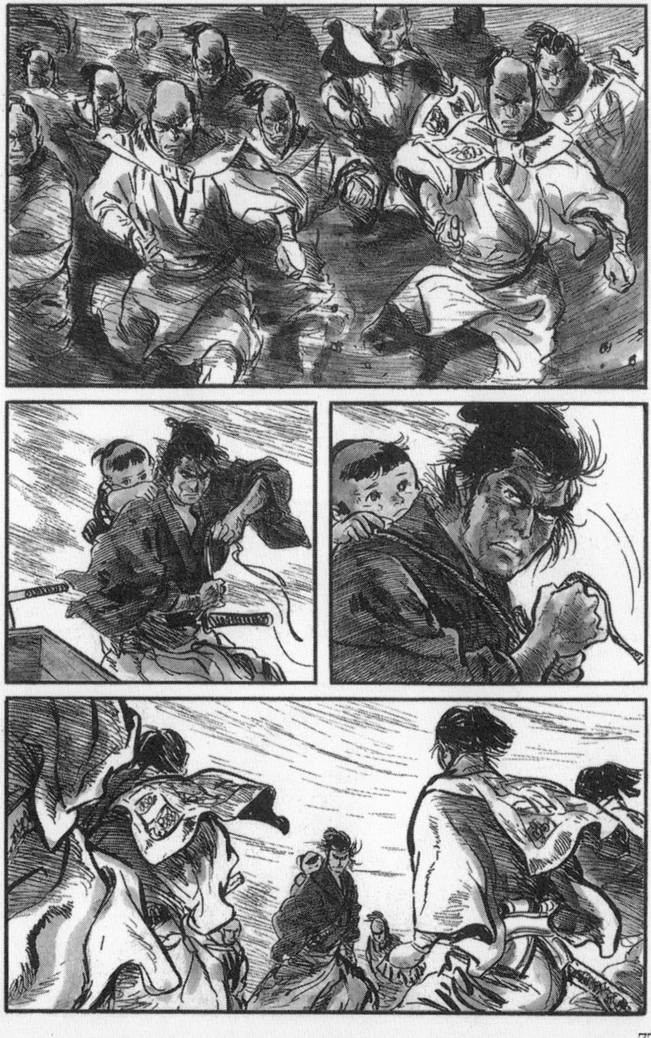

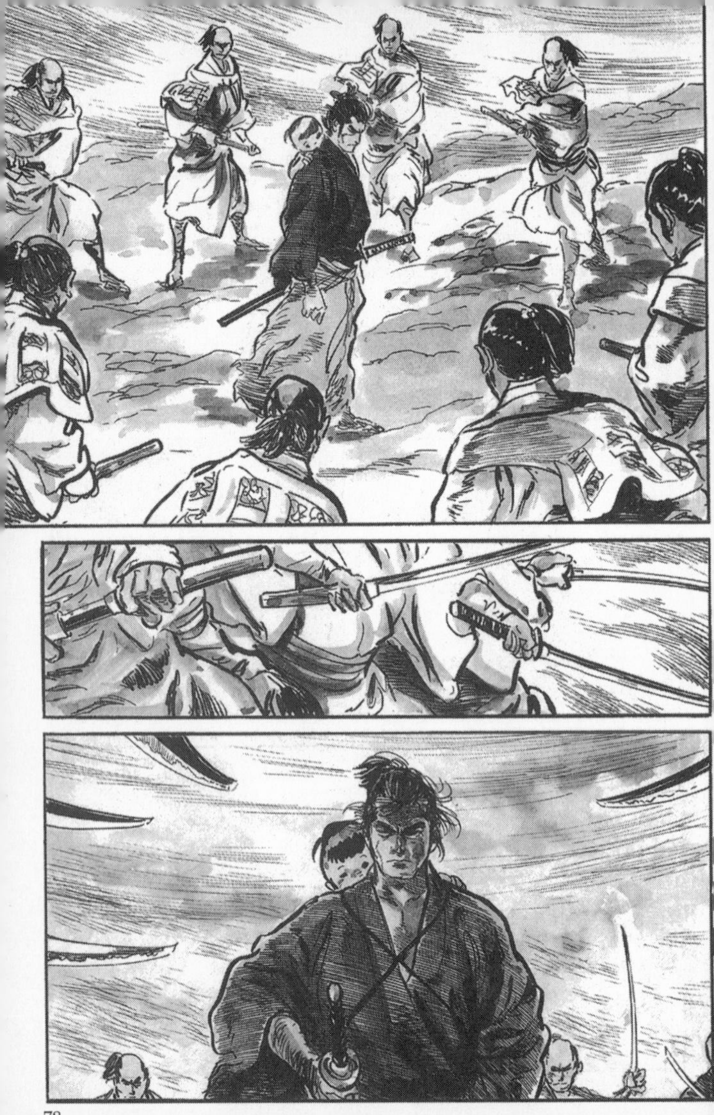

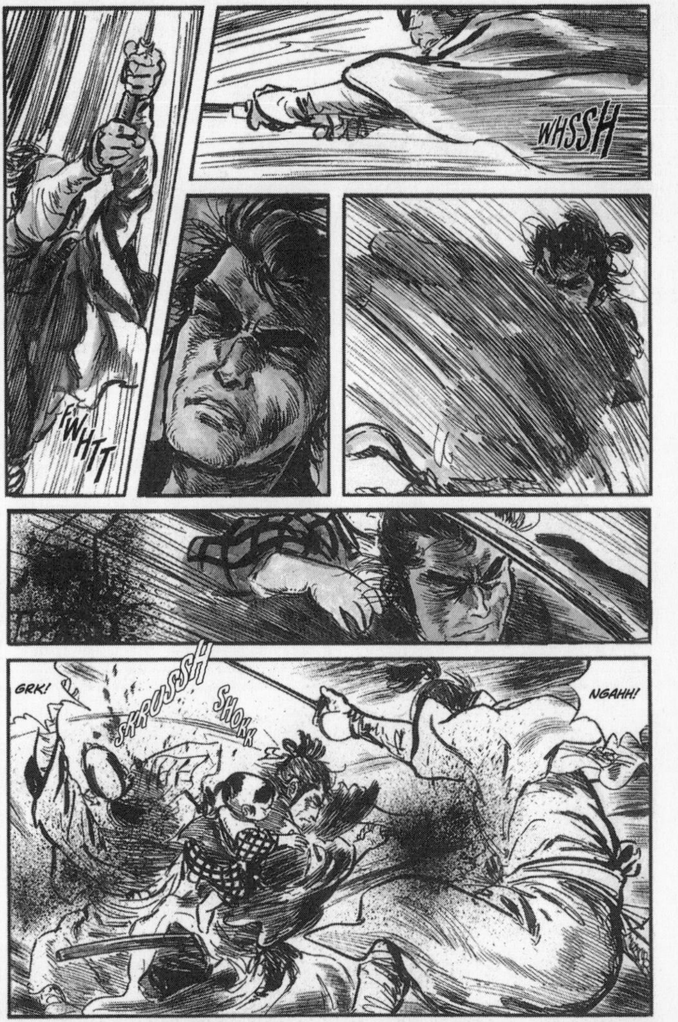
WHSSH
FWHTT
GRK!
SKRUSSSH
SHOKK
NGAHH!

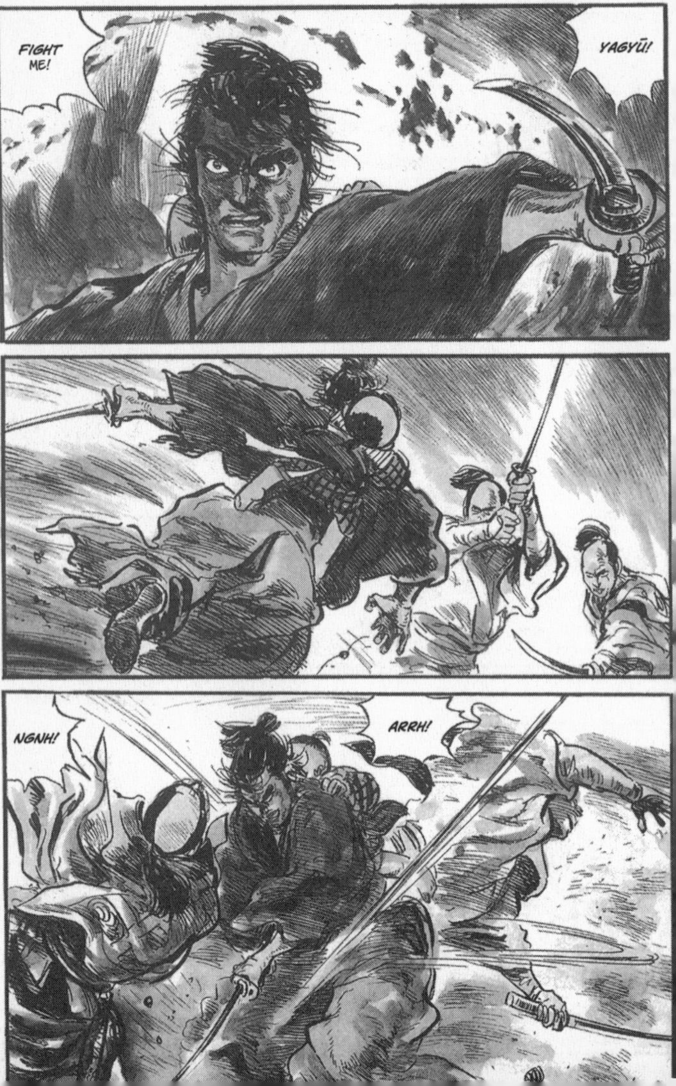
FIGHT ME!
YAGYŪ!
NGNH!
ARRH!

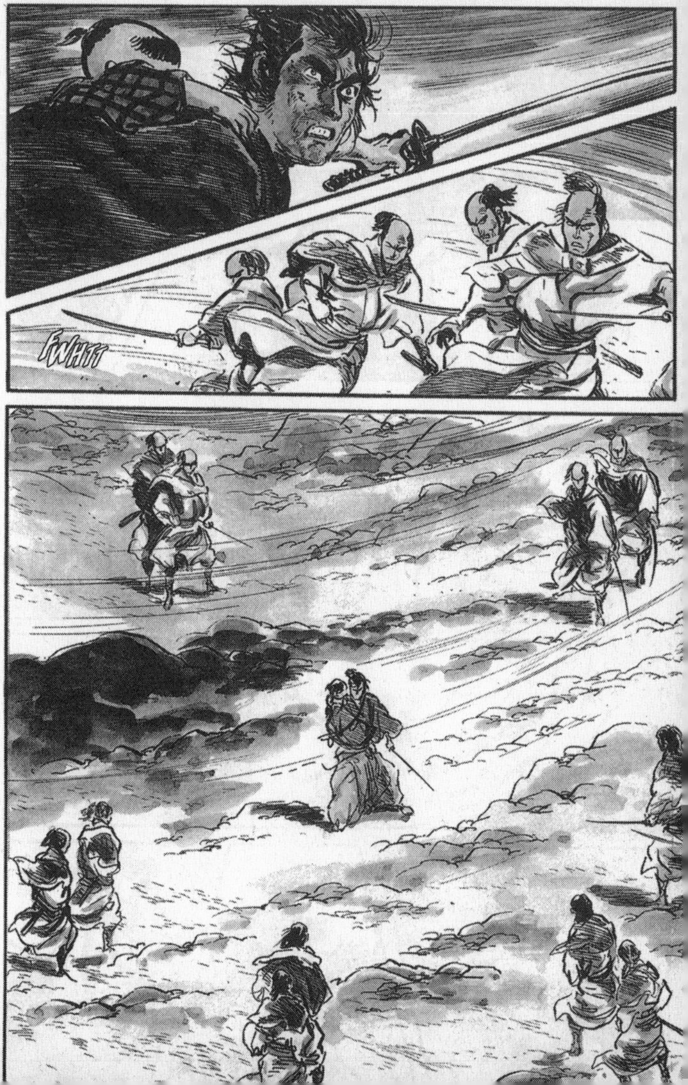
FWHTT

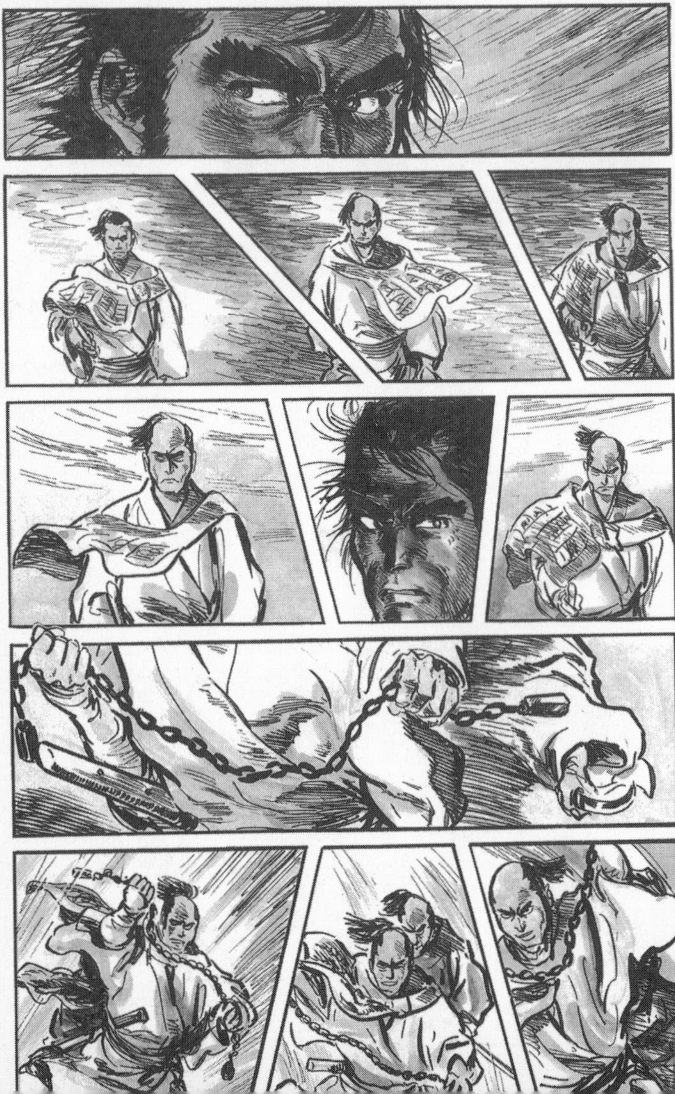

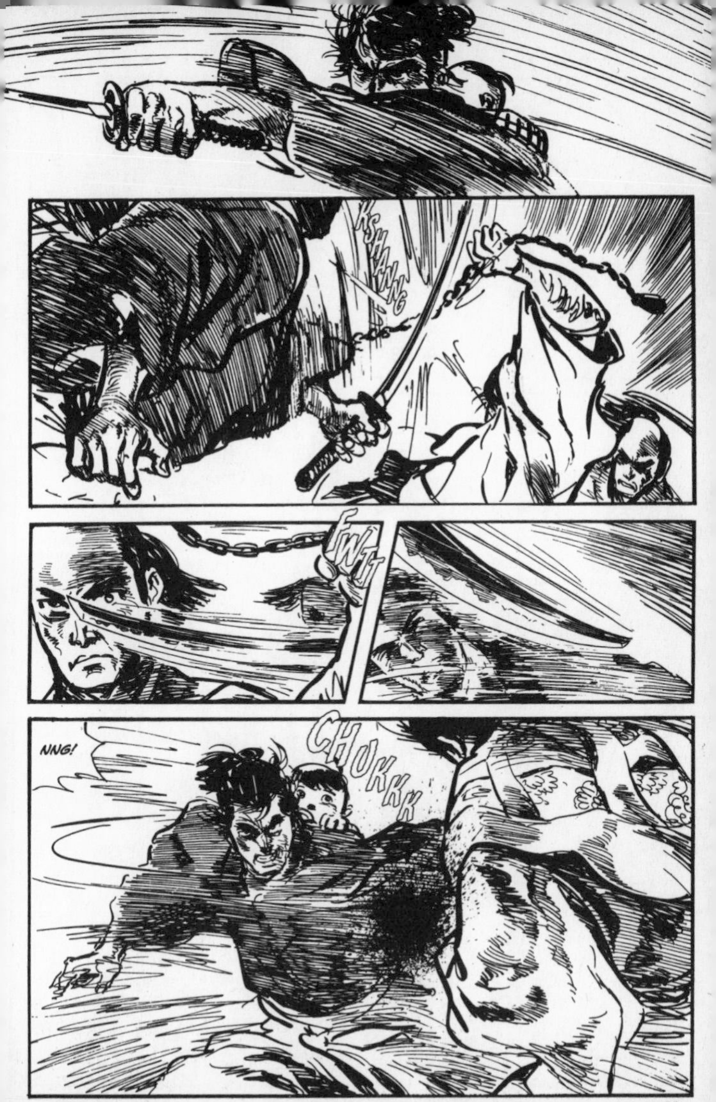
KSHANNG
FWTT
NNG!
CHUKKK

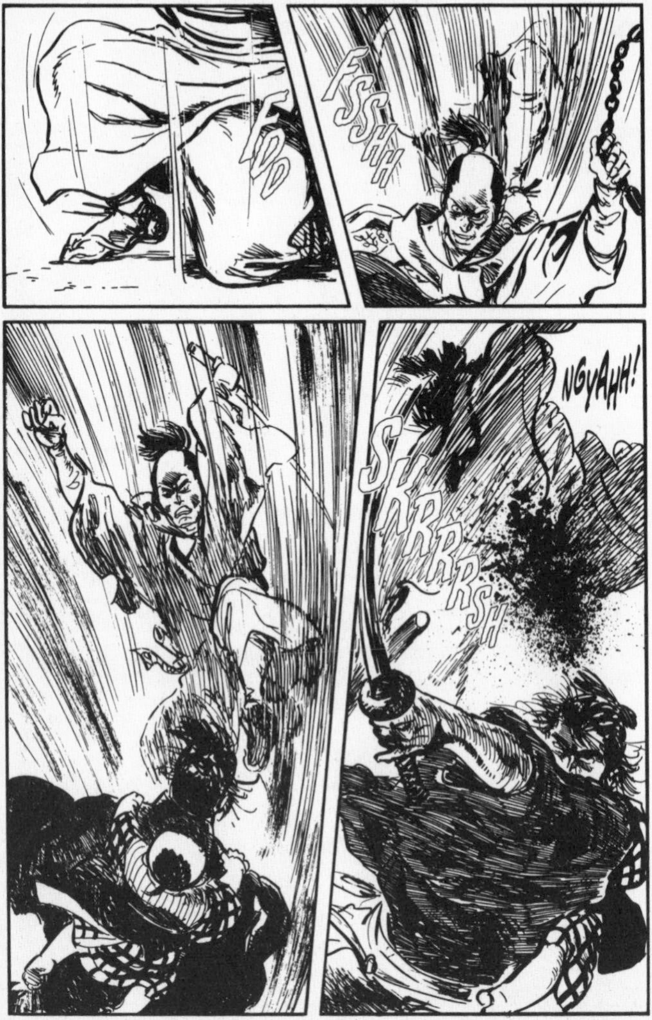
FOO
FSSHH
SHKRRRSH
NGYAHH!

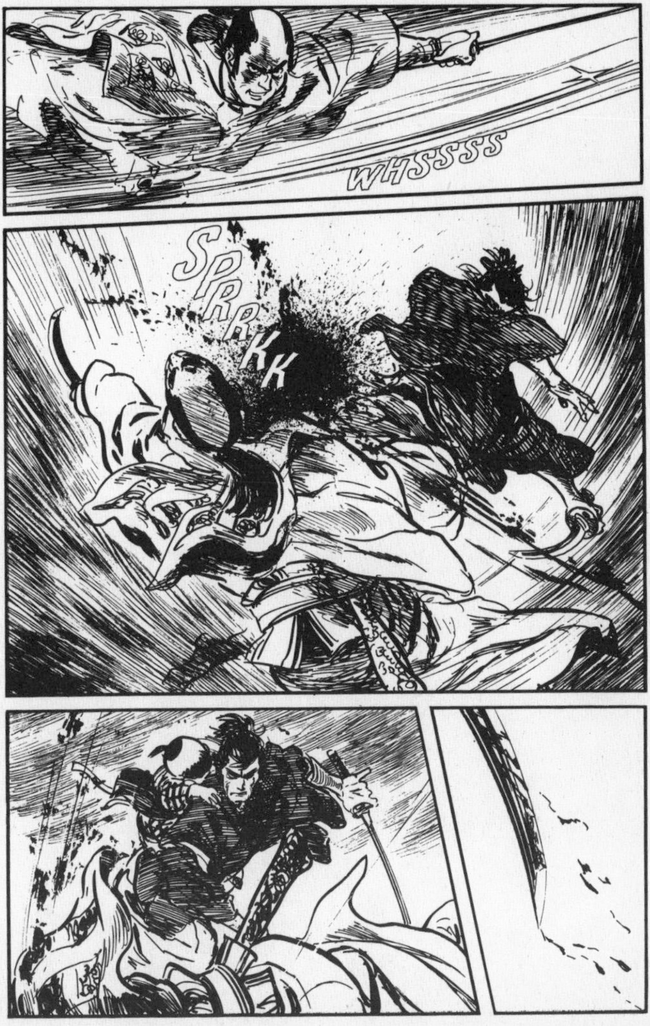
WHSSSSS
SPRRKK

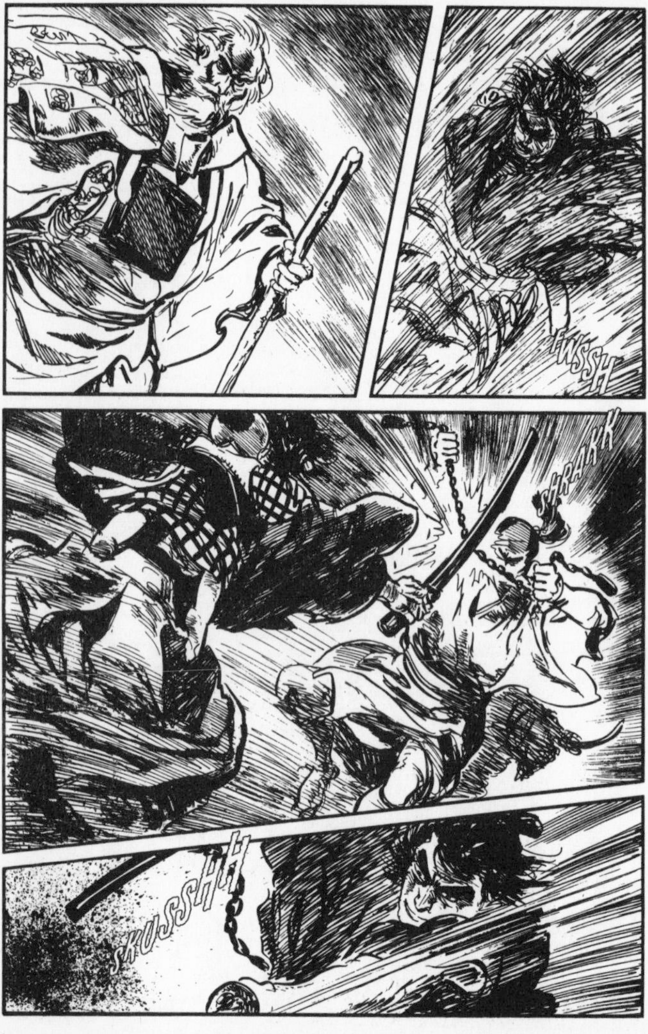
FWSSH
SHRAKK
SKUSSHH

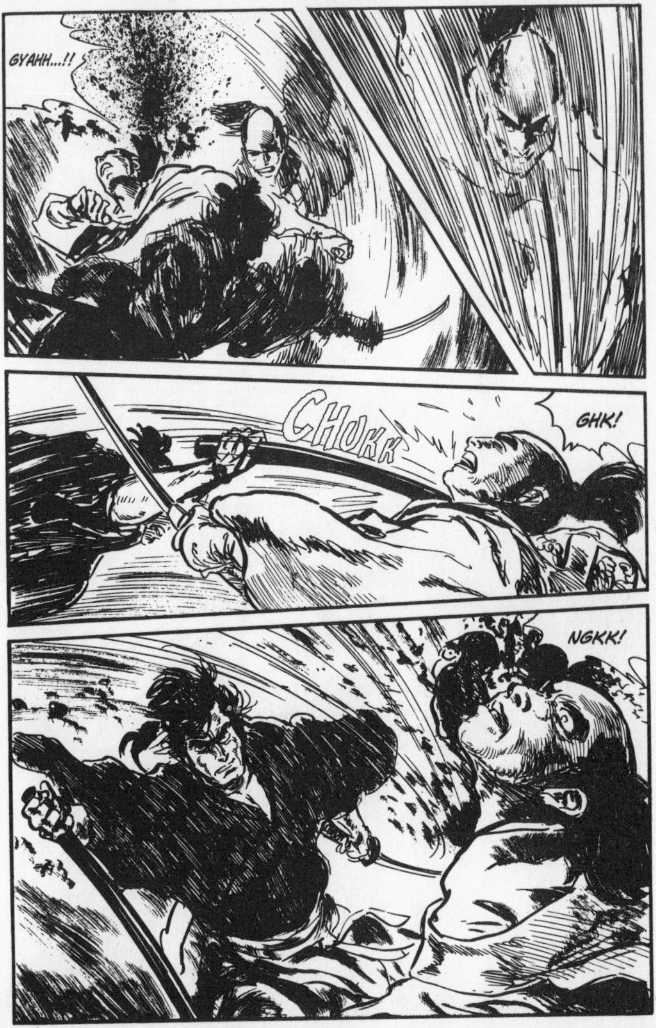
GYAHH...!!
CHOKK
GHK!
NGKK!

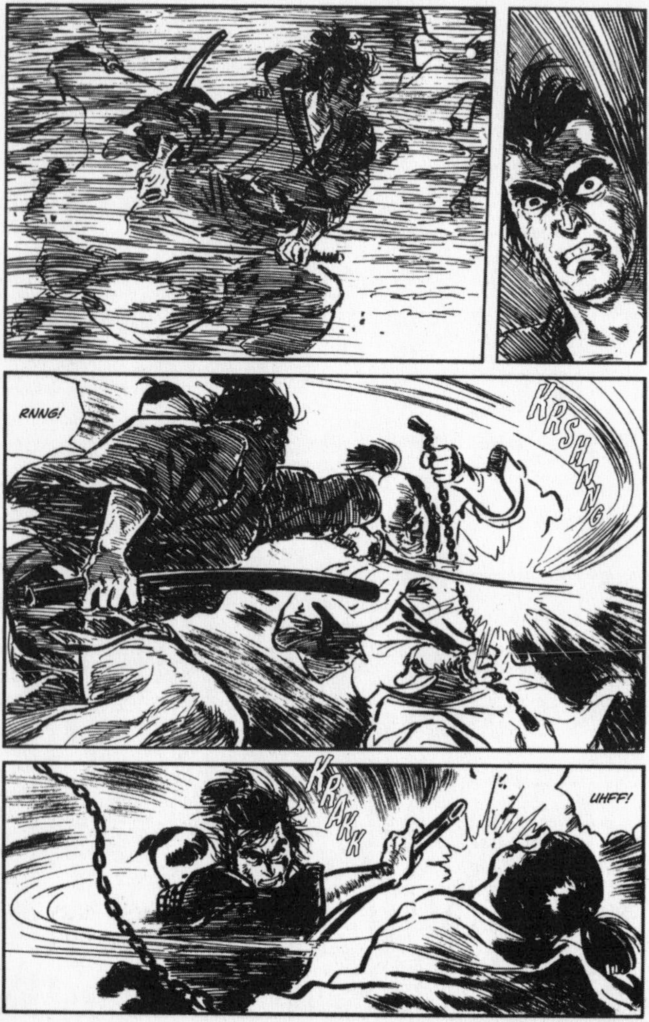
KRSHNNG
RNNG!
UHFF!
KRAKK

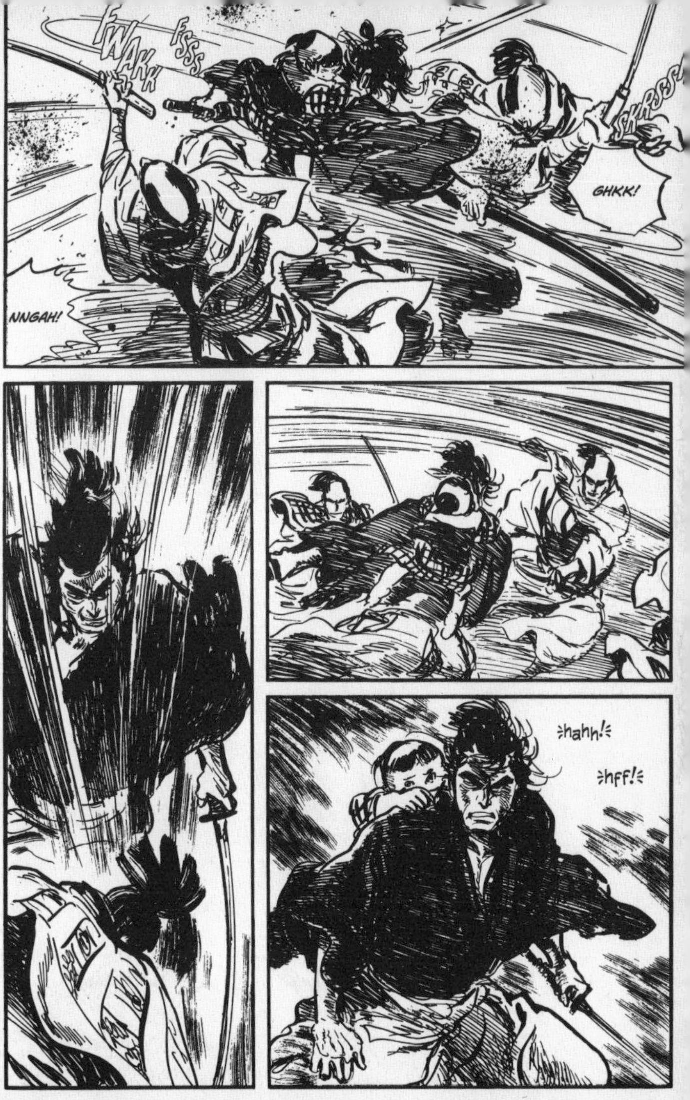
FWAKK
FSSS
SKRSSS
GHKK!
NNGAH!
hahh!
hff!

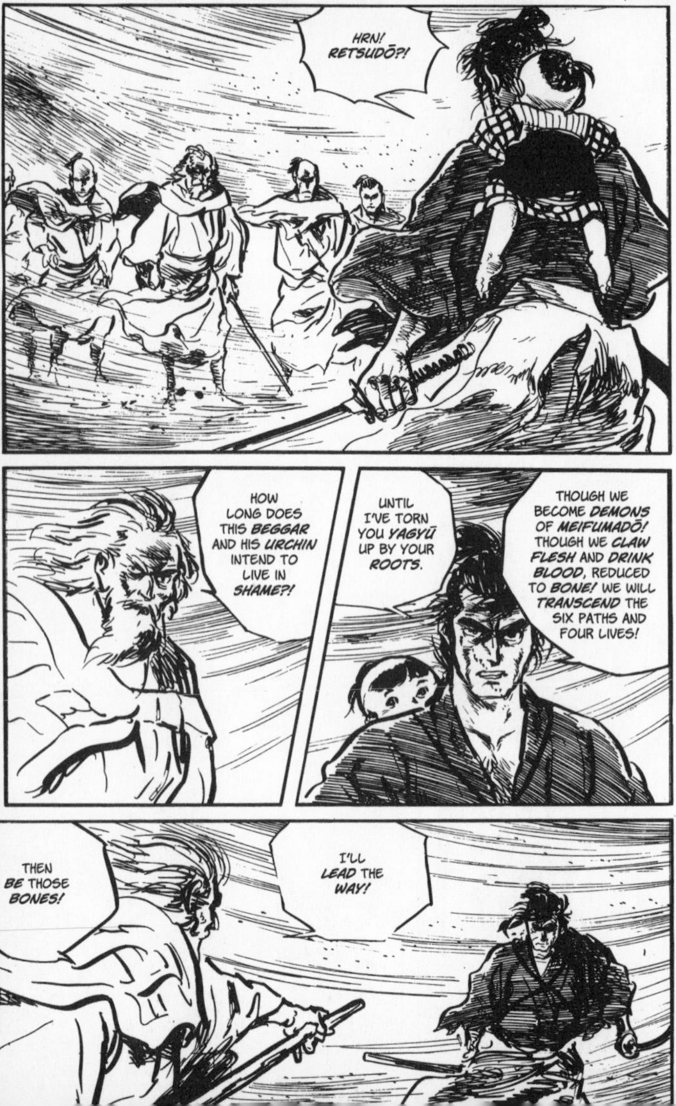
HRN! RETSUDŌ?!
HOW LONG DOES THIS BEGGAR AND HIS URCHIN INTEND TO LIVE IN SHAME?!
UNTIL I'VE TORN YOU YAGYŪ UP BY YOUR ROOTS.
THOUGH WE BECOME DEMONS OF MEIFUMADŌ! THOUGH WE CLAW FLESH AND DRINK BLOOD, REDUCED TO BONE! WE WILL TRANSCEND THE SIX PATHS AND FOUR LIVES!
THEN BE THOSE BONES!
I'LL LEAD THE WAY!

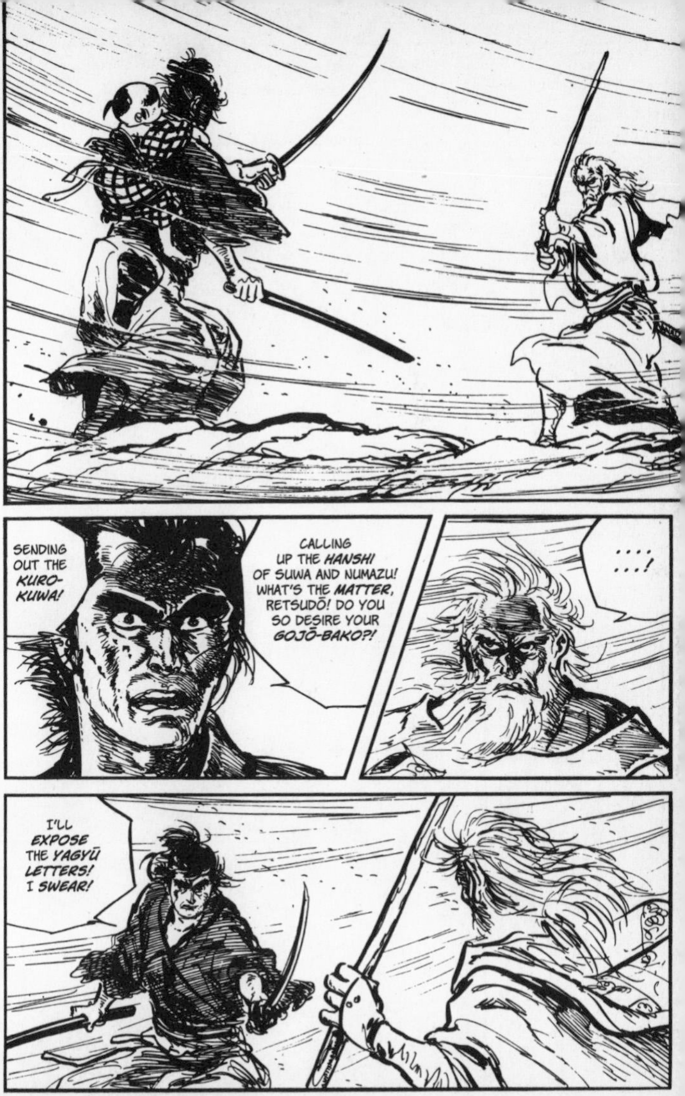
SENDING OUT THE KURO-KUWA!
CALLING UP THE HANSHI OF SUWA AND NUMAZU! WHAT'S THE MATTER, RETSUDŌ! DO YOU SO DESIRE YOUR GOJŌ-BAKO?!
....!
I'LL EXPOSE THE YAGYŪ LETTERS! I SWEAR!

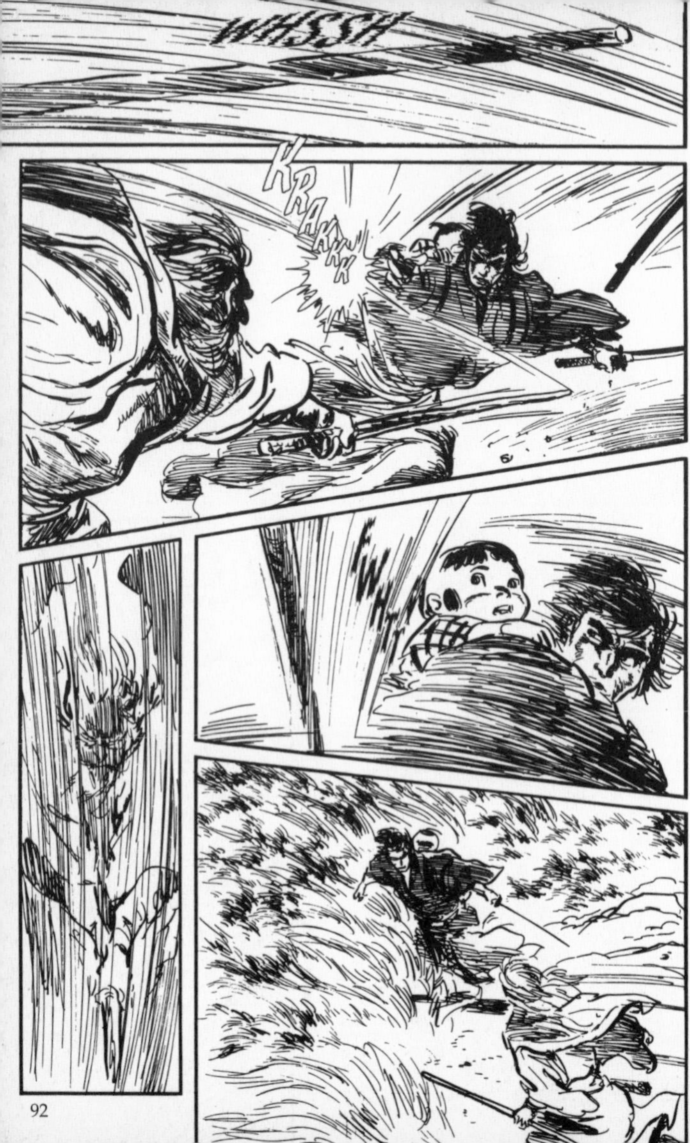
WHSSH
KRAKKKK
FWHT

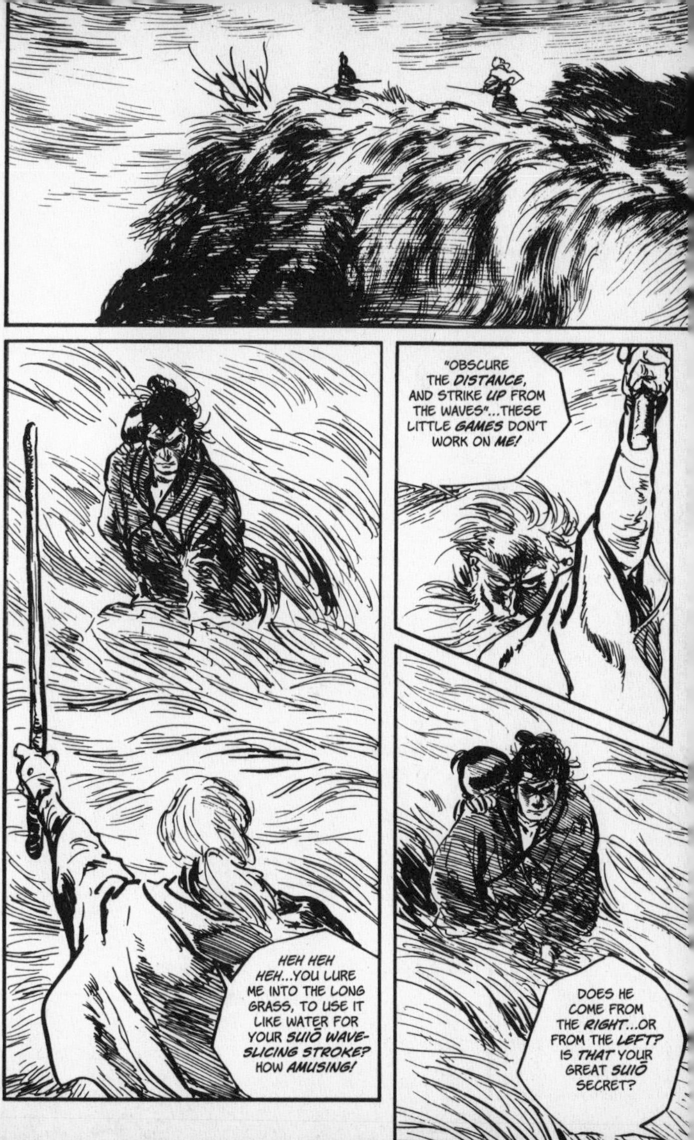

HEH HEH HEH...YOU LURE ME INTO THE LONG GRASS, TO USE IT LIKE WATER FOR YOUR SUIŌ WAVE-SLICING STROKE? HOW AMUSING!
"OBSCURE THE DISTANCE, AND STRIKE UP FROM THE WAVES"...THESE LITTLE GAMES DON'T WORK ON ME!
DOES HE COME FROM THE RIGHT...OR FROM THE LEFT? IS THAT YOUR GREAT SUIŌ SECRET?

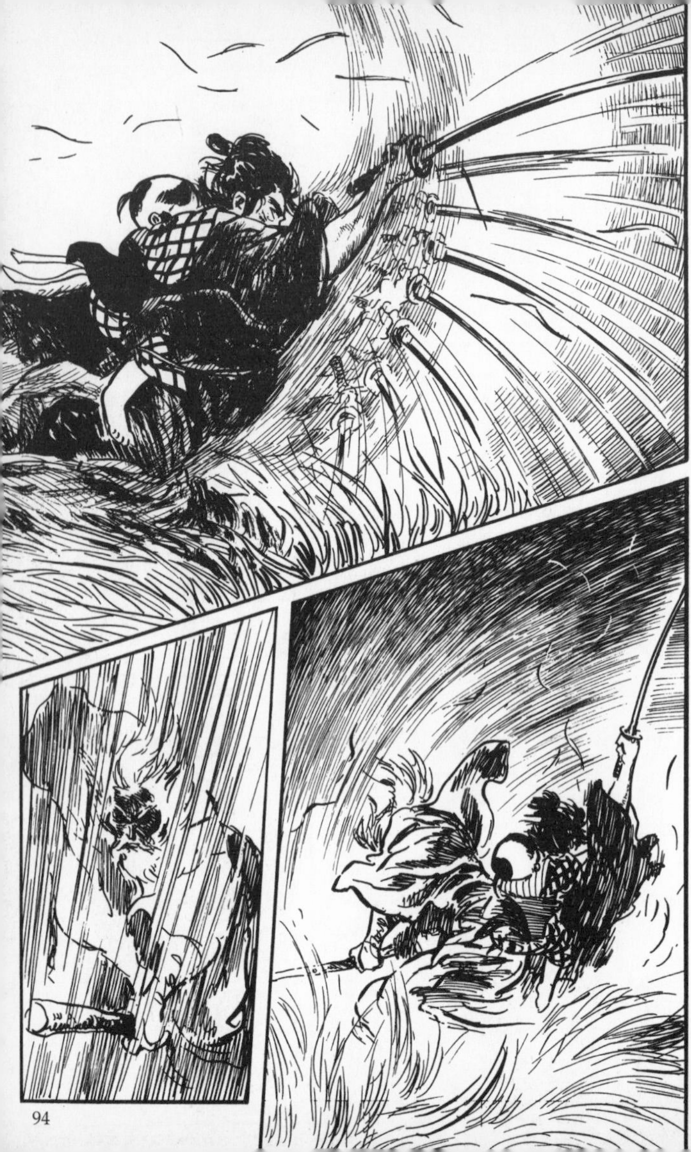

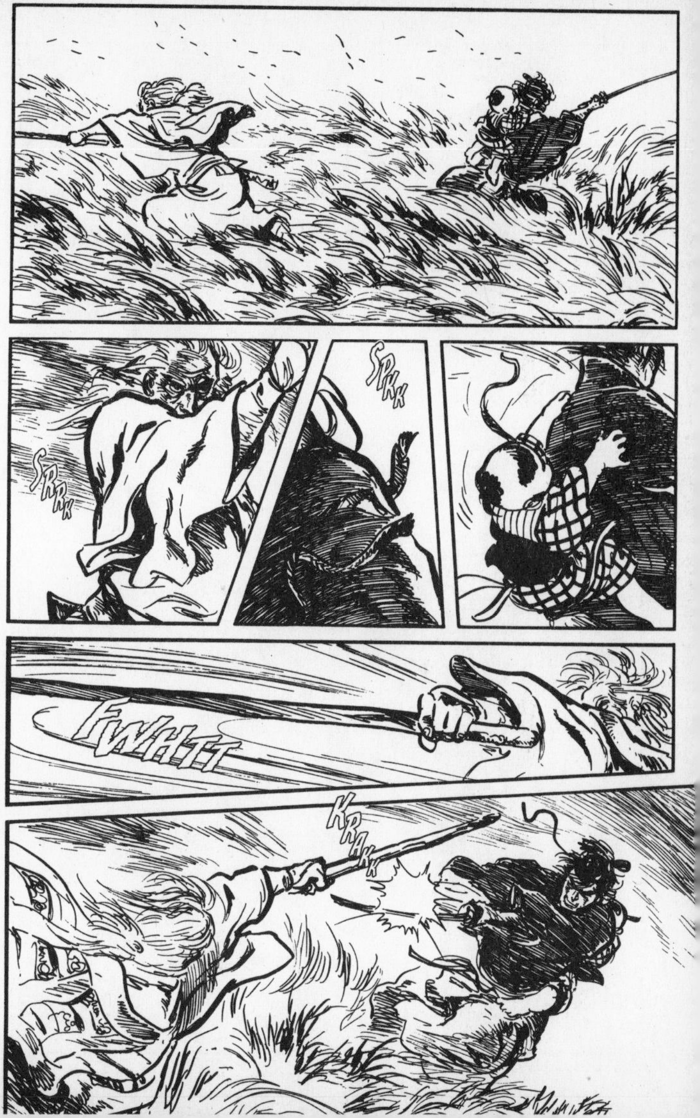
SRRKK
SPKK
FWHTT
KRAKK

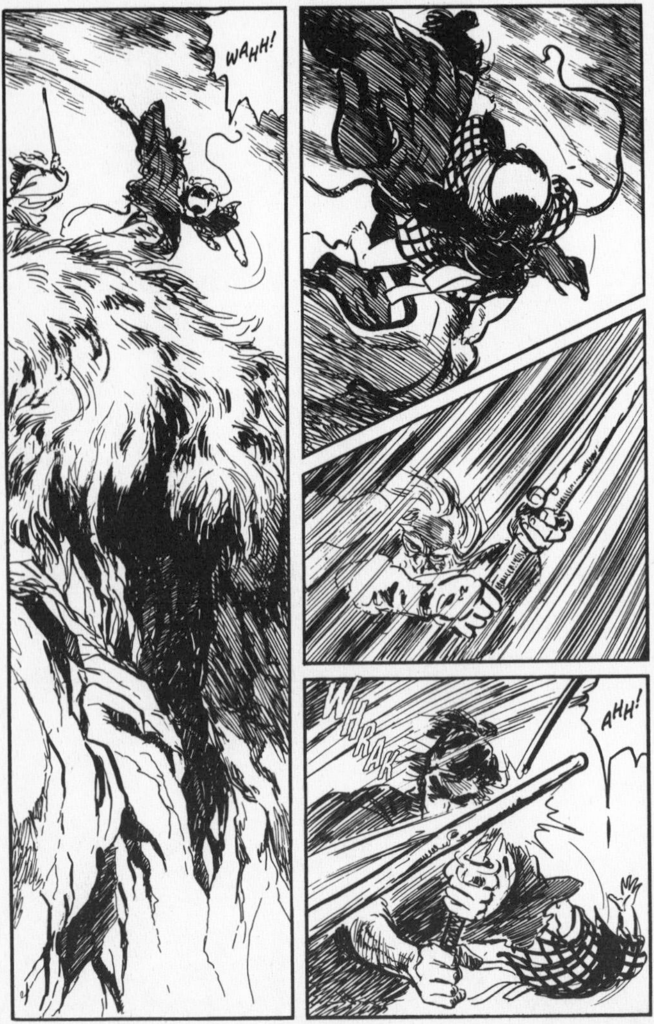
WAHH!
WHRAK
AHH!

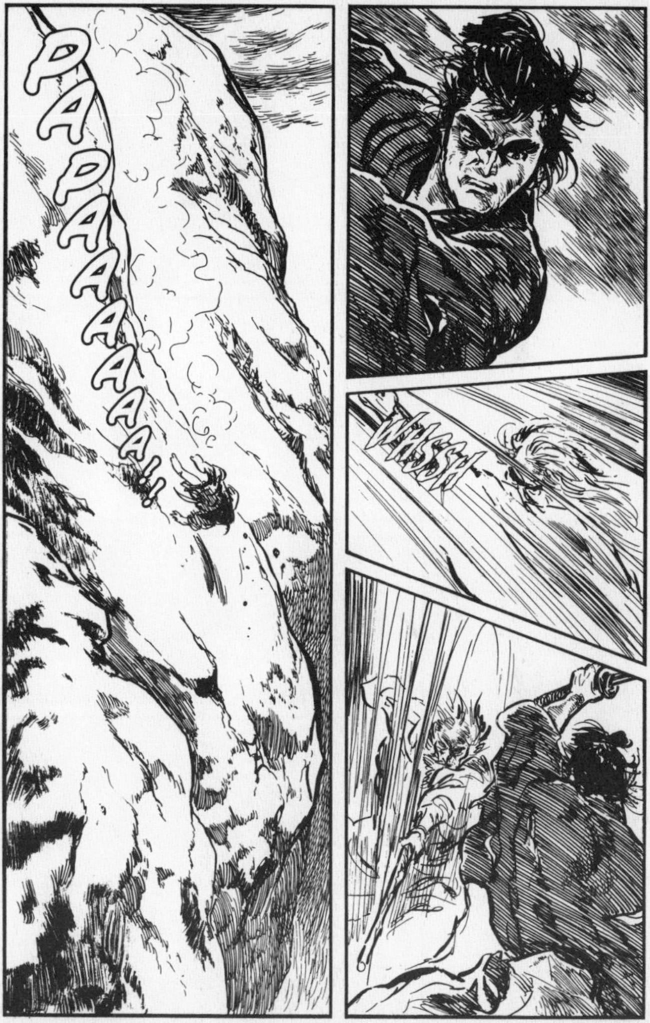
PAPAAAAAA!!!
WHSSH

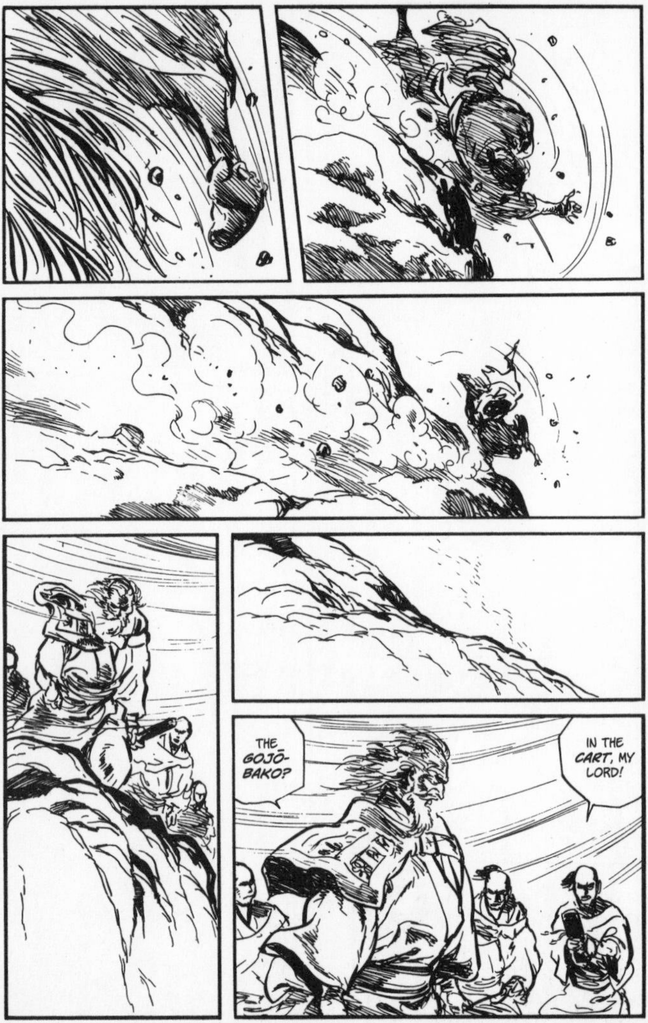
THE *GOJŌ-BAKO?*
IN THE *CART*, MY LORD!

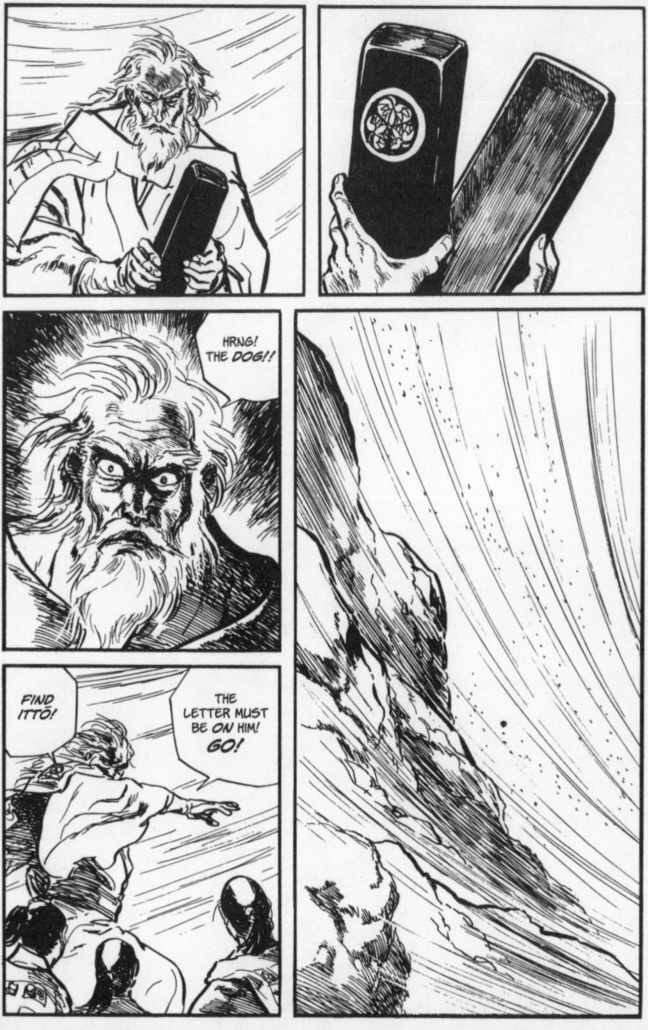
HRNG! THE DOG!!
FIND ITTŌ!
THE LETTER MUST BE ON HIM! GO!

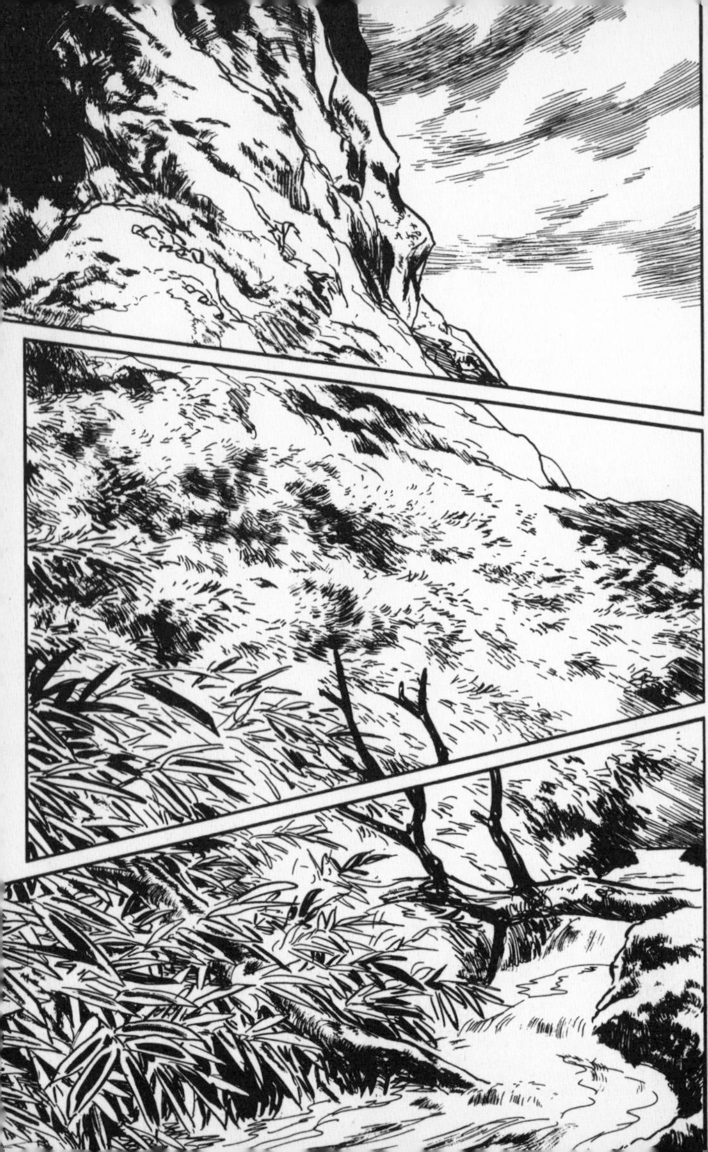

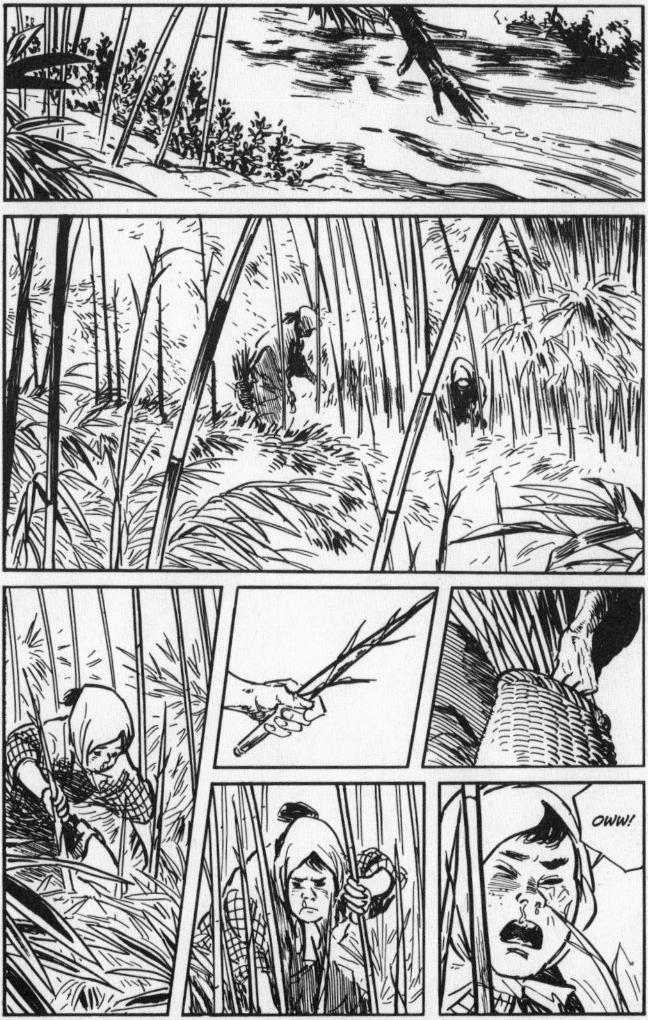
OWW!

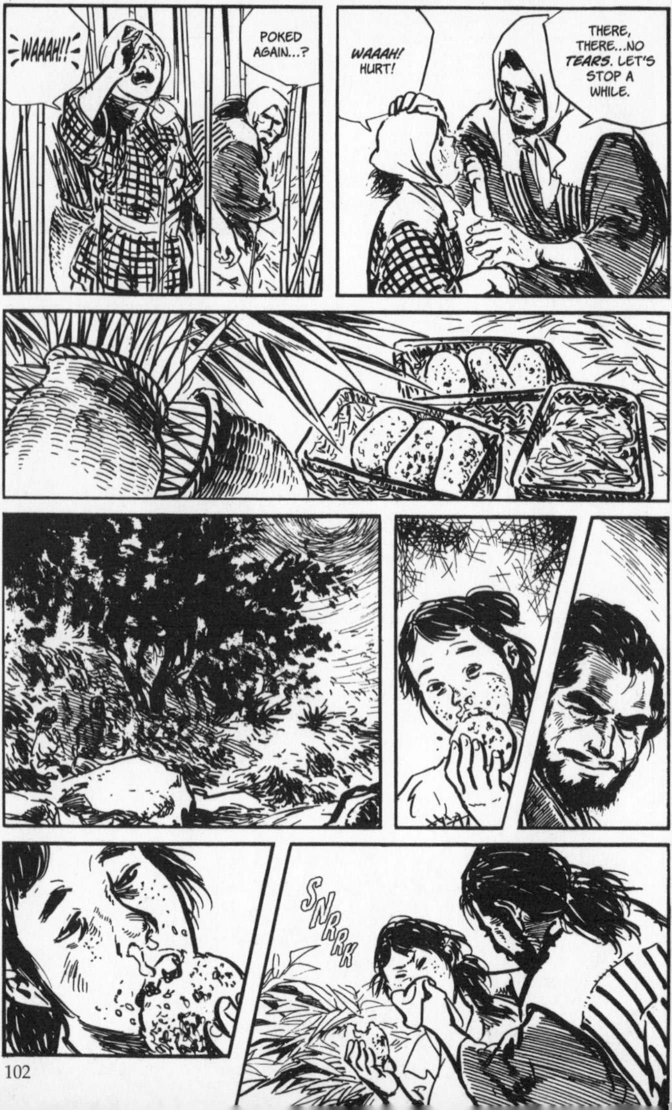
WAAAH!!
POKED AGAIN...?
WAAAH! HURT!
THERE, THERE...NO TEARS. LET'S STOP A WHILE.
SNRRK

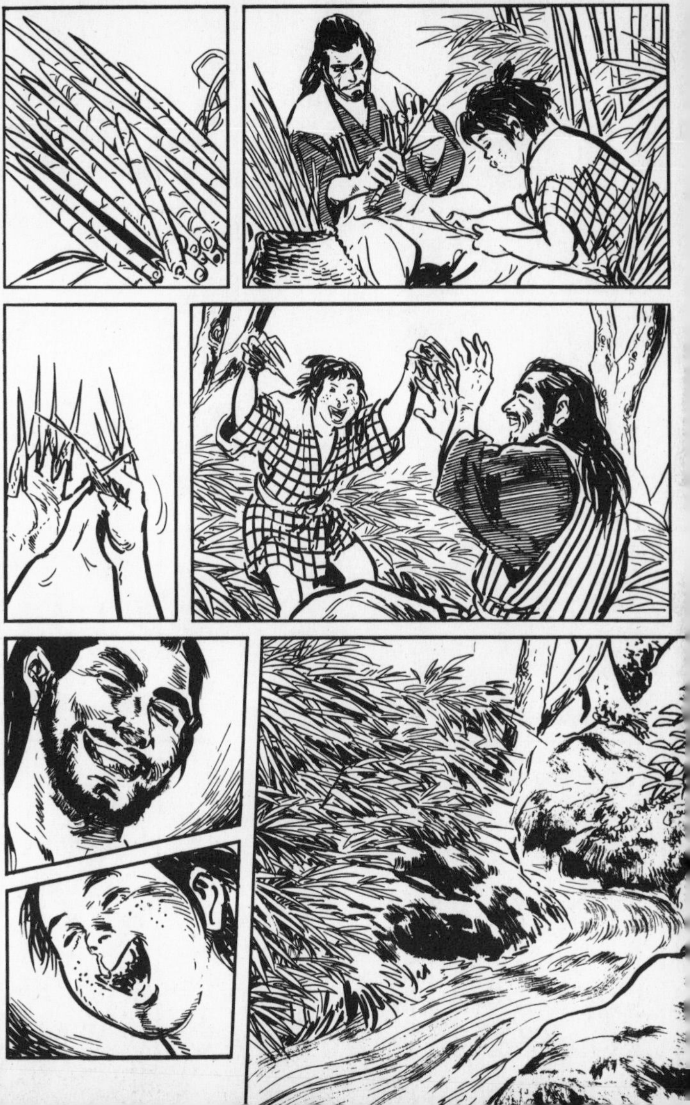

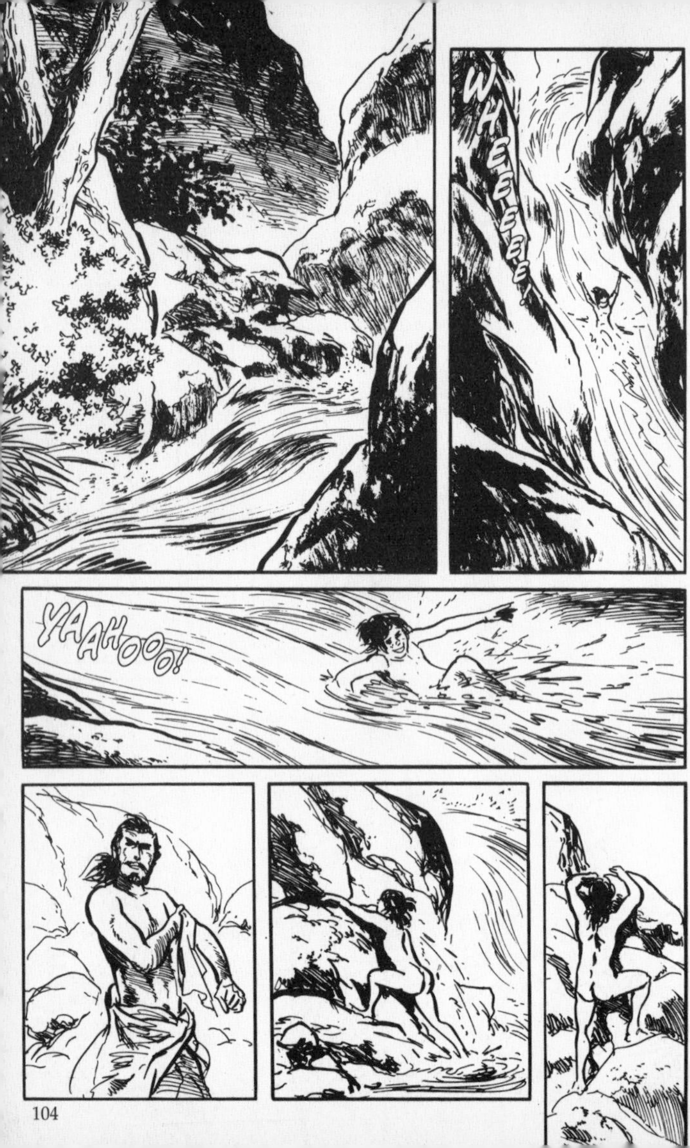
WHEEEEEE!
YAAHOOOO!

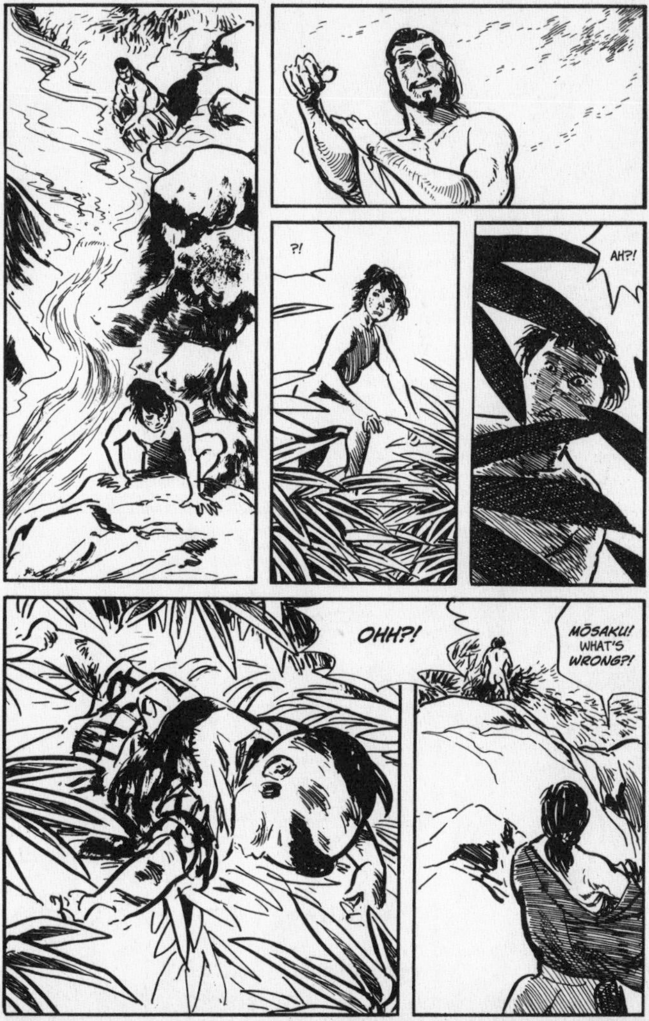
?!
AH?!
OHH?!
MŌSAKU! WHAT'S WRONG?!

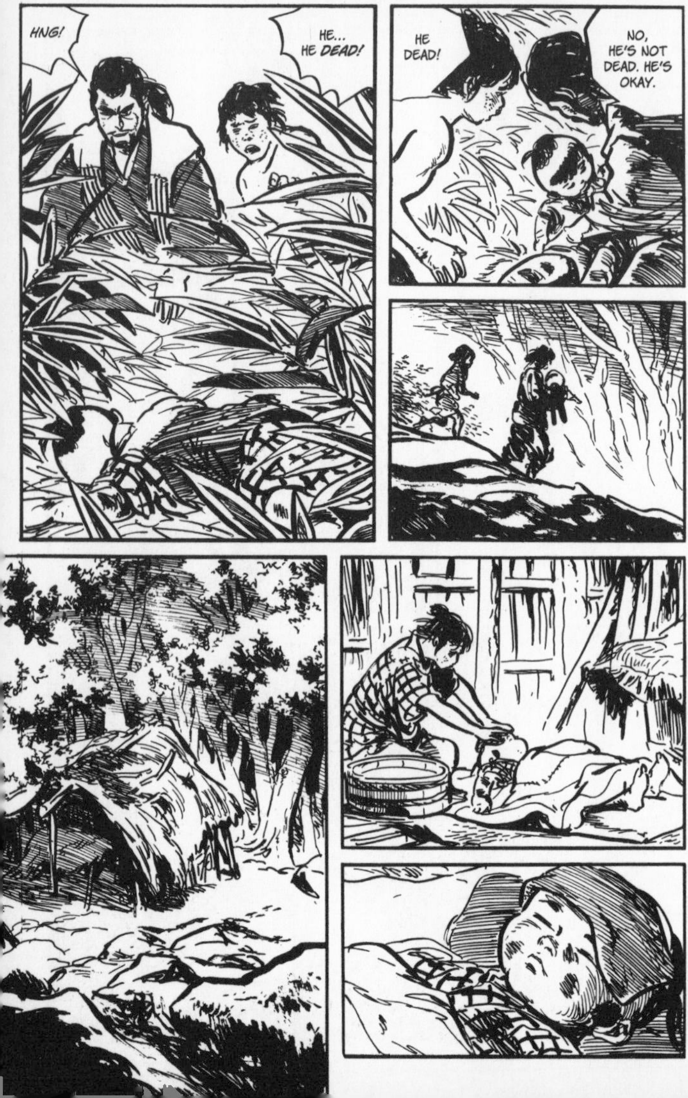
HNG!
HE... HE *DEAD!*
HE DEAD!
NO, HE'S NOT DEAD. HE'S OKAY.

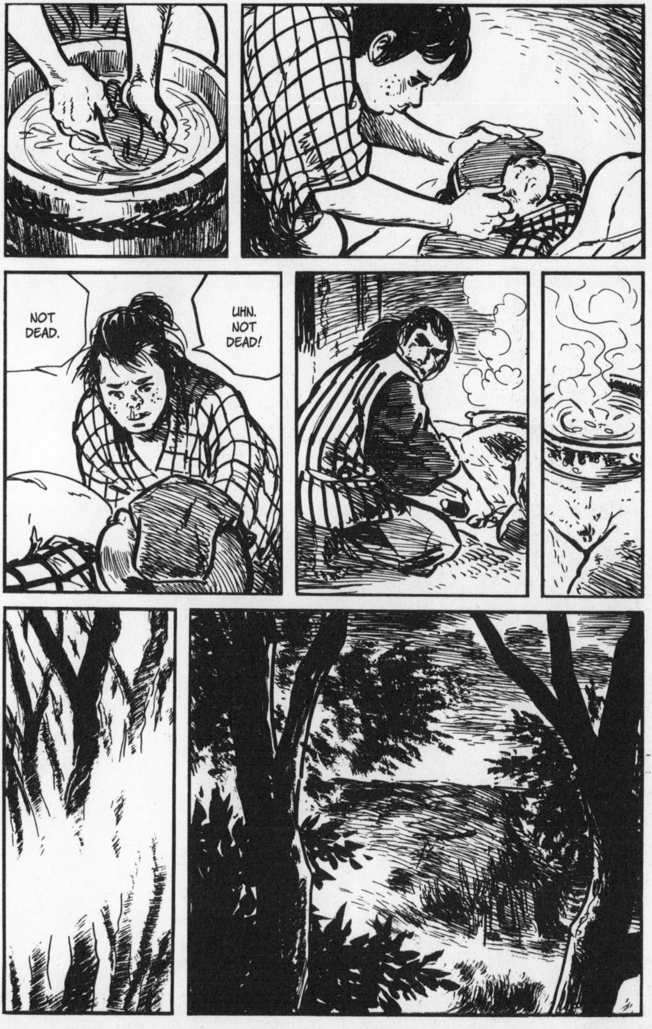
NOT DEAD.
UHN. NOT DEAD!

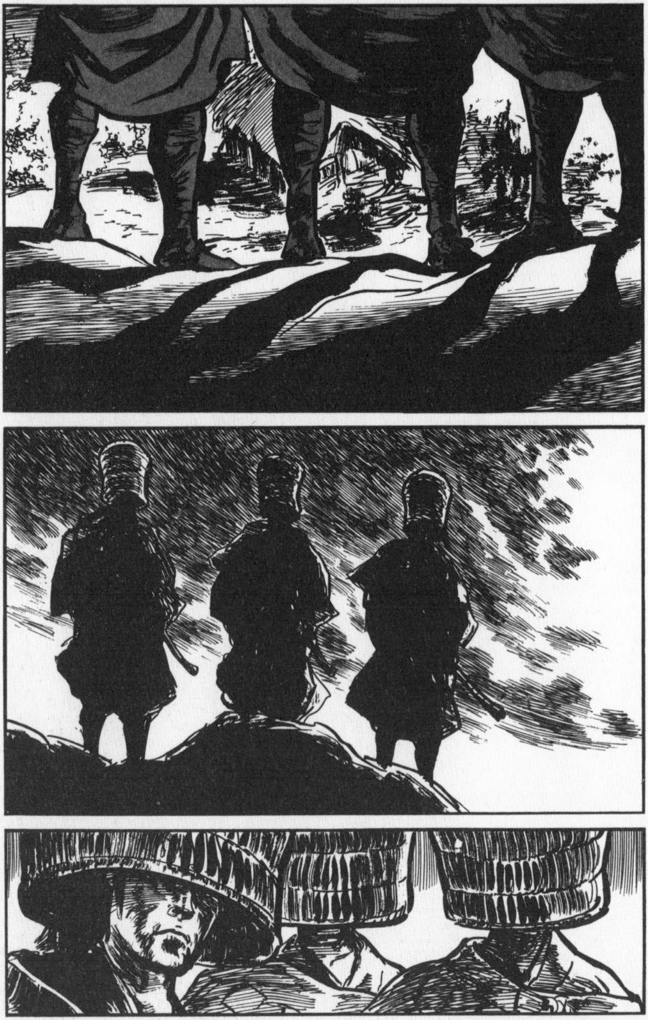

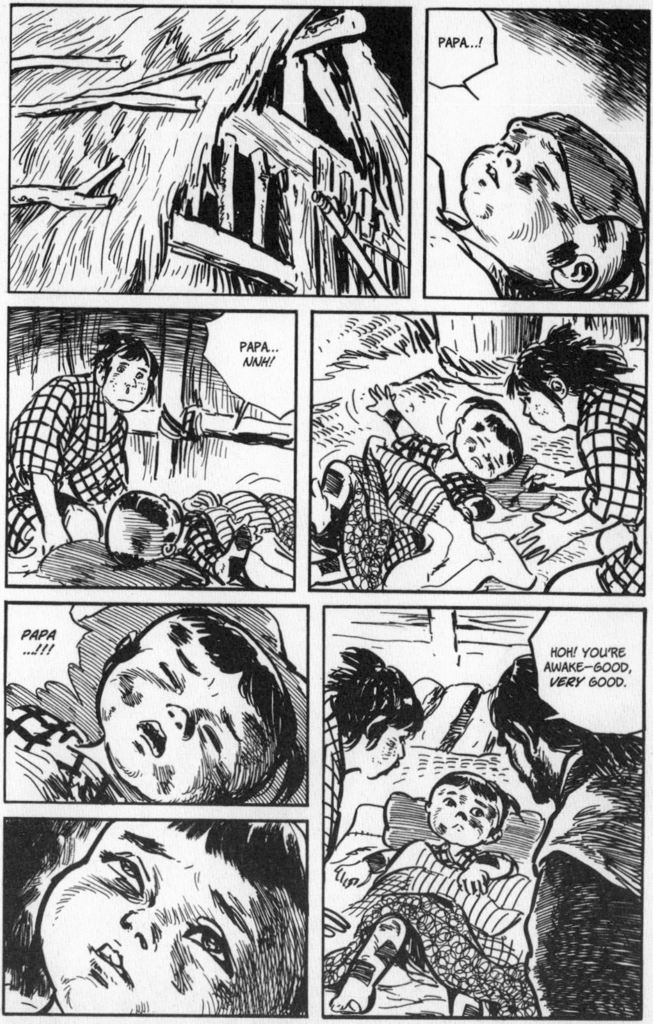
PAPA...!
PAPA.. NNH!
PAPA ...!!!
HOH! YOU'RE AWAKE—GOOD, VERY GOOD.

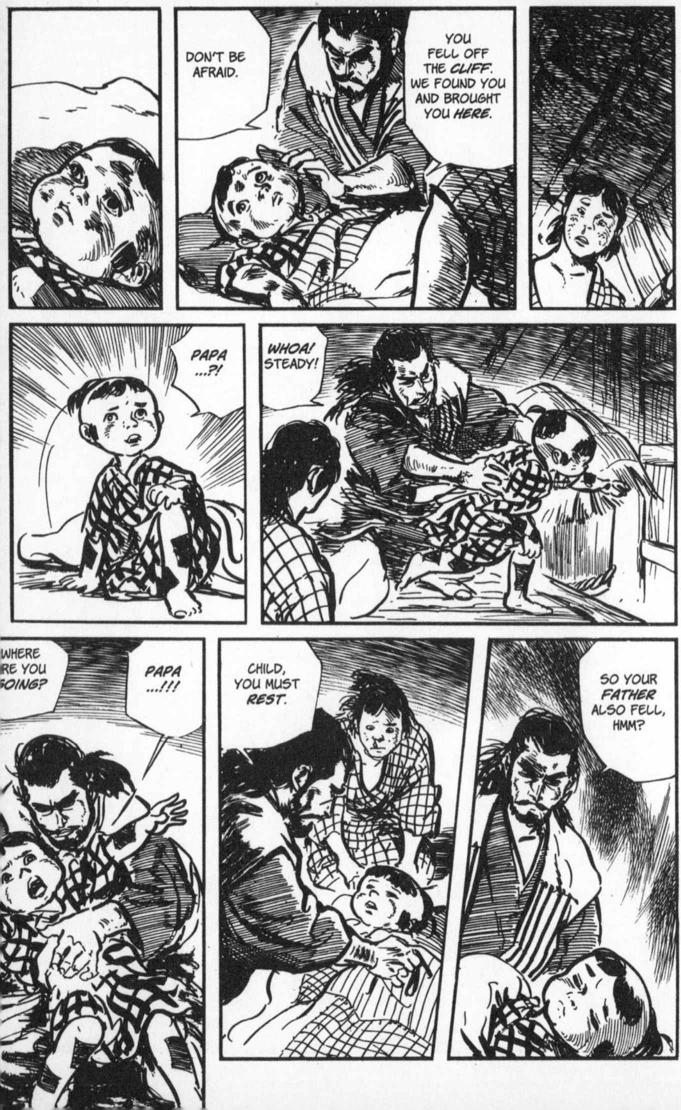
DON'T BE AFRAID.
YOU FELL OFF THE CLIFF. WE FOUND YOU AND BROUGHT YOU HERE.
PAPA ...?!
WHOA! STEADY!
WHERE RE YOU GOING?
PAPA ...!!!
CHILD, YOU MUST REST.
SO YOUR FATHER ALSO FELL, HMM?

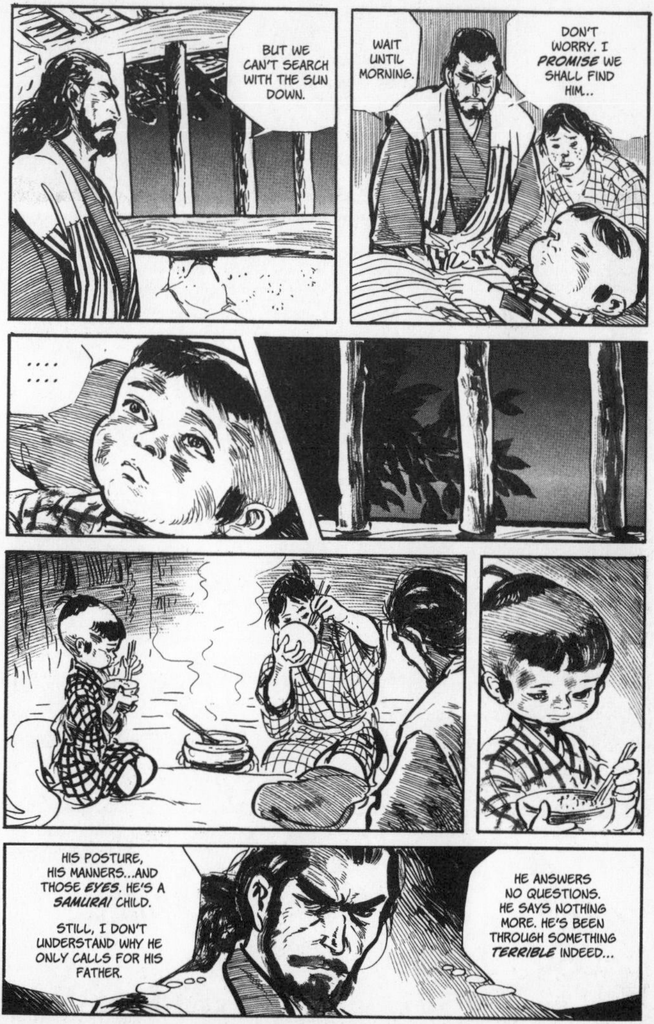

BUT WE CAN'T SEARCH WITH THE SUN DOWN.
WAIT UNTIL MORNING.
DON'T WORRY. I *PROMISE* WE SHALL FIND HIM...
....
....
HIS POSTURE, HIS MANNERS...AND THOSE *EYES*. HE'S A *SAMURAI* CHILD.
STILL, I DON'T UNDERSTAND WHY HE ONLY CALLS FOR HIS FATHER.
HE ANSWERS NO QUESTIONS. HE SAYS NOTHING MORE. HE'S BEEN THROUGH SOMETHING *TERRIBLE* INDEED...

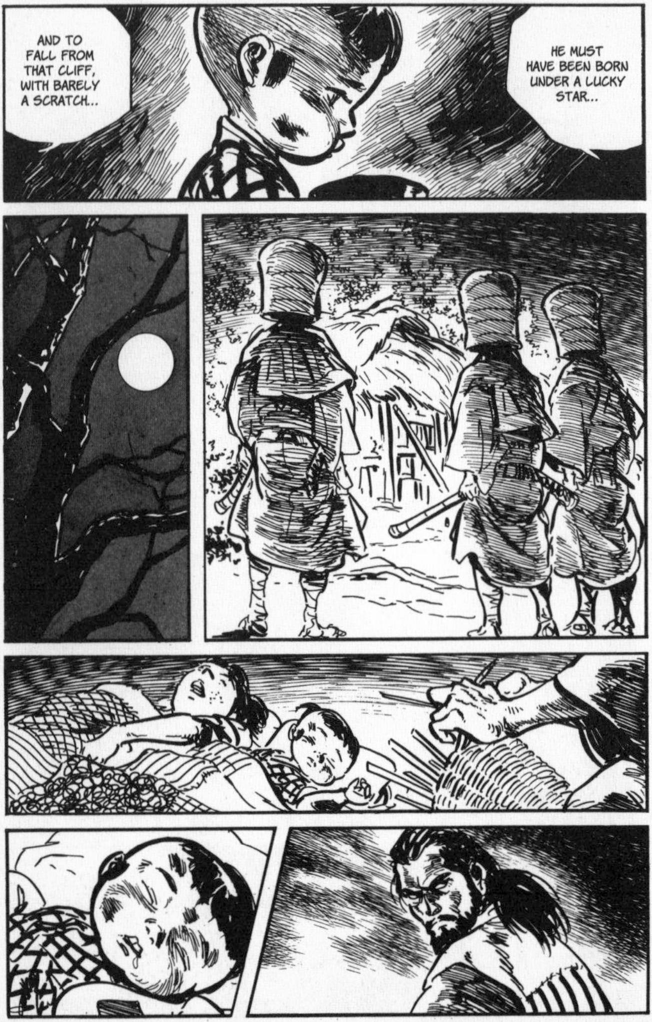
AND TO FALL FROM THAT CLIFF, WITH BARELY A SCRATCH...
HE MUST HAVE BEEN BORN UNDER A LUCKY STAR...

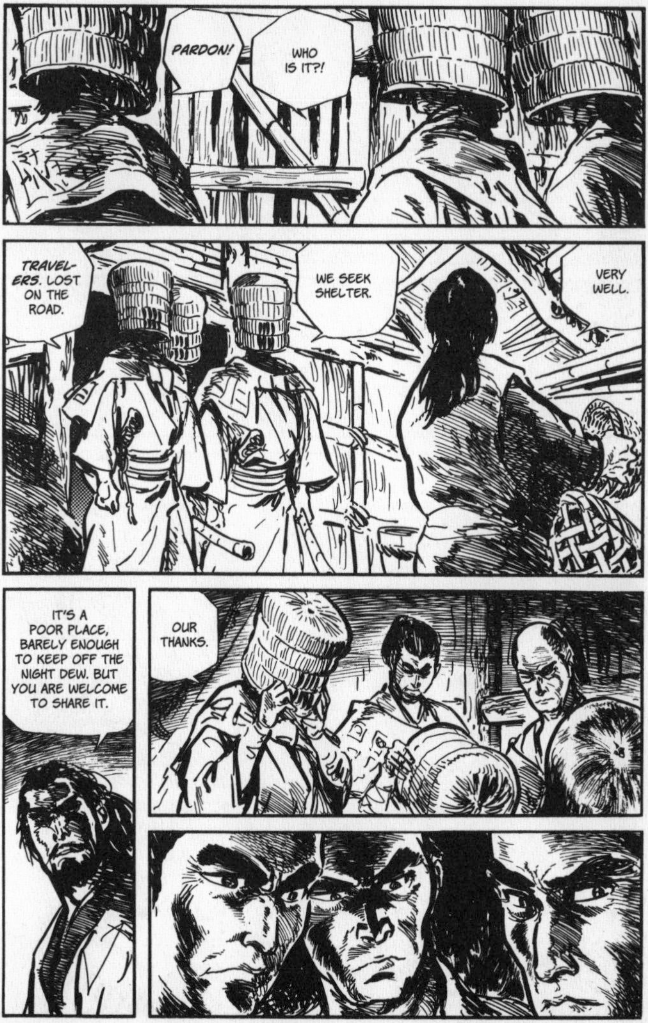
PARDON!
WHO IS IT?!
TRAVELERS. LOST ON THE ROAD.
WE SEEK SHELTER.
VERY WELL.
IT'S A POOR PLACE, BARELY ENOUGH TO KEEP OFF THE NIGHT DEW. BUT YOU ARE WELCOME TO SHARE IT.
OUR THANKS.

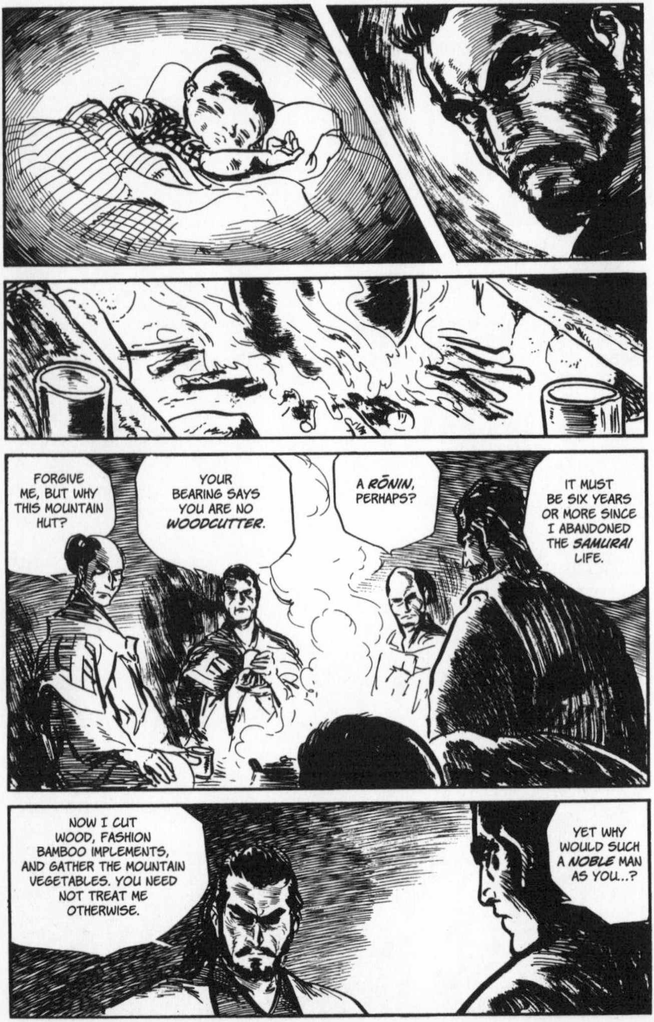
FORGIVE ME, BUT WHY THIS MOUNTAIN HUT?
YOUR BEARING SAYS YOU ARE NO *WOODCUTTER*.
A *RŌNIN*, PERHAPS?
IT MUST BE SIX YEARS OR MORE SINCE I ABANDONED THE *SAMURAI* LIFE.
NOW I CUT WOOD, FASHION BAMBOO IMPLEMENTS, AND GATHER THE MOUNTAIN VEGETABLES. YOU NEED NOT TREAT ME OTHERWISE.
YET WHY WOULD SUCH A *NOBLE* MAN AS YOU...?

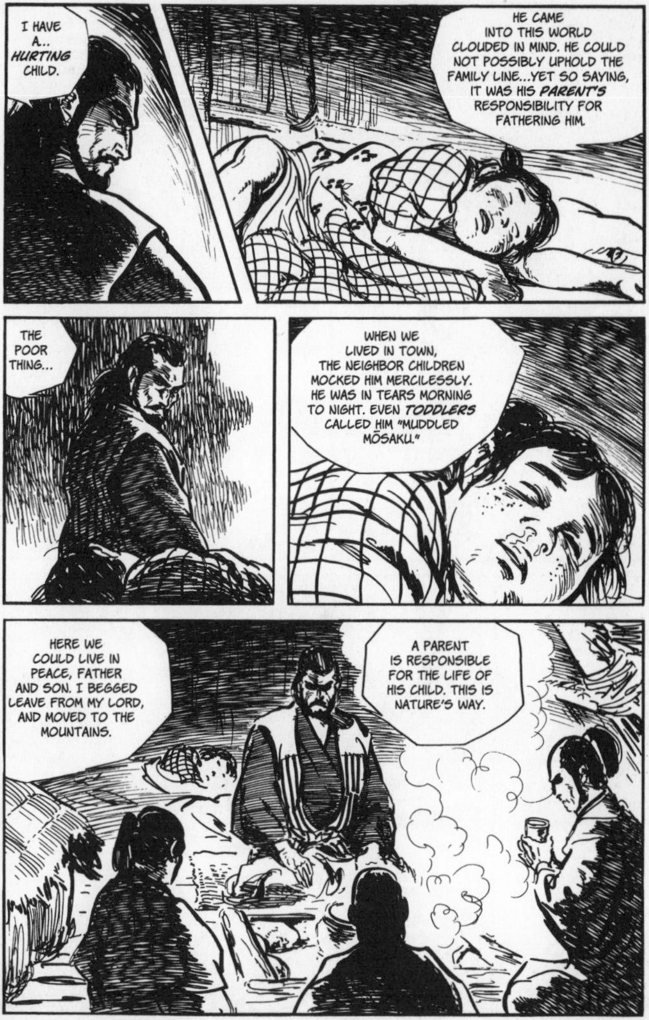
I HAVE A... *HURTING* CHILD.
HE CAME INTO THIS WORLD CLOUDED IN MIND. HE COULD NOT POSSIBLY UPHOLD THE FAMILY LINE...YET SO SAYING, IT WAS HIS *PARENT'S* RESPONSIBILITY FOR FATHERING HIM.
THE POOR THING...
WHEN WE LIVED IN TOWN, THE NEIGHBOR CHILDREN MOCKED HIM MERCILESSLY. HE WAS IN TEARS MORNING TO NIGHT. EVEN *TODDLERS* CALLED HIM "MUDDLED MŌSAKU."
HERE WE COULD LIVE IN PEACE, FATHER AND SON. I BEGGED LEAVE FROM MY LORD, AND MOVED TO THE MOUNTAINS.
A PARENT IS RESPONSIBLE FOR THE LIFE OF HIS CHILD. THIS IS NATURE'S WAY.

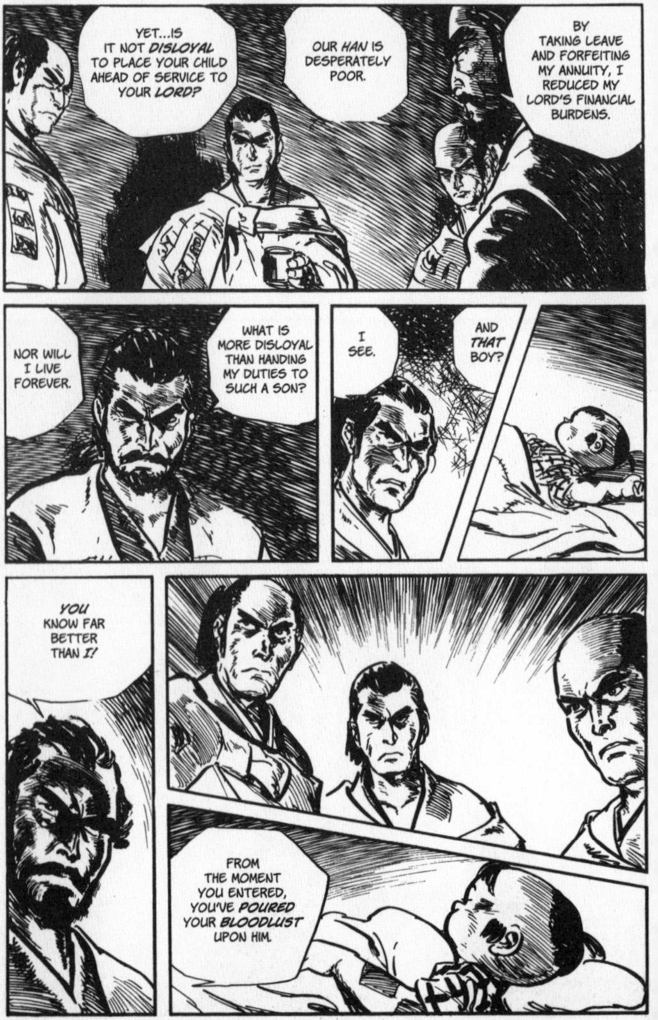
YET...IS IT NOT *DISLOYAL* TO PLACE YOUR CHILD AHEAD OF SERVICE TO YOUR *LORD?*
OUR *HAN* IS DESPERATELY POOR.
BY TAKING LEAVE AND FORFEITING MY ANNUITY, I REDUCED MY LORD'S FINANCIAL BURDENS.
NOR WILL I LIVE FOREVER.
WHAT IS MORE DISLOYAL THAN HANDING MY DUTIES TO SUCH A SON?
I SEE.
AND *THAT* BOY?
YOU KNOW FAR BETTER THAN *I!*
FROM THE MOMENT YOU ENTERED, YOU'VE *POURED* YOUR *BLOODLUST* UPON HIM.

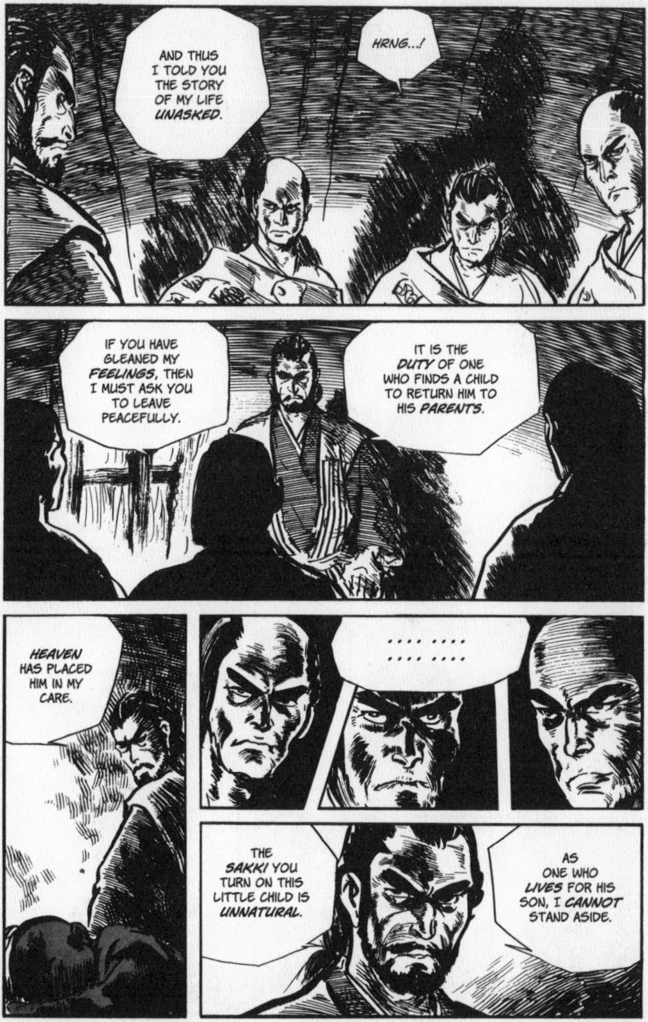
AND THUS I TOLD YOU THE STORY OF MY LIFE *UNASKED*.
HRNG...!
IF YOU HAVE GLEANED MY *FEELINGS*, THEN I MUST ASK YOU TO LEAVE PEACEFULLY.
IT IS THE *DUTY* OF ONE WHO FINDS A CHILD TO RETURN HIM TO HIS *PARENTS*.
HEAVEN HAS PLACED HIM IN MY CARE.
....
....
THE *SAKKI* YOU TURN ON THIS LITTLE CHILD IS *UNNATURAL*.
AS ONE WHO *LIVES* FOR HIS SON, I *CANNOT* STAND ASIDE.

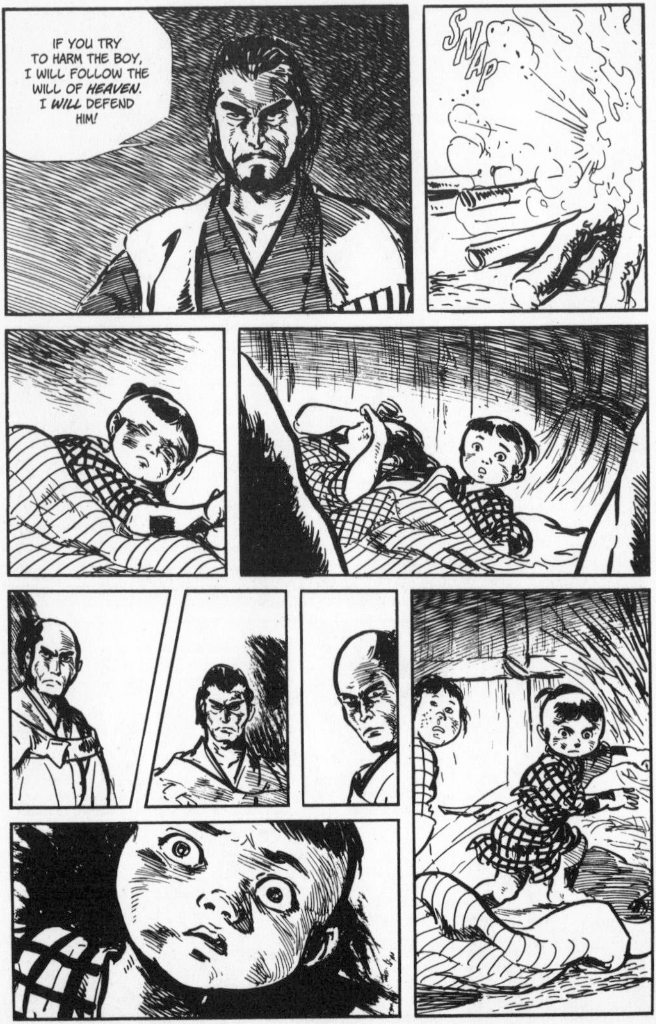
IF YOU TRY TO HARM THE BOY, I WILL FOLLOW THE WILL OF *HEAVEN*. I *WILL* DEFEND HIM!
SNAP

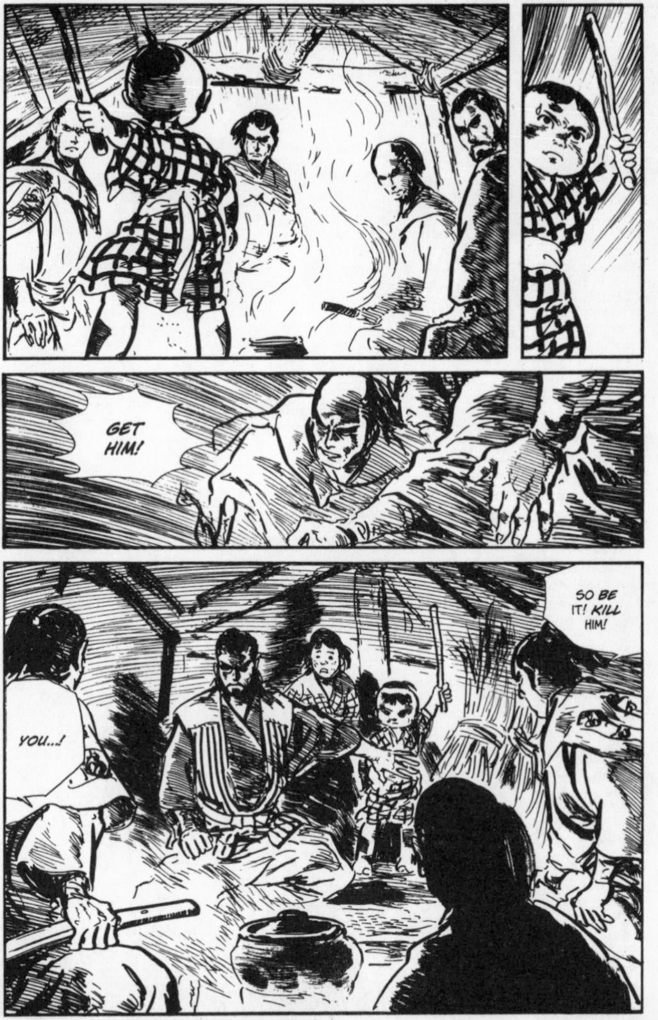
GET HIM!
YOU...!
SO BE IT! KILL HIM!

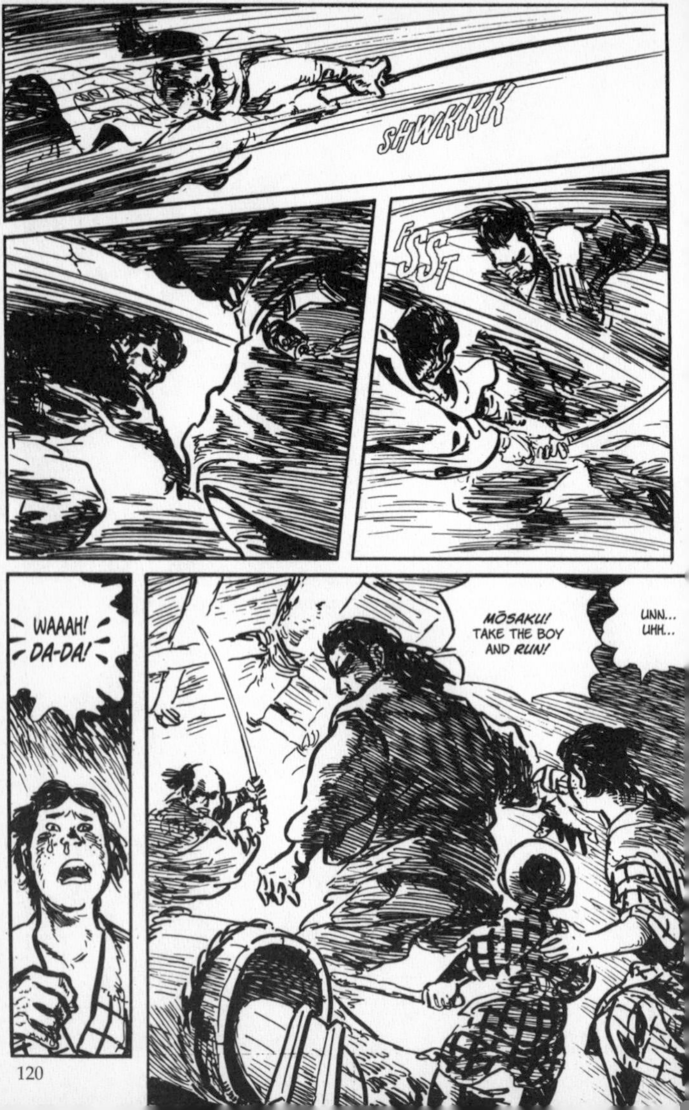
SHWKKK
FSST
WAAAH! DA-DA!
MŌSAKU! TAKE THE BOY AND RUN!
UNN... UHH...

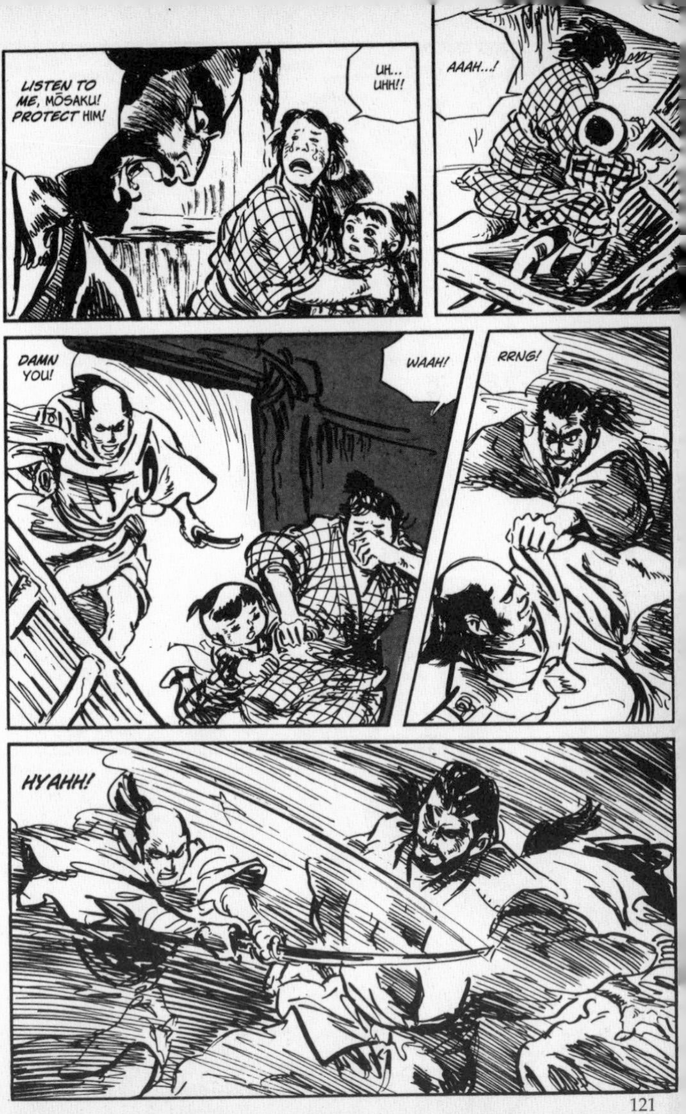
LISTEN TO ME, MŌSAKU! PROTECT HIM!
UH... UHH!!
AAAH...!
DAMN YOU!
WAAH!
RRNG!
HYAHH!

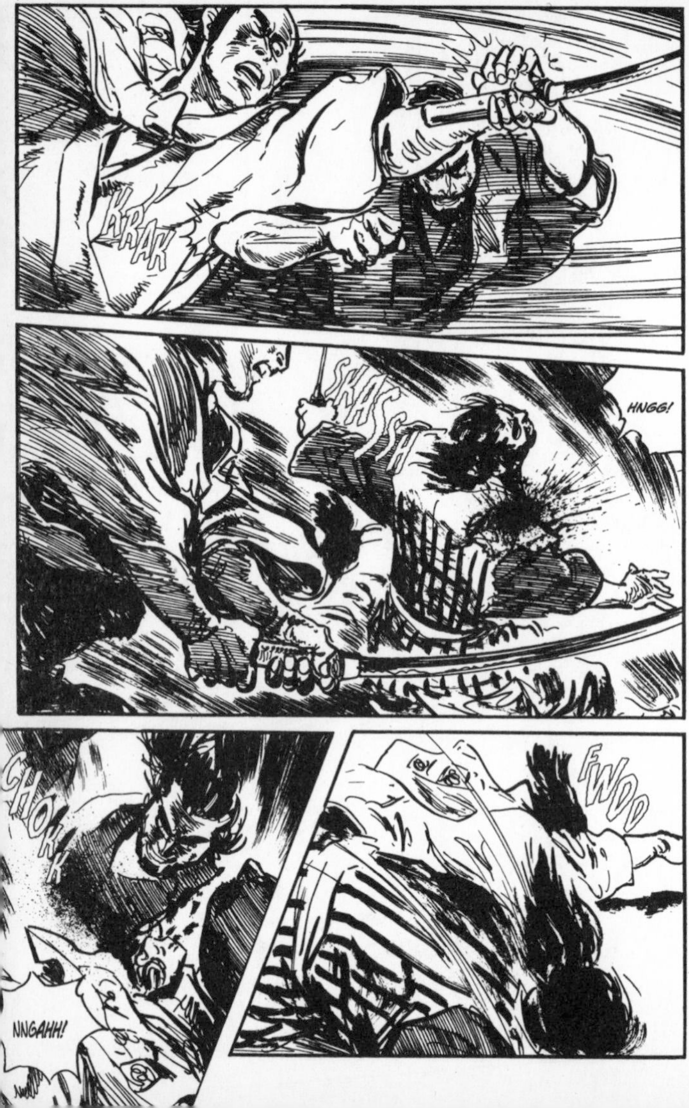
KRAK
SKASCH
HNGG!
CHOKK
NNGAHH!
FWOO

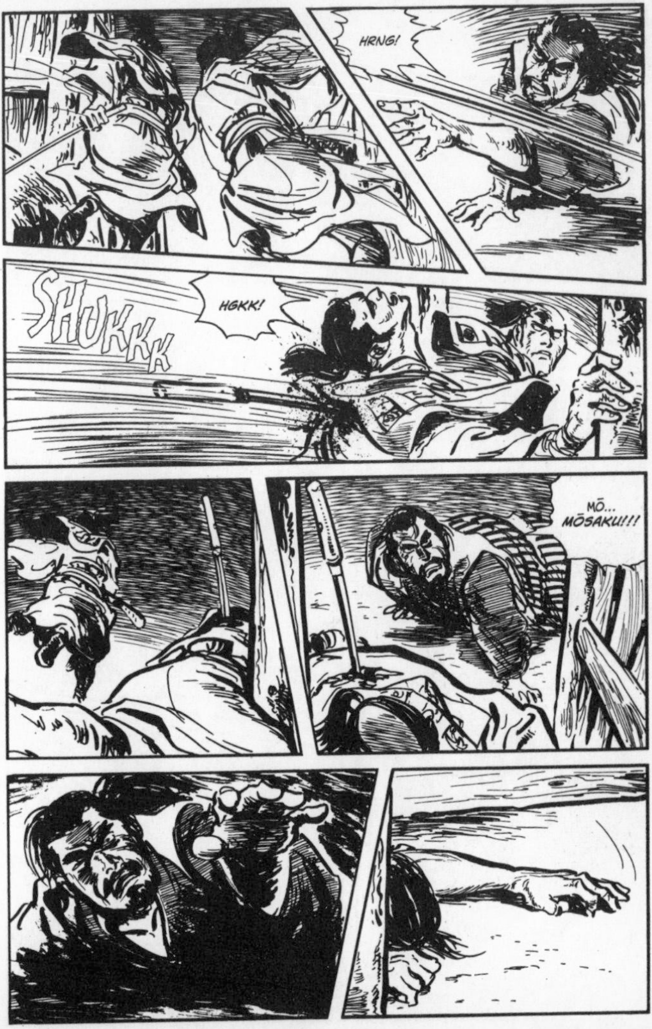
HRNG!
SHUKKK
HGKK!
MŌ...
MŌSAKU!!!

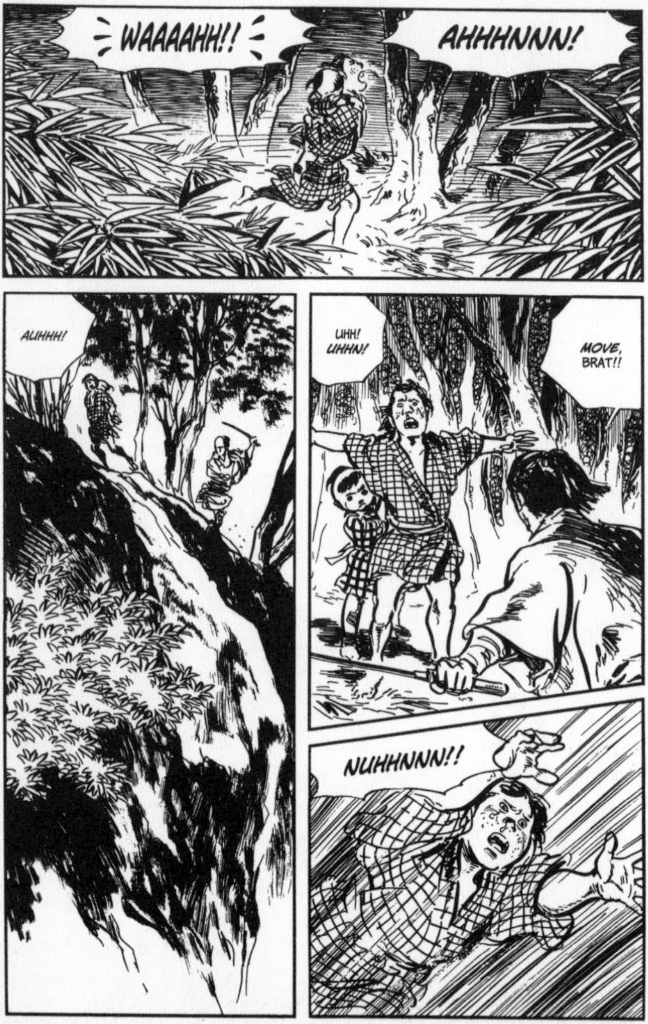
WAAAAHH!!
AHHHNNN!
AUHHH!
UHH! UHHN!
MOVE, BRAT!!
NUHHNNN!!

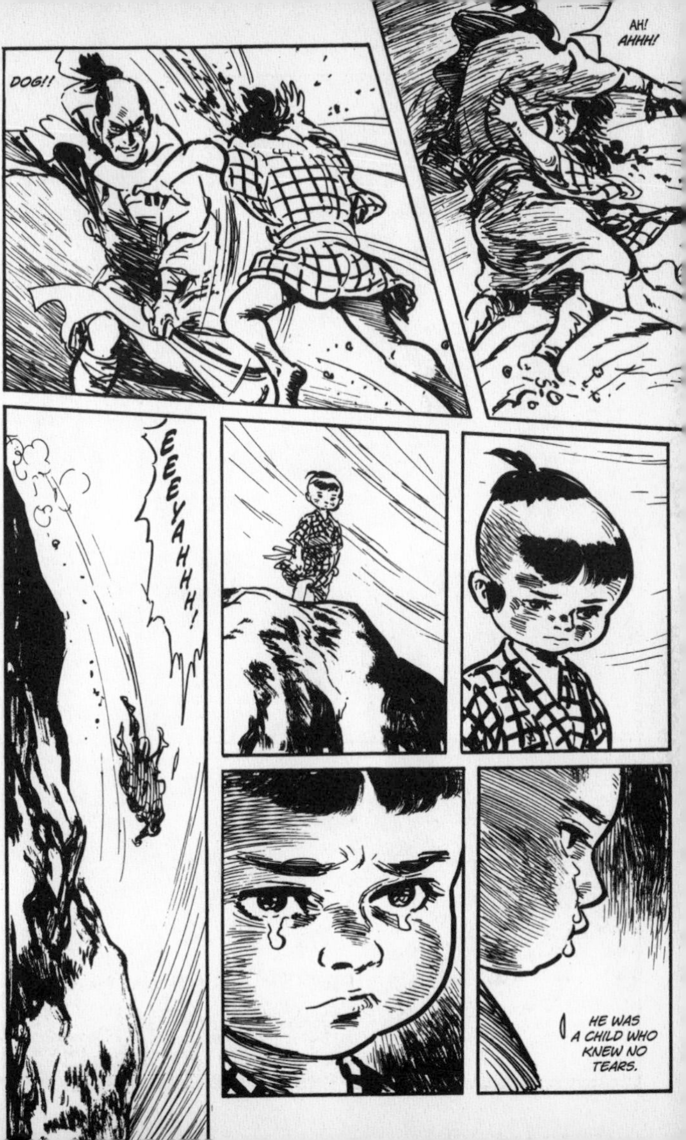
DOG!!
AH! AHHH!
EEEYAHHHH!
HE WAS A CHILD WHO KNEW NO TEARS.

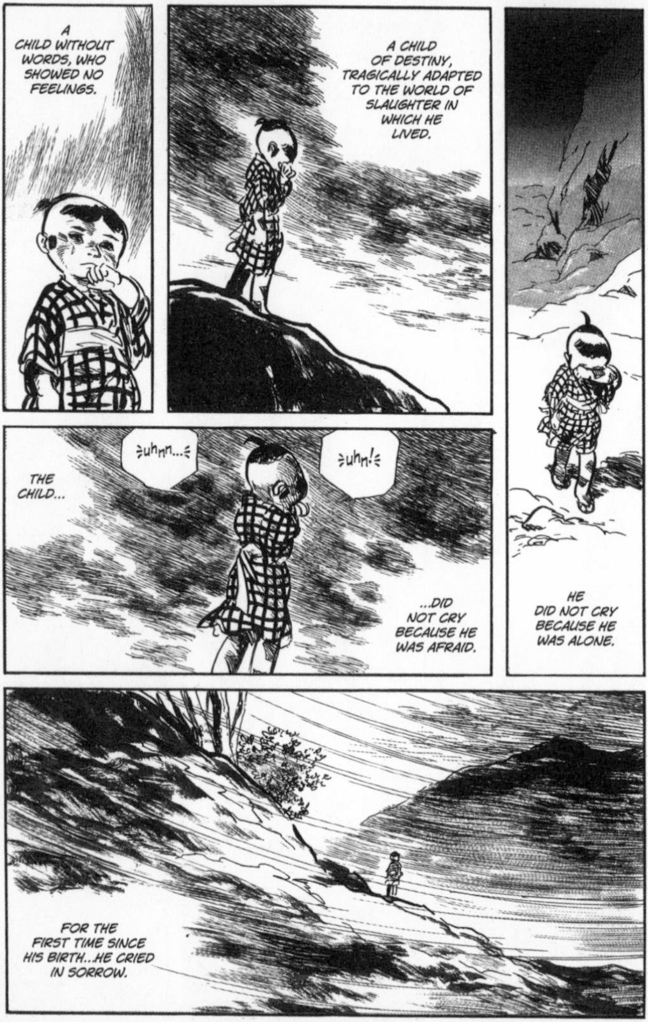
A CHILD WITHOUT WORDS, WHO SHOWED NO FEELINGS.
A CHILD OF DESTINY, TRAGICALLY ADAPTED TO THE WORLD OF SLAUGHTER IN WHICH HE LIVED.
THE CHILD...
uhnn...
uhn!
...DID NOT CRY BECAUSE HE WAS AFRAID.
HE DID NOT CRY BECAUSE HE WAS ALONE.
FOR THE FIRST TIME SINCE HIS BIRTH...HE CRIED IN SORROW.

the fifty-second

The Fisher-woman's Love

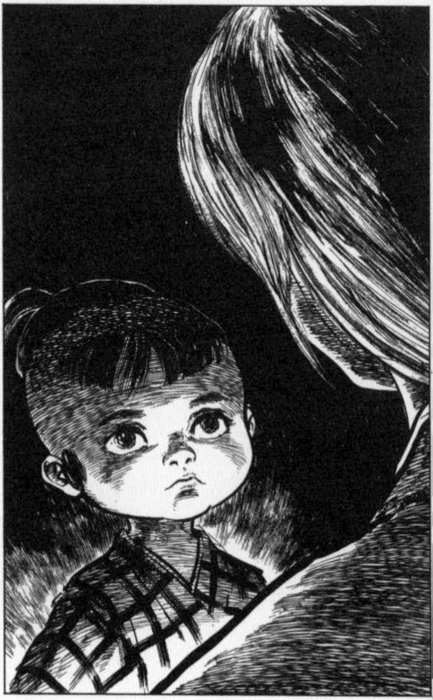

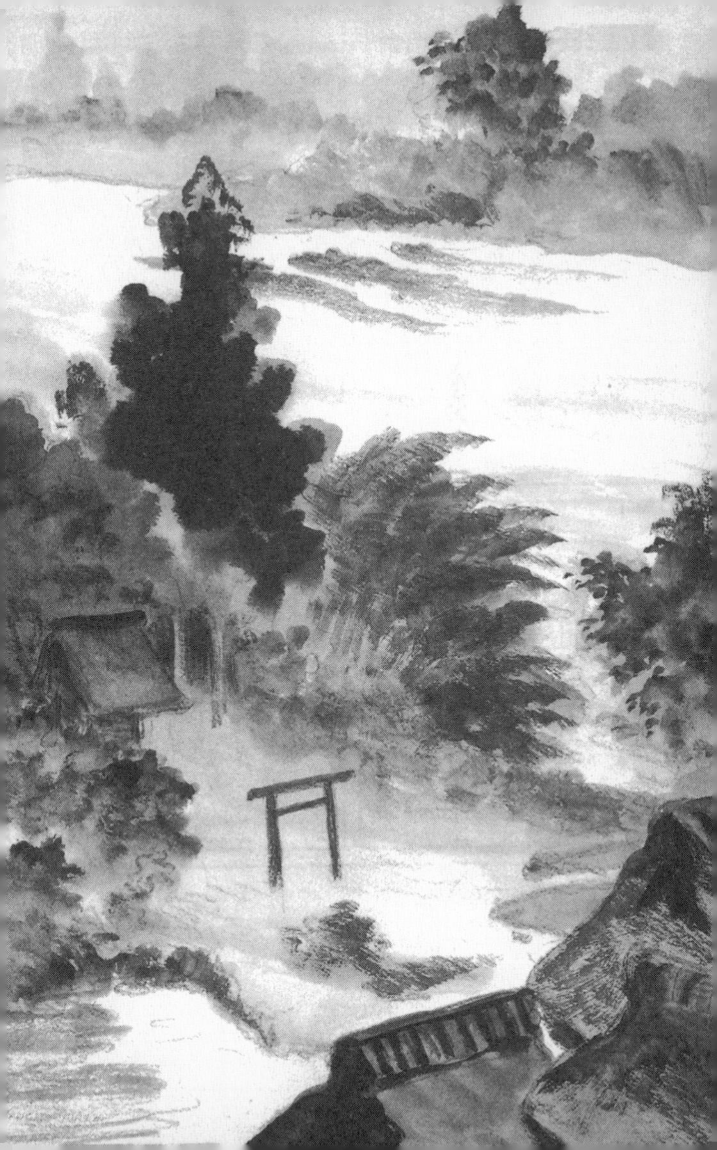

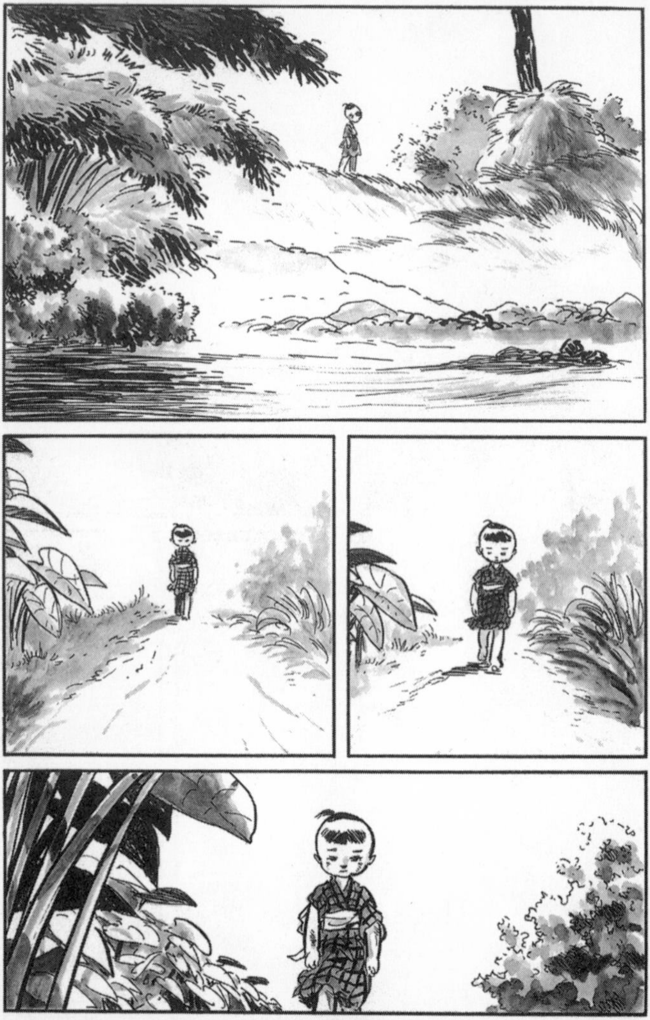

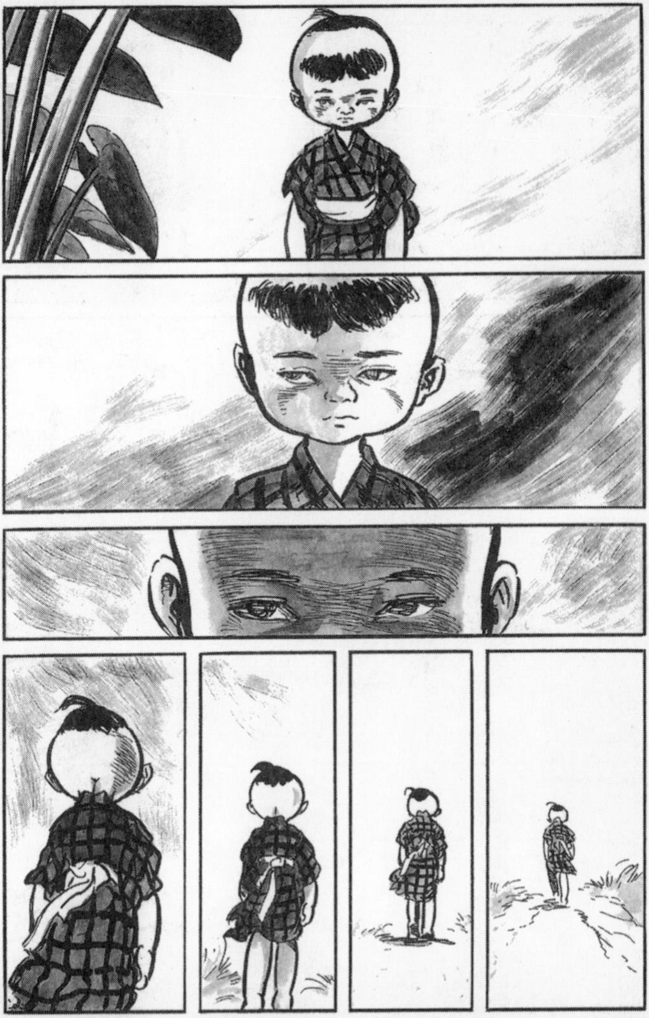

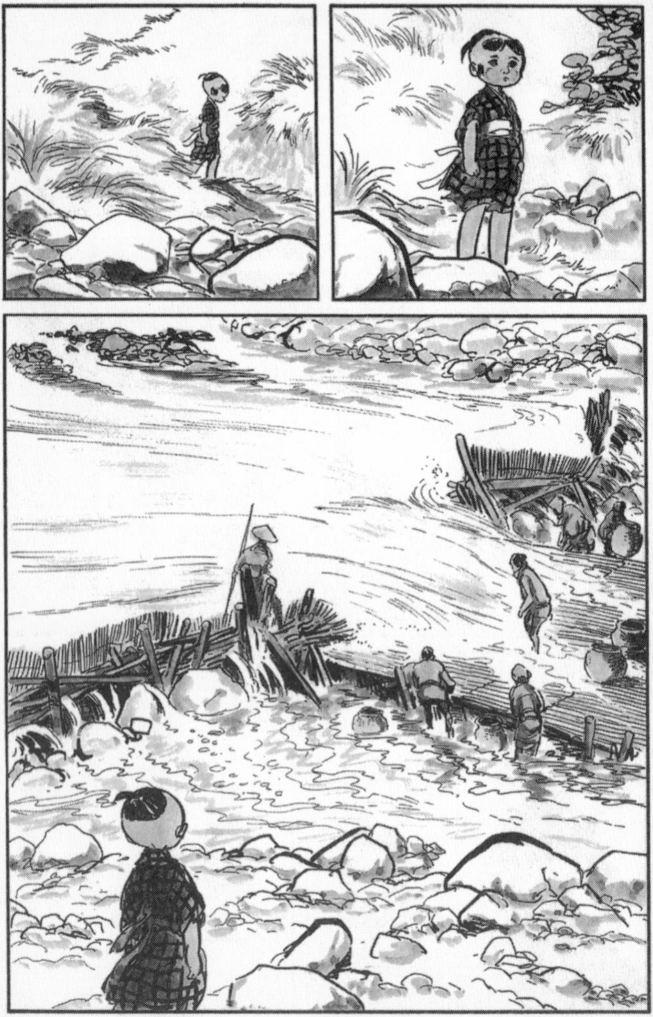

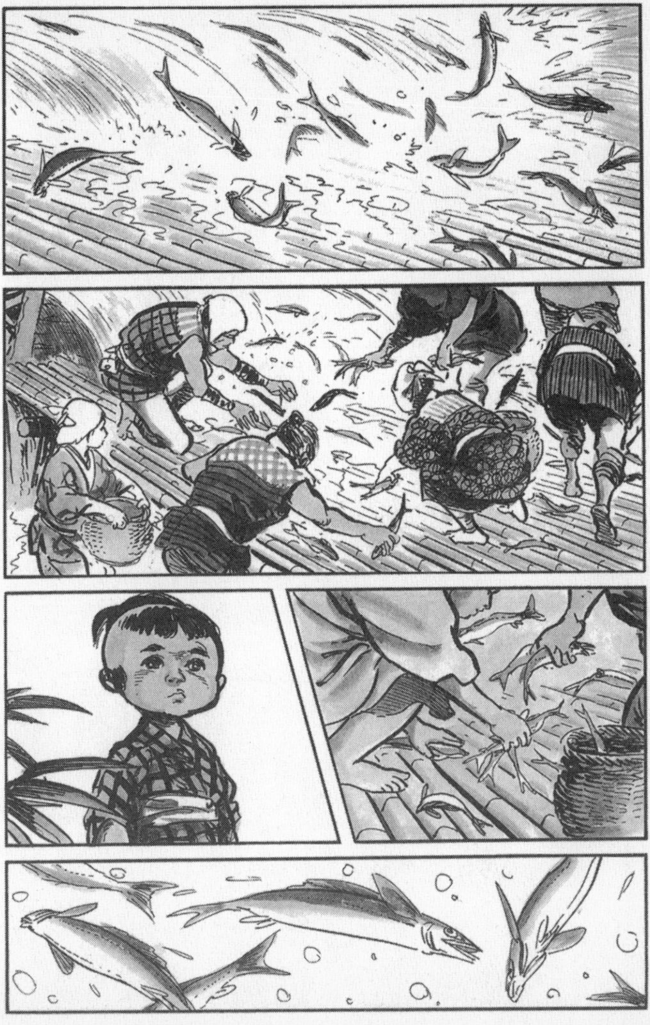

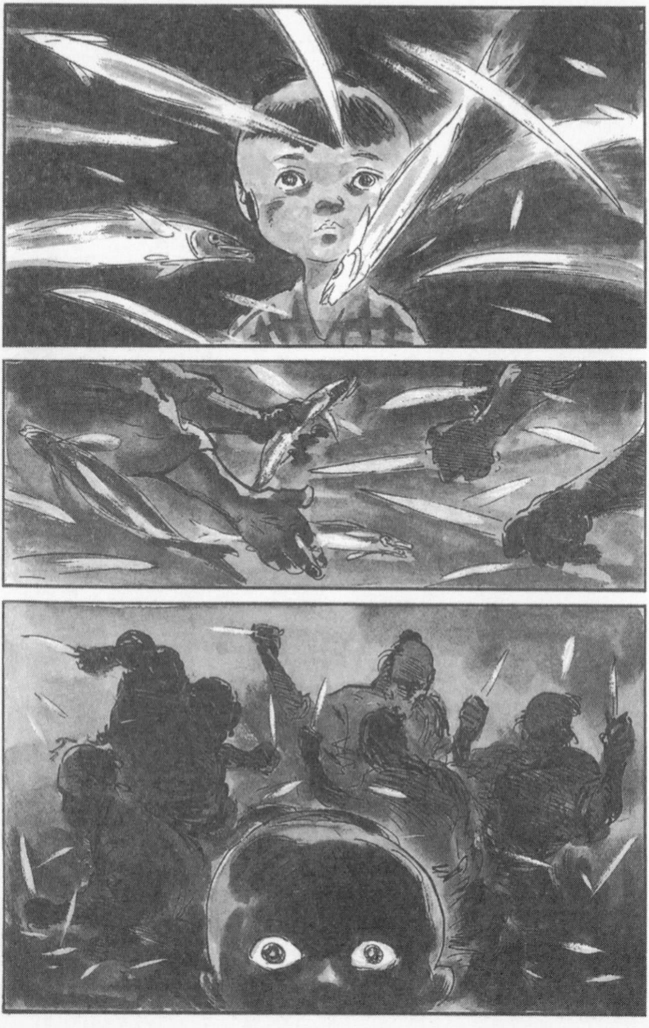

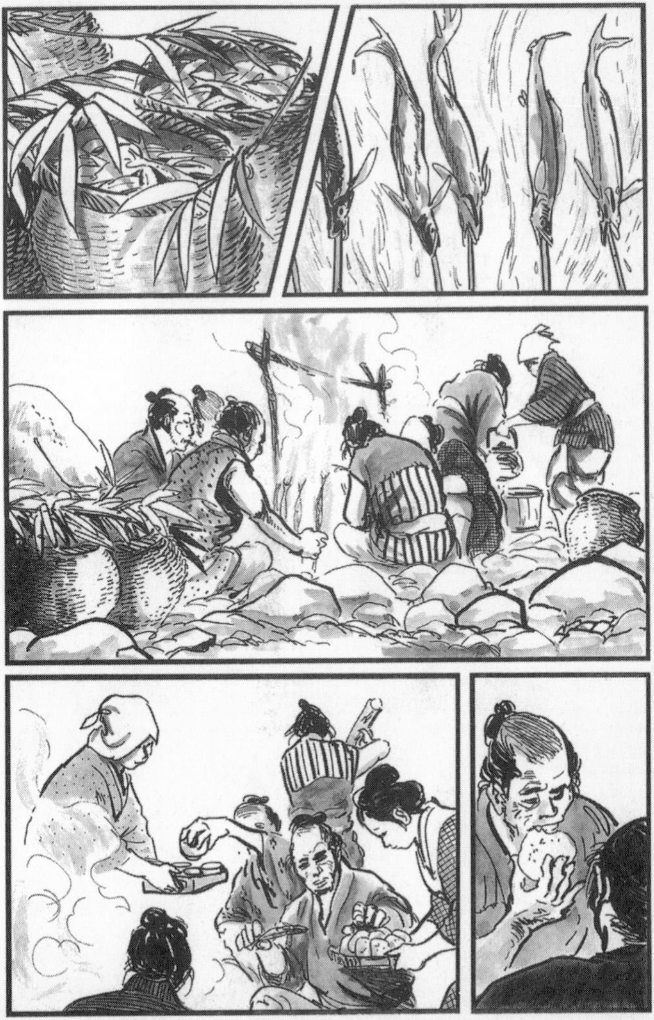

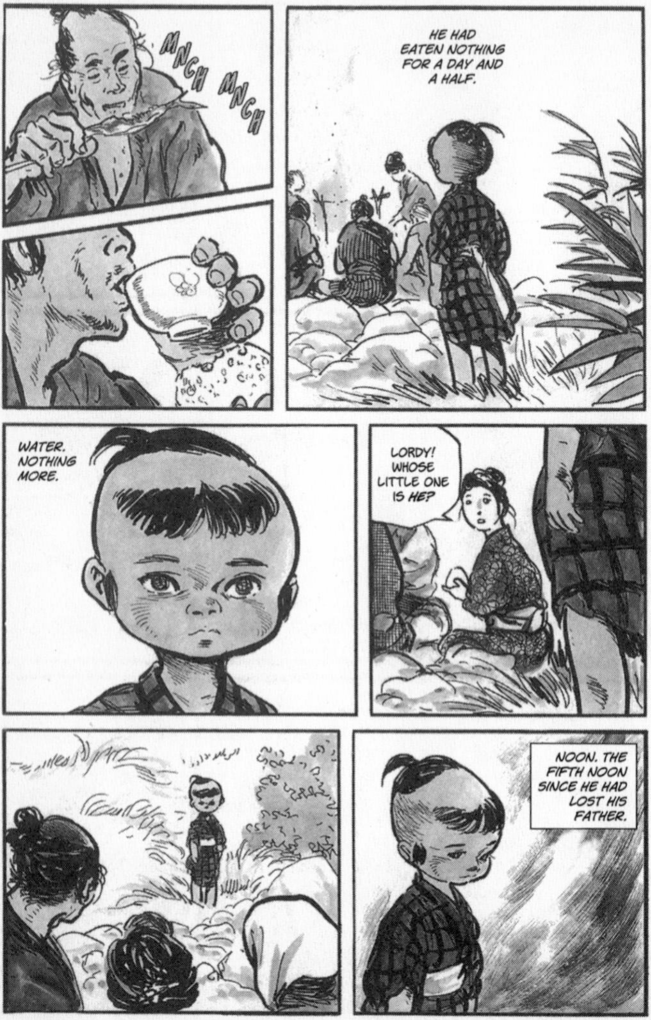
MNCH MNCH
HE HAD EATEN NOTHING FOR A DAY AND A HALF.
WATER. NOTHING MORE.
LORDY! WHOSE LITTLE ONE IS *HE?*
NOON. THE FIFTH NOON SINCE HE HAD LOST HIS FATHER.

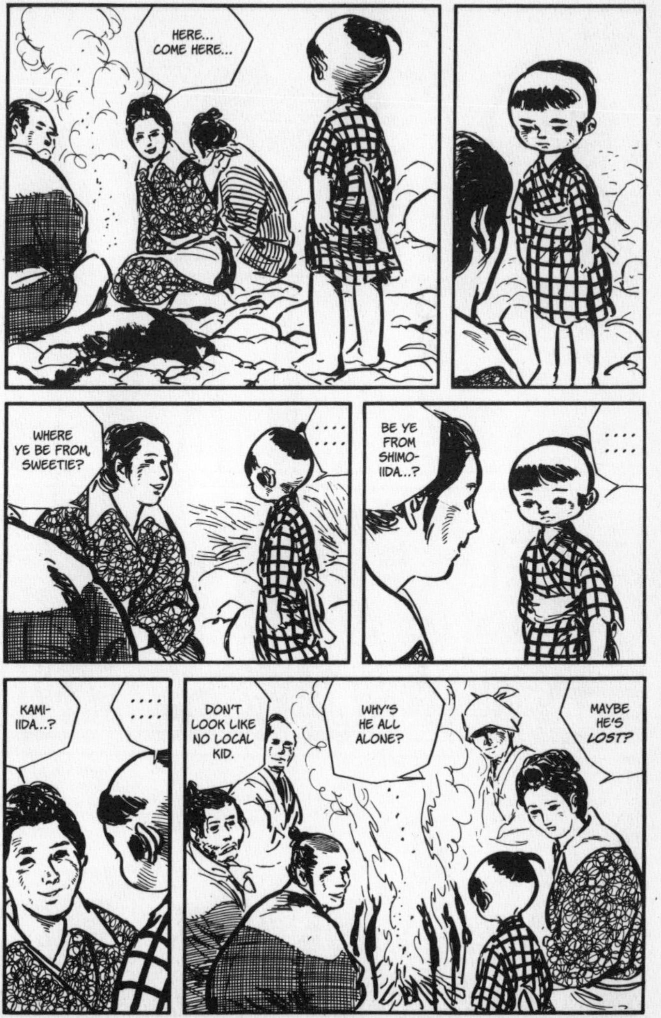
HERE... COME HERE...
WHERE YE BE FROM, SWEETIE?
....
....
BE YE FROM SHIMO-IIDA..?
....
....
KAMI-IIDA..?
....
....
DON'T LOOK LIKE NO LOCAL KID.
WHY'S HE ALL ALONE?
MAYBE HE'S *LOST?*

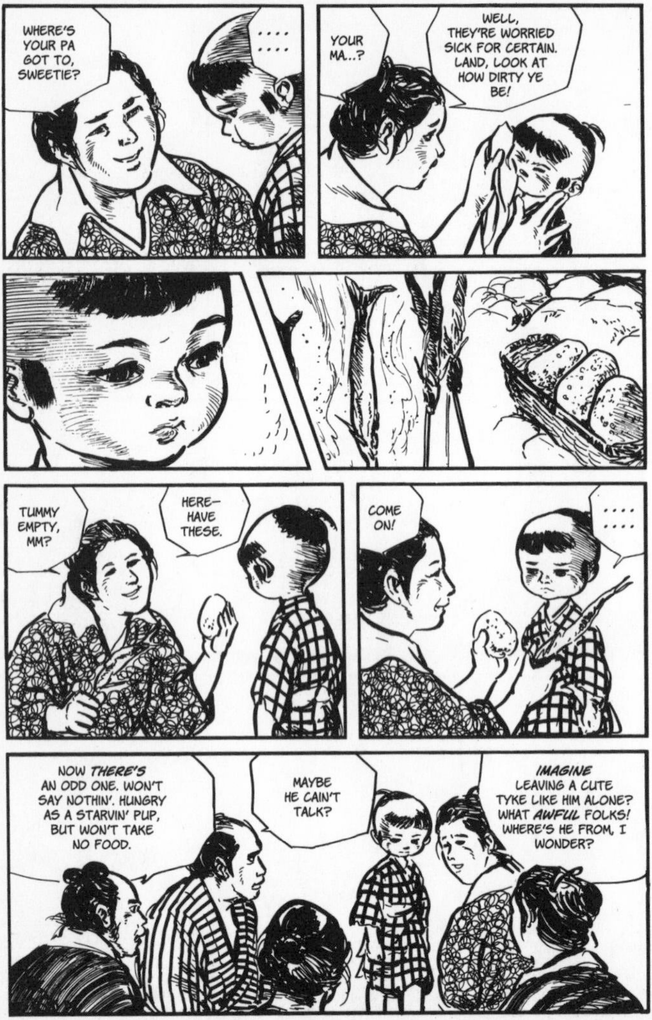
WHERE'S YOUR PA GOT TO, SWEETIE?
....
....
YOUR MA...?
WELL, THEY'RE WORRIED SICK FOR CERTAIN. LAND, LOOK AT HOW DIRTY YE BE!
TUMMY EMPTY, MM?
HERE— HAVE THESE.
COME ON!
....
....
NOW *THERE'S* AN ODD ONE. WON'T SAY NOTHIN'. HUNGRY AS A STARVIN' PUP, BUT WON'T TAKE NO FOOD.
MAYBE HE CAIN'T TALK?
IMAGINE LEAVING A CUTE TYKE LIKE HIM ALONE? WHAT *AWFUL* FOLKS! WHERE'S HE FROM, I WONDER?

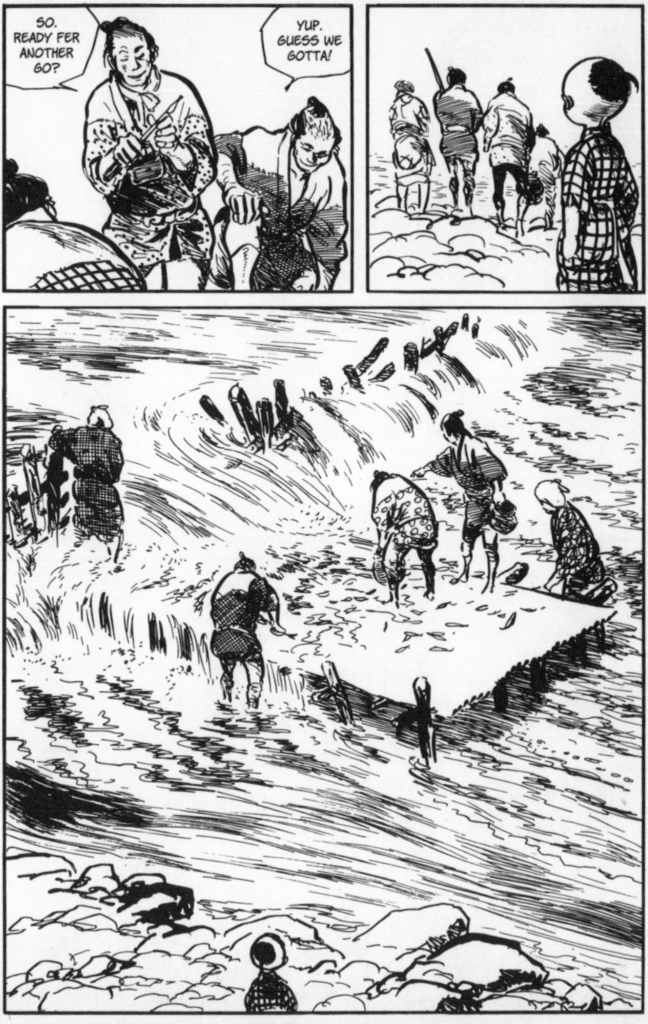
SO. READY FER ANOTHER GO?
YUP. GUESS WE GOTTA!

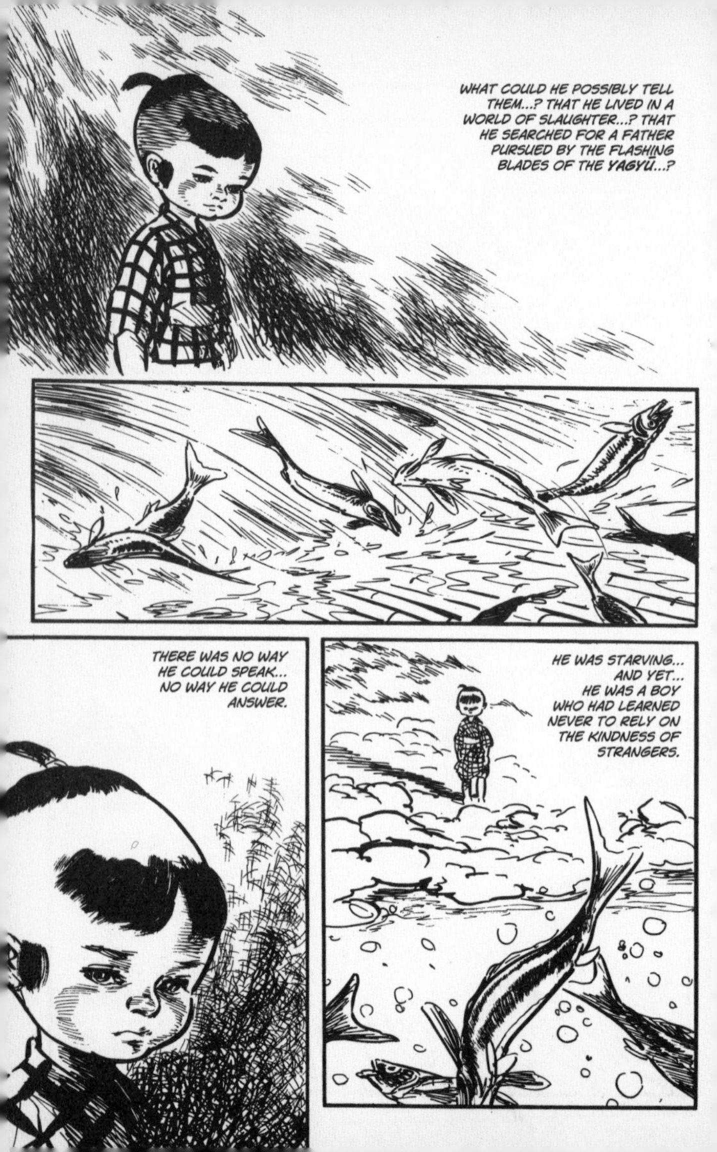
WHAT COULD HE POSSIBLY TELL THEM...? THAT HE LIVED IN A WORLD OF SLAUGHTER...? THAT HE SEARCHED FOR A FATHER PURSUED BY THE FLASHING BLADES OF THE YAGYŪ...?
THERE WAS NO WAY HE COULD SPEAK... NO WAY HE COULD ANSWER.
HE WAS STARVING... AND YET... HE WAS A BOY WHO HAD LEARNED NEVER TO RELY ON THE KINDNESS OF STRANGERS.

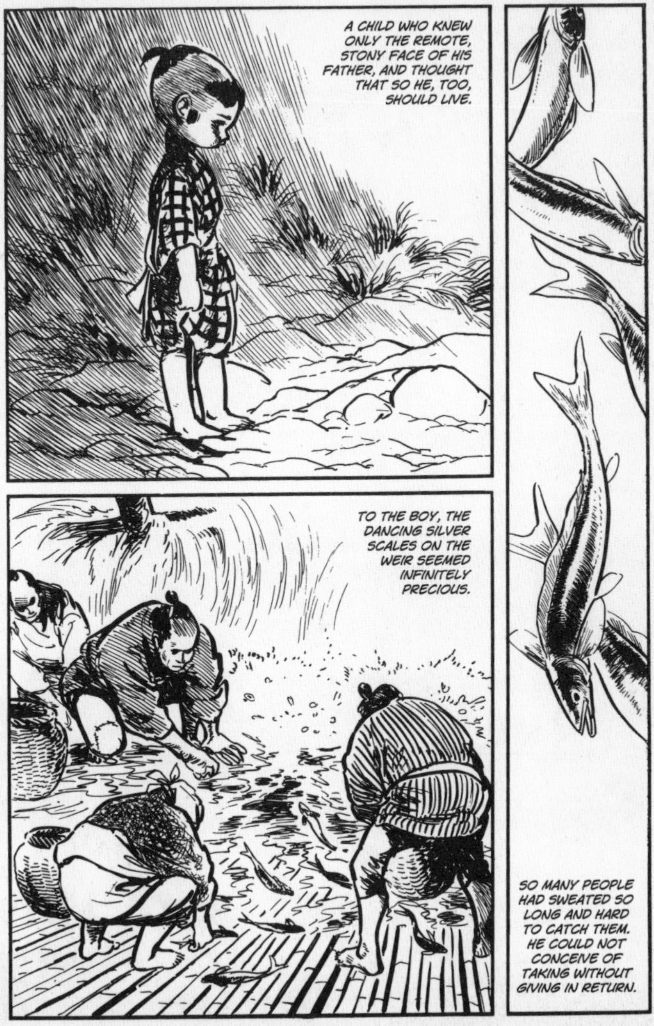
A CHILD WHO KNEW ONLY THE REMOTE, STONY FACE OF HIS FATHER, AND THOUGHT THAT SO HE, TOO, SHOULD LIVE.
TO THE BOY, THE DANCING SILVER SCALES ON THE WEIR SEEMED INFINITELY PRECIOUS.
SO MANY PEOPLE HAD SWEATED SO LONG AND HARD TO CATCH THEM. HE COULD NOT CONCEIVE OF TAKING WITHOUT GIVING IN RETURN.

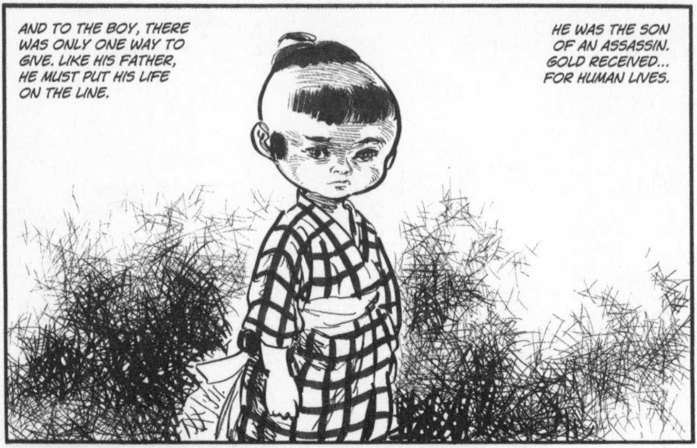
AND TO THE BOY, THERE WAS ONLY ONE WAY TO GIVE. LIKE HIS FATHER, HE MUST PUT HIS LIFE ON THE LINE.
HE WAS THE SON OF AN ASSASSIN. GOLD RECEIVED... FOR HUMAN LIVES.

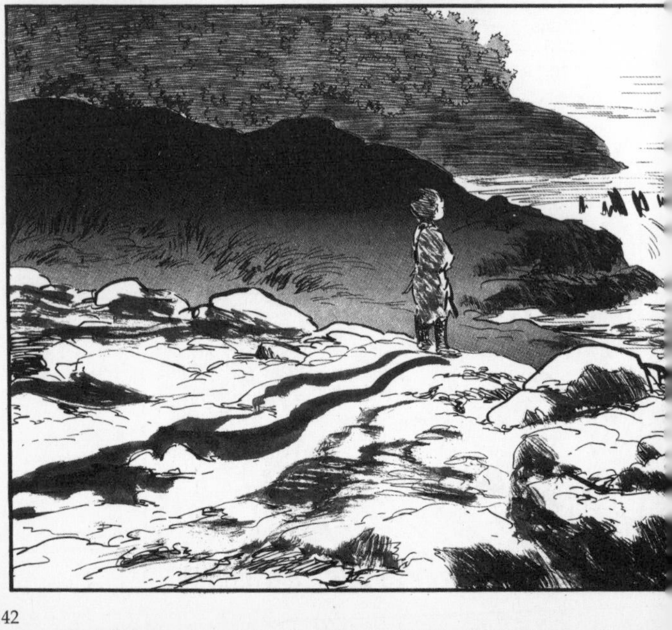

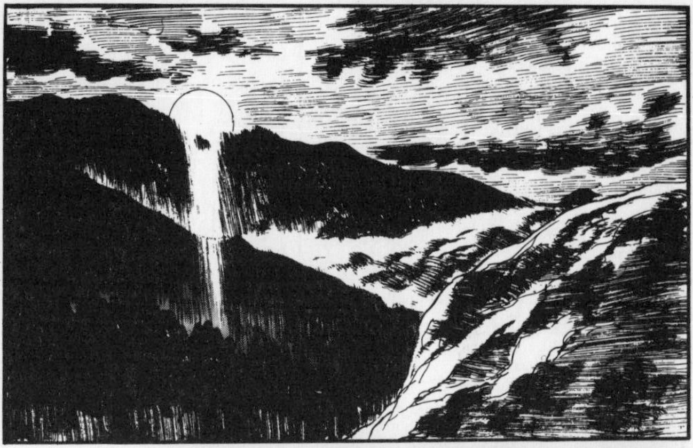
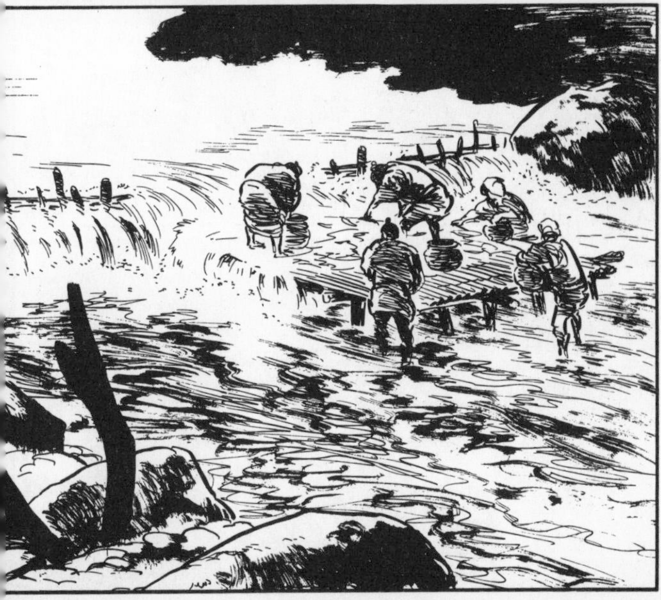

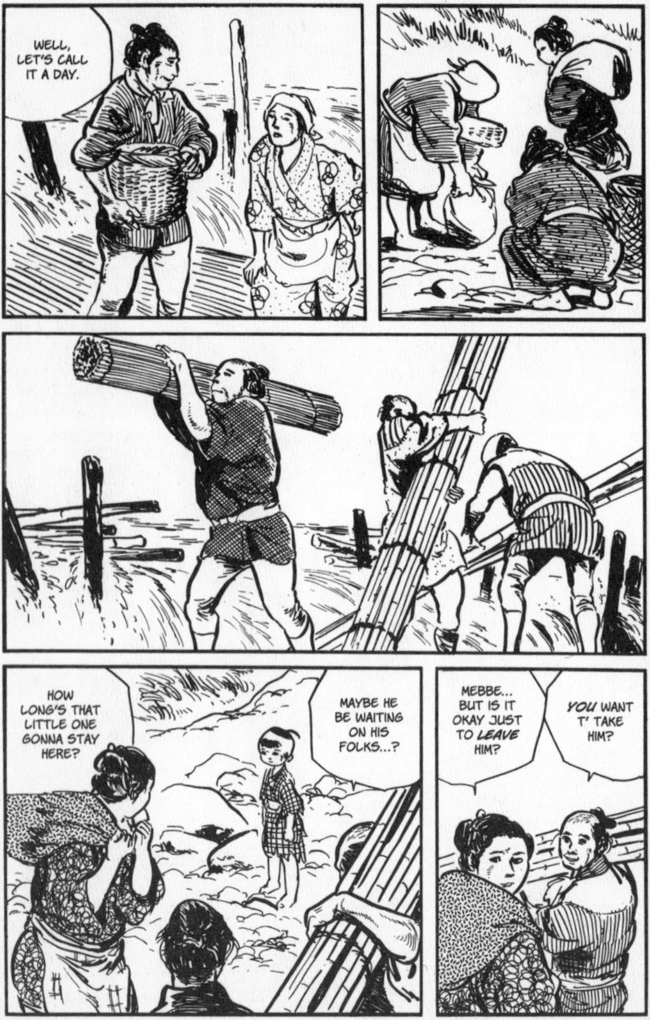
WELL, LET'S CALL IT A DAY.
HOW LONG'S THAT LITTLE ONE GONNA STAY HERE?
MAYBE HE BE WAITING ON HIS FOLKS...?
MEBBE... BUT IS IT OKAY JUST TO *LEAVE* HIM?
YOU WANT T' TAKE HIM?

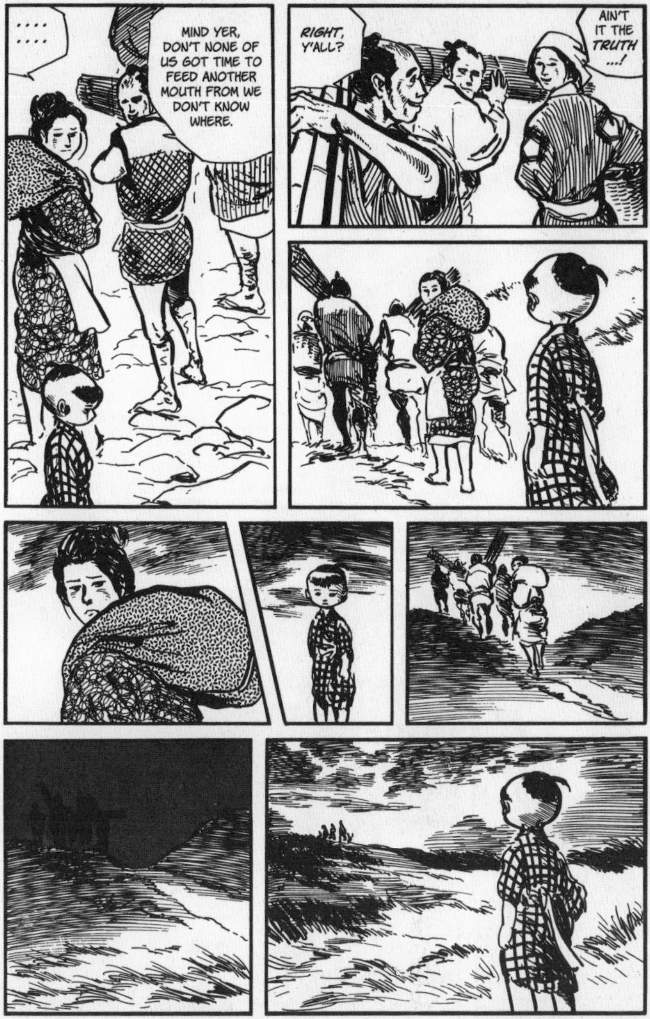
. . . .
. . . .
MIND YER, DON'T NONE OF US GOT TIME TO FEED ANOTHER MOUTH FROM WE DON'T KNOW WHERE.
RIGHT, Y'ALL?
AIN'T IT THE TRUTH ...!

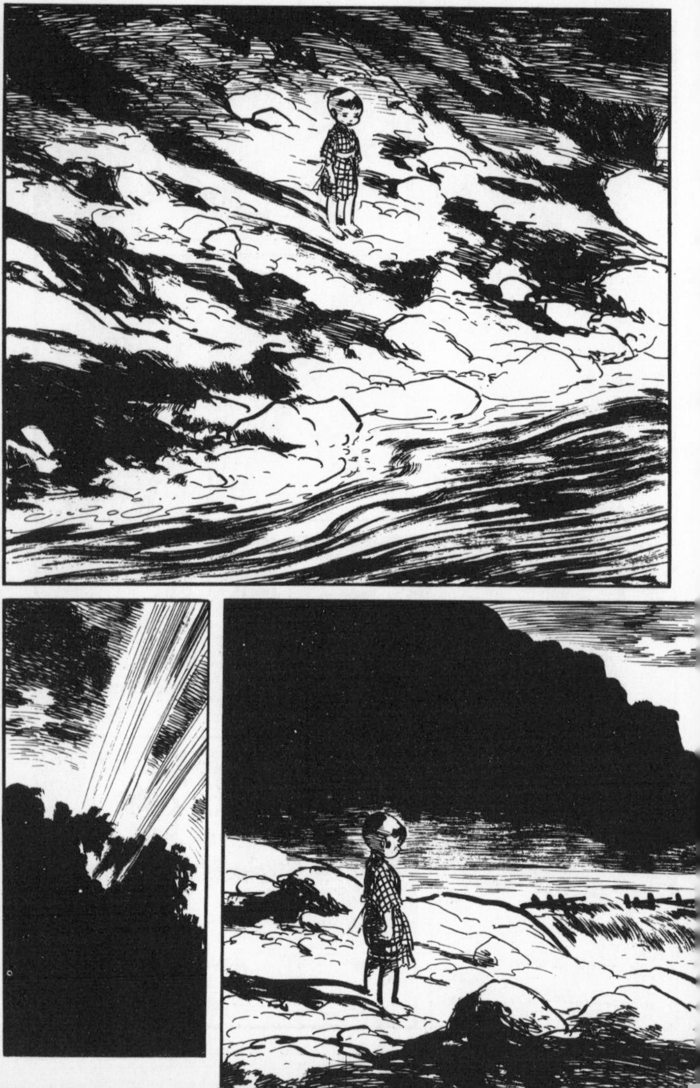

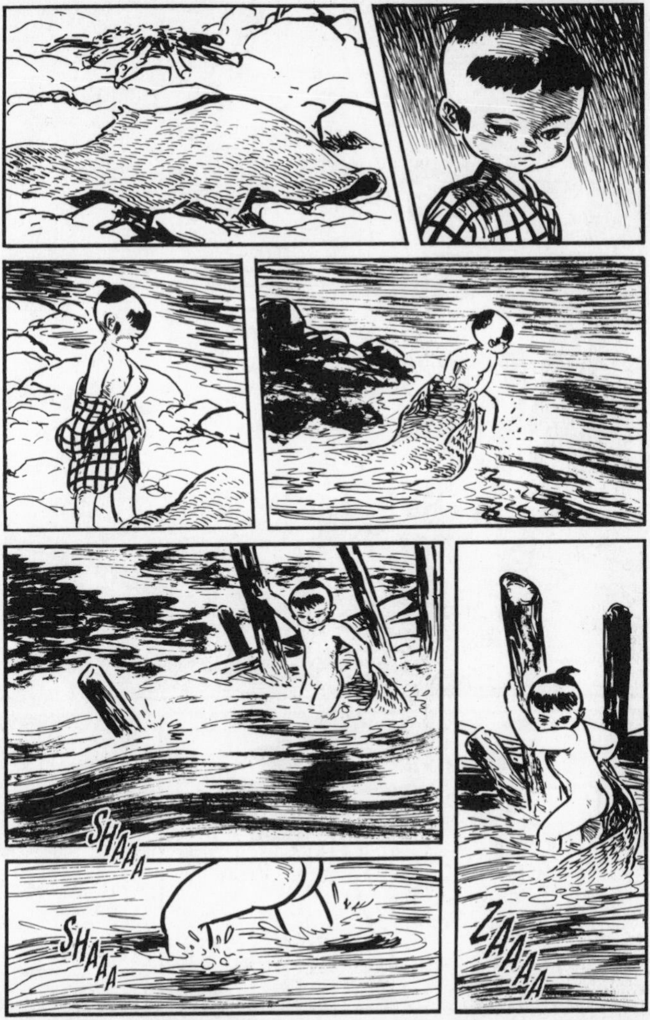
SHAAA
SHAAA
ZAAAA

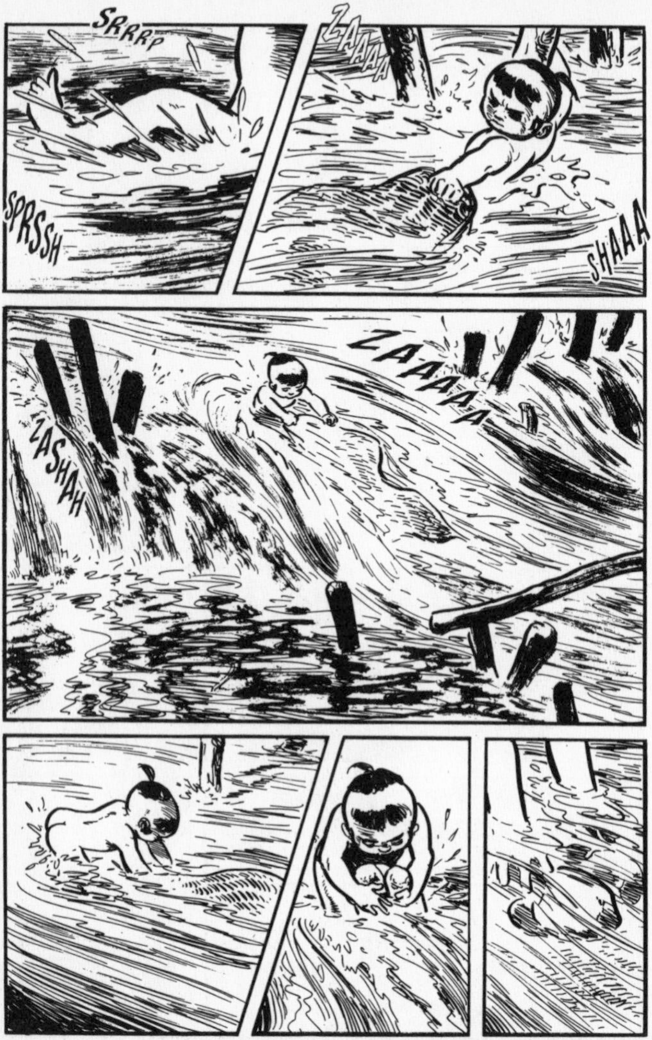

SRRRP
SPRSSH
ZAAAA
SHAAA
ZAAAAAA
ZASHAH

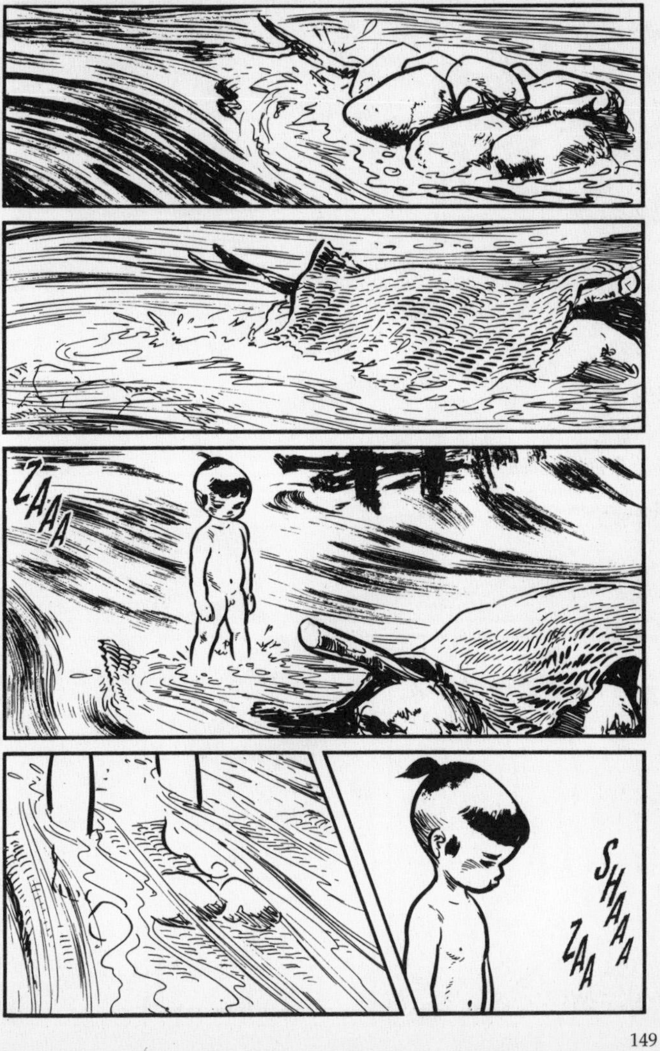
ZAAA
SHAAAA
ZAA

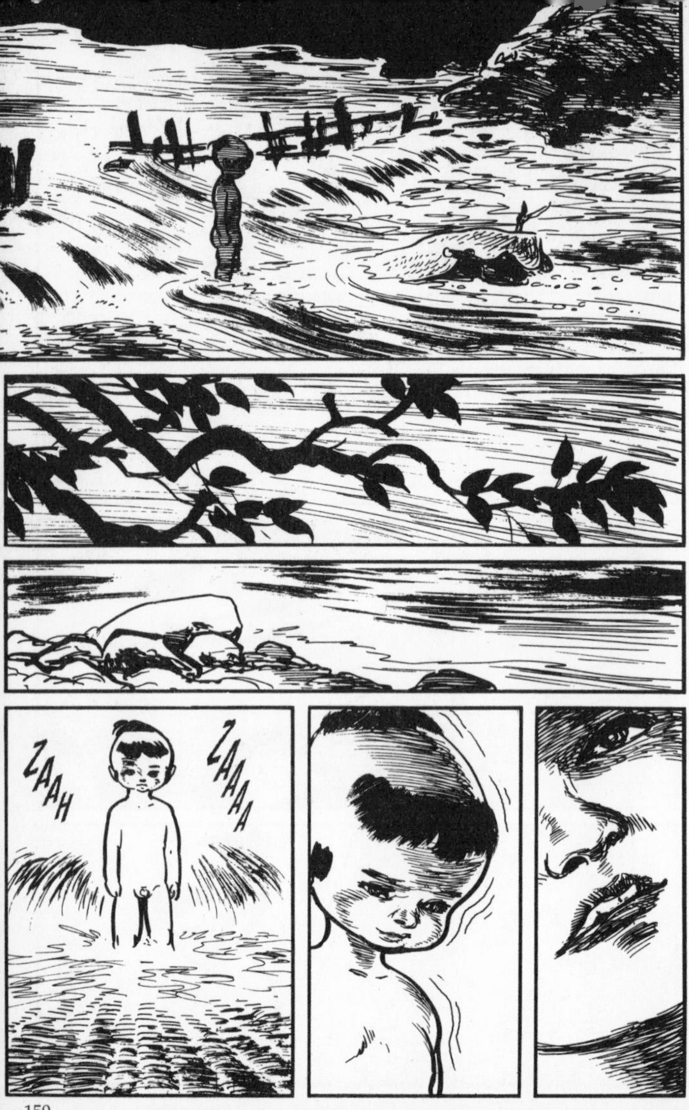
ZAAH
ZAAAAA

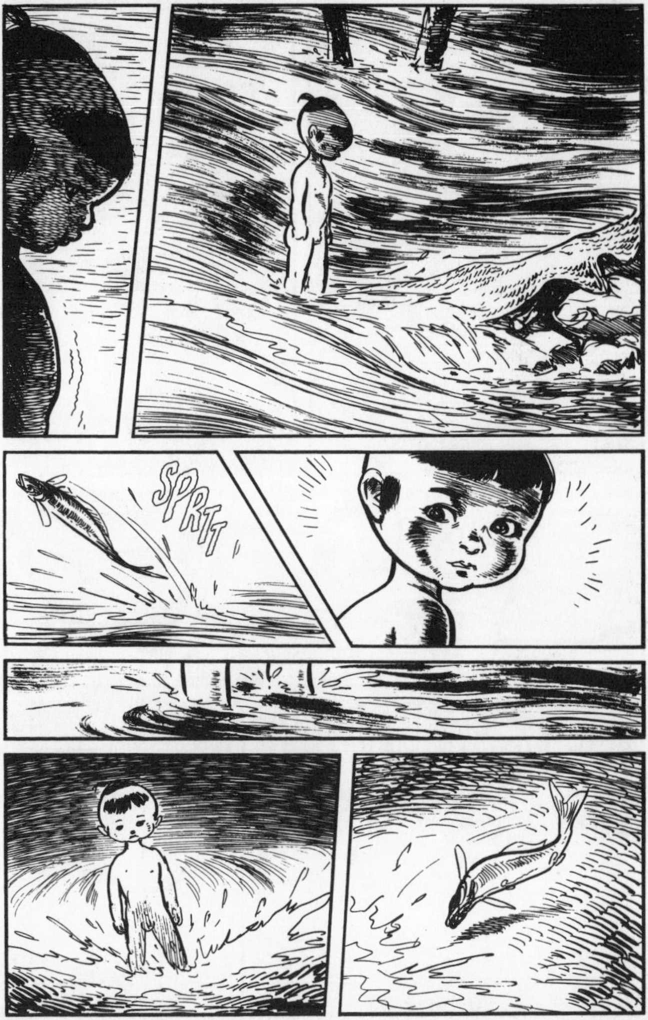
SPRTT

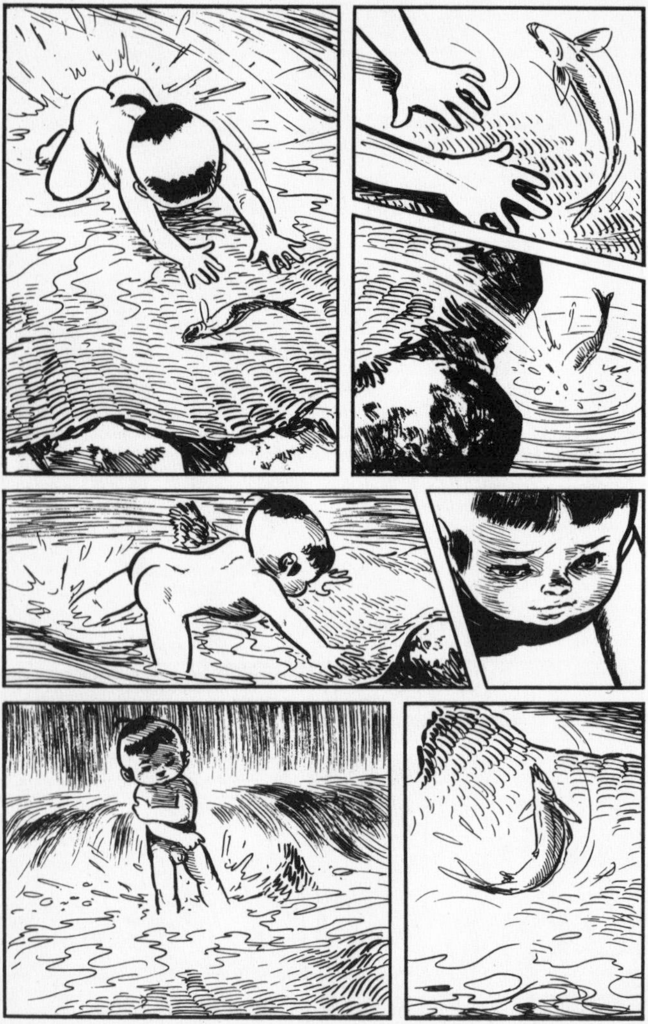

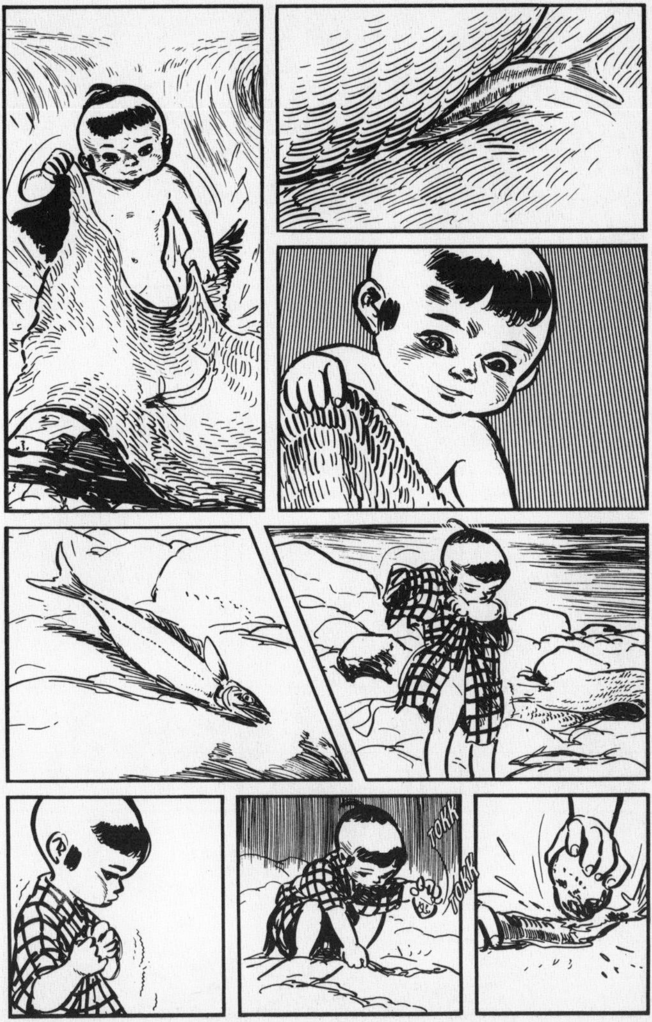
TOKK
TOKK

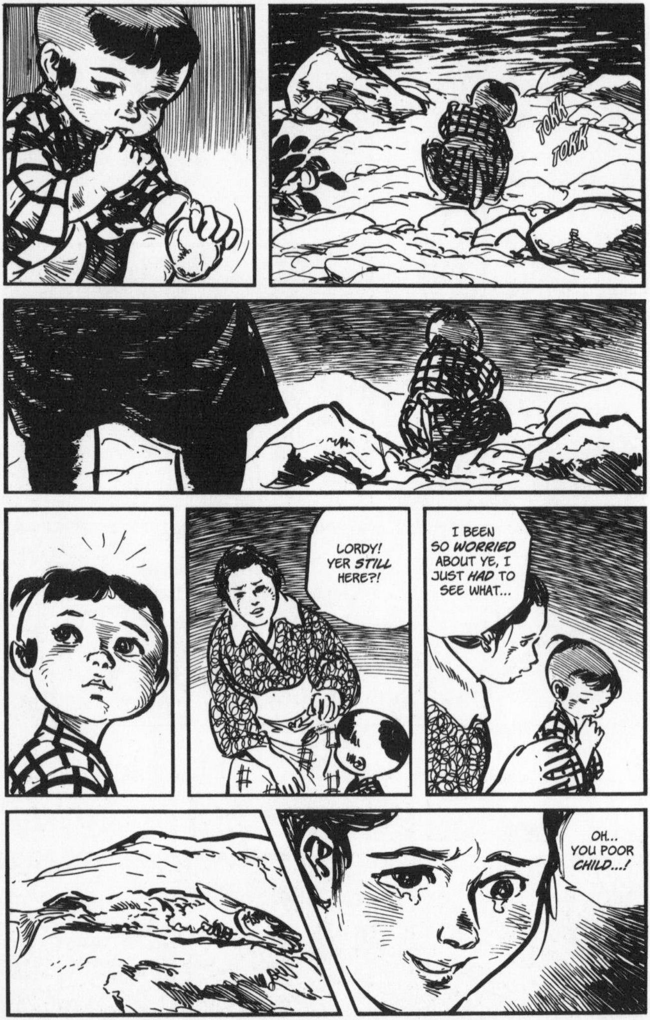
TOKK
TOKK
LORDY! YER STILL HERE?!
I BEEN SO WORRIED ABOUT YE, I JUST HAD TO SEE WHAT...
OH... YOU POOR CHILD...!

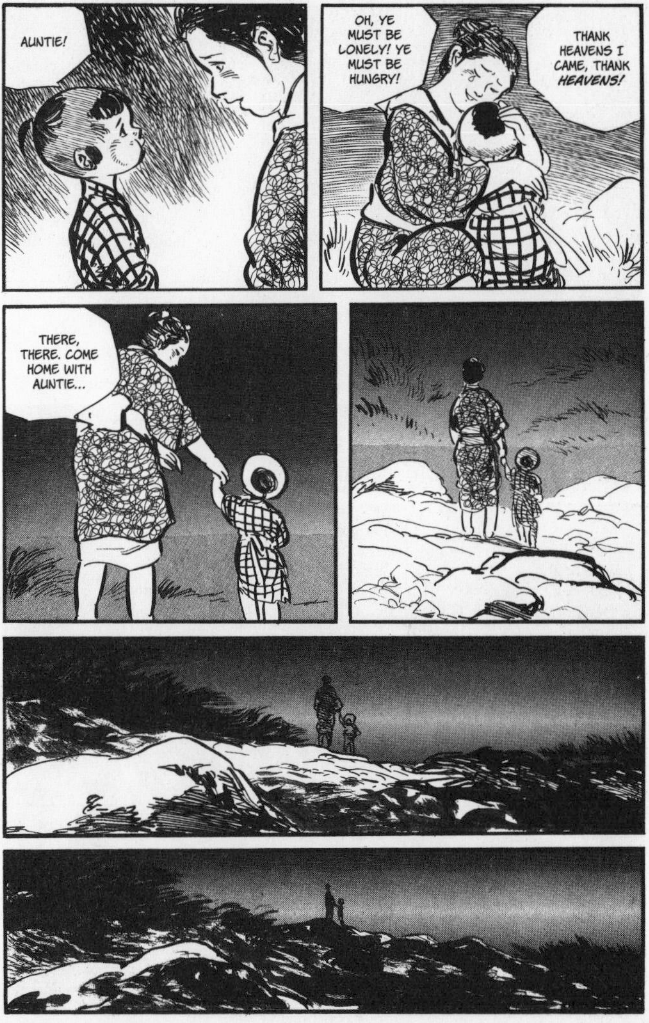
AUNTIE!
OH, YE MUST BE LONELY! YE MUST BE HUNGRY!
THANK HEAVENS I CAME, THANK *HEAVENS!*
THERE, THERE. COME HOME WITH AUNTIE...

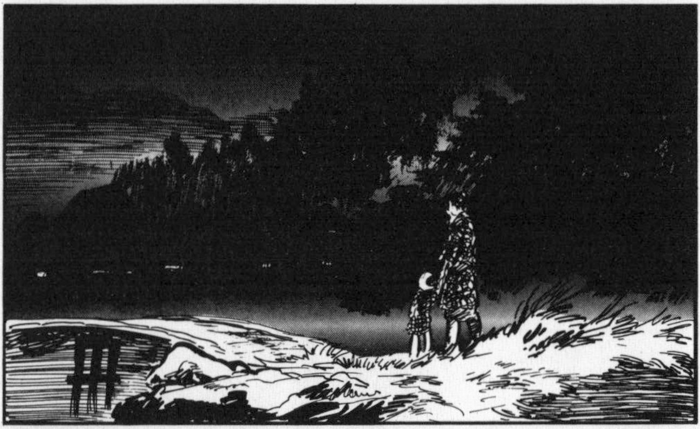

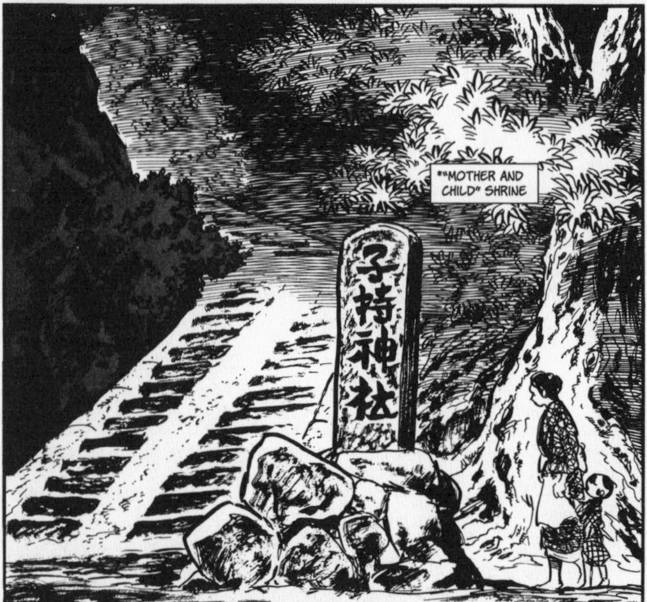
*"MOTHER AND CHILD" SHRINE
子持神社

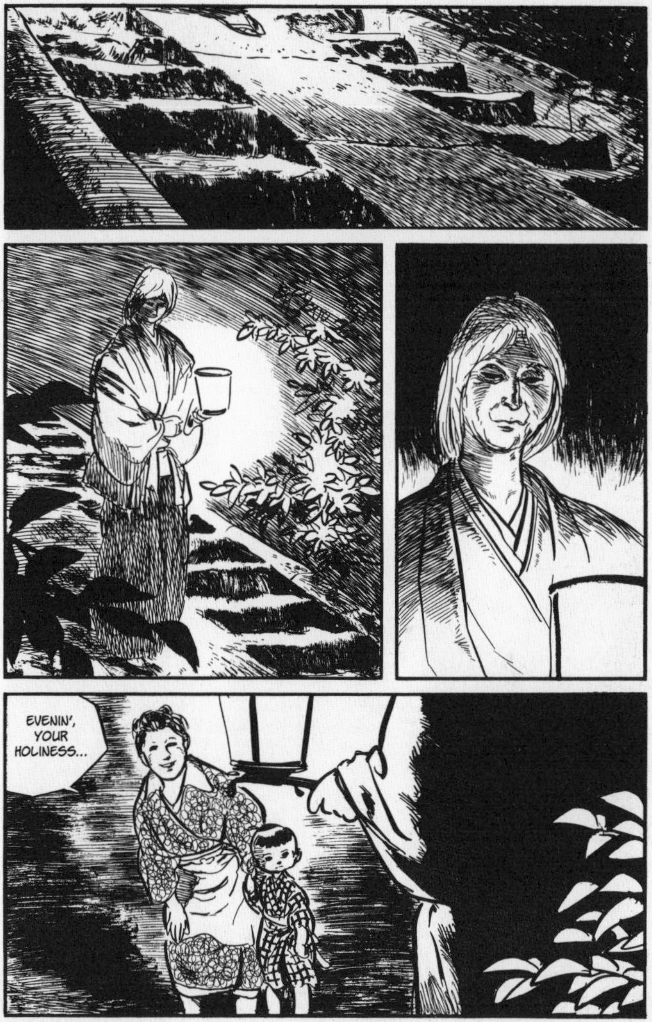
EVENIN', YOUR HOLINESS...

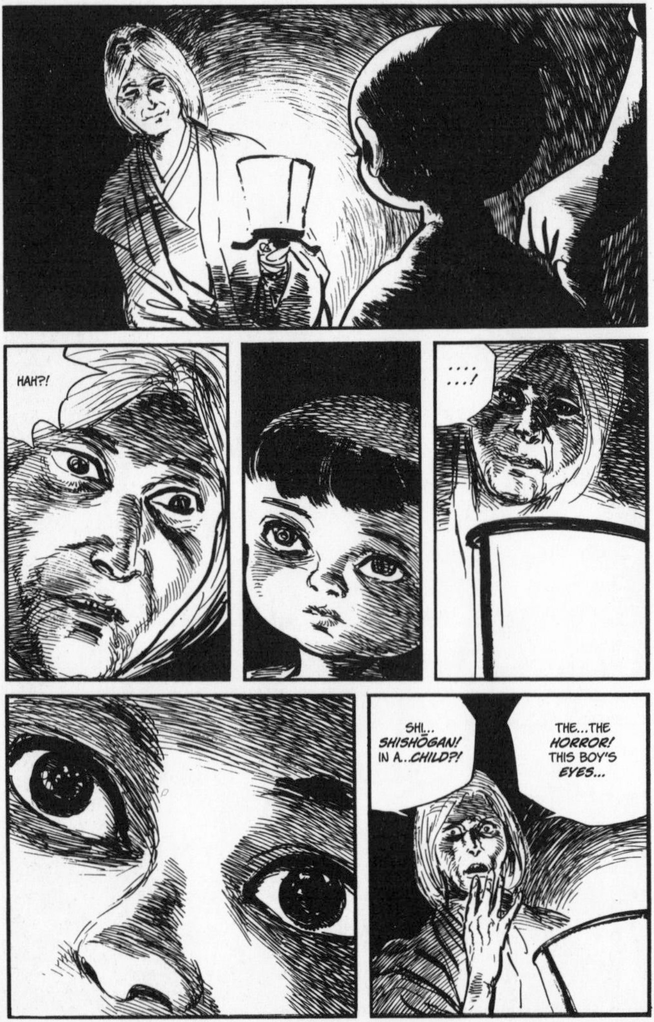
HAH?!
...,
...?
SHI... SHISHŌGAN! IN A..CHILD?!
THE...THE HORROR! THIS BOY'S EYES...

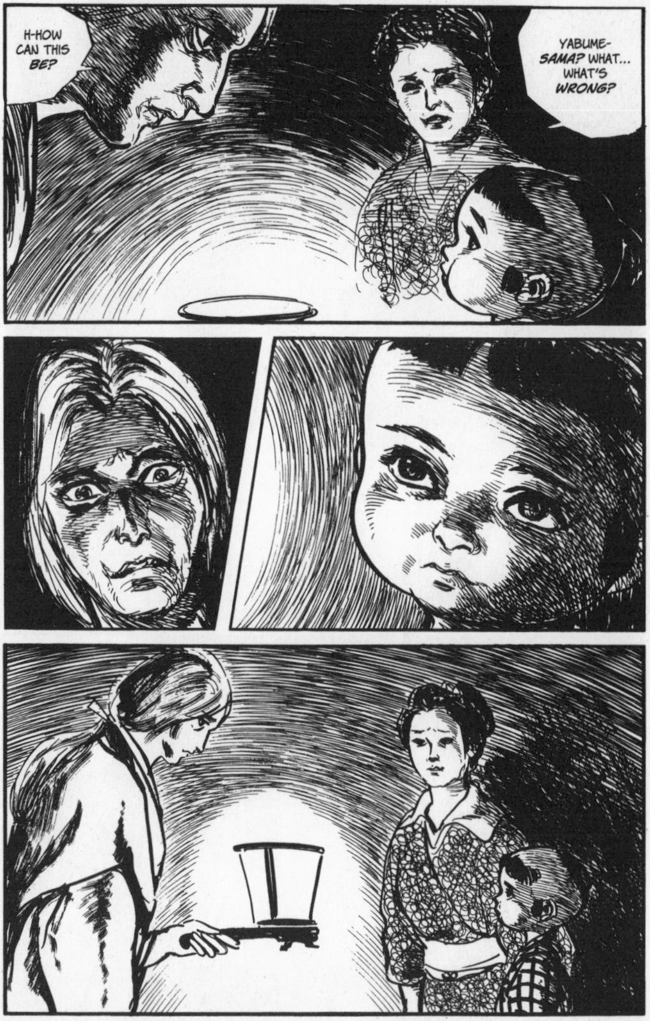
H-HOW CAN THIS BE?
YABUME-SAMA? WHAT... WHAT'S WRONG?

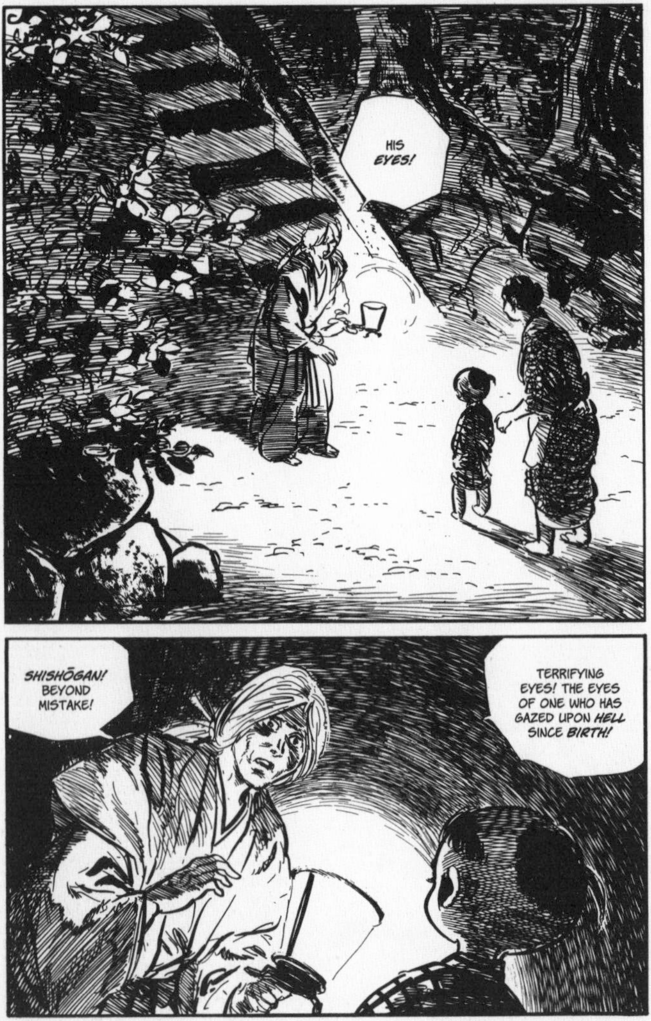
HIS EYES!
SHISHŌGAN! BEYOND MISTAKE!
TERRIFYING EYES! THE EYES OF ONE WHO HAS GAZED UPON HELL SINCE BIRTH!

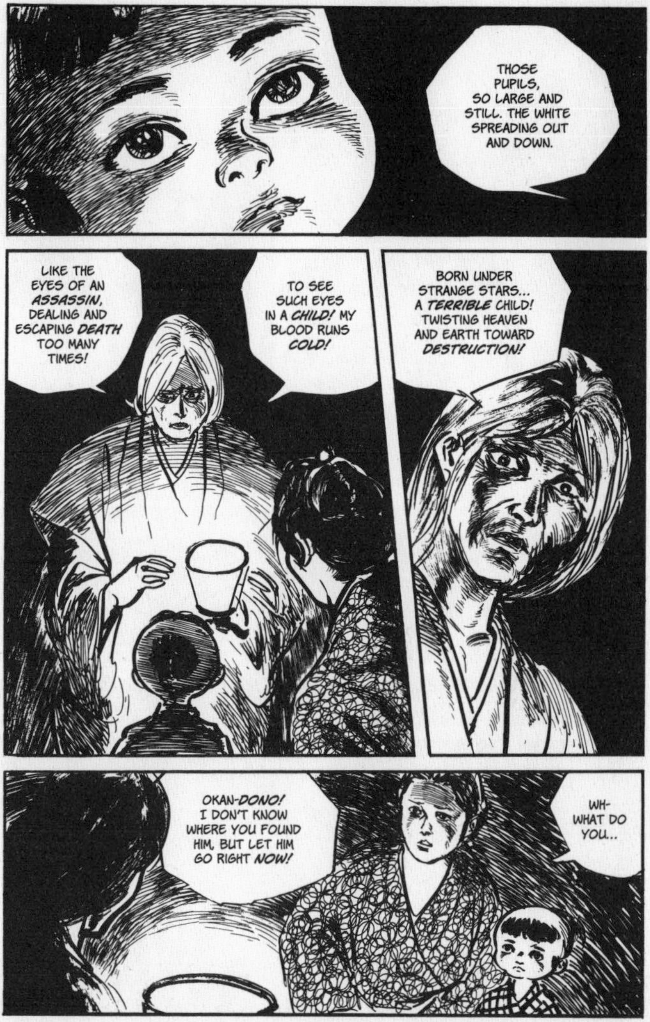
THOSE PUPILS, SO LARGE AND STILL. THE WHITE SPREADING OUT AND DOWN.
LIKE THE EYES OF AN *ASSASSIN*, DEALING AND ESCAPING *DEATH* TOO MANY TIMES!
TO SEE SUCH EYES IN A *CHILD!* MY BLOOD RUNS *COLD!*
BORN UNDER STRANGE STARS... A *TERRIBLE* CHILD! TWISTING HEAVEN AND EARTH TOWARD *DESTRUCTION!*
OKAN-*DONO!* I DON'T KNOW WHERE YOU FOUND HIM, BUT LET HIM GO RIGHT *NOW!*
WH- WHAT DO YOU...

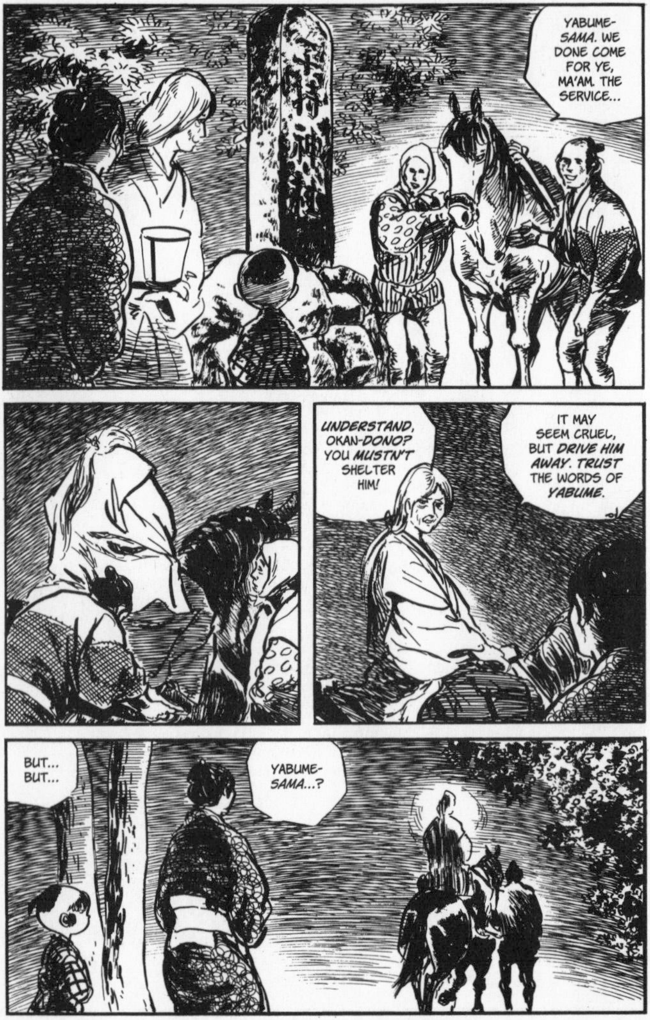
YABUME-SAMA. WE DONE COME FOR YE, MA'AM. THE SERVICE...
UNDERSTAND, OKAN-DONO? YOU MUSTN'T SHELTER HIM!
IT MAY SEEM CRUEL, BUT DRIVE HIM AWAY. TRUST THE WORDS OF YABUME.
BUT... BUT...
YABUME-SAMA...?

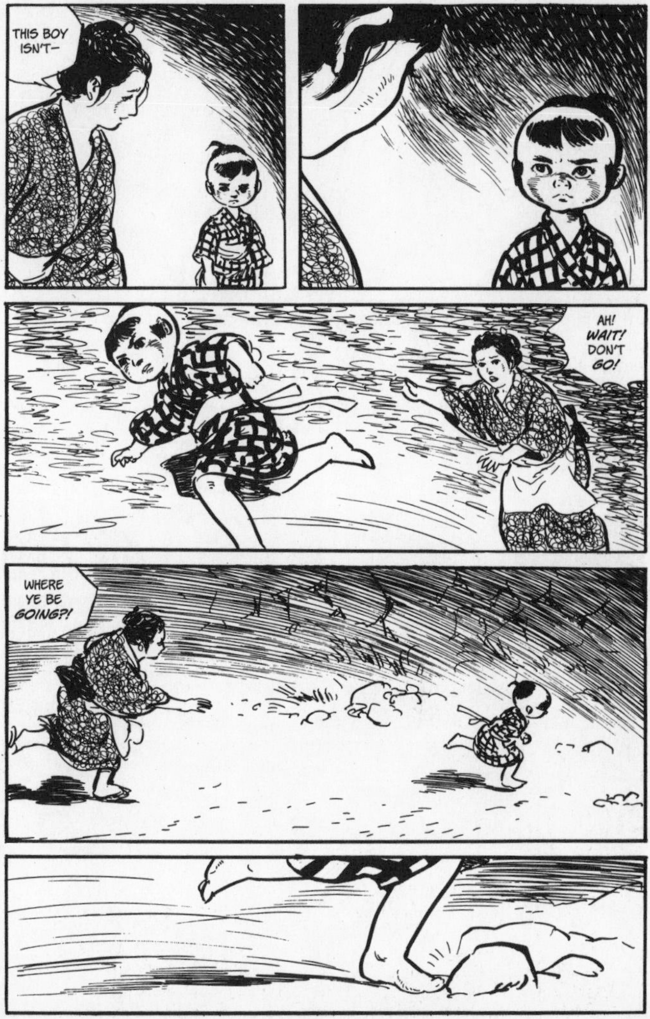
THIS BOY ISN'T-
AH! WAIT! DON'T GO!
WHERE YE BE GOING?!

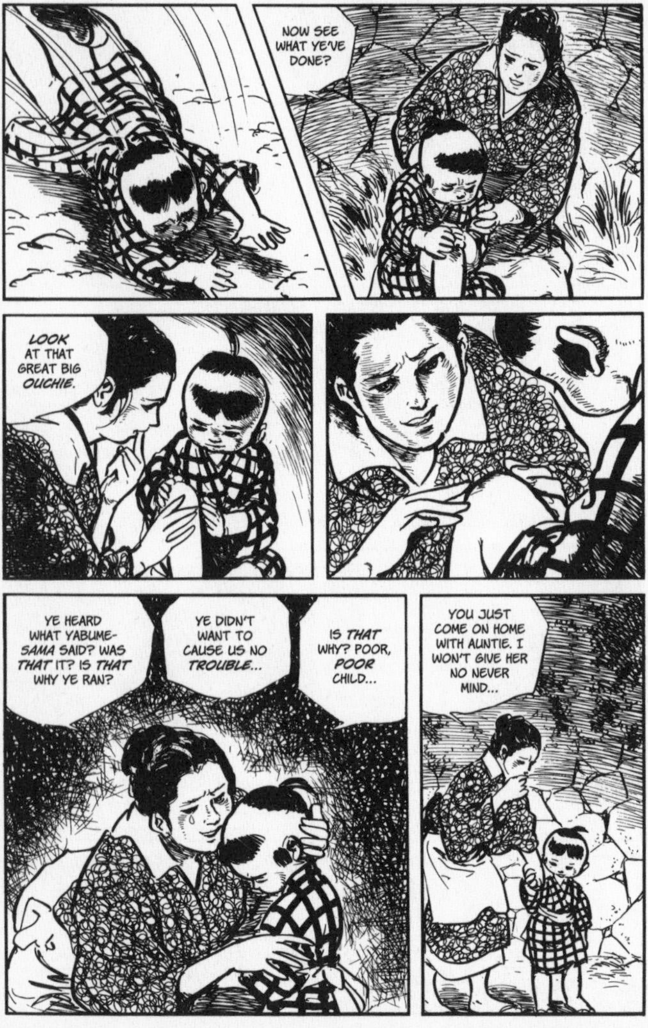
NOW SEE WHAT YE'VE DONE?
LOOK AT THAT GREAT BIG OUCHIE.
YE HEARD WHAT YABUME-SAMA SAID? WAS THAT IT? IS THAT WHY YE RAN?
YE DIDN'T WANT TO CAUSE US NO TROUBLE...
IS THAT WHY? POOR, POOR CHILD...
YOU JUST COME ON HOME WITH AUNTIE. I WON'T GIVE HER NO NEVER MIND...

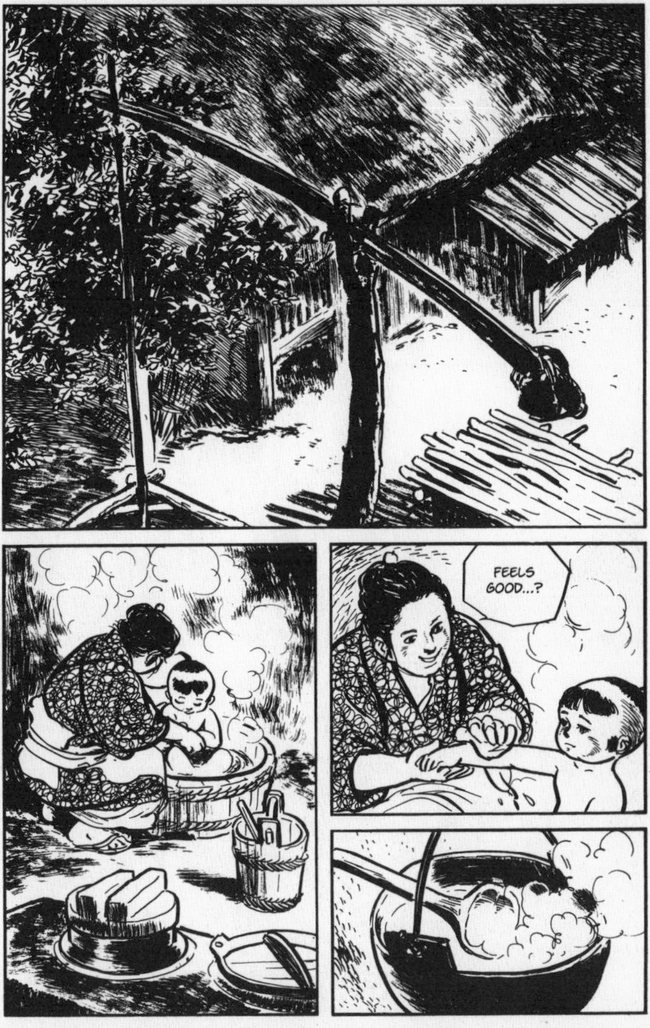
FEELS GOOD...?

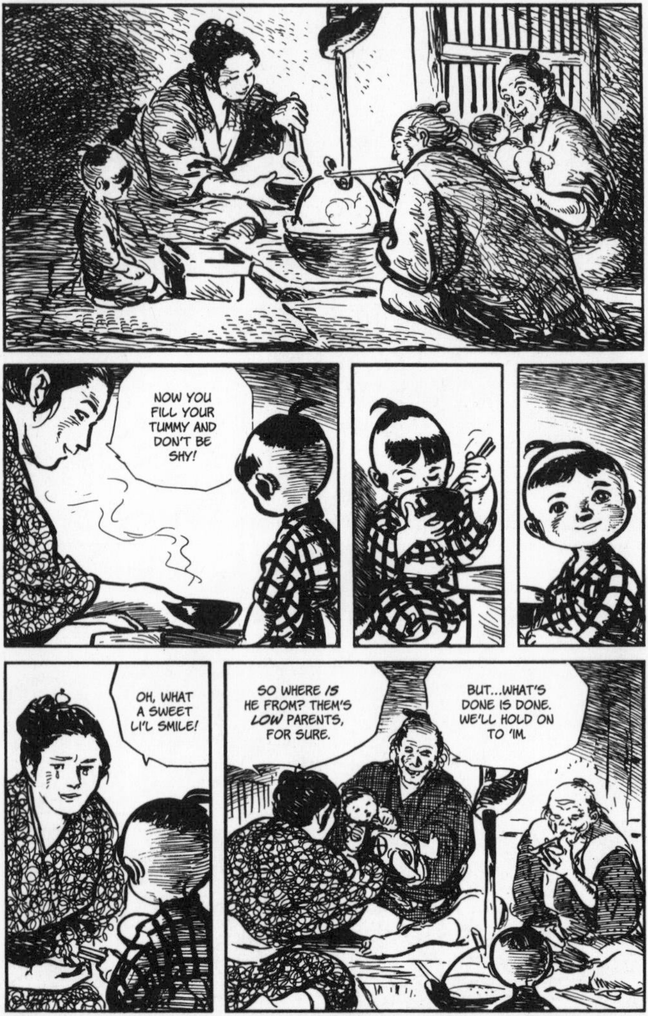
NOW YOU FILL YOUR TUMMY AND DON'T BE SHY!
OH, WHAT A SWEET LI'L SMILE!
SO WHERE *IS* HE FROM? THEM'S *LOW* PARENTS, FOR SURE.
BUT...WHAT'S DONE IS DONE. WE'LL HOLD ON TO 'IM.

AYE, THAT BE GOOD!
CUTE LI'L TYKE...
GOOD MANNERS, TOO!
FHT
AHH! NOT AG'IN! THAT'S DANGEROUS, GRANPAPPY!

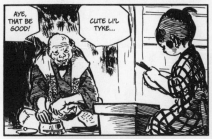

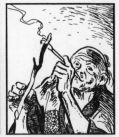

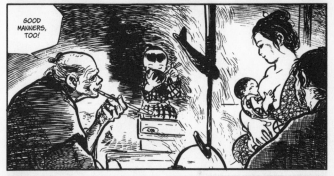

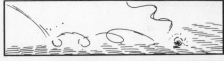

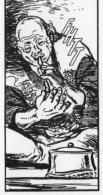

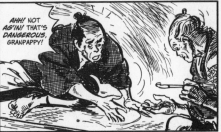

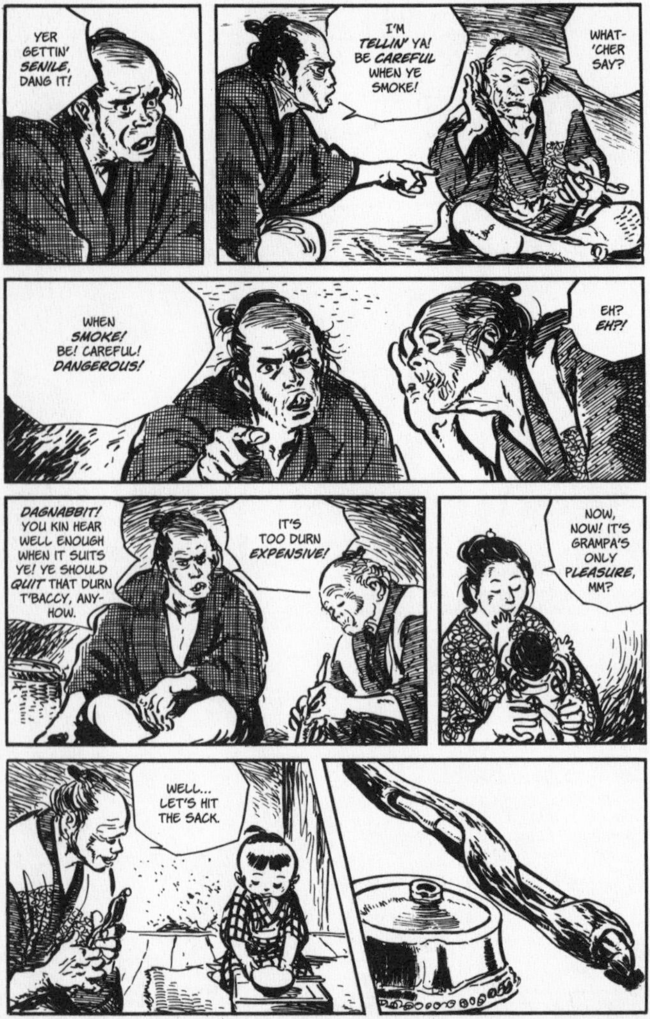
YER GETTIN' *SENILE*, DANG IT!
I'M *TELLIN'* YA! BE *CAREFUL* WHEN YE SMOKE!
WHAT-'CHER SAY?
WHEN *SMOKE!* BE! CAREFUL! *DANGEROUS!*
EH? *EH?!*
DAGNABBIT! YOU KIN HEAR WELL ENOUGH WHEN IT SUITS YE! YE SHOULD *QUIT* THAT DURN T'BACCY, ANY-HOW.
IT'S TOO DURN *EXPENSIVE!*
NOW, NOW! IT'S GRAMPA'S ONLY *PLEASURE*, MM?
WELL... LET'S HIT THE SACK.

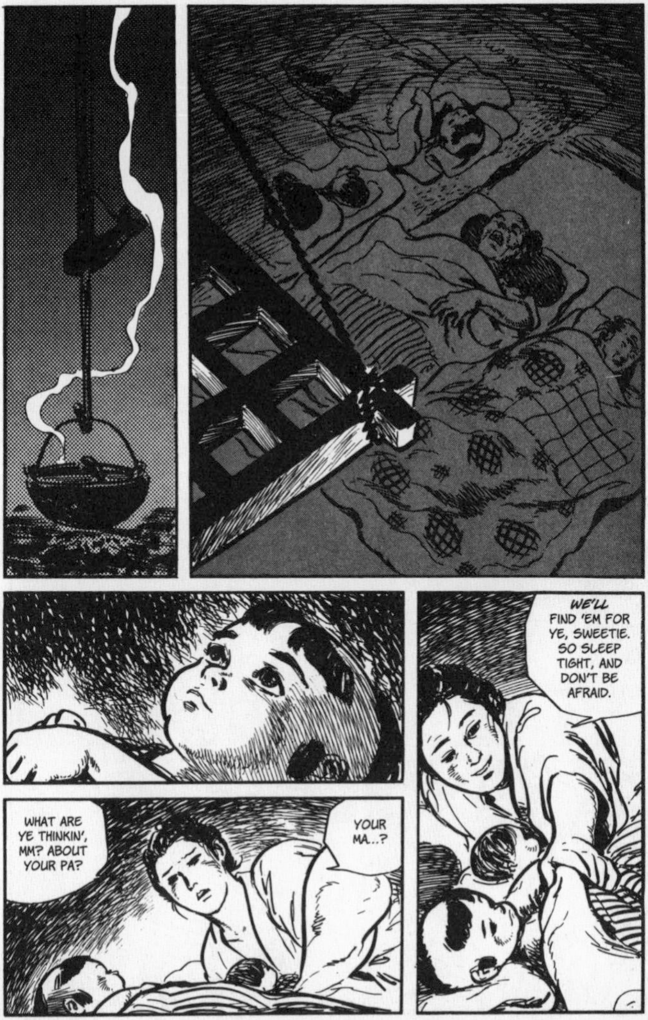
WHAT ARE YE THINKIN', MM? ABOUT YOUR PA?
YOUR MA...?
WE'LL FIND 'EM FOR YE, SWEETIE. SO SLEEP TIGHT, AND DON'T BE AFRAID.

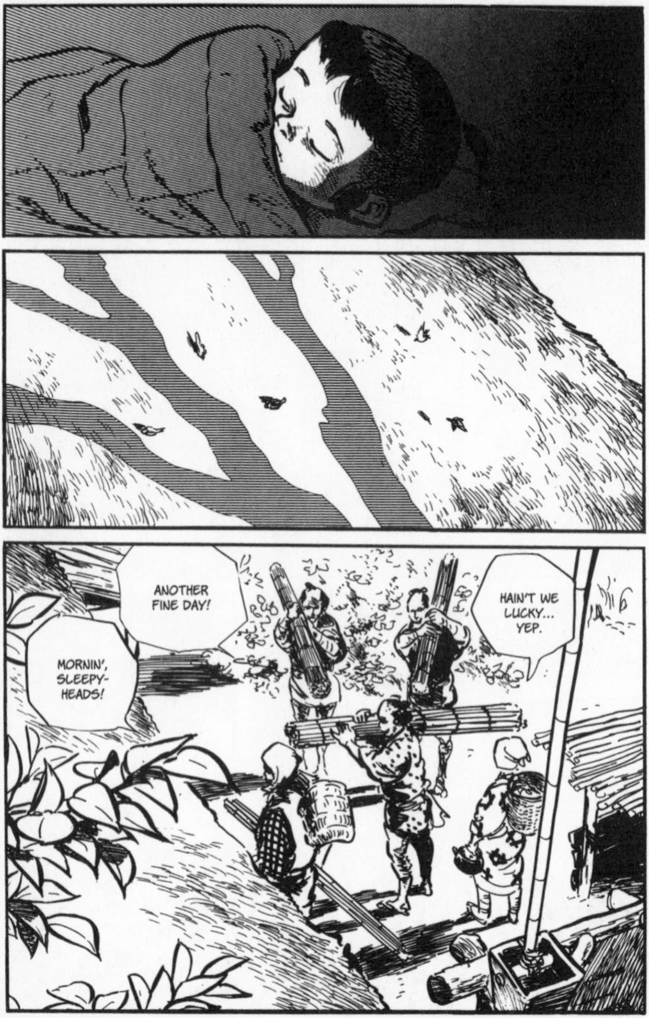
MORNIN', SLEEPY-HEADS!
ANOTHER FINE DAY!
HAIN'T WE LUCKY... YEP.

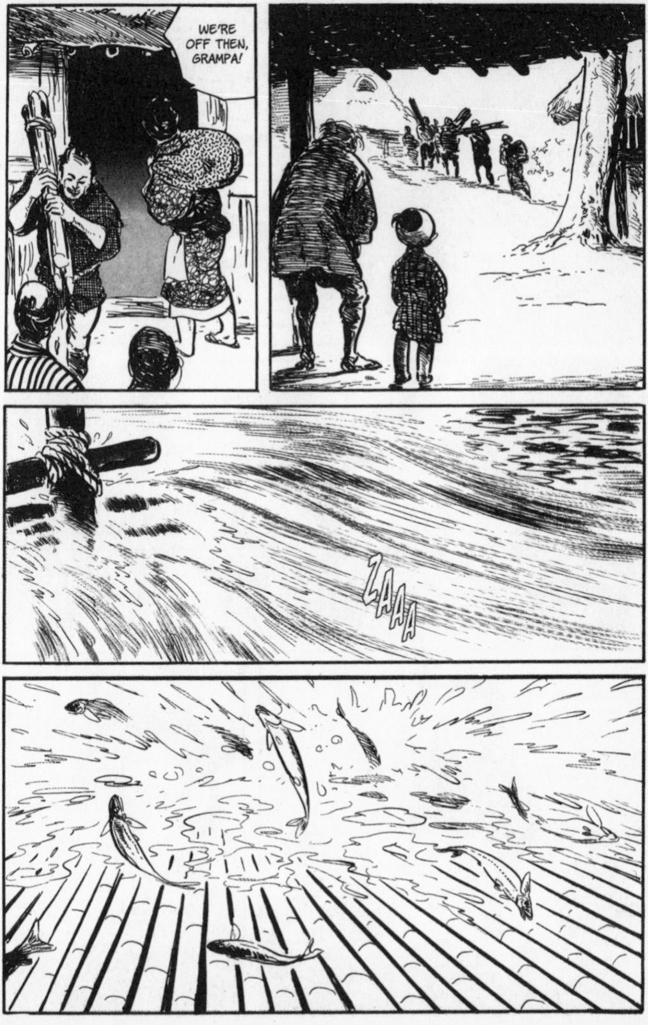
WE'RE OFF THEN, GRAMPA!
ZAAA

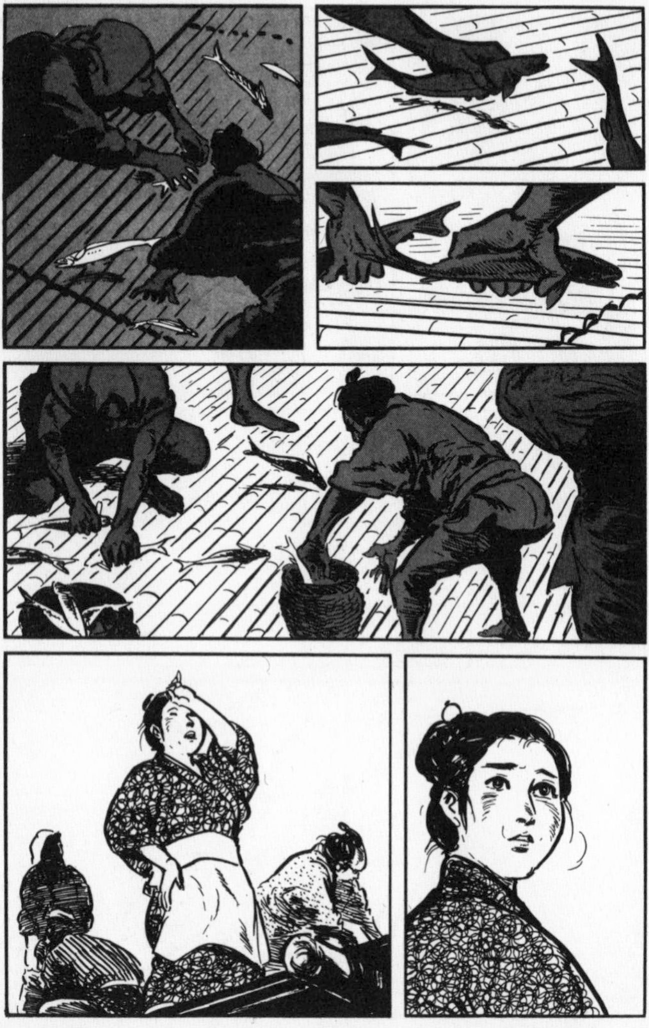

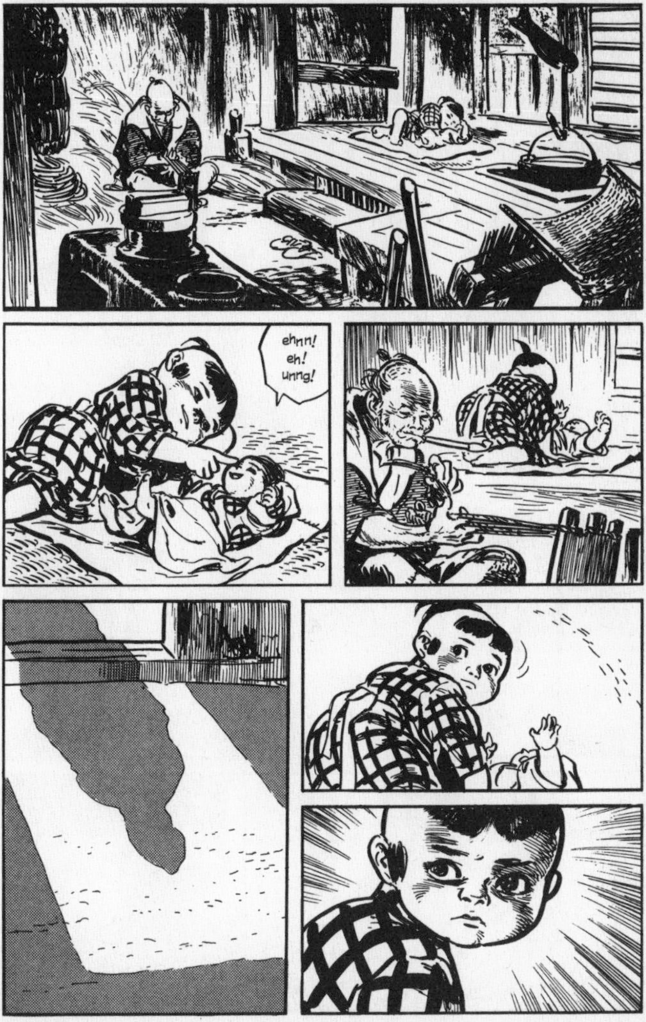
ehnn!
eh!
unng!

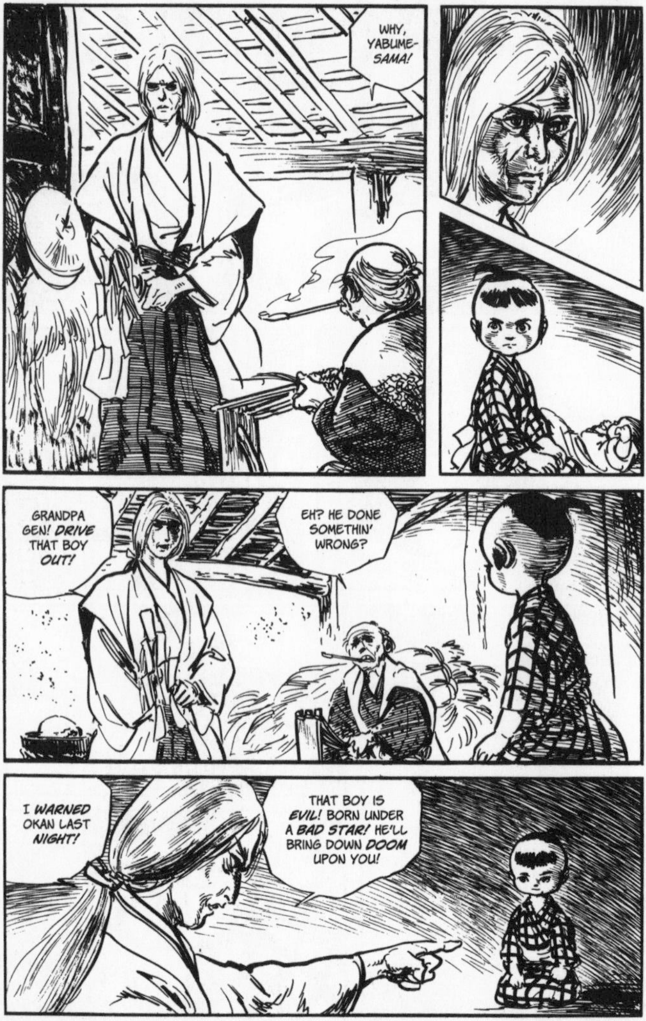
WHY, YABUME-SAMA!
GRANDPA GEN! *DRIVE* THAT BOY *OUT!*
EH? HE DONE SOMETHIN' WRONG?
I *WARNED* OKAN LAST *NIGHT!*
THAT BOY IS *EVIL!* BORN UNDER A *BAD STAR!* HE'LL BRING DOWN *DOOM* UPON YOU!

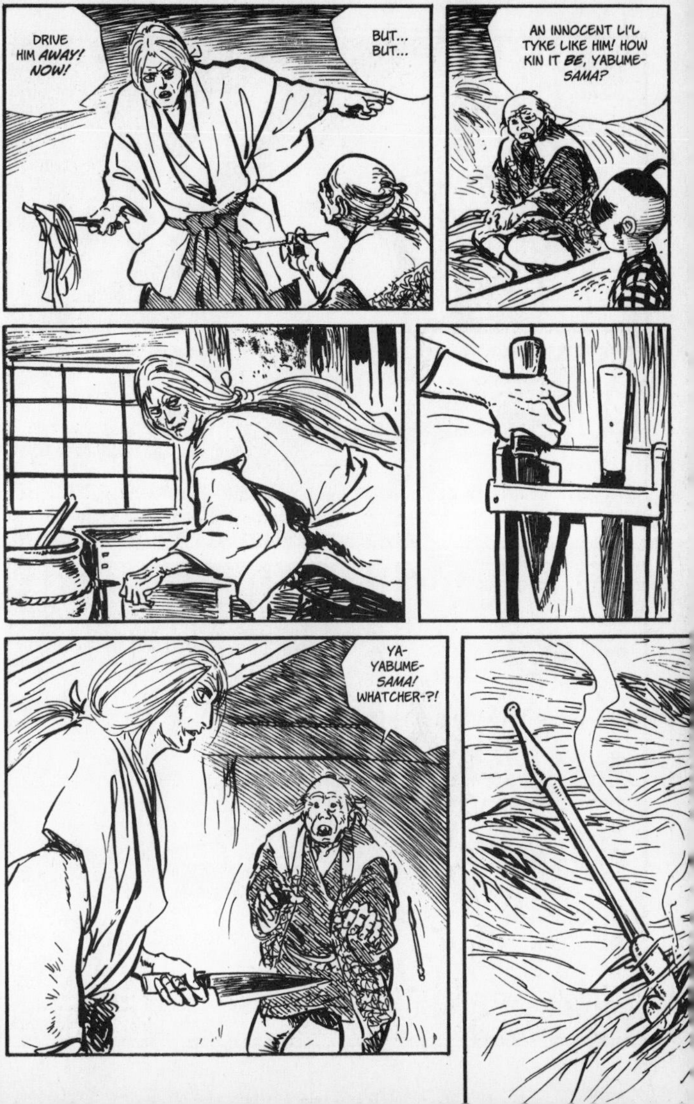
DRIVE HIM AWAY! NOW!
BUT... BUT...
AN INNOCENT LI'L TYKE LIKE HIM! HOW KIN IT BE, YABUME-SAMA?
YA-YABUME-SAMA! WHATCHER-?!

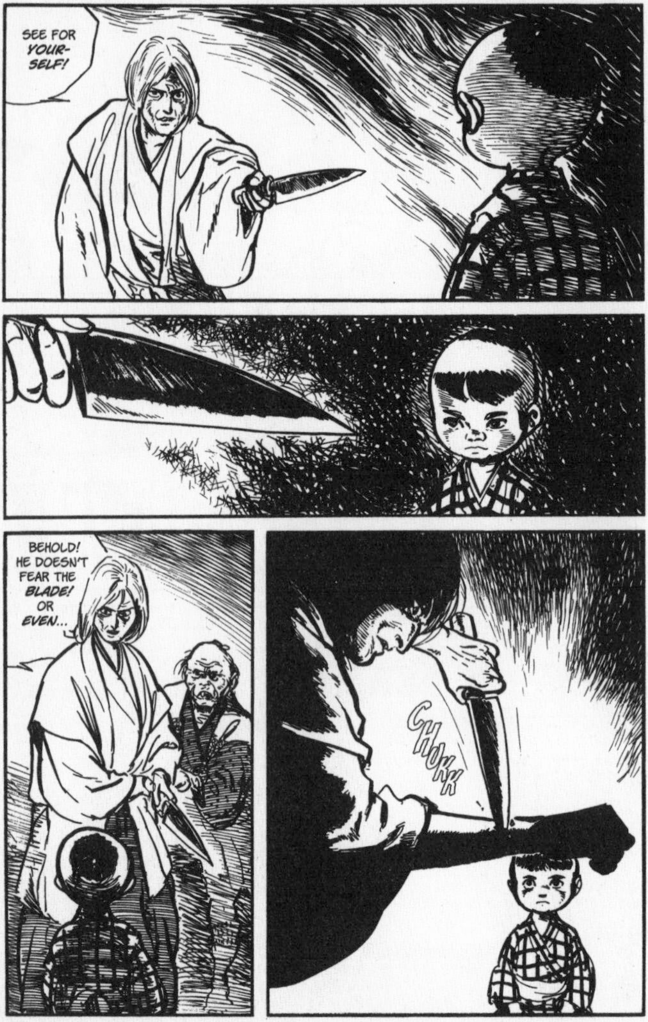
SEE FOR *YOURSELF!*
BEHOLD! HE DOESN'T FEAR THE *BLADE!* OR *EVEN...*
CHUKK

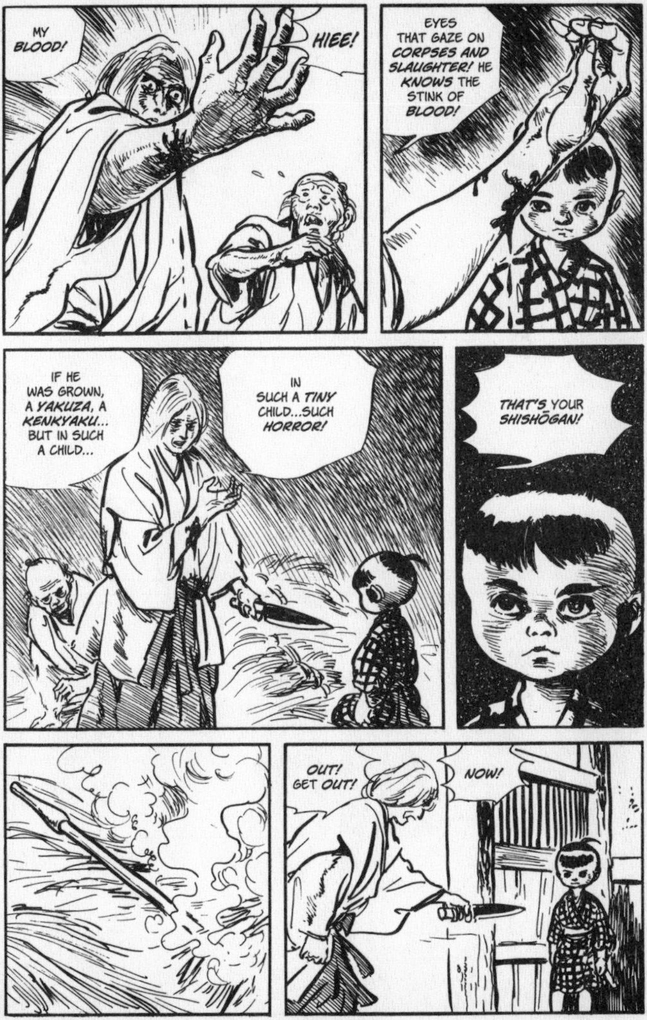
MY BLOOD!
HIEE!
EYES THAT GAZE ON CORPSES AND SLAUGHTER! HE KNOWS THE STINK OF BLOOD!
IF HE WAS GROWN, A YAKUZA, A KENKYAKU... BUT IN SUCH A CHILD...
IN SUCH A TINY CHILD...SUCH HORROR!
THAT'S YOUR SHISHŌGAN!
OUT! GET OUT!
NOW!

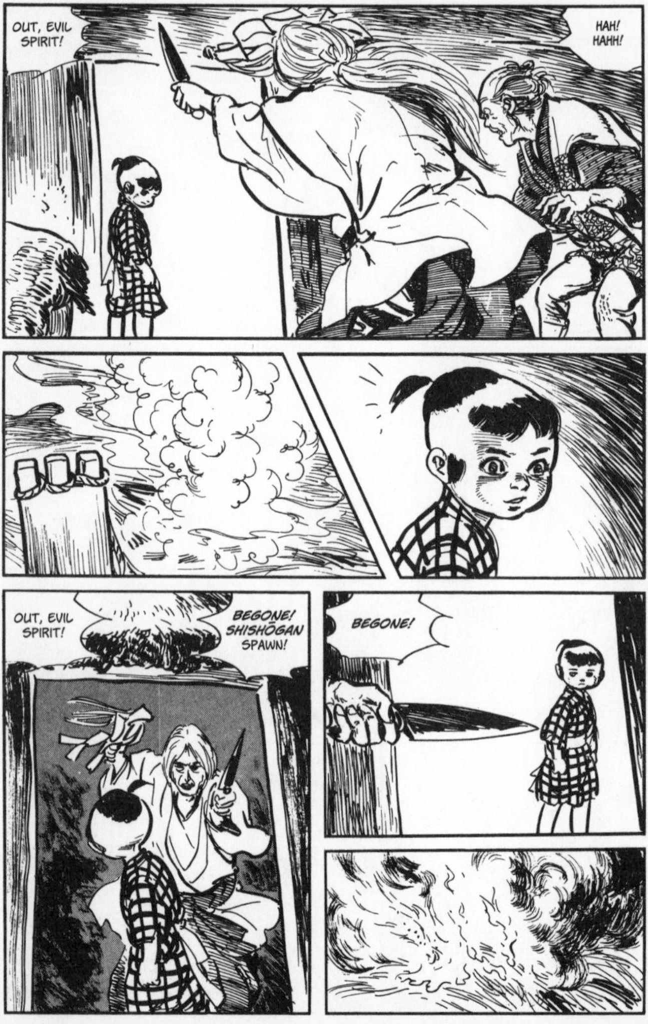
OUT, EVIL SPIRIT!
HAH! HAHH!
OUT, EVIL SPIRIT!
BEGONE! SHISHŌGAN SPAWN!
BEGONE!

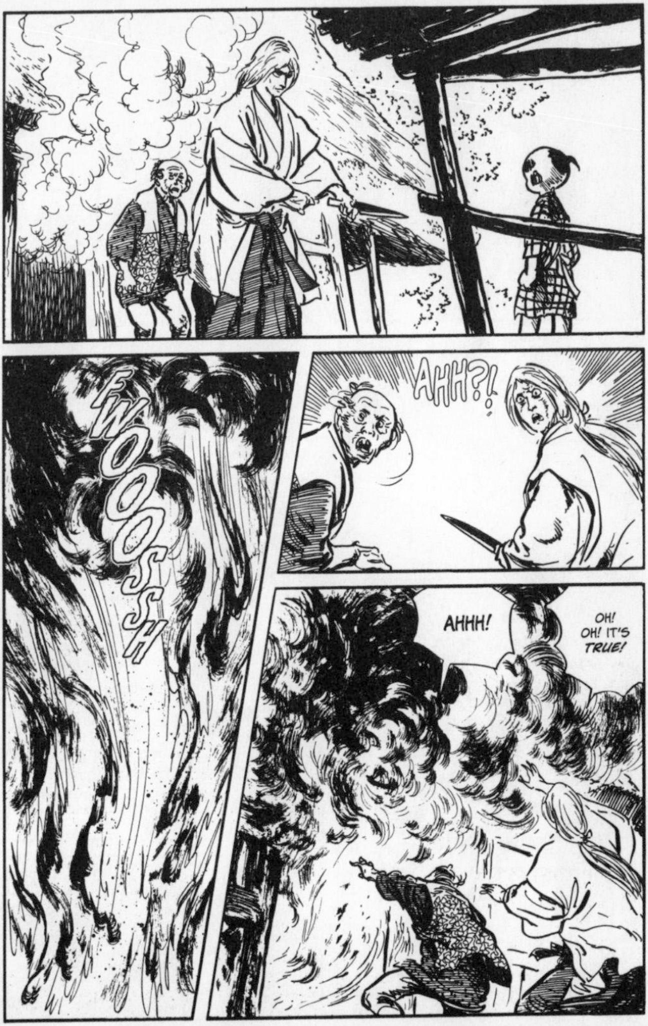
AHH?!
OH! OH! IT'S *TRUE!*
AHHH!
FWOOOSSH

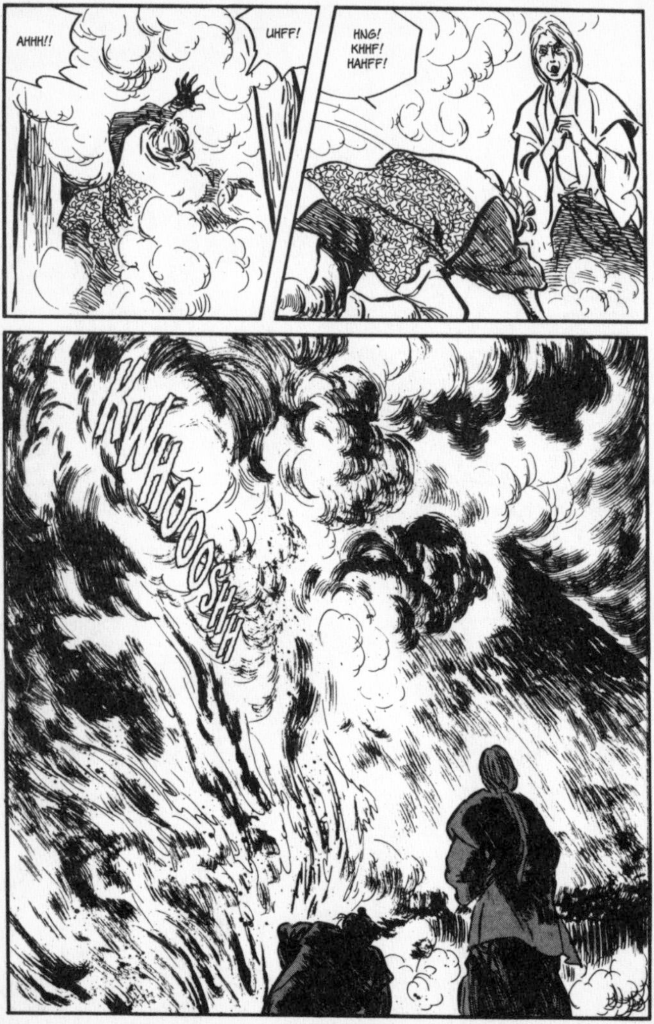
AHHH!!
UHFF!
HNG! KHHF! HAHFF!
KWHOOOSHH

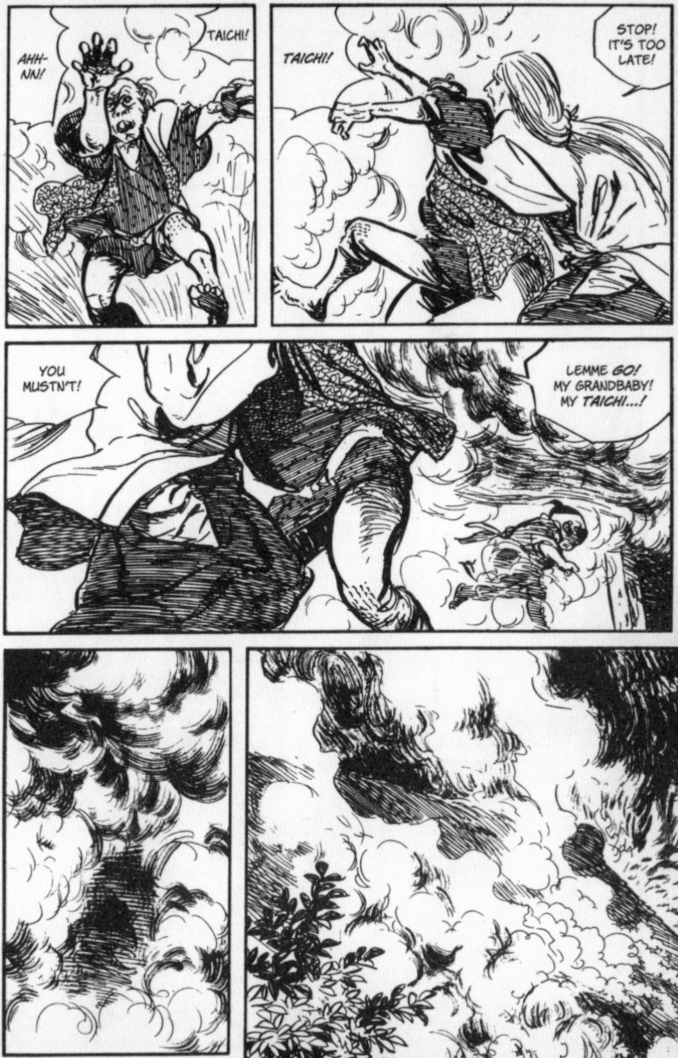
AHH-NN!
TAICHI!
TAICHI!
STOP! IT'S TOO LATE!
YOU MUSTN'T!
LEMME GO! MY GRANDBABY! MY TAICHI...!

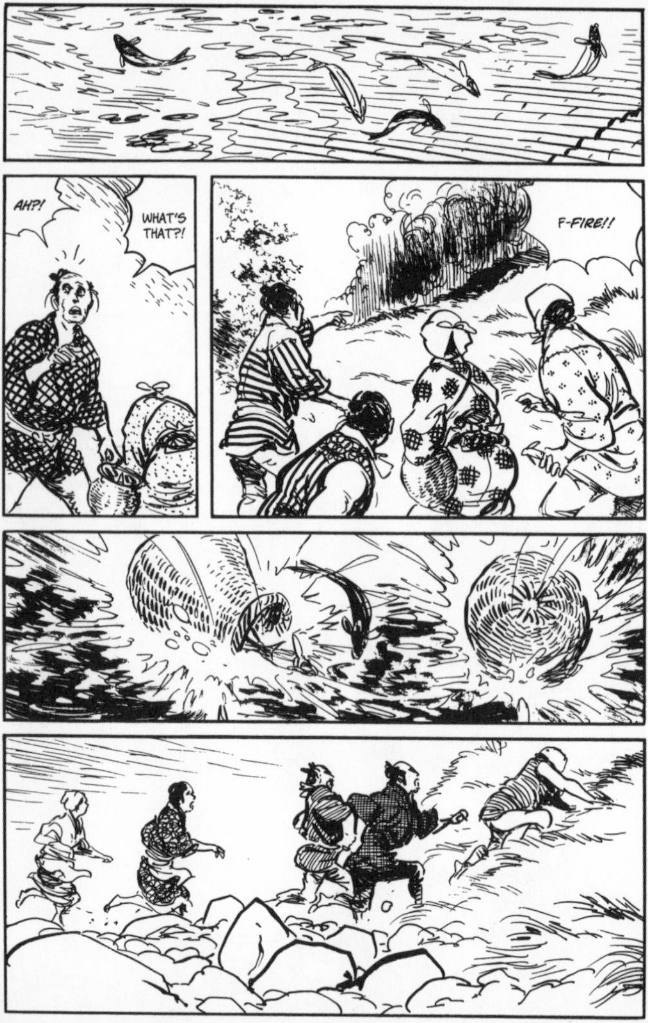
AH?!
WHAT'S THAT?!
F-FIRE!!

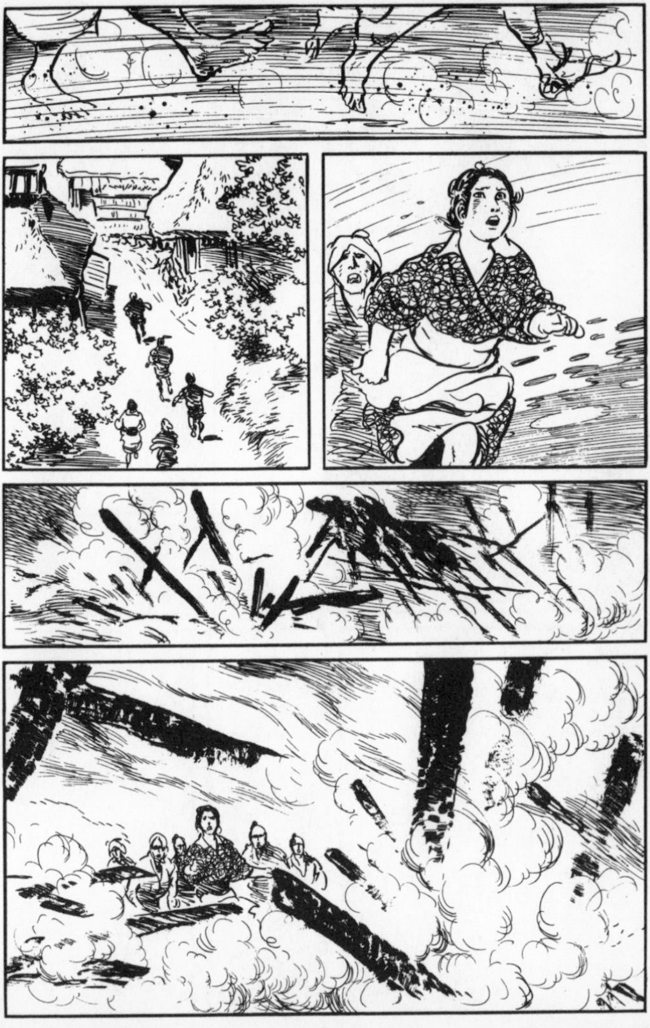

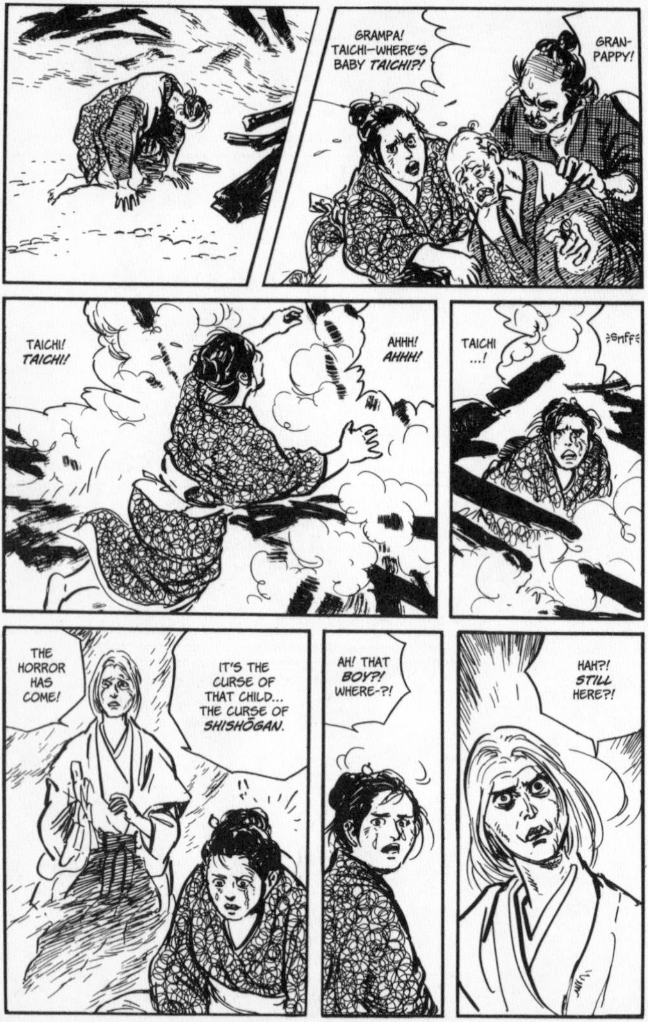
GRAMPA! TAICHI—WHERE'S BABY TAICHI?!
GRAN-PAPPY!
TAICHI! TAICHI!
AHHH! AHHH!
TAICHI ...!
SNFF
THE HORROR HAS COME!
IT'S THE CURSE OF THAT CHILD... THE CURSE OF SHISHŌGAN.
AH! THAT BOY?! WHERE-?!
HAH?! STILL HERE?!

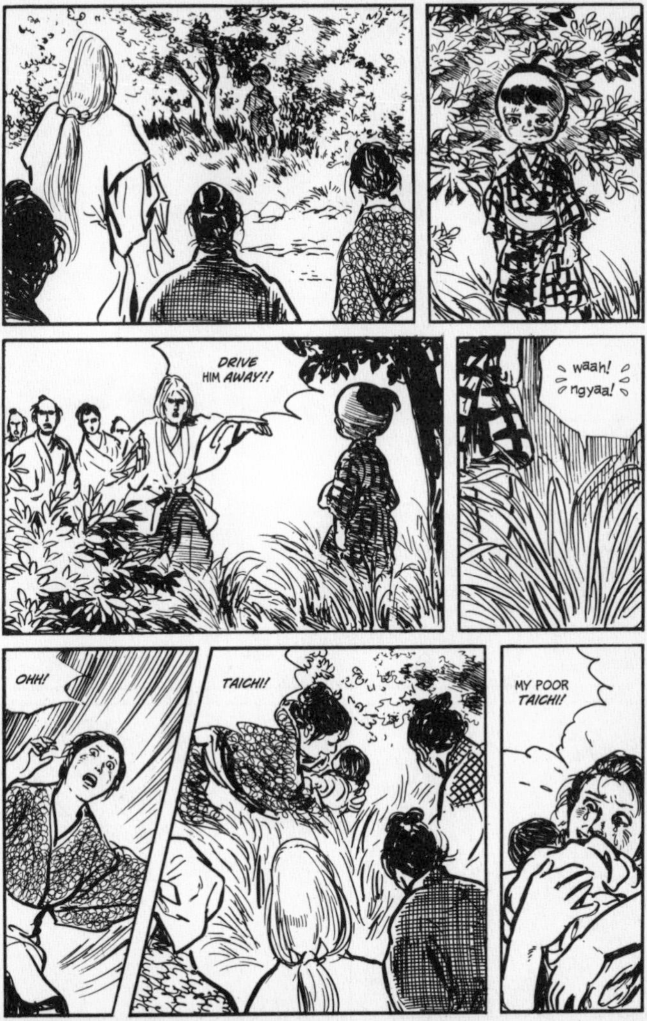
DRIVE HIM AWAY!!
waah! ngyaa!
OHH!
TAICHI!
MY POOR TAICHI!

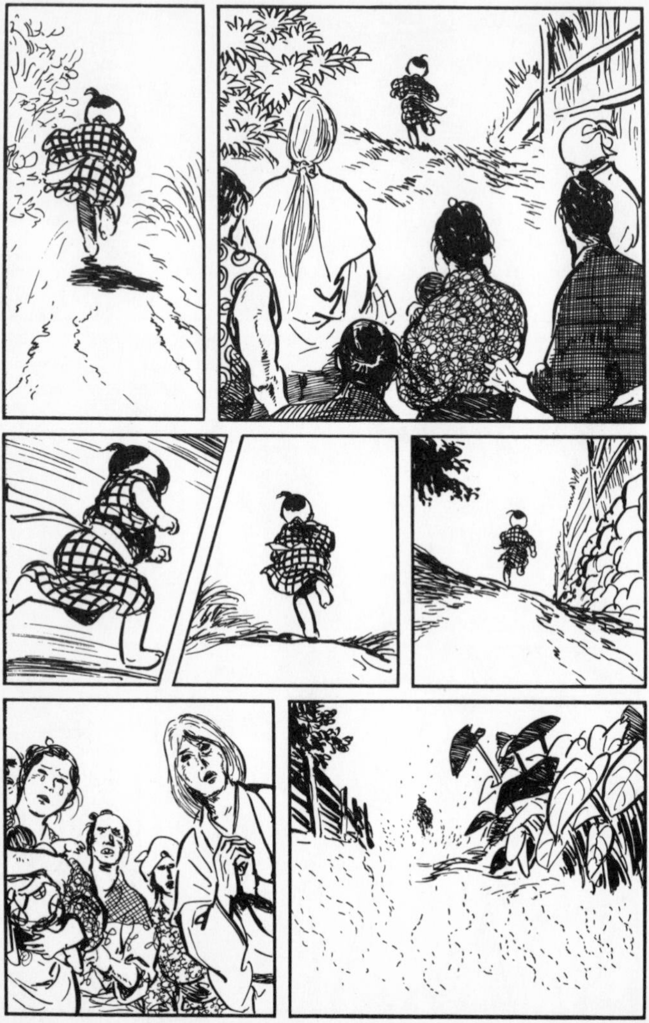

the fifty-third

Drifting Shadows

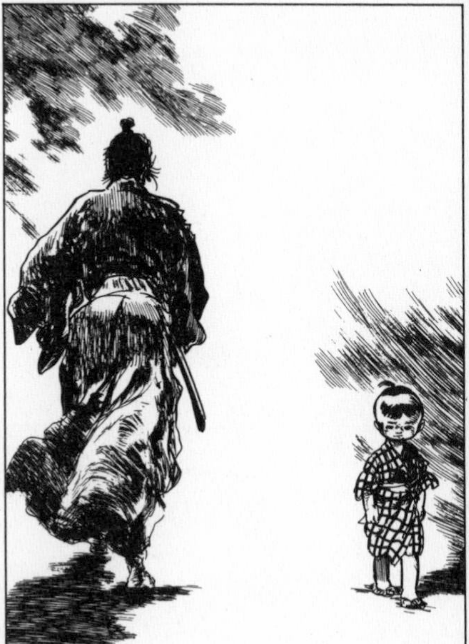

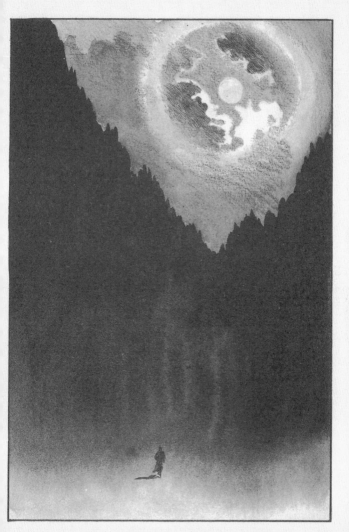

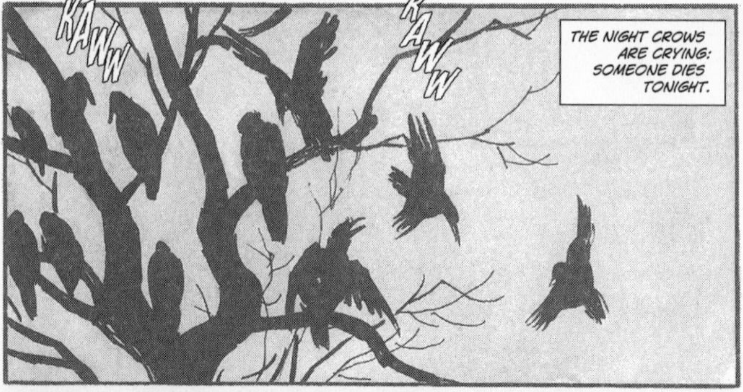
KAWW
KAWW
THE NIGHT CROWS ARE CRYING: SOMEONE DIES TONIGHT.

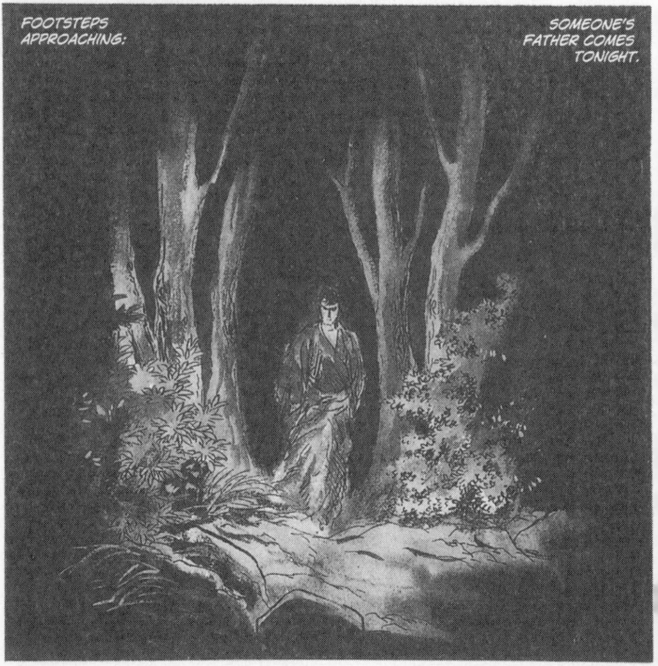
FOOTSTEPS APPROACHING:
SOMEONE'S FATHER COMES TONIGHT.

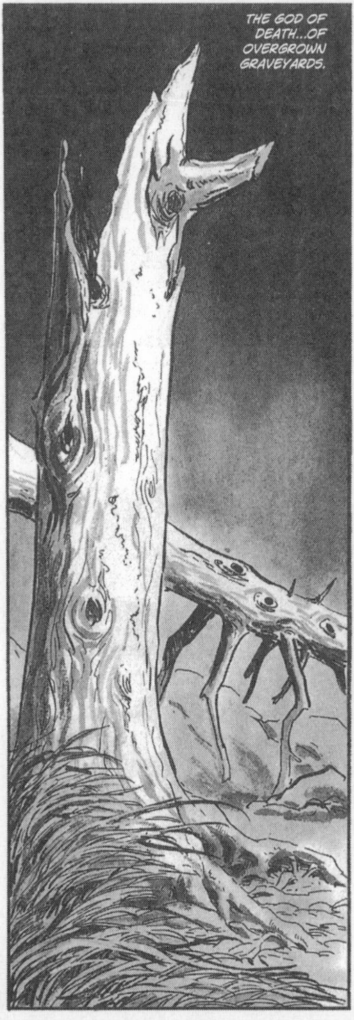
THE GOD OF DEATH...OF OVERGROWN GRAVEYARDS.

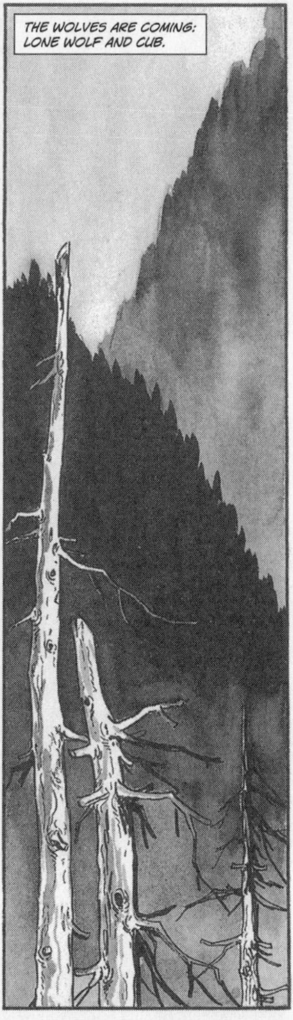
THE WOLVES ARE COMING: LONE WOLF AND CUB.

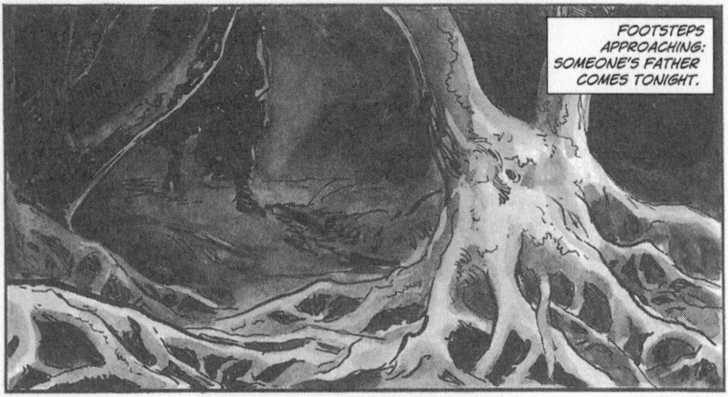
FOOTSTEPS APPROACHING: SOMEONE'S FATHER COMES TONIGHT.

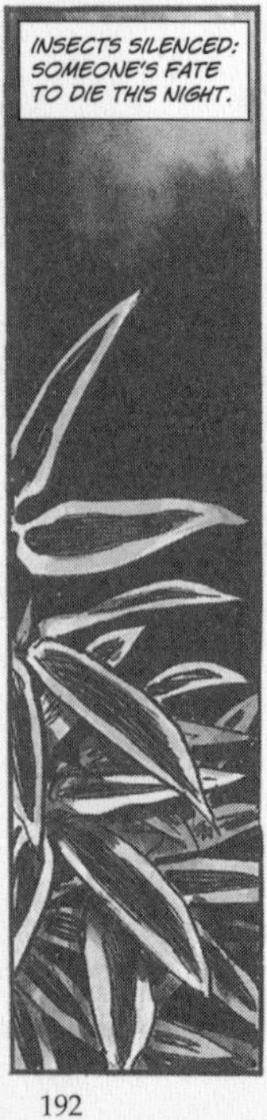
INSECTS SILENCED: SOMEONE'S FATE TO DIE THIS NIGHT.

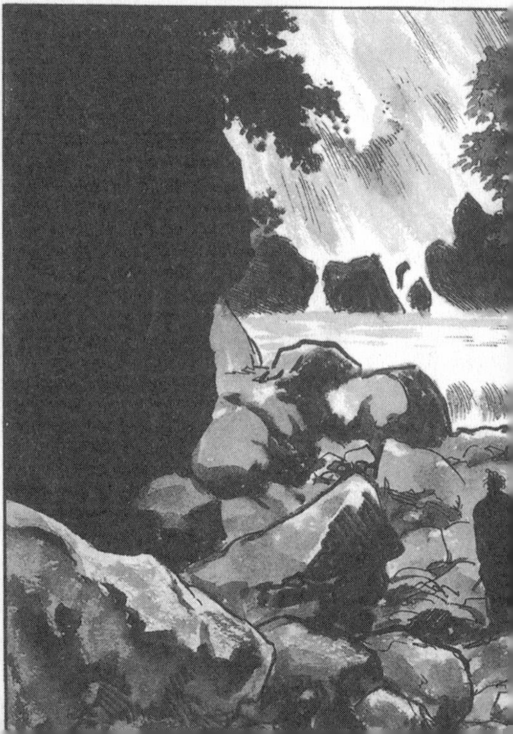

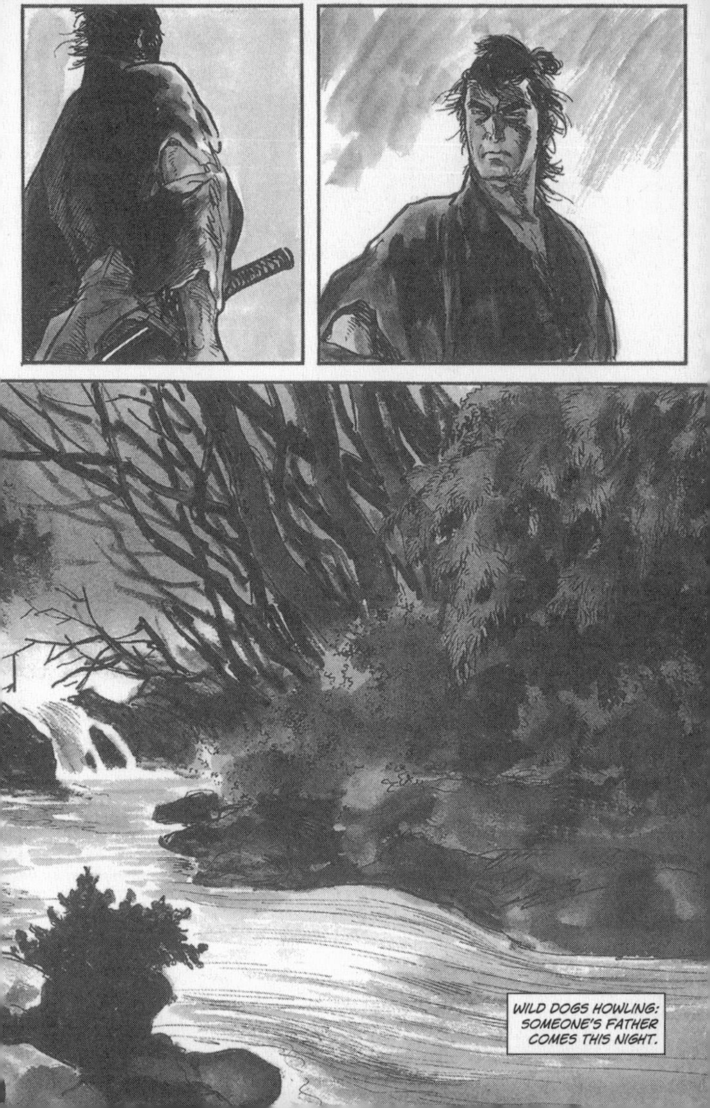
WILD DOGS HOWLING: SOMEONE'S FATHER COMES THIS NIGHT.

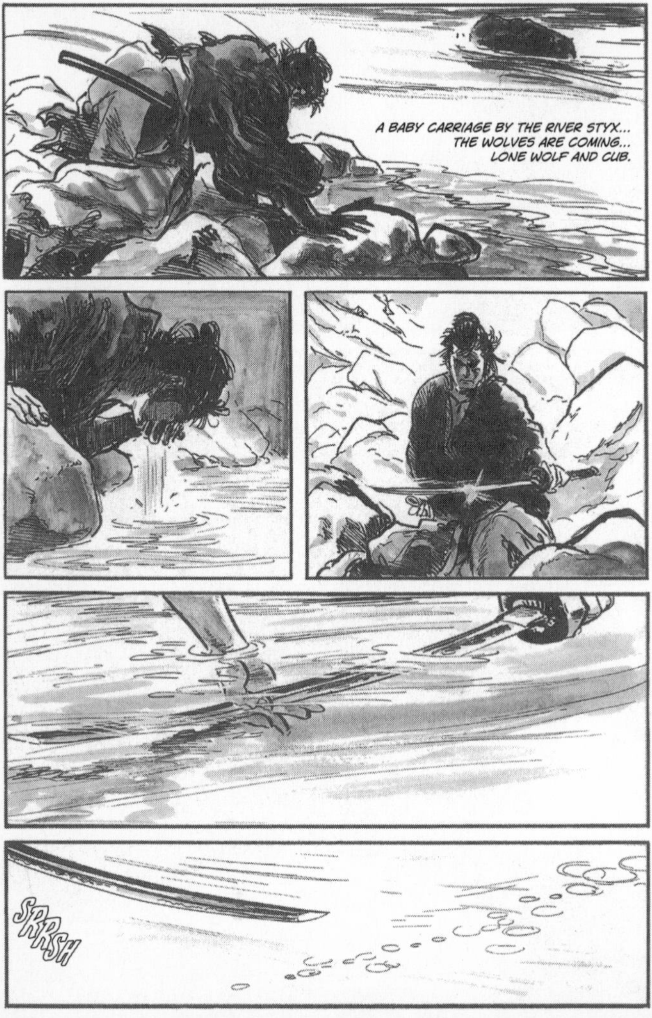
A BABY CARRIAGE BY THE RIVER STYX...
THE WOLVES ARE COMING...
LONE WOLF AND CUB.
SRRSH

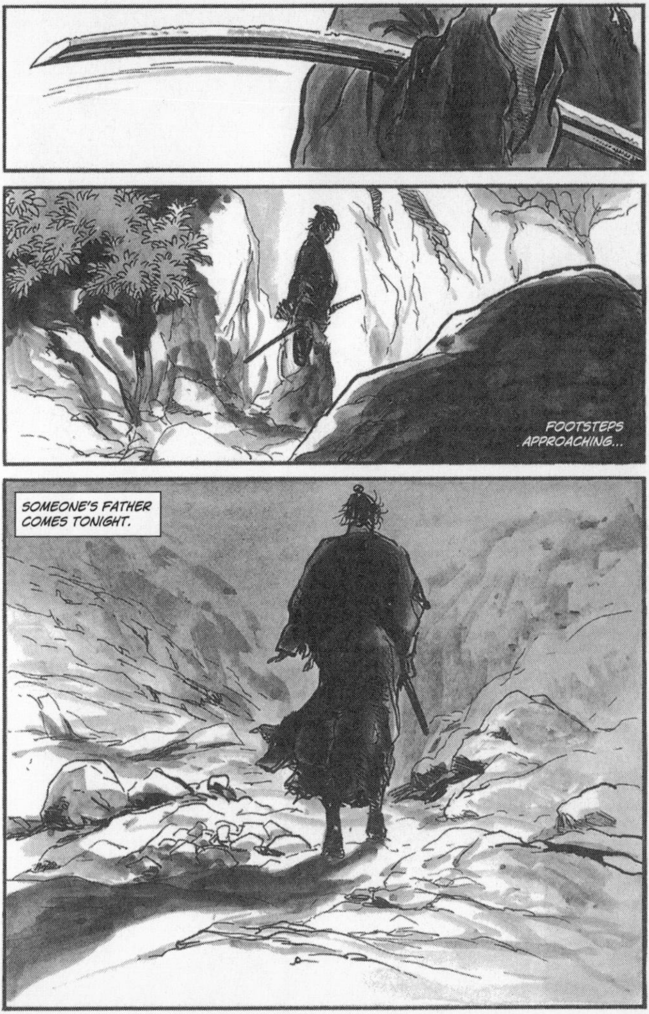
FOOTSTEPS
APPROACHING...
SOMEONE'S FATHER
COMES TONIGHT.

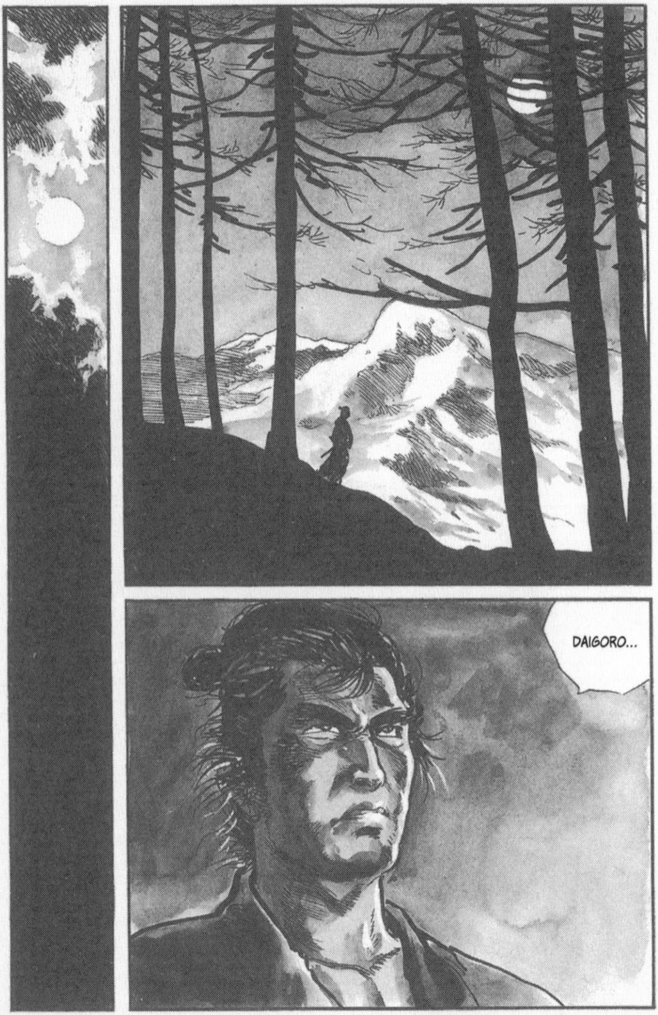
DAIGORO...

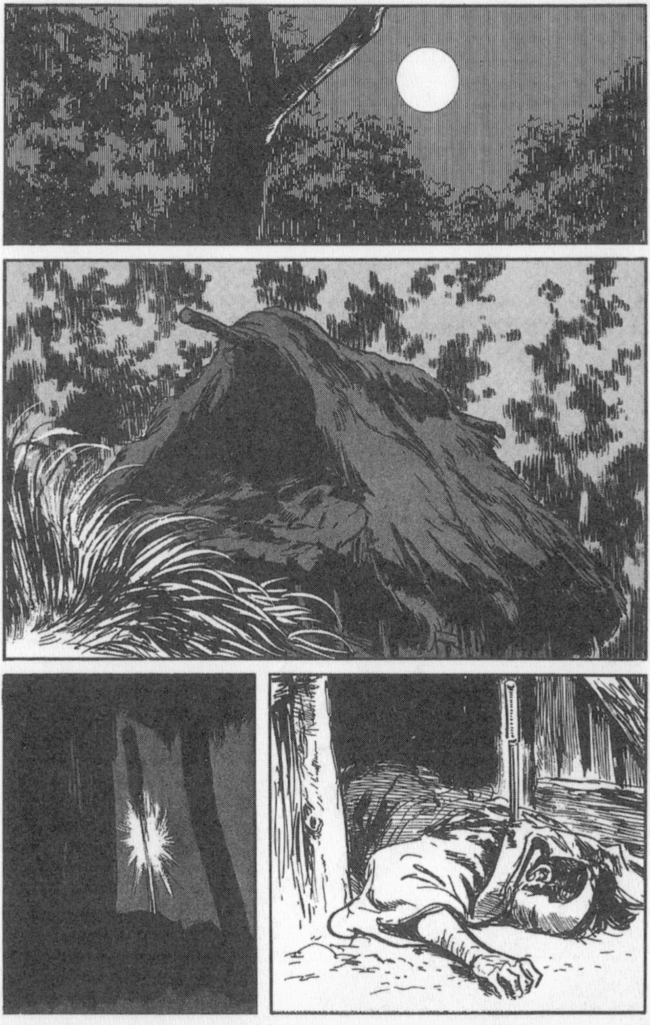

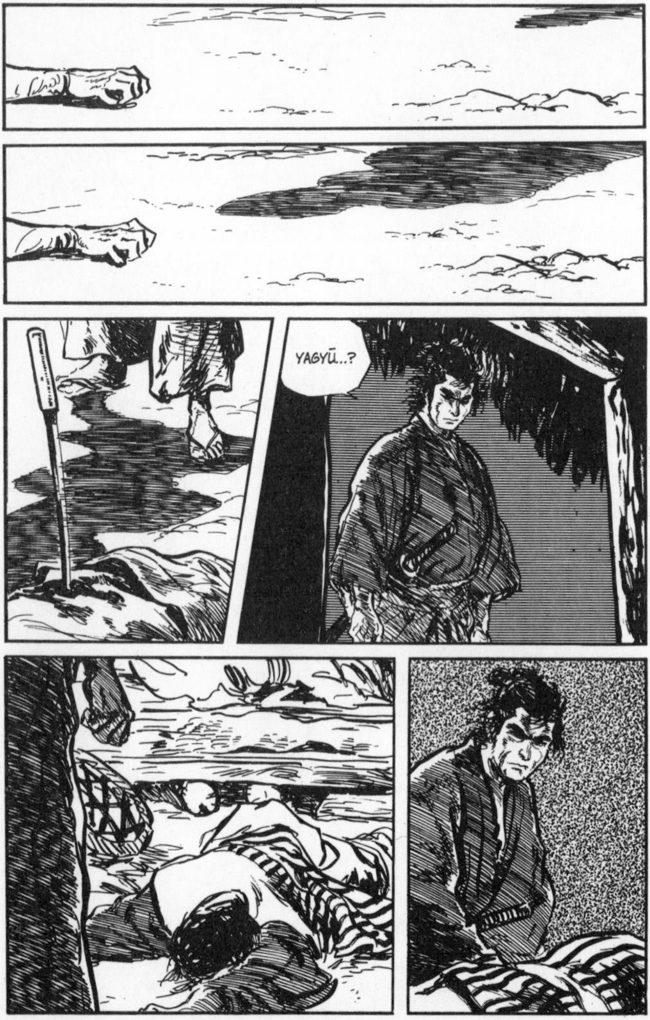
YAGYŪ...?

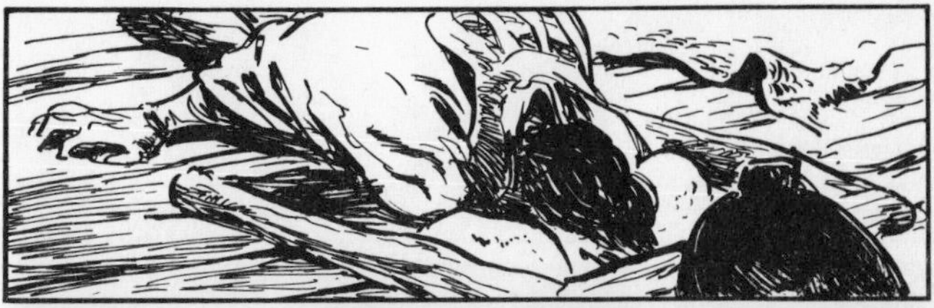

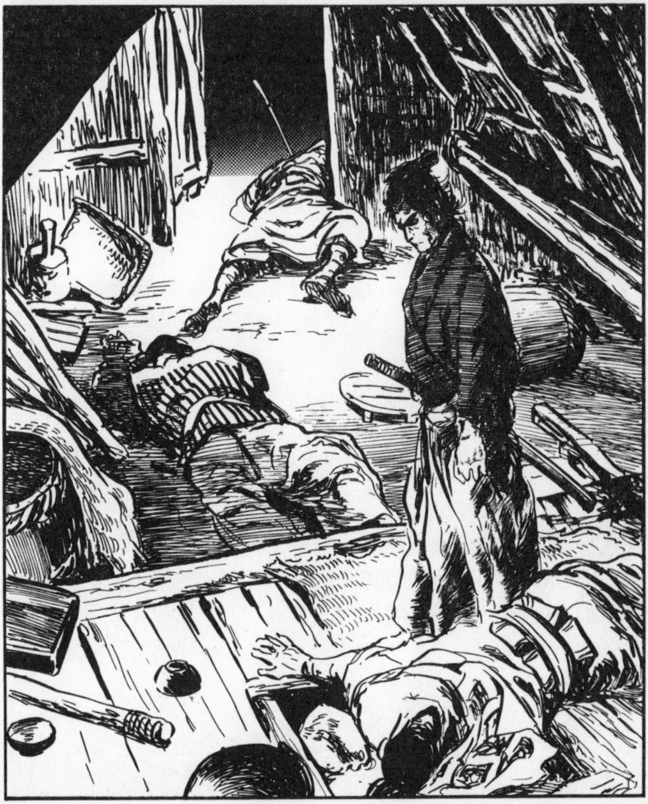

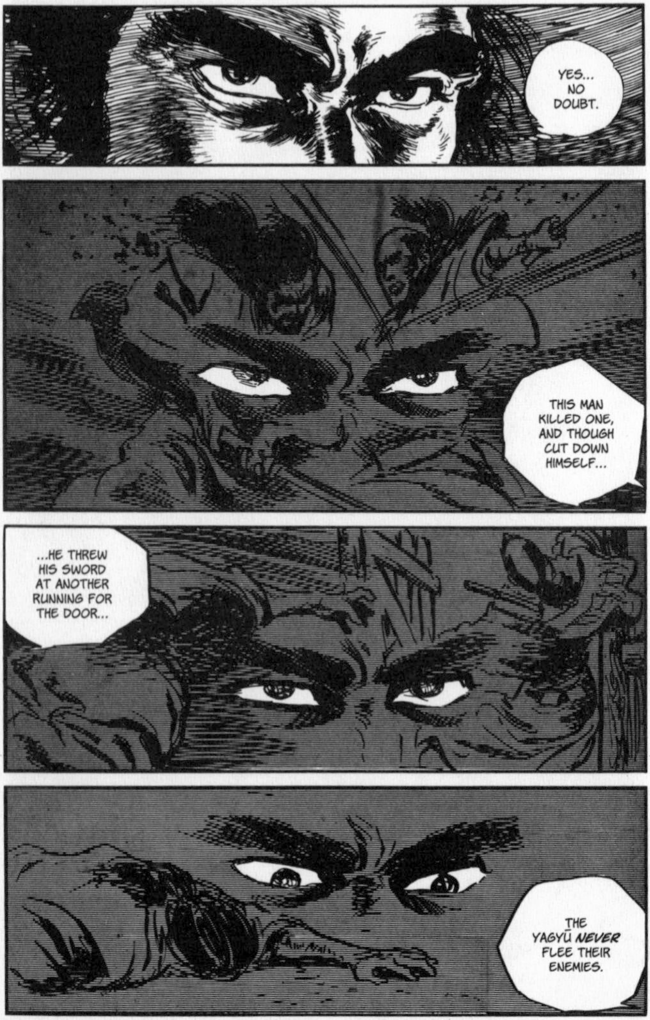
YES... NO DOUBT.
THIS MAN KILLED ONE, AND THOUGH CUT DOWN HIMSELF...
...HE THREW HIS SWORD AT ANOTHER RUNNING FOR THE DOOR...
THE YAGYŪ *NEVER* FLEE THEIR ENEMIES.

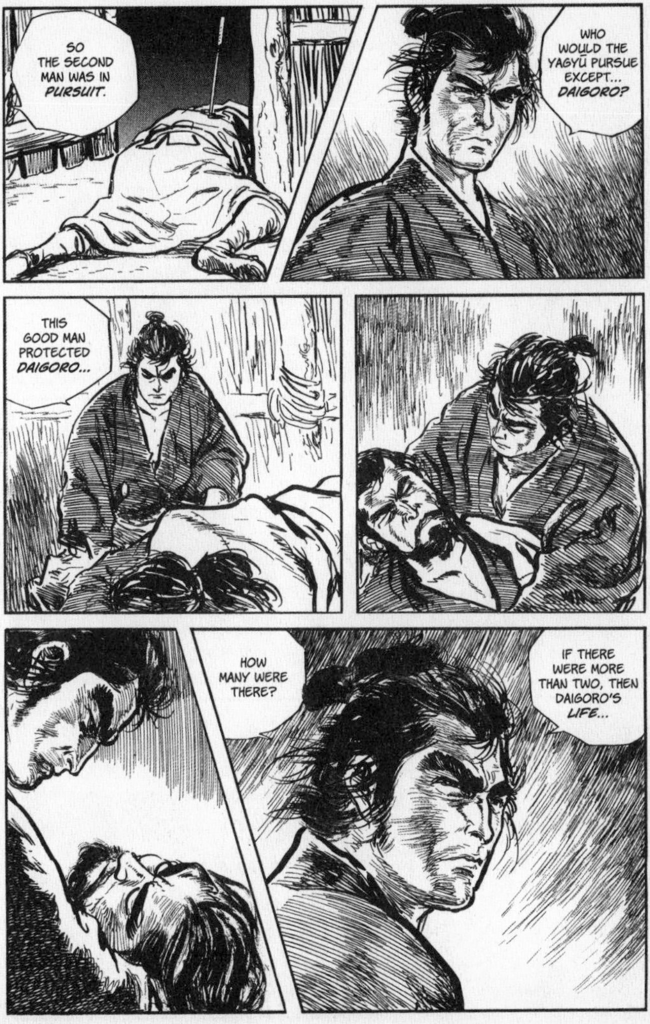
SO THE SECOND MAN WAS IN PURSUIT.
WHO WOULD THE YAGYŪ PURSUE EXCEPT... DAIGORO?
THIS GOOD MAN PROTECTED DAIGORO...
HOW MANY WERE THERE?
IF THERE WERE MORE THAN TWO, THEN DAIGORO'S LIFE...

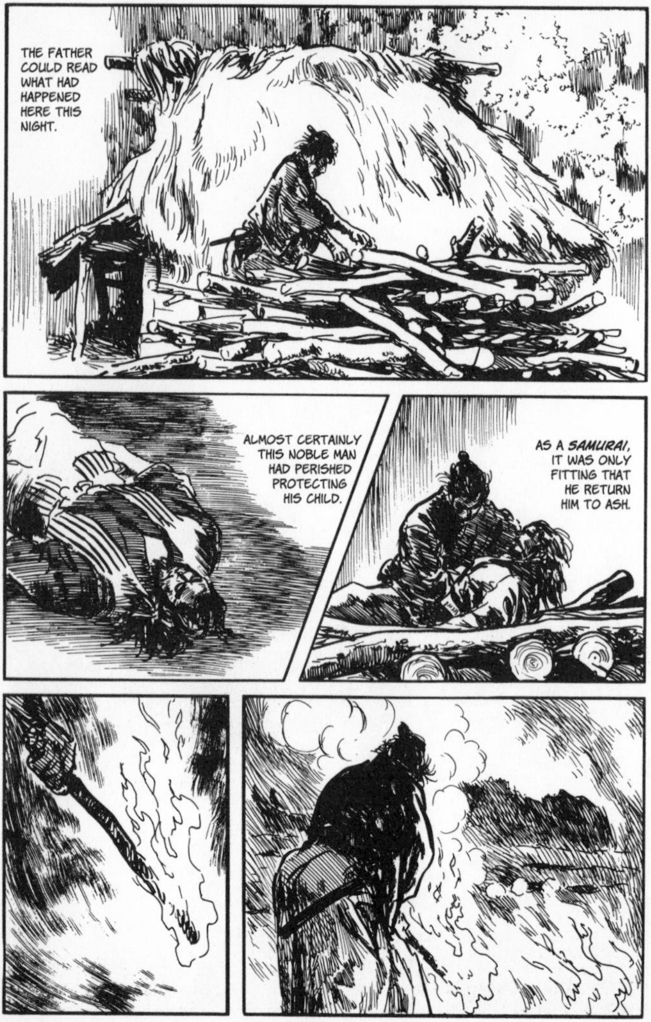
THE FATHER COULD READ WHAT HAD HAPPENED HERE THIS NIGHT.
ALMOST CERTAINLY THIS NOBLE MAN HAD PERISHED PROTECTING HIS CHILD.
AS A *SAMURAI*, IT WAS ONLY FITTING THAT HE RETURN HIM TO ASH.

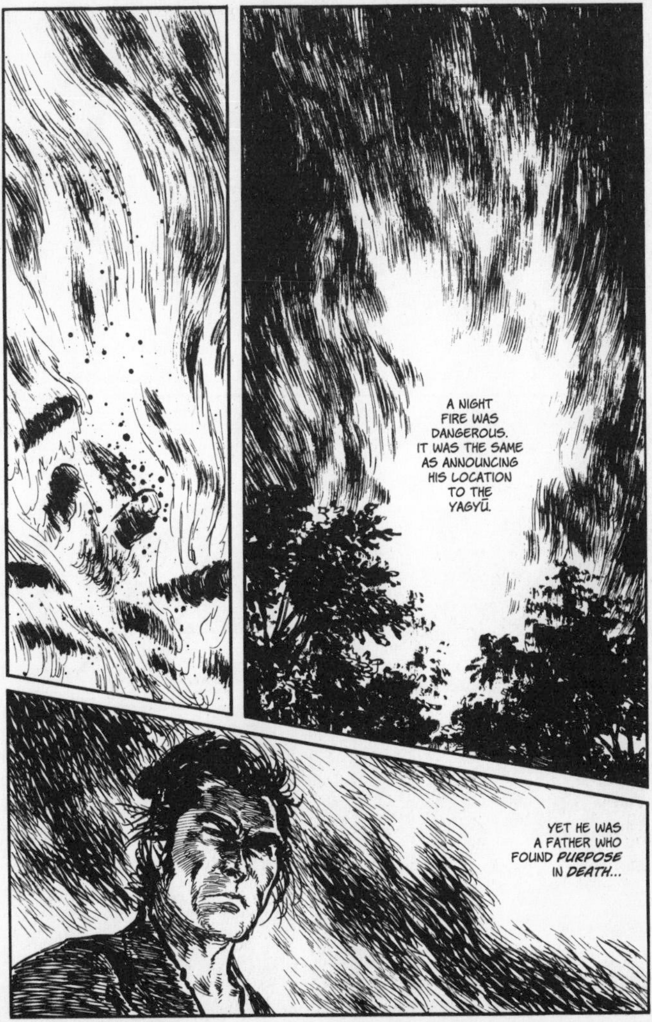
A NIGHT FIRE WAS DANGEROUS. IT WAS THE SAME AS ANNOUNCING HIS LOCATION TO THE YAGYŪ.
YET HE WAS A FATHER WHO FOUND *PURPOSE* IN *DEATH*...

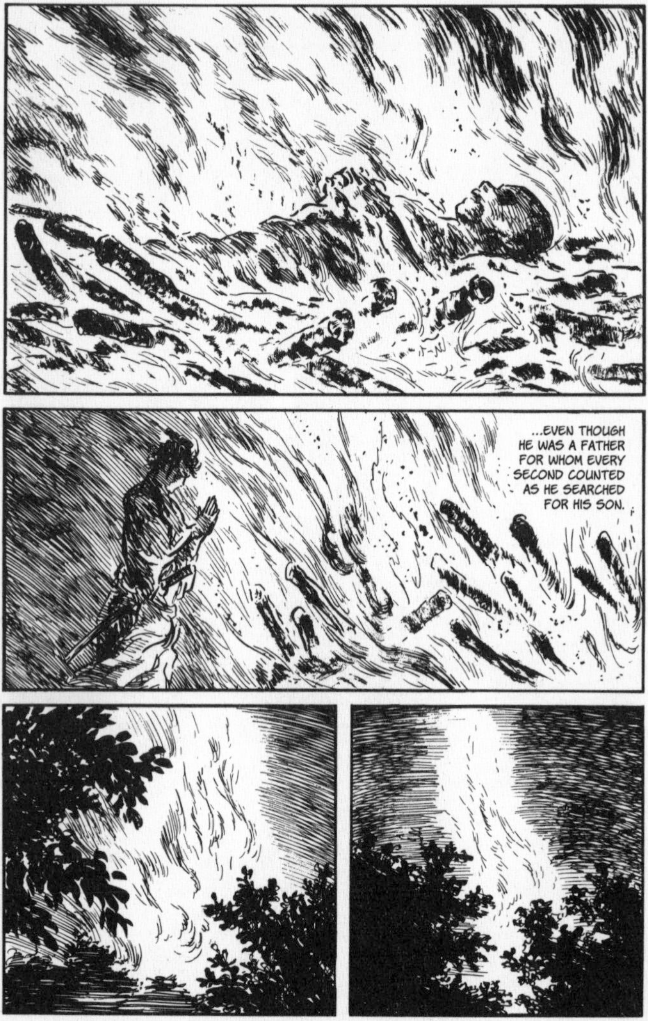
...EVEN THOUGH HE WAS A FATHER FOR WHOM EVERY SECOND COUNTED AS HE SEARCHED FOR HIS SON.

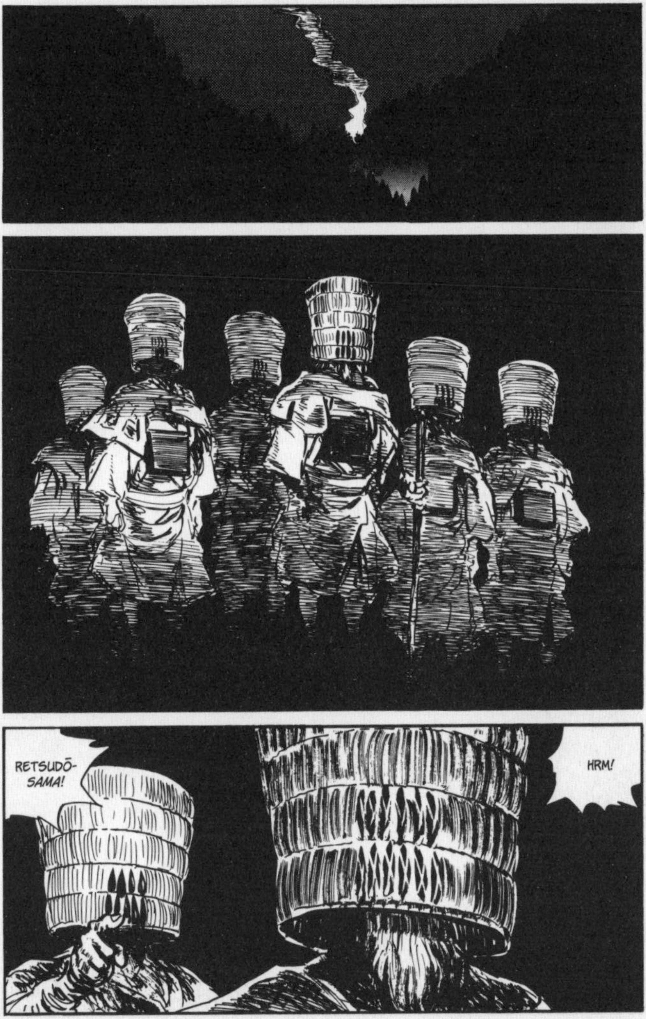
RETSUDŌ-SAMA!
HRM!

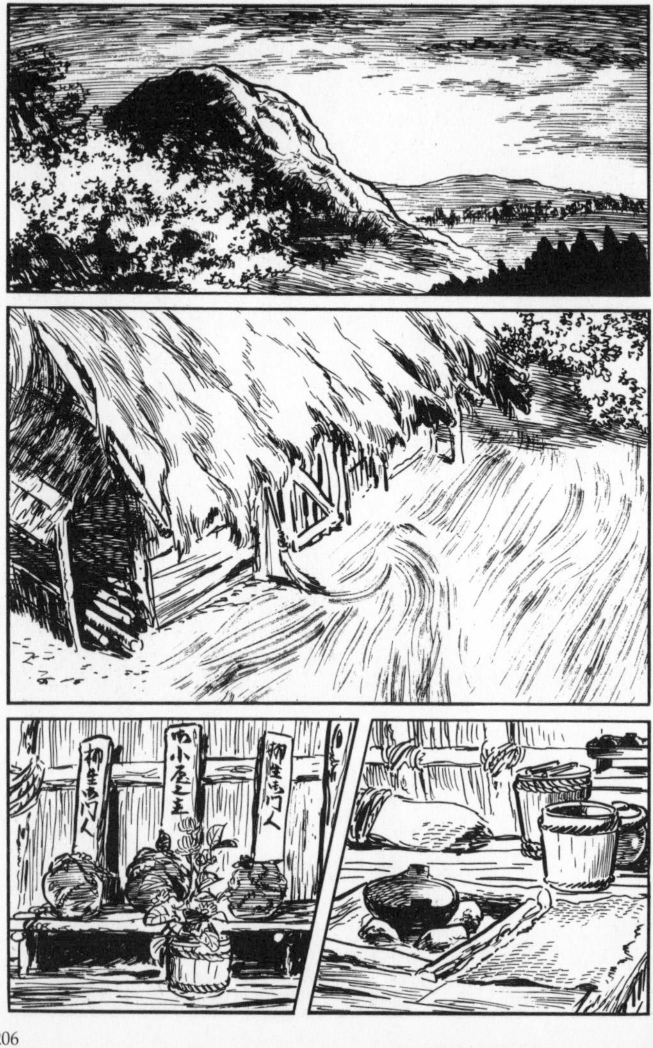
柳生門人
小屋之主
柳生門人

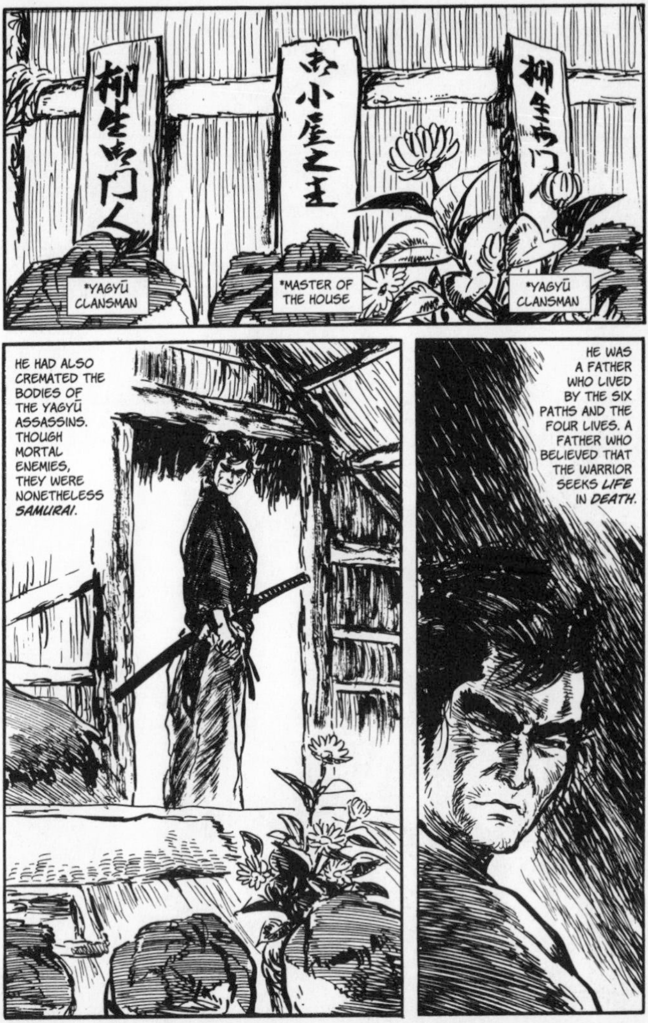
*YAGYŪ CLANSMAN
*MASTER OF THE HOUSE
*YAGYŪ CLANSMAN
HE HAD ALSO CREMATED THE BODIES OF THE YAGYŪ ASSASSINS. THOUGH MORTAL ENEMIES, THEY WERE NONETHELESS *SAMURAI*.
HE WAS A FATHER WHO LIVED BY THE SIX PATHS AND THE FOUR LIVES. A FATHER WHO BELIEVED THAT THE WARRIOR SEEKS *LIFE* IN *DEATH*.

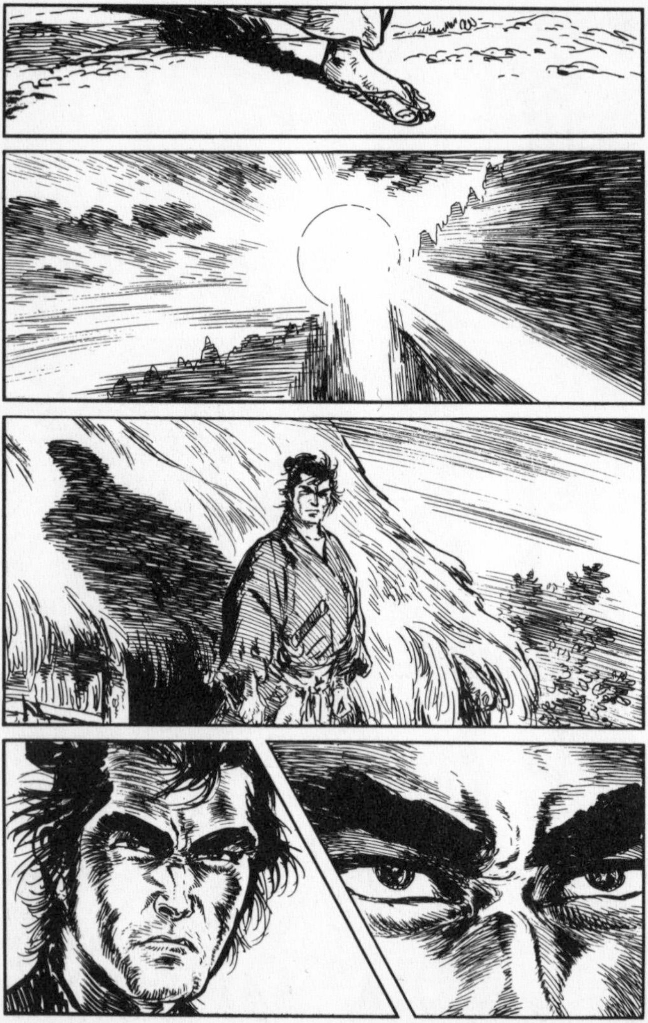

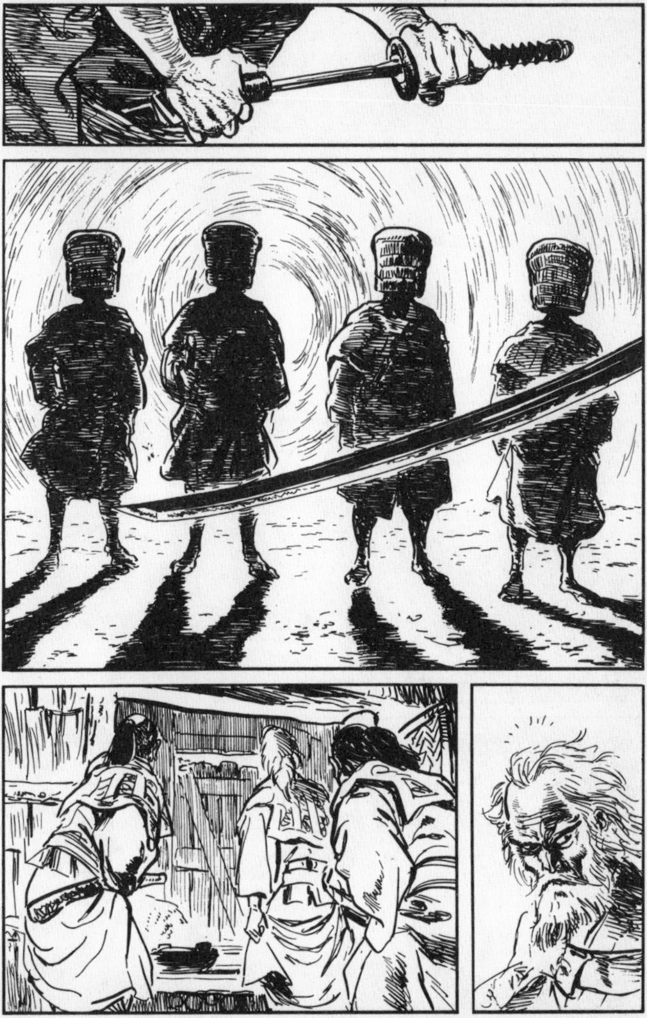

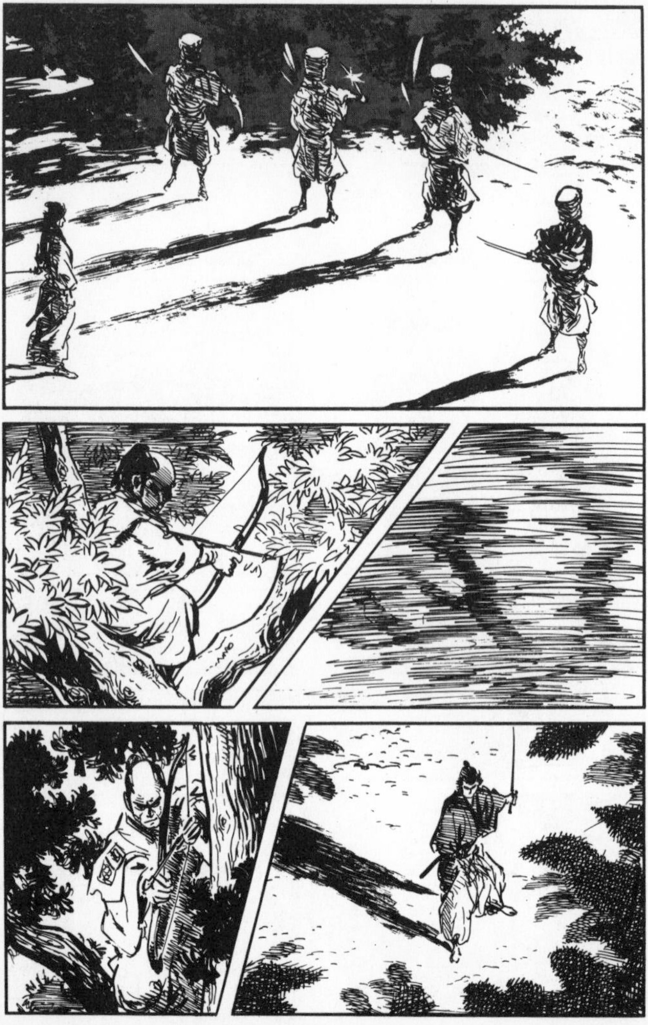

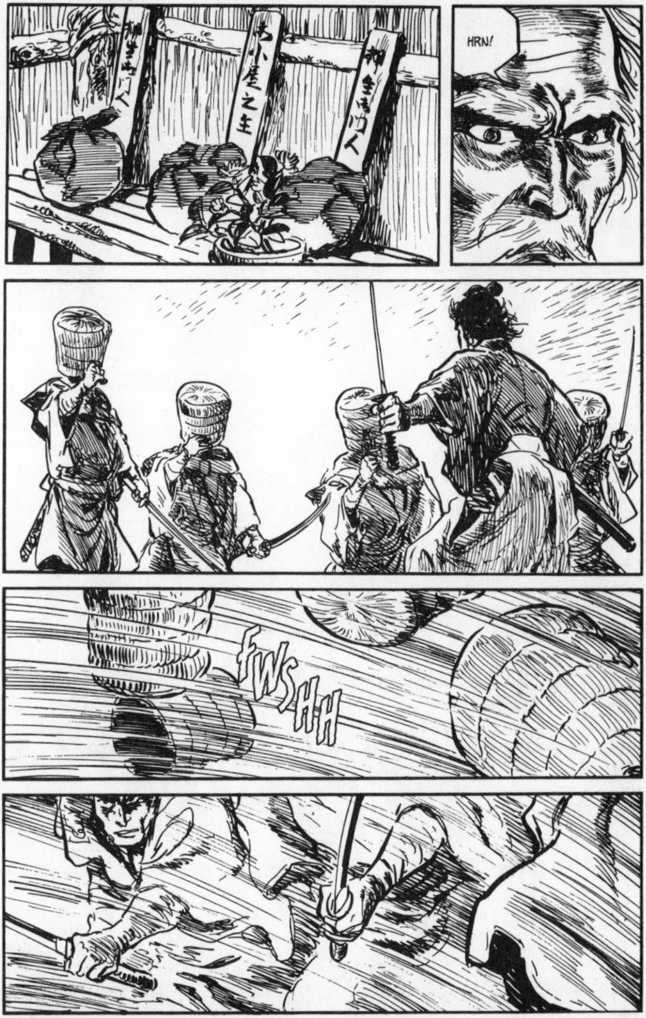
HRN!
FWSHH

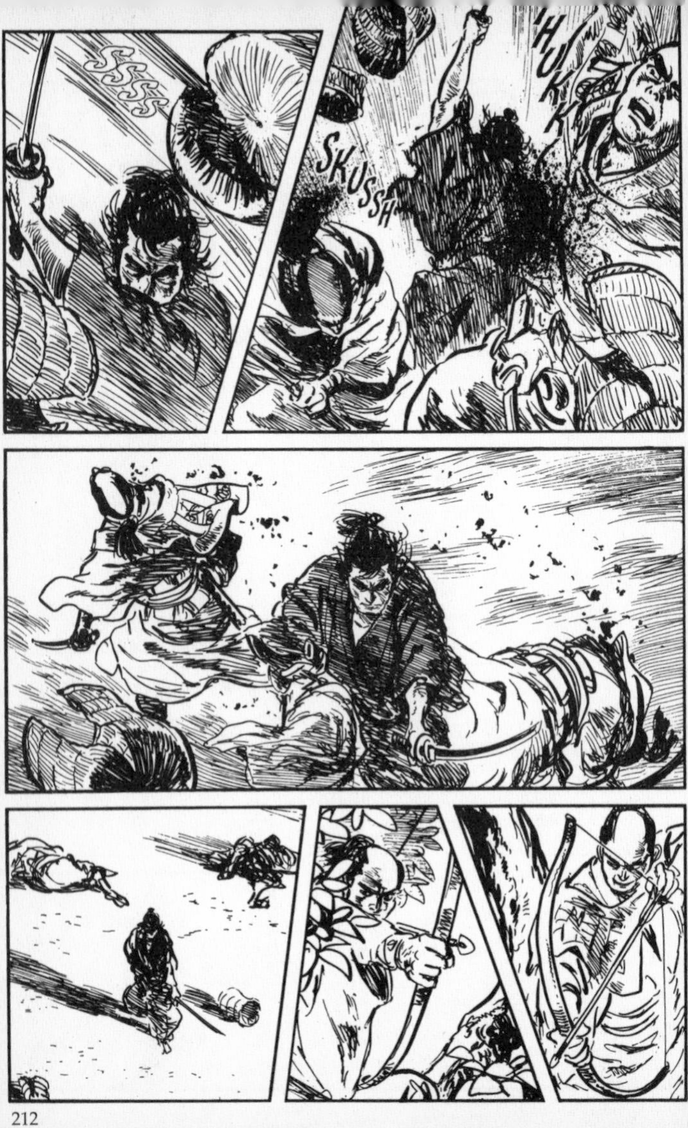
SSSS
SKUSSH
HUK

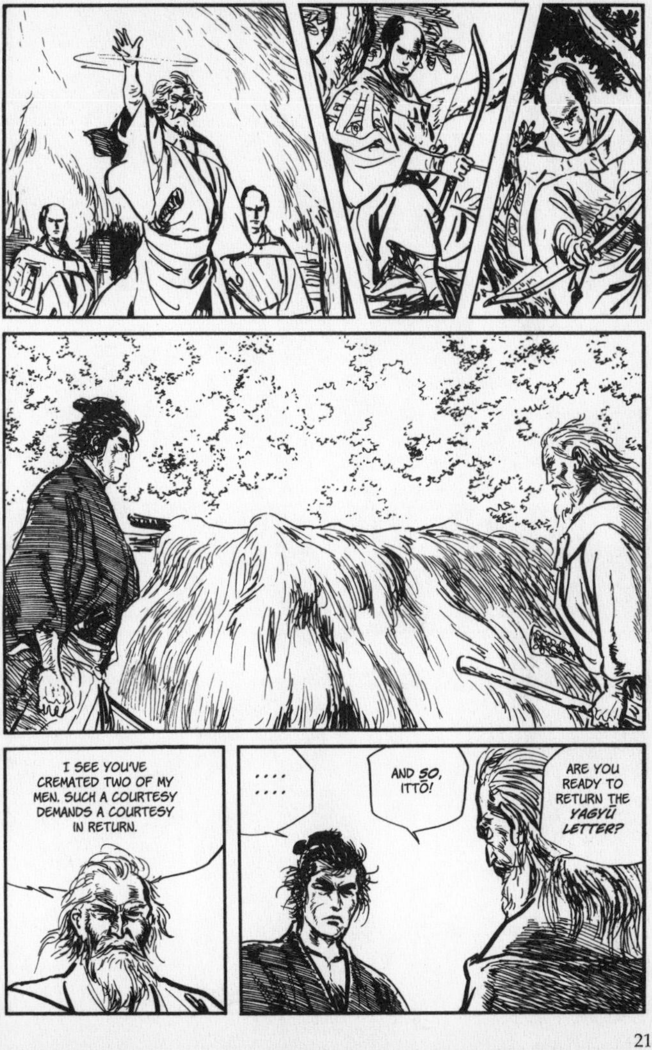
I SEE YOU'VE CREMATED TWO OF MY MEN. SUCH A COURTESY DEMANDS A COURTESY IN RETURN.
....
....
AND *SO*, ITTŌ!
ARE YOU READY TO RETURN THE *YAGYŪ LETTER?*

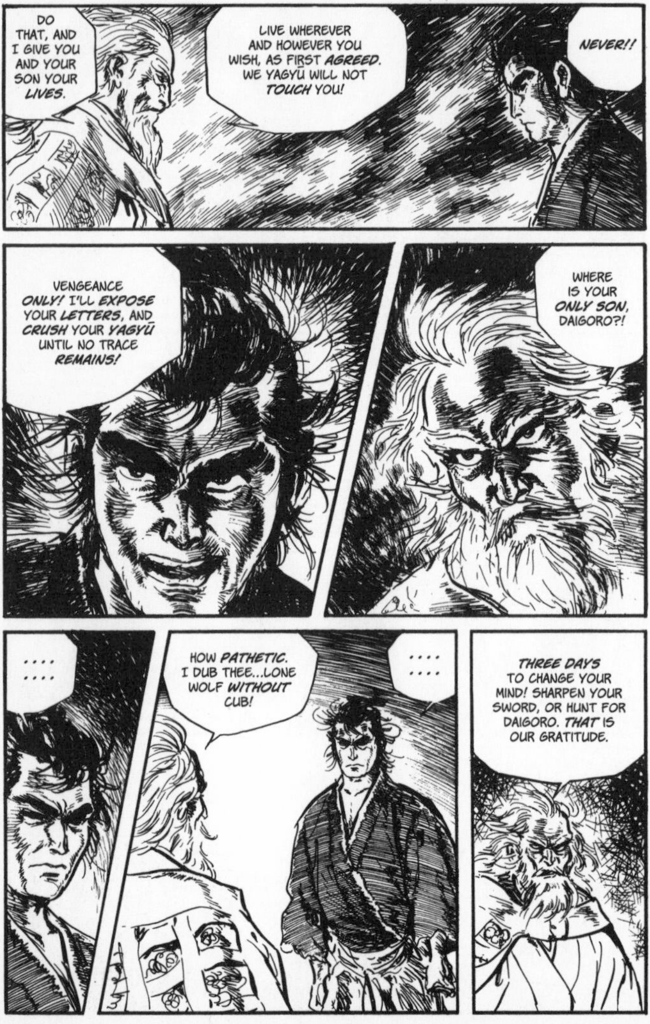
DO THAT, AND I GIVE YOU AND YOUR SON YOUR *LIVES*.
LIVE WHEREVER AND HOWEVER YOU WISH, AS FIRST *AGREED*. WE YAGYŪ WILL NOT *TOUCH* YOU!
NEVER!!
VENGEANCE *ONLY!* I'LL *EXPOSE* YOUR *LETTERS*, AND *CRUSH* YOUR *YAGYŪ* UNTIL NO TRACE *REMAINS!*
WHERE IS YOUR *ONLY SON*, DAIGORO?!
....
HOW *PATHETIC*. I DUB THEE...LONE WOLF *WITHOUT* CUB!
....
THREE DAYS TO CHANGE YOUR MIND! SHARPEN YOUR SWORD, OR HUNT FOR DAIGORO. *THAT* IS OUR GRATITUDE.

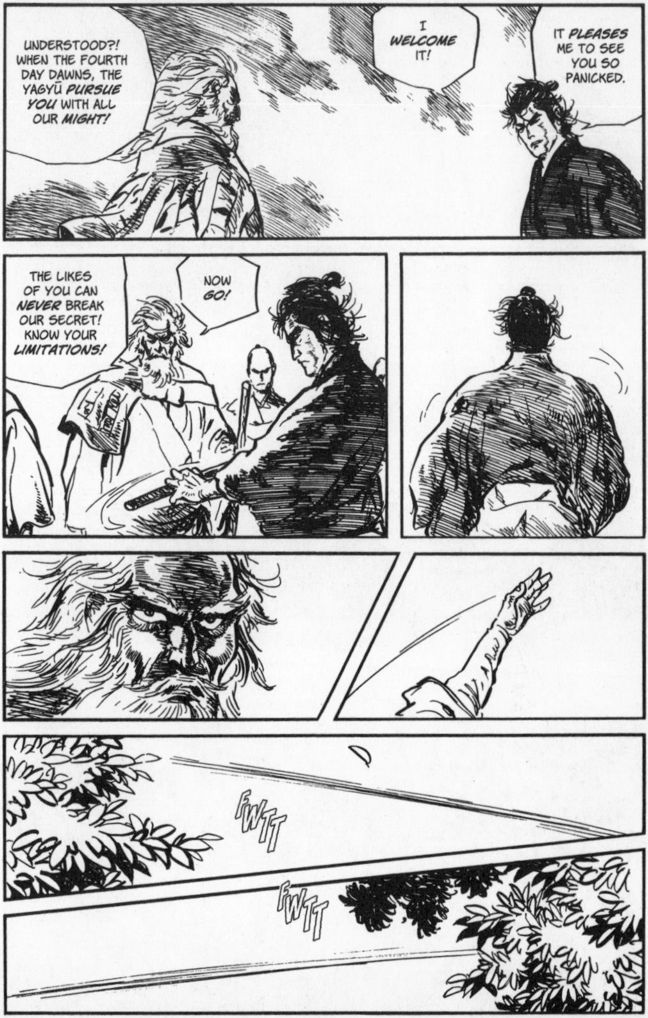
UNDERSTOOD?! WHEN THE FOURTH DAY DAWNS, THE YAGYŪ *PURSUE YOU* WITH ALL OUR *MIGHT!*
I *WELCOME* IT!
IT *PLEASES* ME TO SEE YOU SO PANICKED.
THE LIKES OF YOU CAN *NEVER* BREAK OUR SECRET! KNOW YOUR *LIMITATIONS!*
NOW *GO!*
FWTT
FWTT

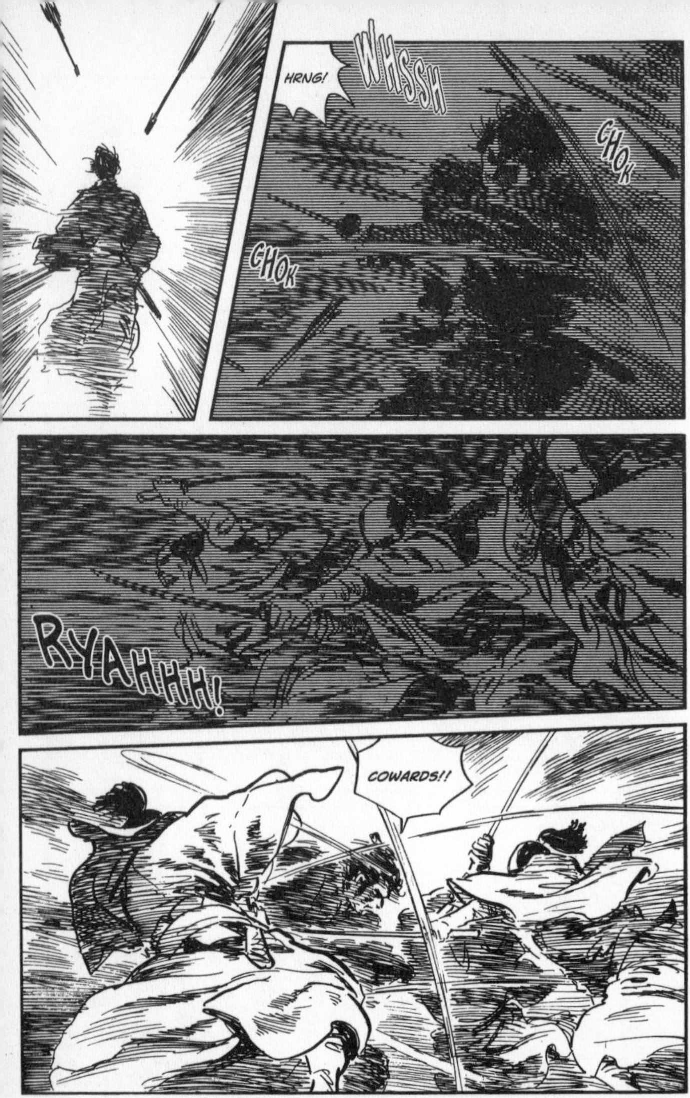
HRNG!
WHSSSH
CHOK
CHOK
RYAHHHH!
COWARDS!!

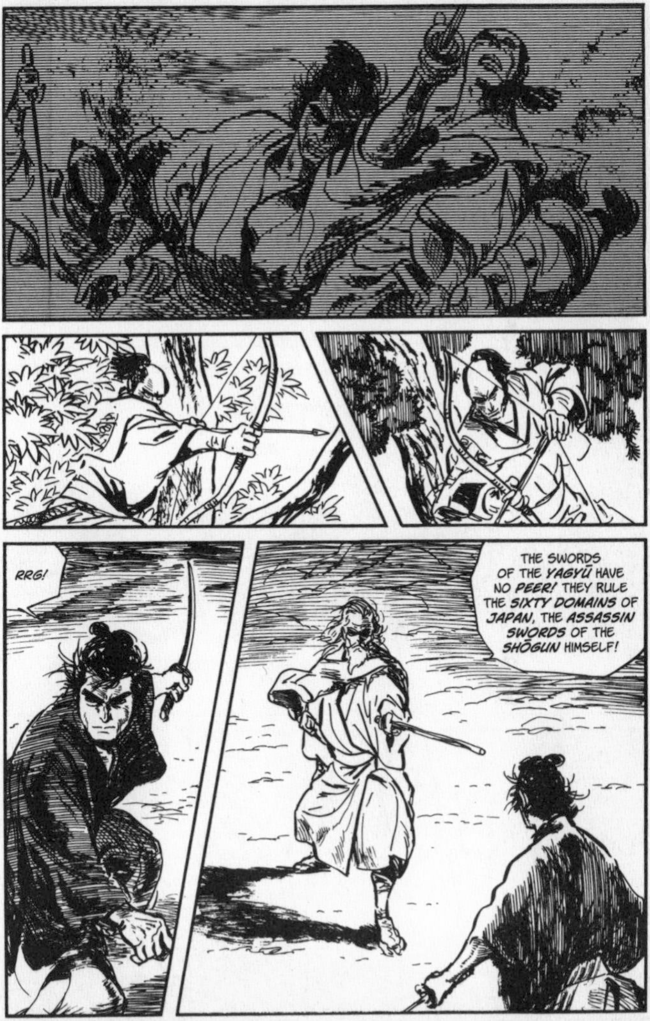
RRG!
THE SWORDS OF THE *YAGYŪ* HAVE NO *PEER!* THEY RULE THE *SIXTY DOMAINS* OF *JAPAN*, THE *ASSASSIN SWORDS* OF THE *SHŌGUN* HIMSELF!

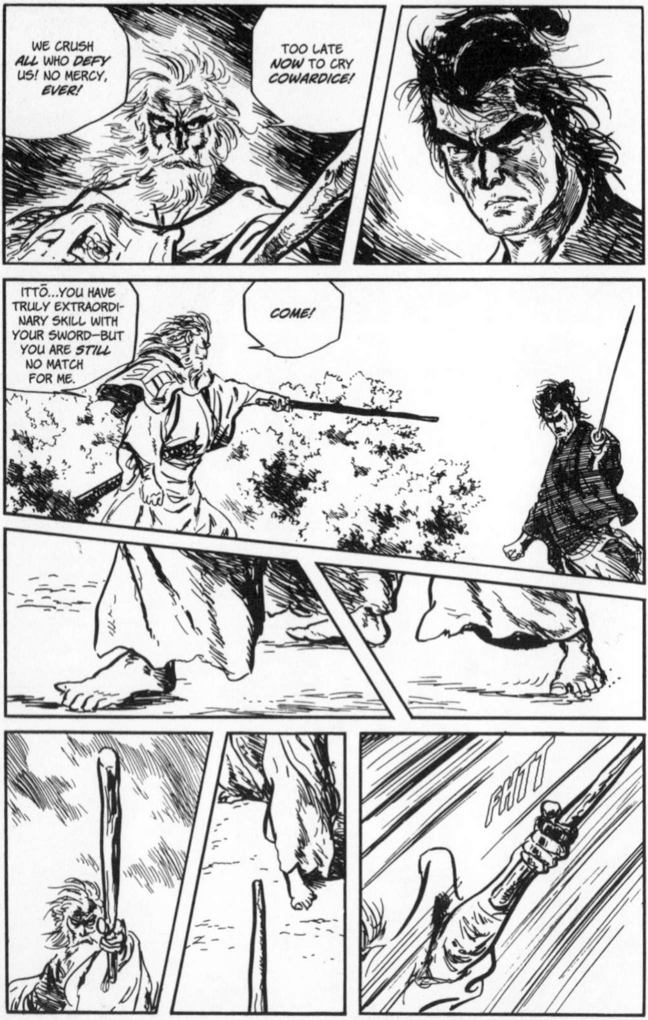
WE CRUSH ALL WHO DEFY US! NO MERCY, EVER!
TOO LATE NOW TO CRY COWARDICE!
ITTŌ...YOU HAVE TRULY EXTRAORDINARY SKILL WITH YOUR SWORD—BUT YOU ARE STILL NO MATCH FOR ME.
COME!
FHTT

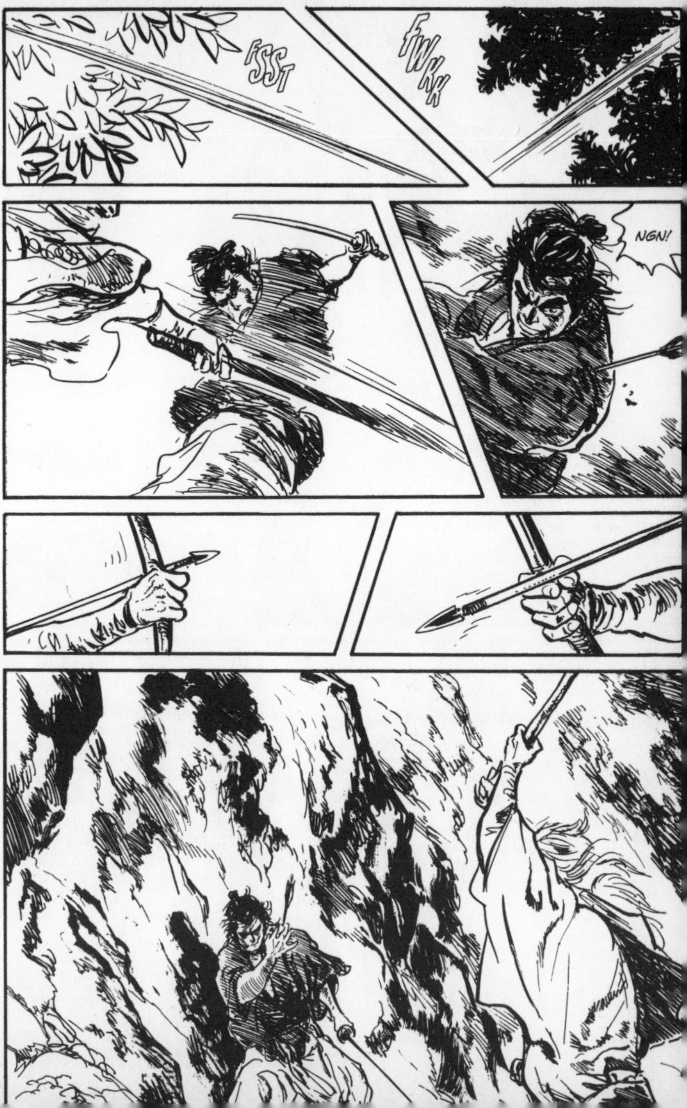
FSST
FWKK
NGN!

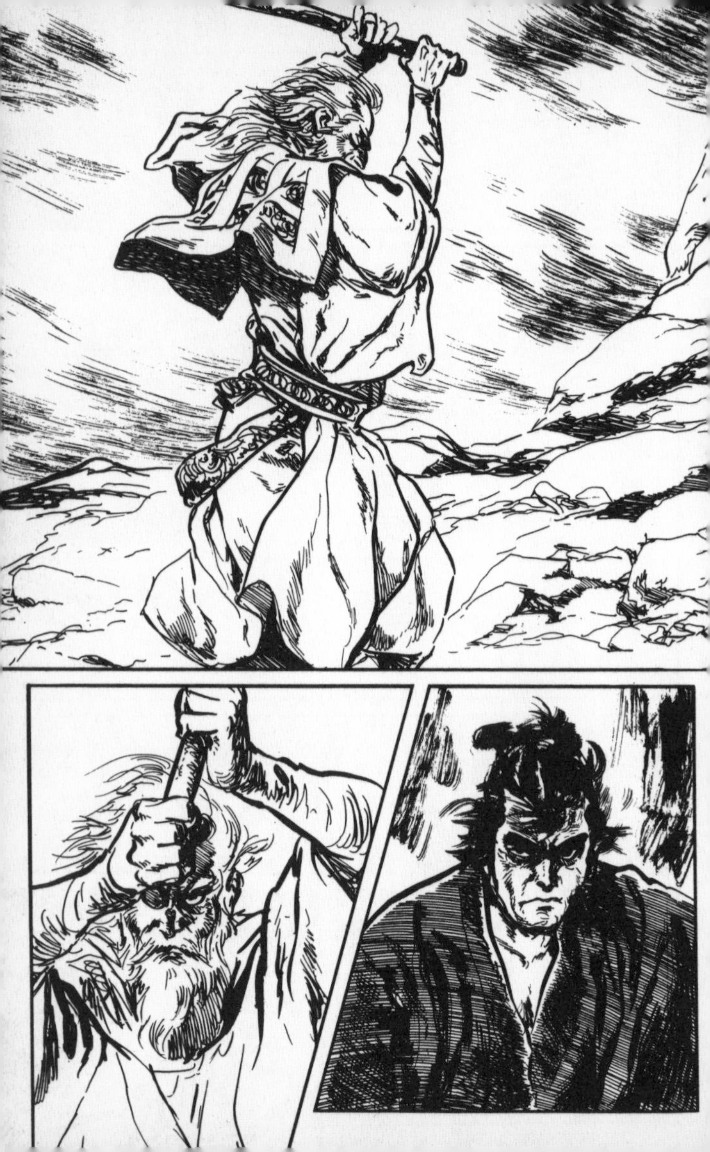

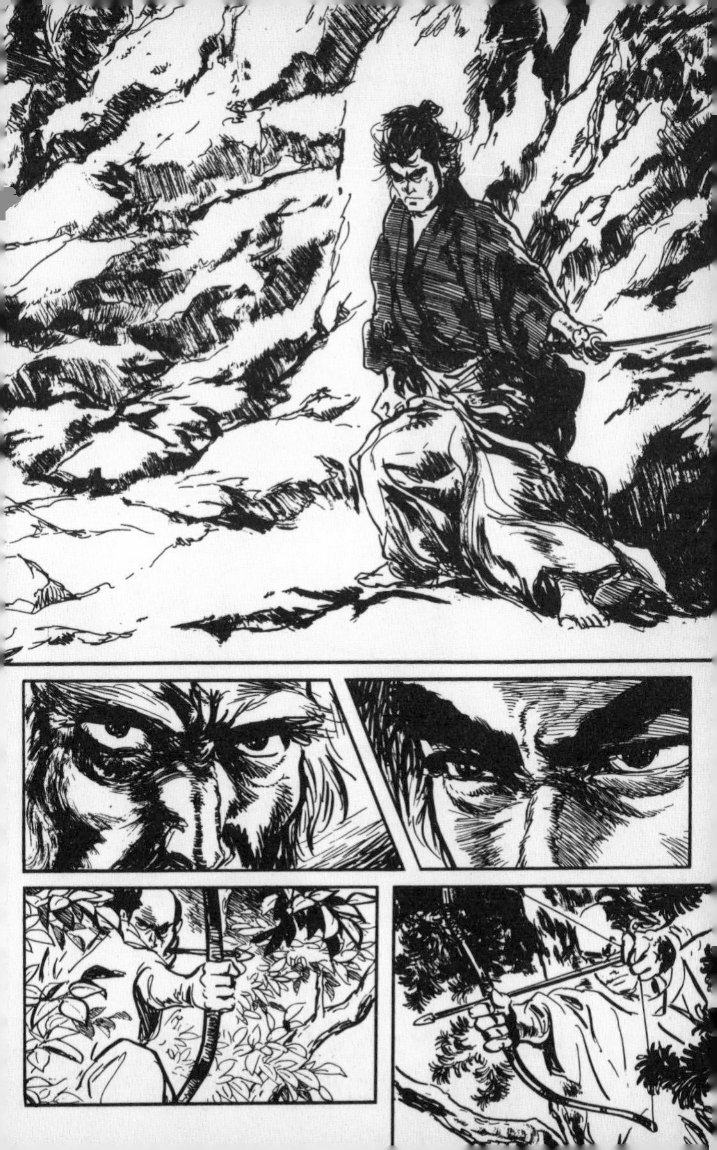

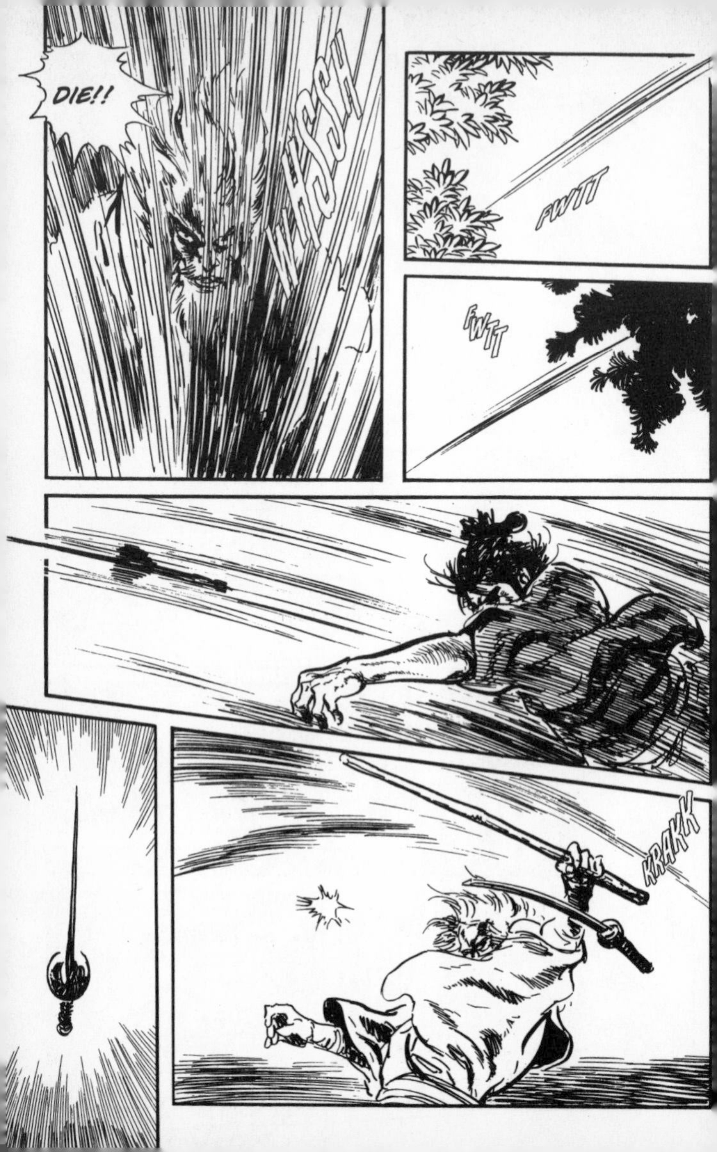

DIE!!
WHSSH
FWTT
FWTT
KRAKK

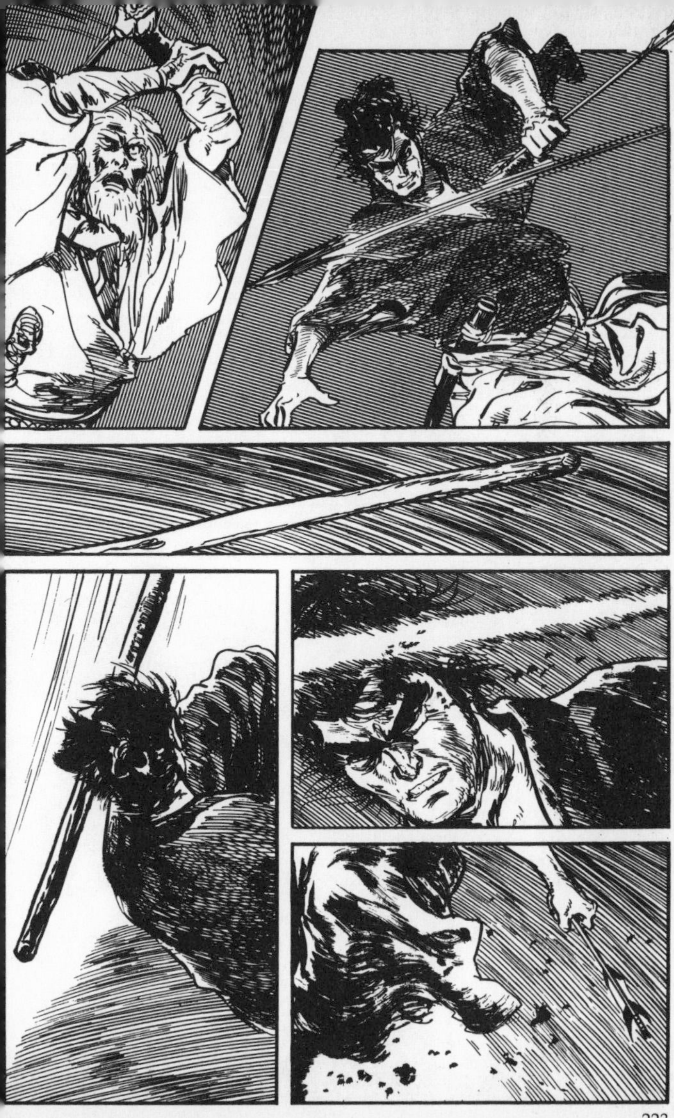

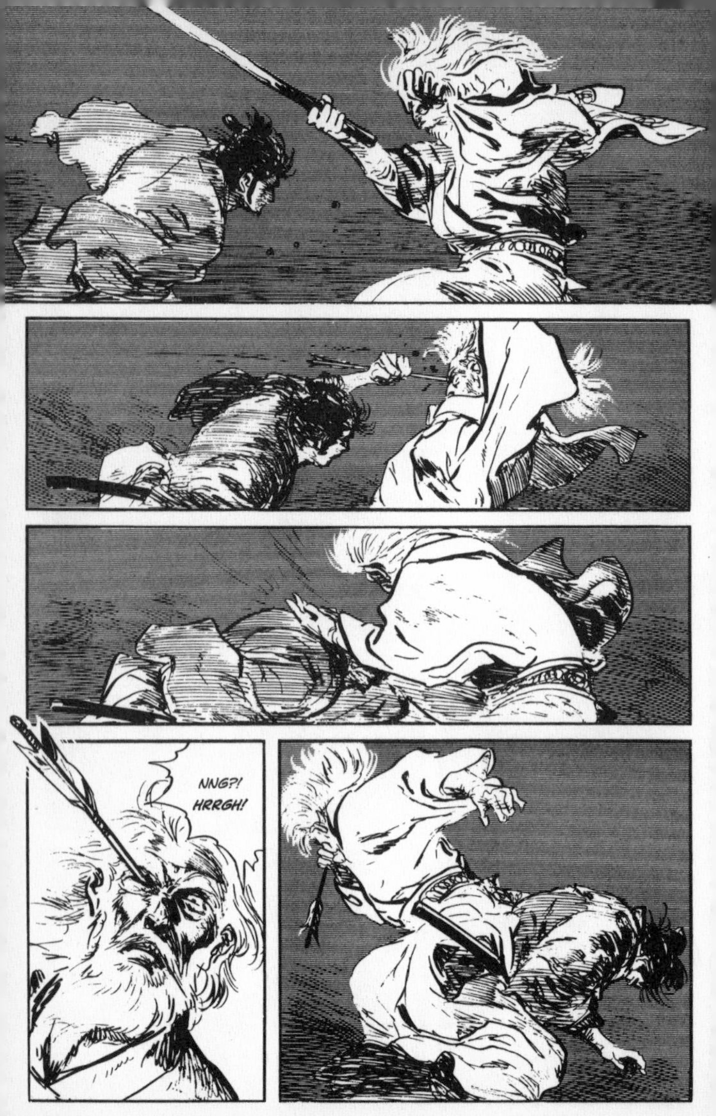
NNG?!
HRRGH!

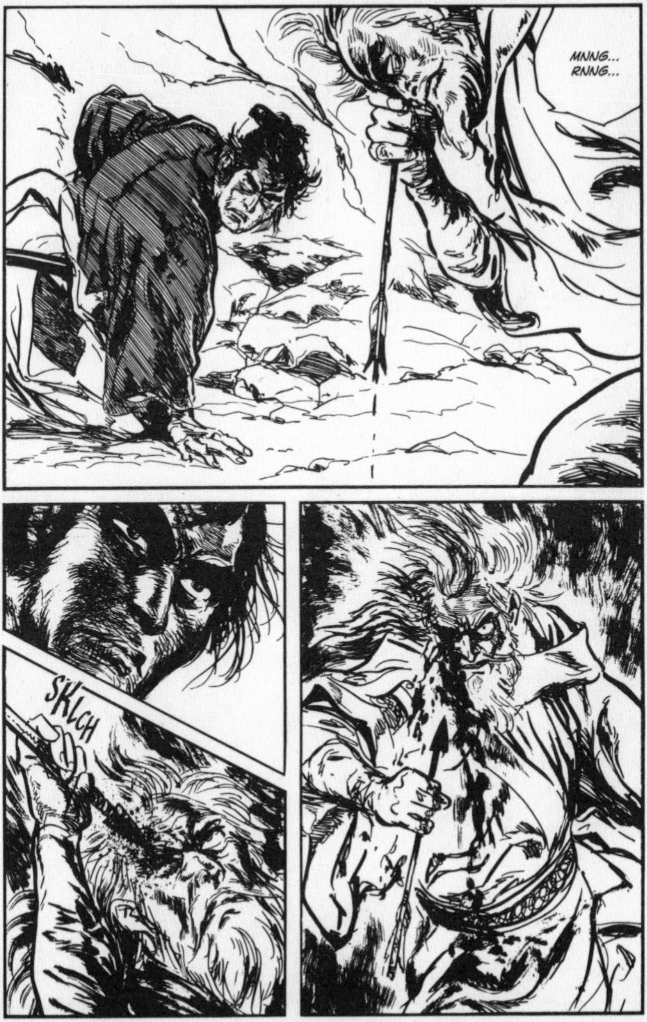
MNNG...
RNNG...
SKLCH

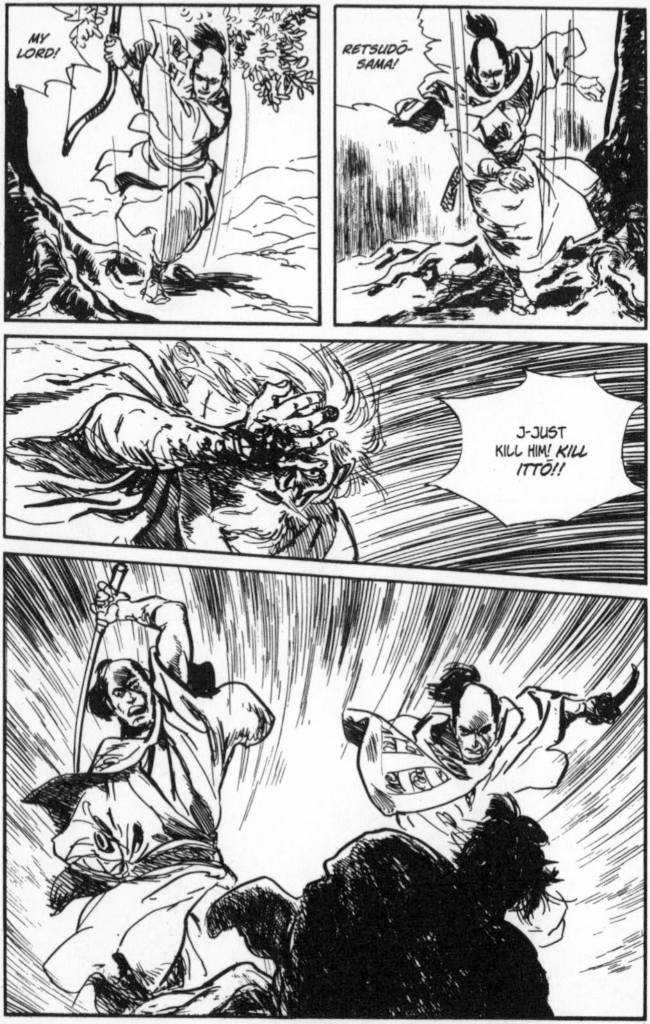
MY LORD!
RETSUDŌ-SAMA!
J-JUST KILL HIM! *KILL ITTŌ!!*

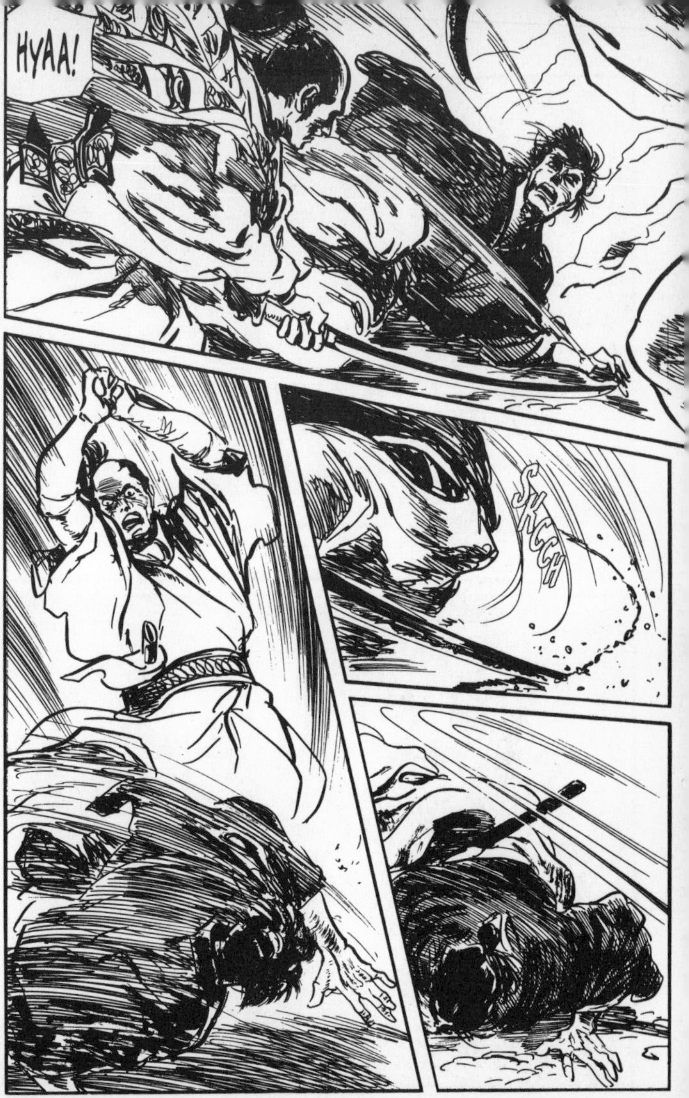
HYAA!
SKCCH

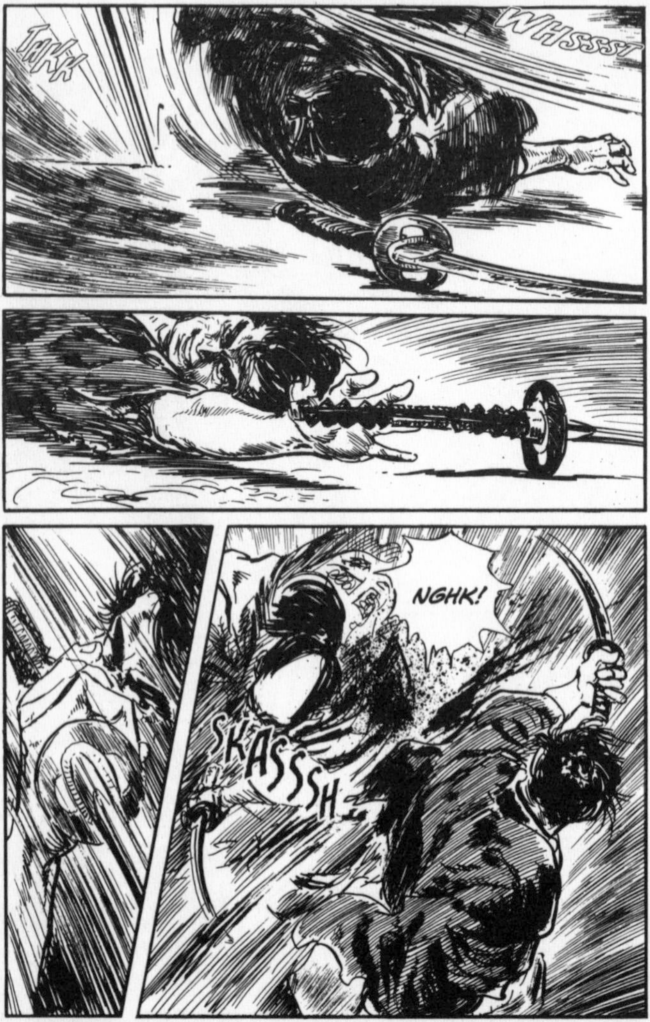
THKK
WHSSSST
NGHK!
SKASSSH

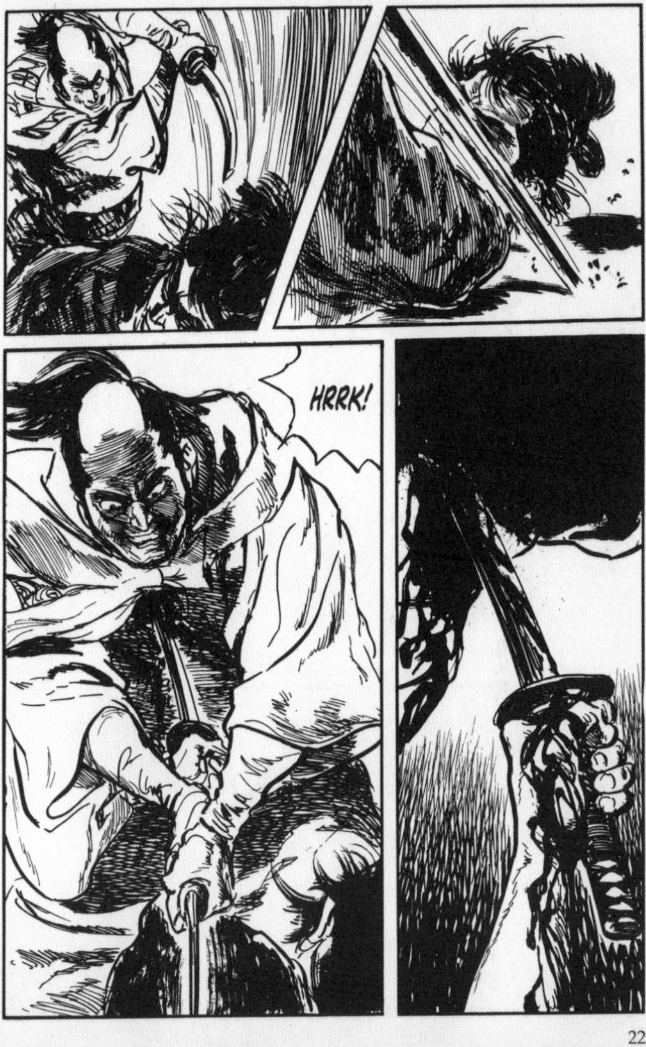
HRRK!

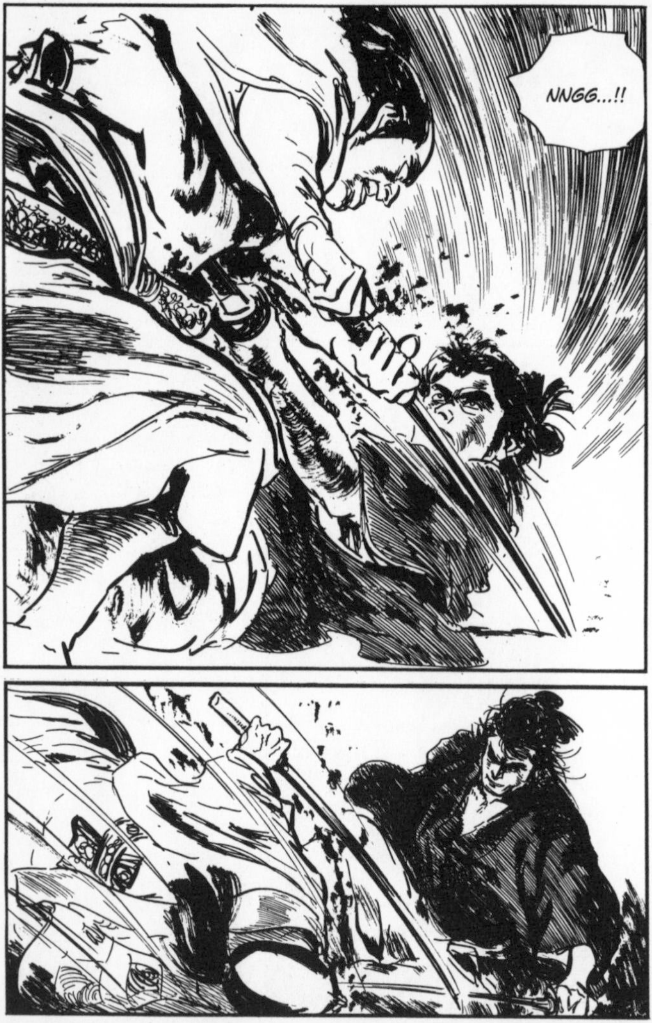
NNGG...!!

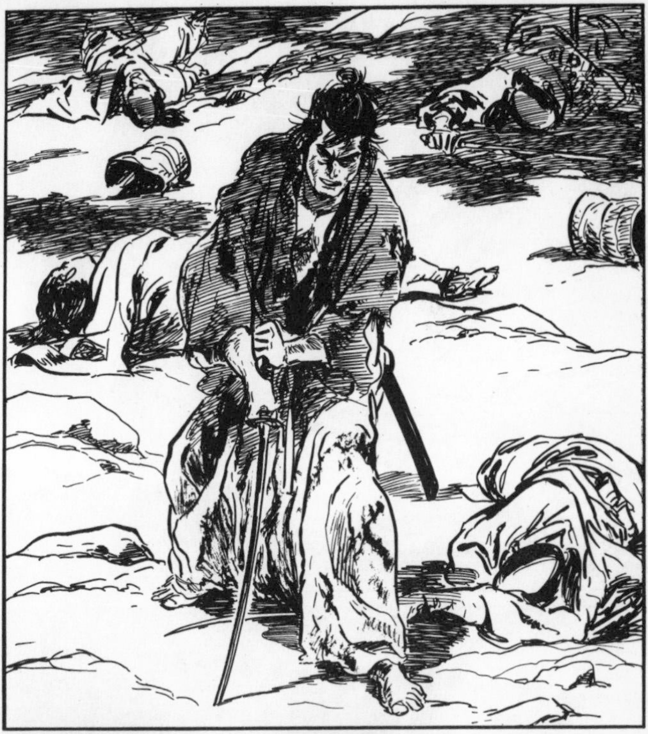

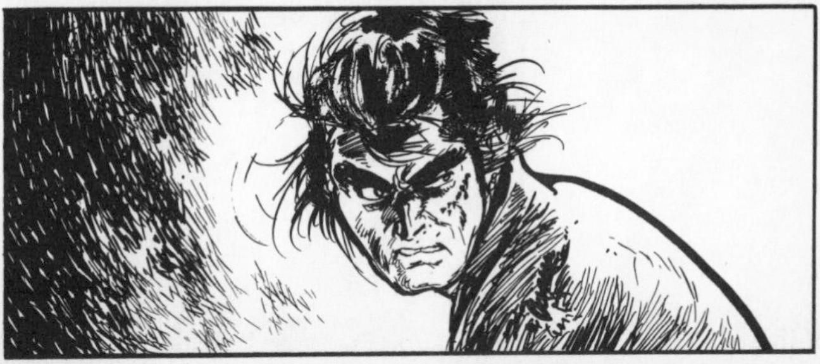

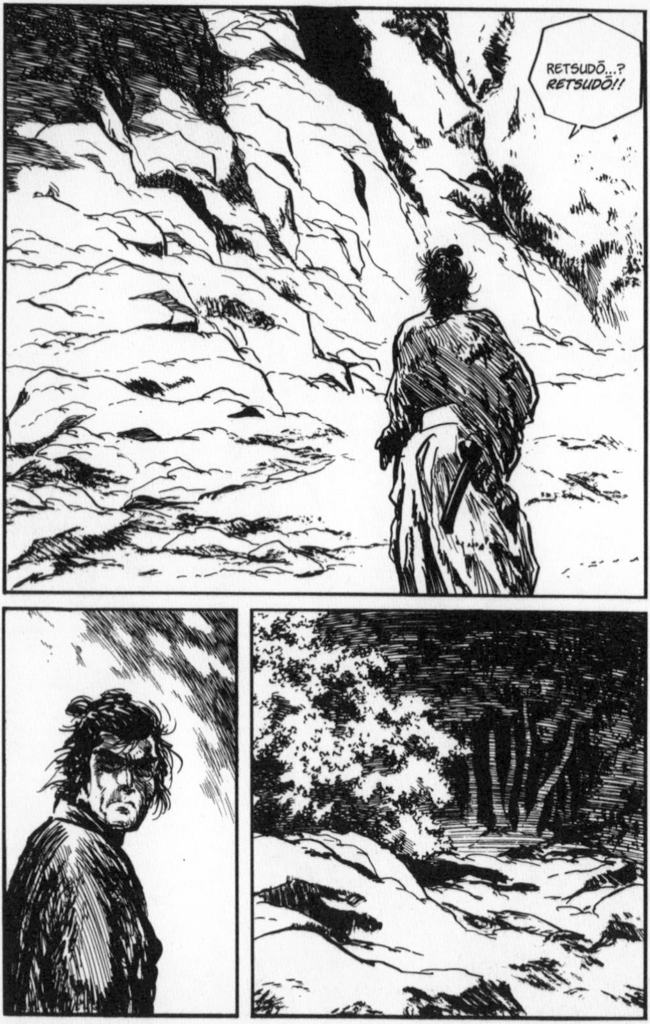
RETSUDŌ...? RETSUDŌ!!

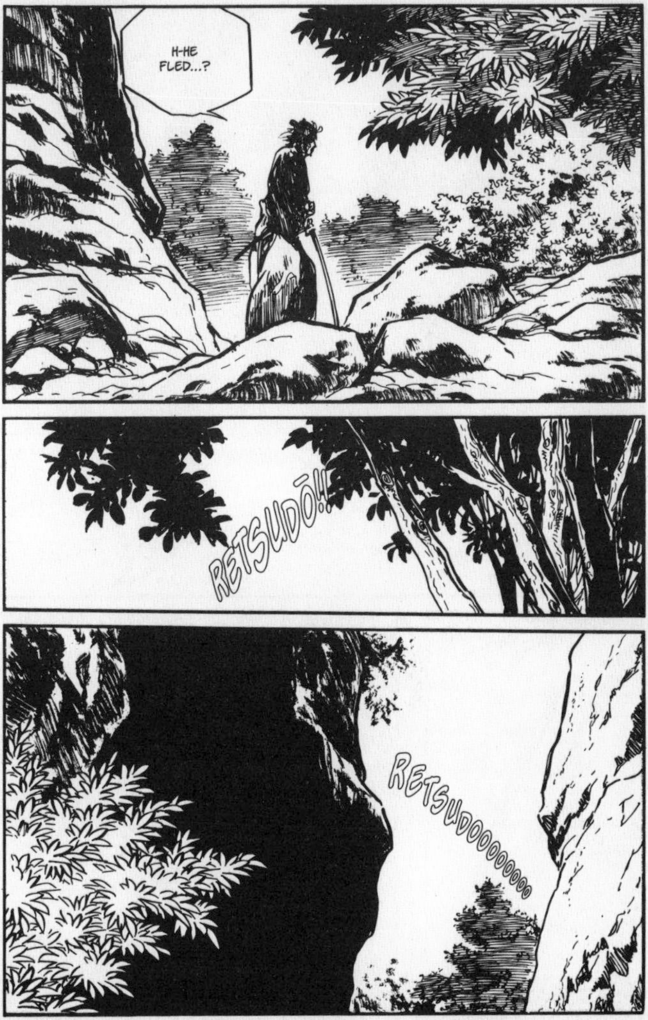
H-HE FLED...?
RETSUDŌ!!
RETSUDOOOOOOO

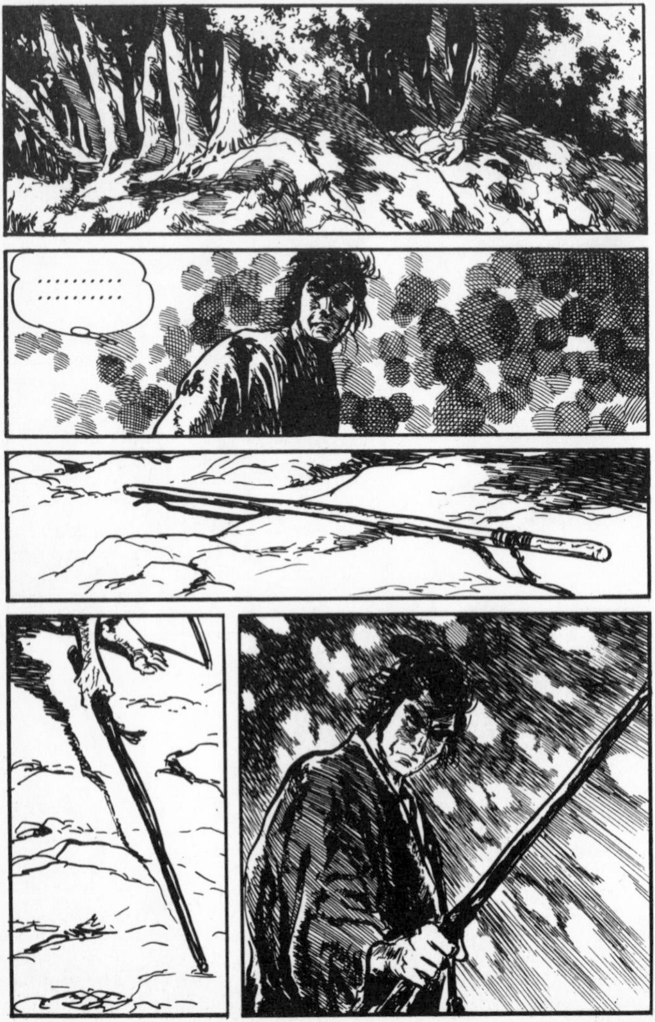
....
....

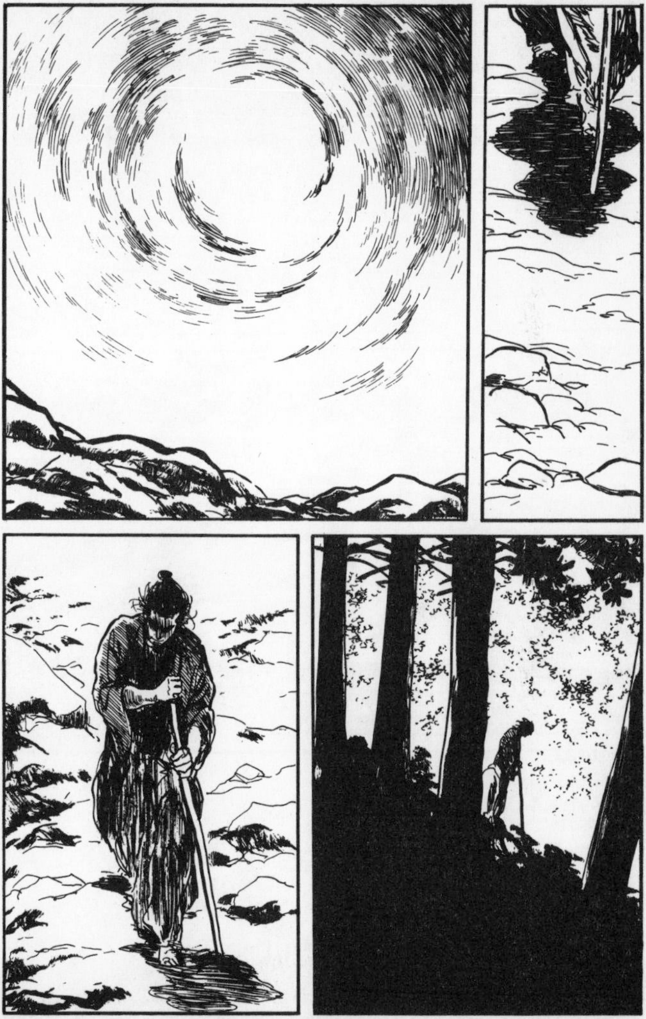

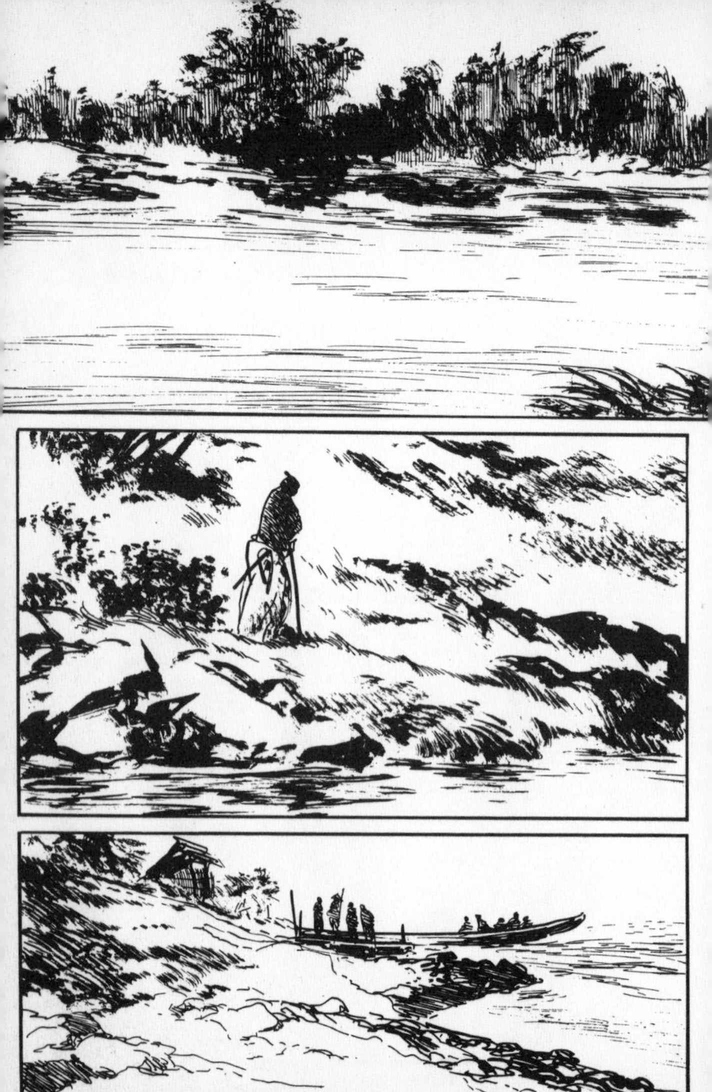

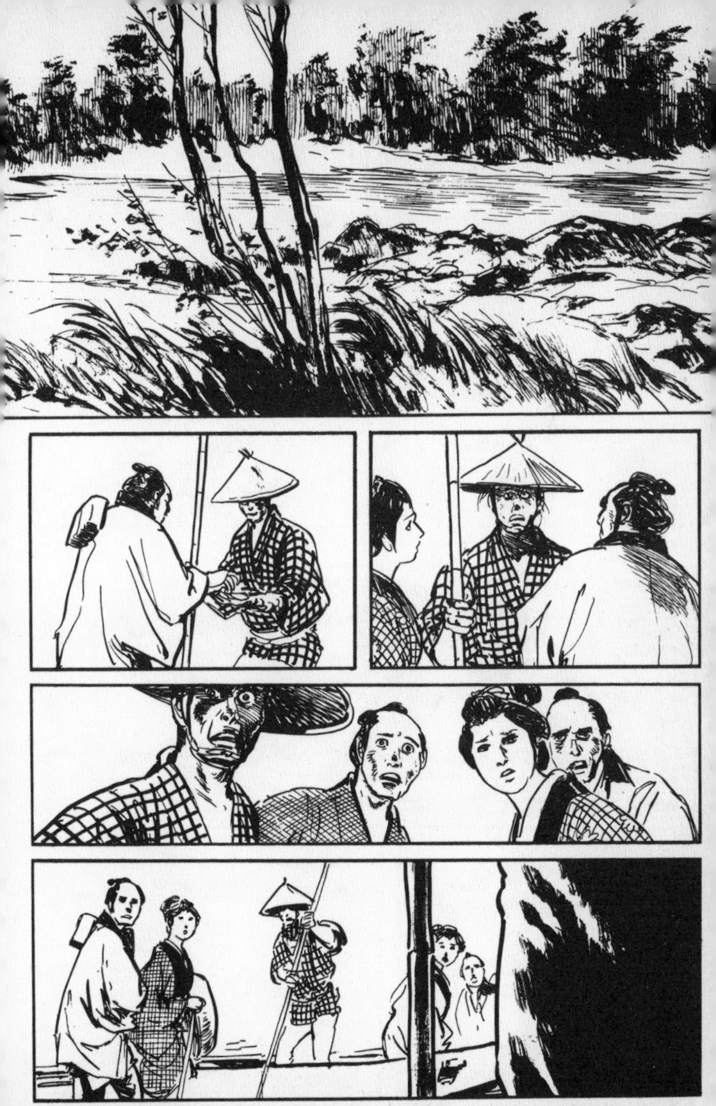

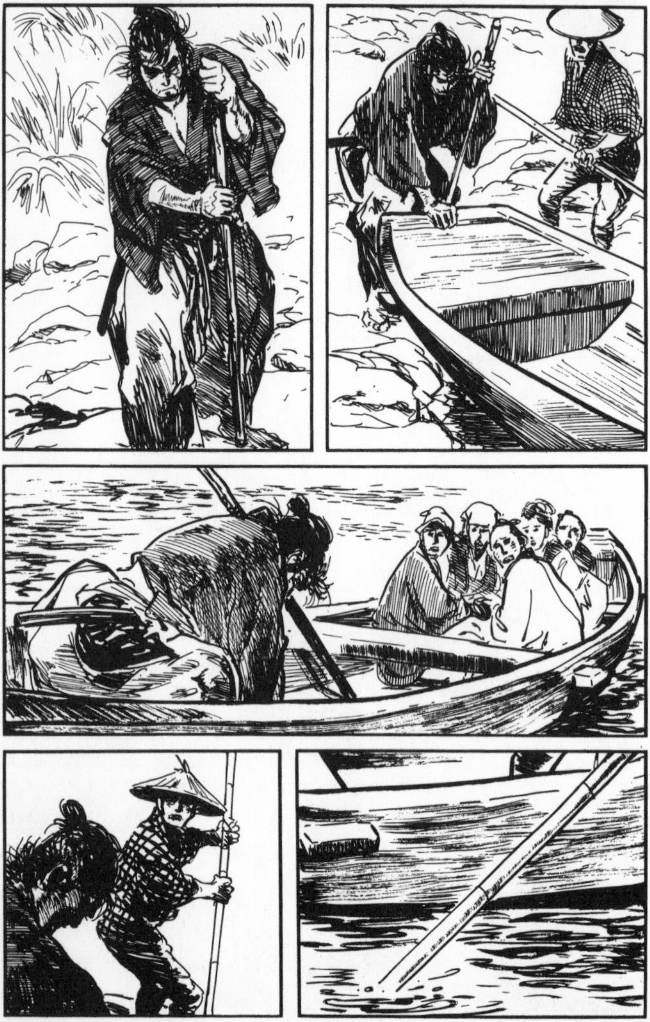

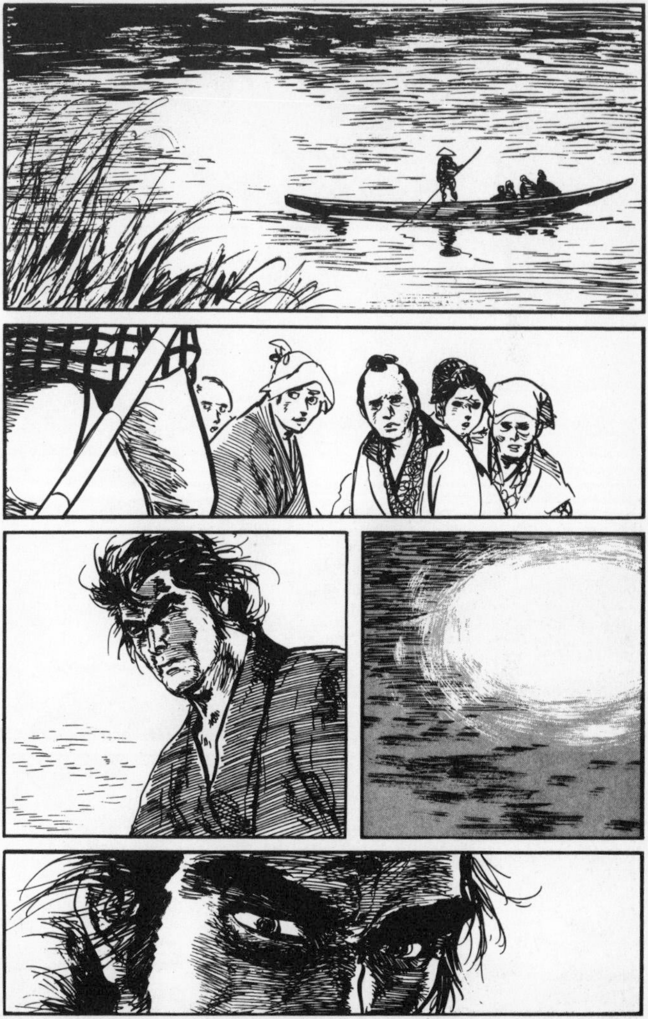

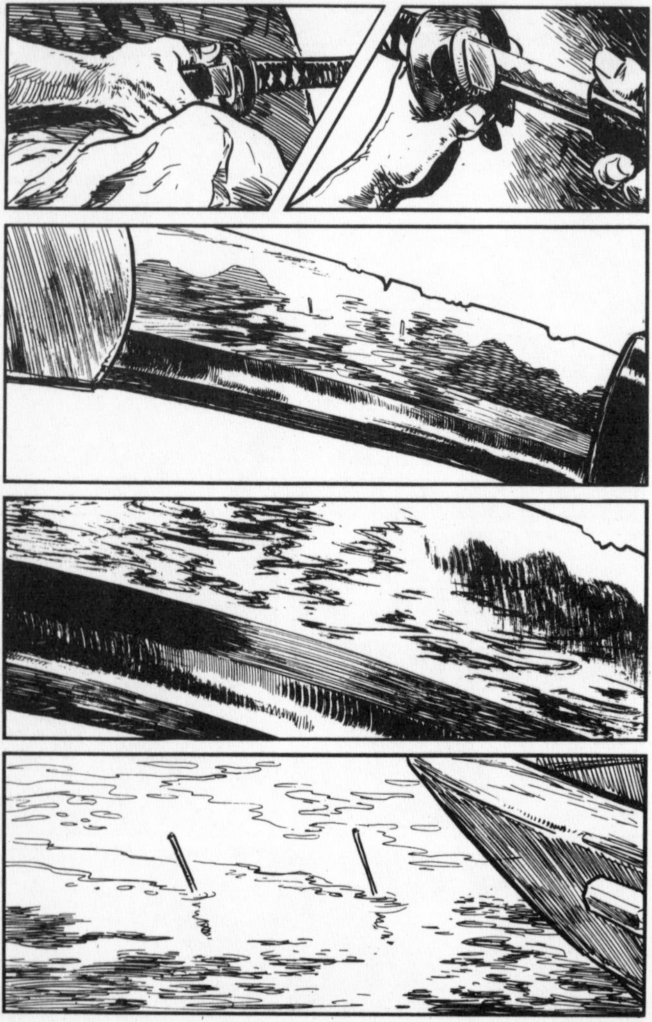

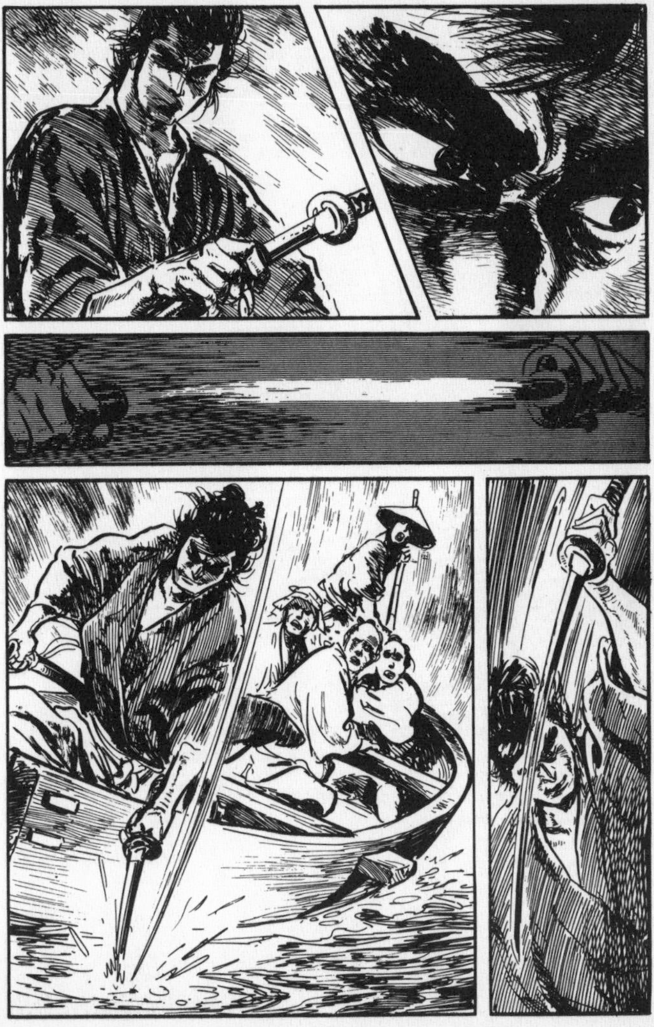

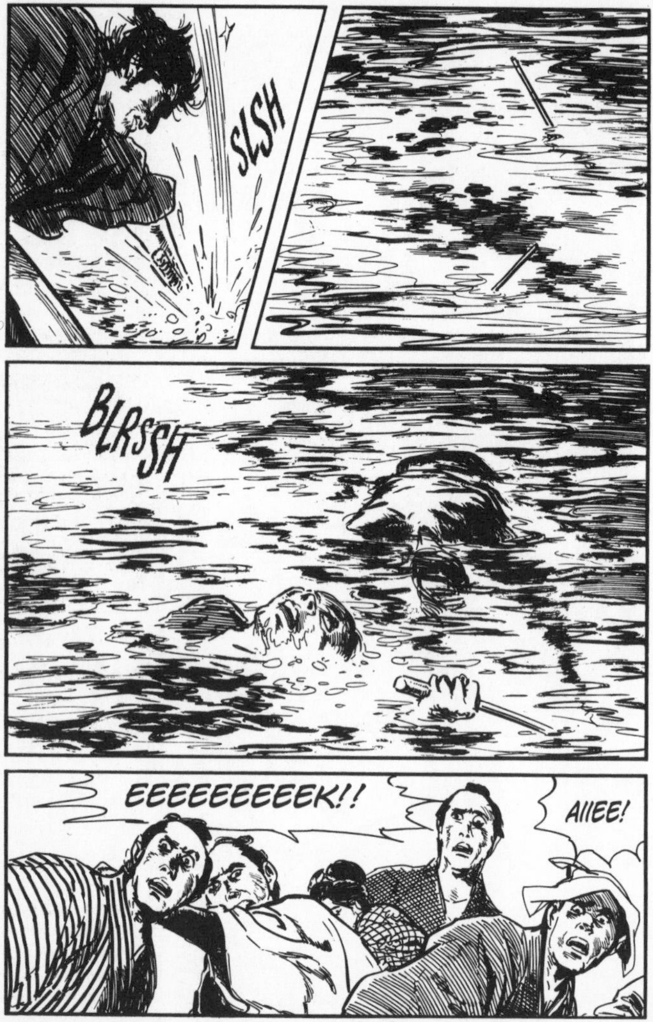
SLSH
BLRSSH
EEEEEEEEEK!!
AIIEE!

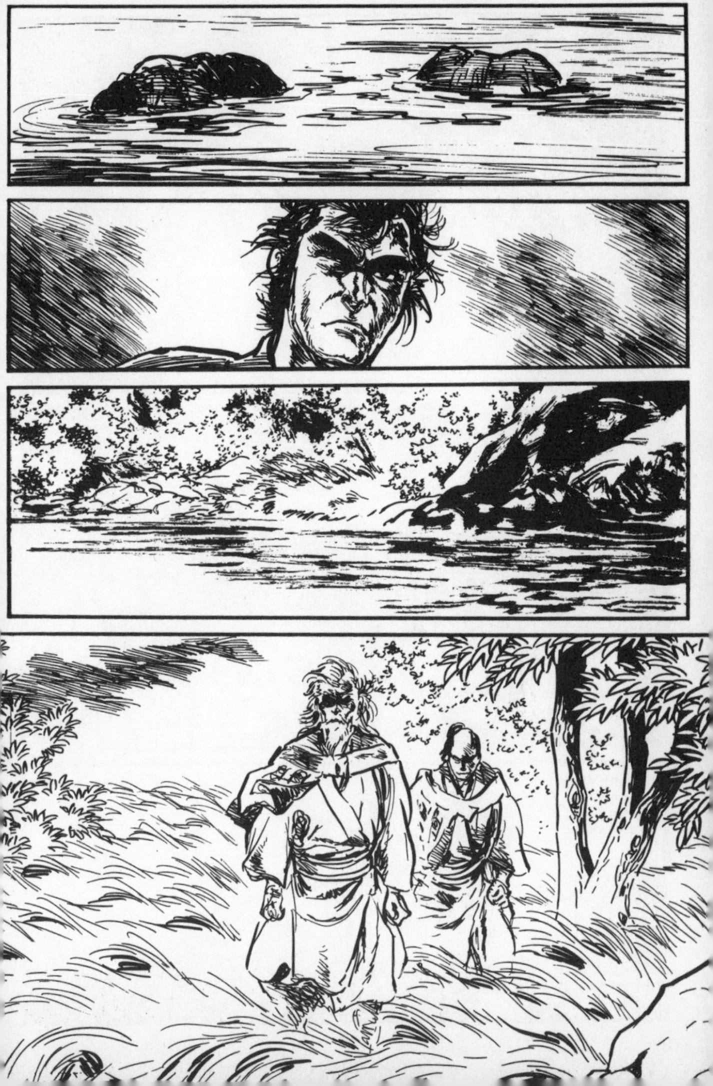

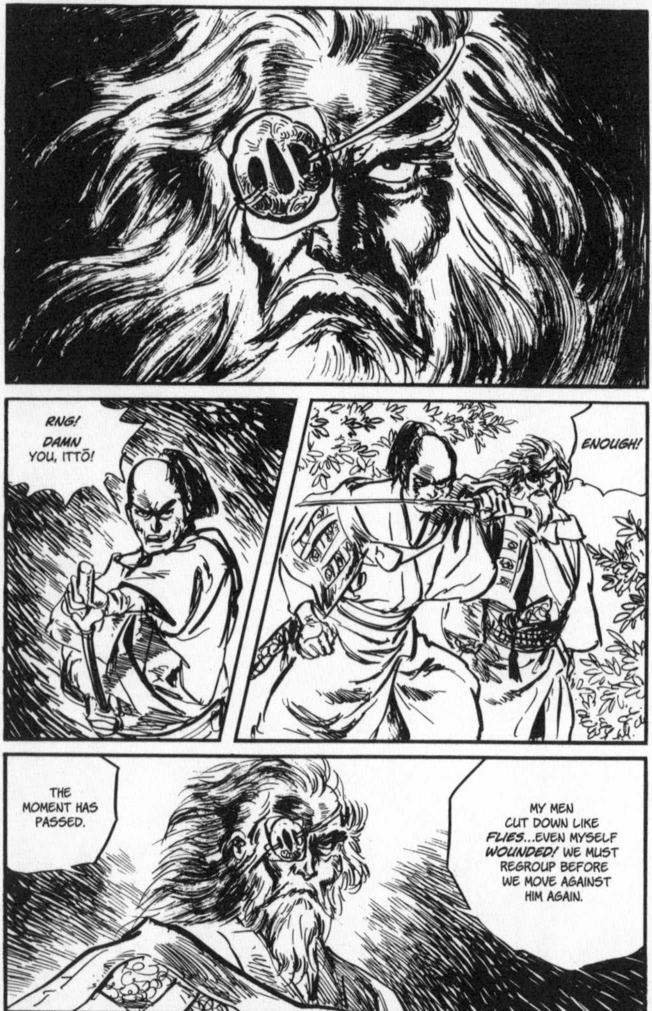

RNG!
DAMN YOU, ITTŌ!
ENOUGH!
THE MOMENT HAS PASSED.
MY MEN CUT DOWN LIKE *FLIES*...EVEN MYSELF *WOUNDED!* WE MUST REGROUP BEFORE WE MOVE AGAINST HIM AGAIN.

YET, ENEMY THOUGH HE BE... *MAGNIFICENT!* A MASTER OF *SUIŌ ZANBATŌ.*

NO ONE, *PAST* NOR *PRESENT,* HAS GIVEN US SUCH A CHALLENGE.

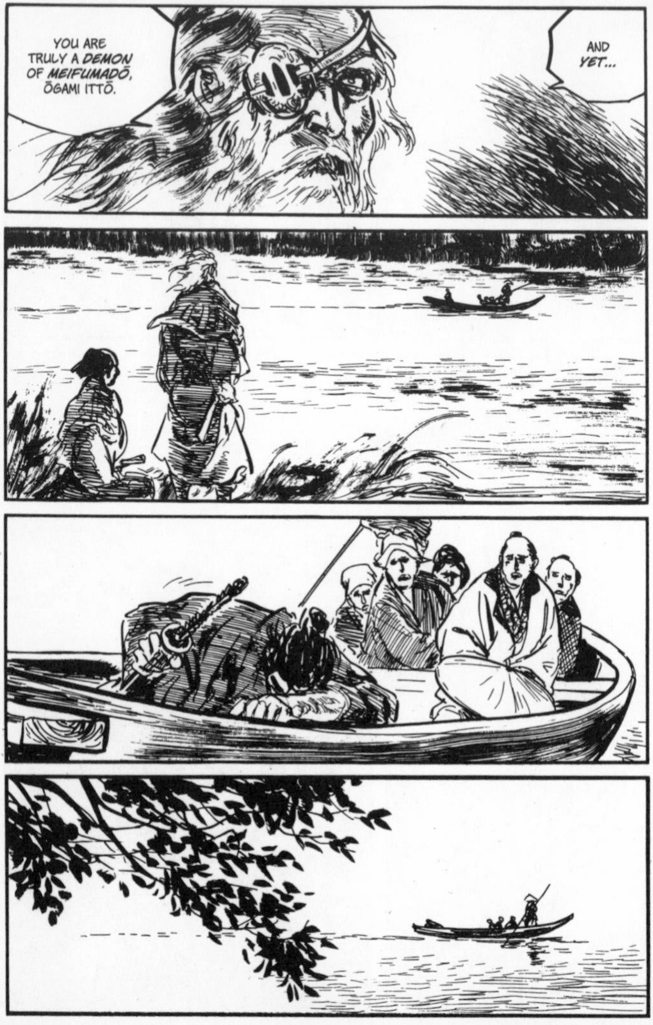

YOU ARE TRULY A *DEMON* OF *MEIFUMADŌ*, ŌGAMI ITTŌ.
AND *YET...*

the fifty-fourth

Straw Boy

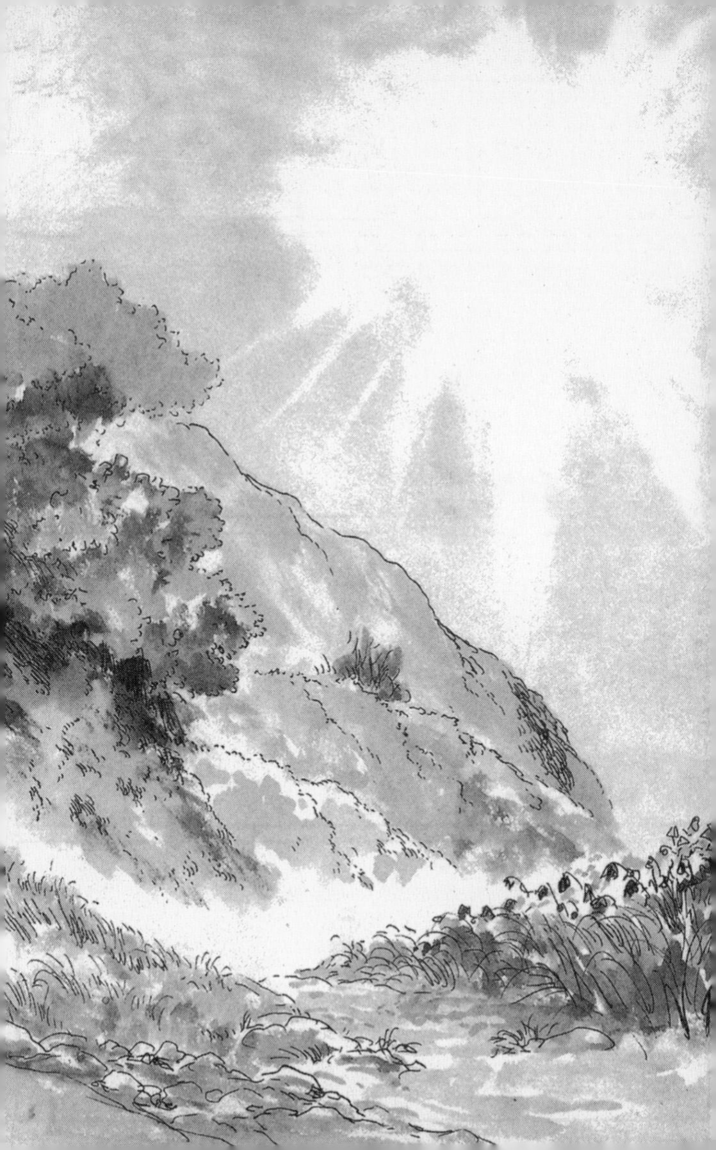

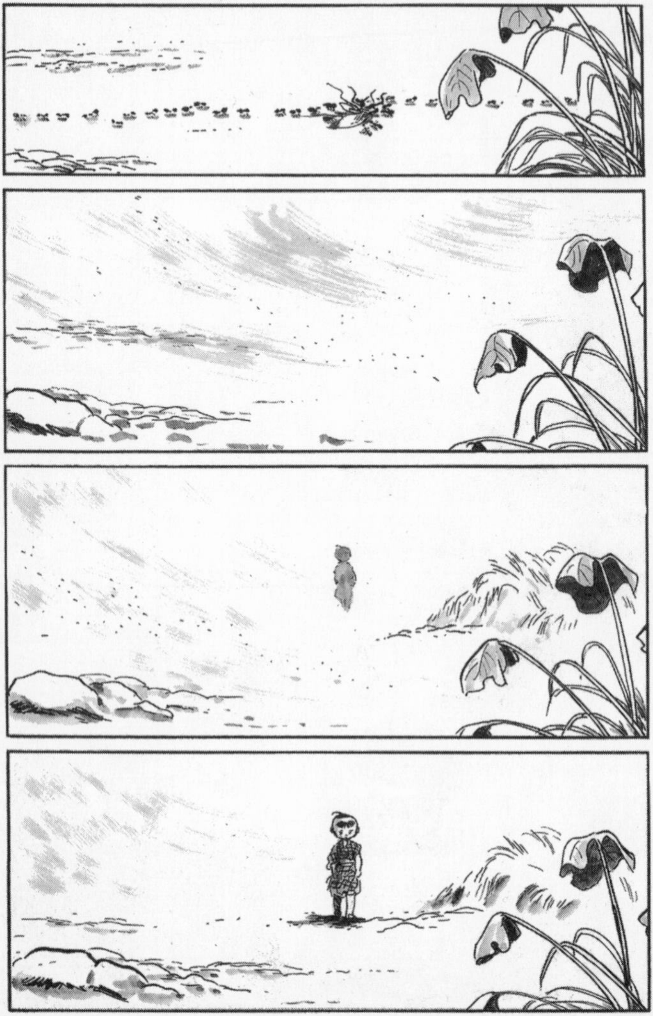

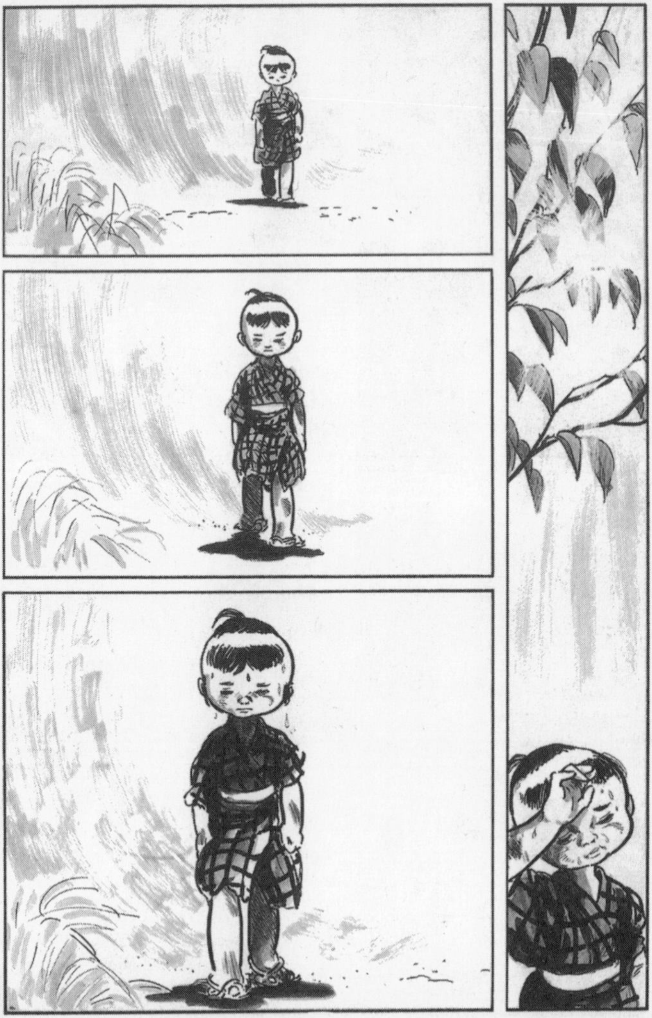

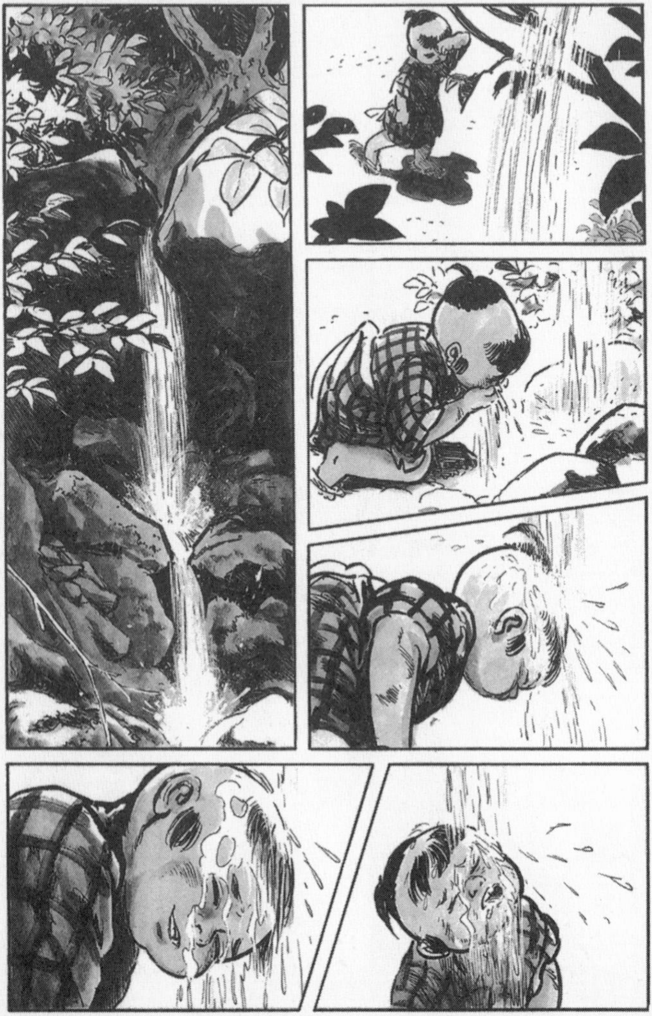

HE WAS STARVING. HE WAS BOILING. HIS STOMACH SLOSHED FULL OF WATER.

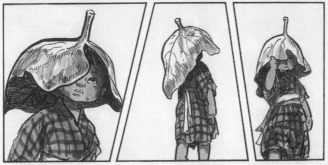

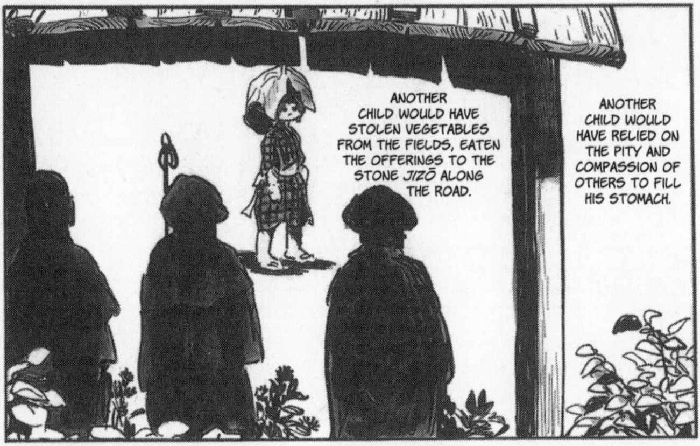
ANOTHER CHILD WOULD HAVE STOLEN VEGETABLES FROM THE FIELDS, EATEN THE OFFERINGS TO THE STONE *JIZŌ* ALONG THE ROAD.
ANOTHER CHILD WOULD HAVE RELIED ON THE PITY AND COMPASSION OF OTHERS TO FILL HIS STOMACH.

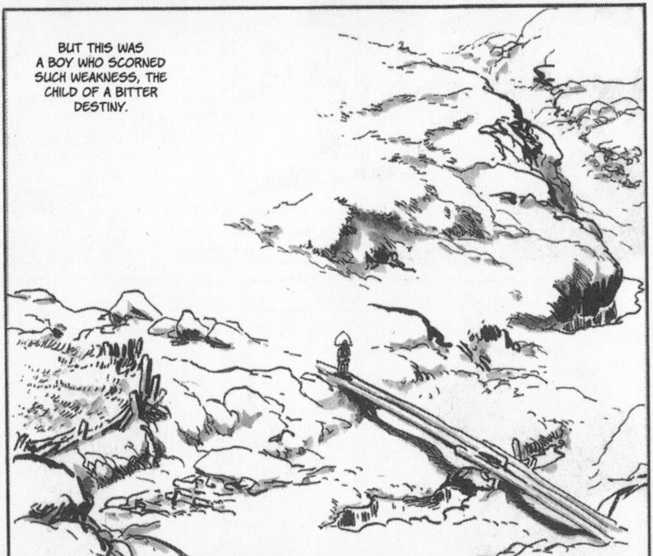
BUT THIS WAS A BOY WHO SCORNED SUCH WEAKNESS, THE CHILD OF A BITTER DESTINY.

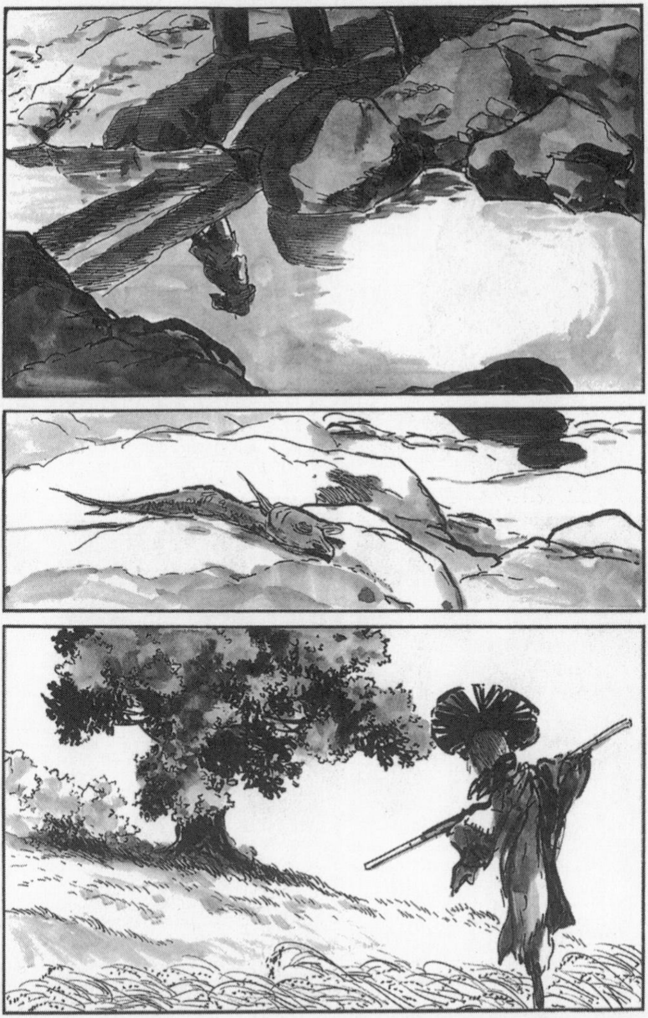

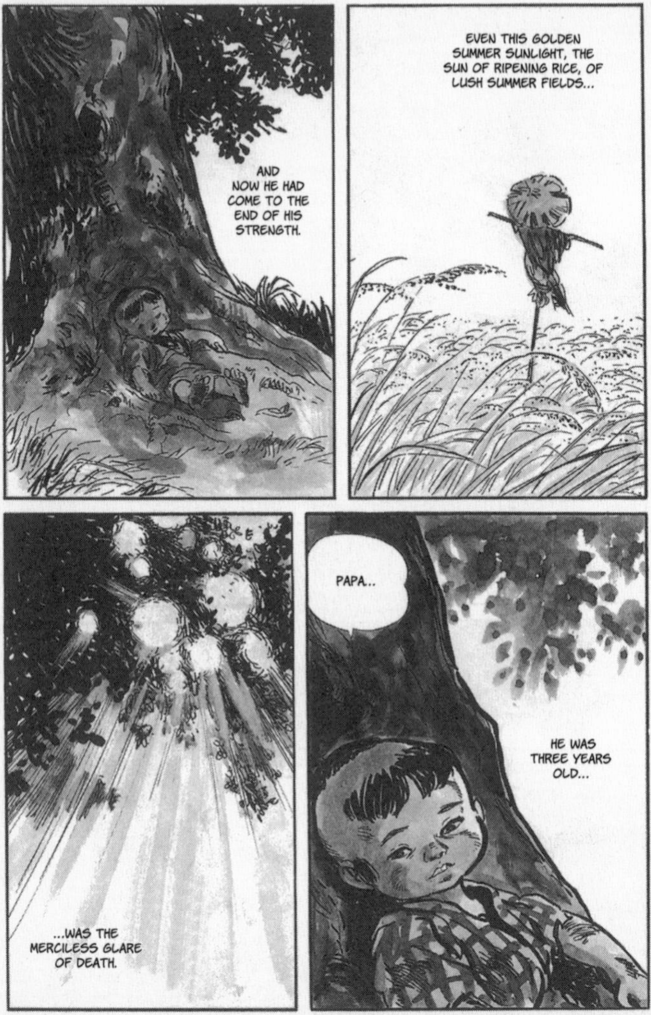

AND NOW HE HAD COME TO THE END OF HIS STRENGTH.
EVEN THIS GOLDEN SUMMER SUNLIGHT, THE SUN OF RIPENING RICE, OF LUSH SUMMER FIELDS...
...WAS THE MERCILESS GLARE OF DEATH.
PAPA..
HE WAS THREE YEARS OLD...

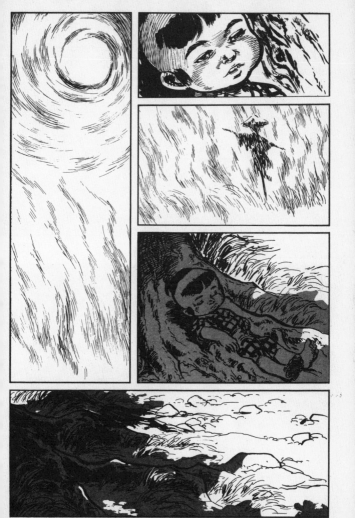

257

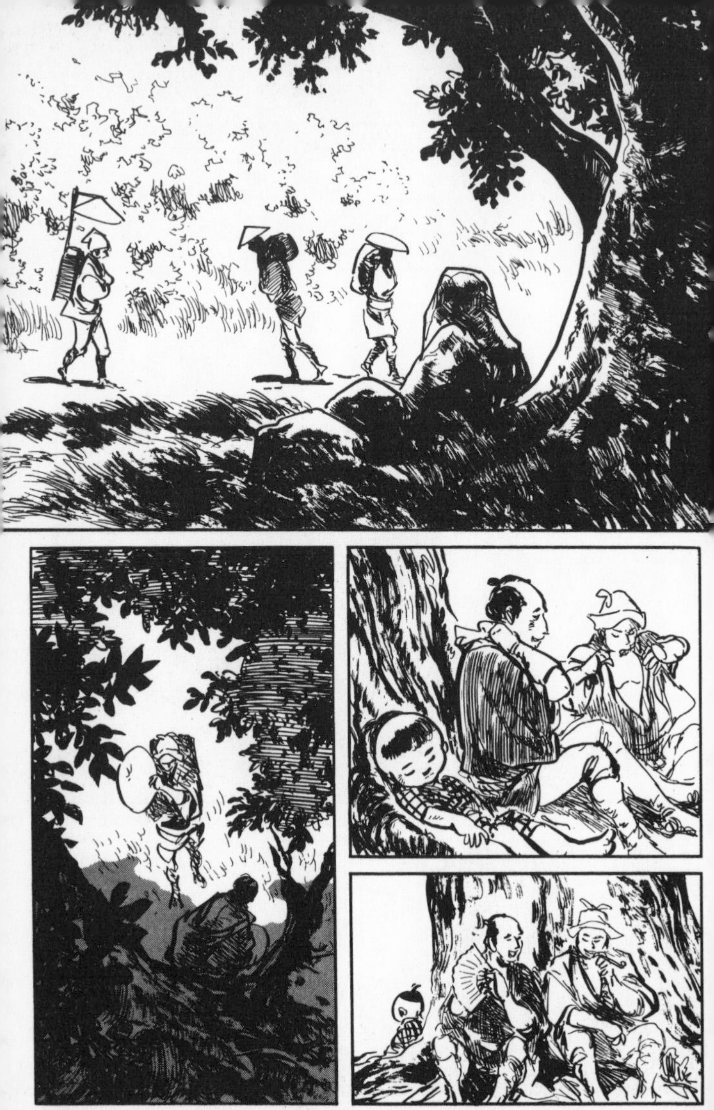

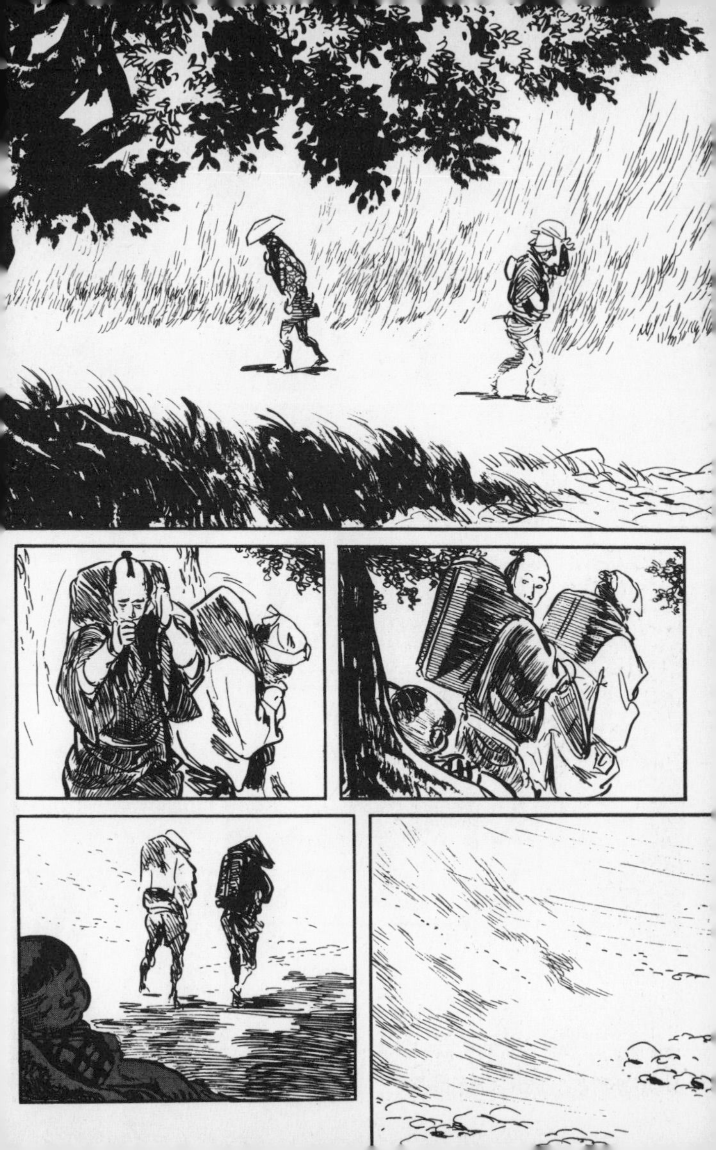

KRNCH CHKK CHRKK

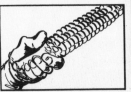

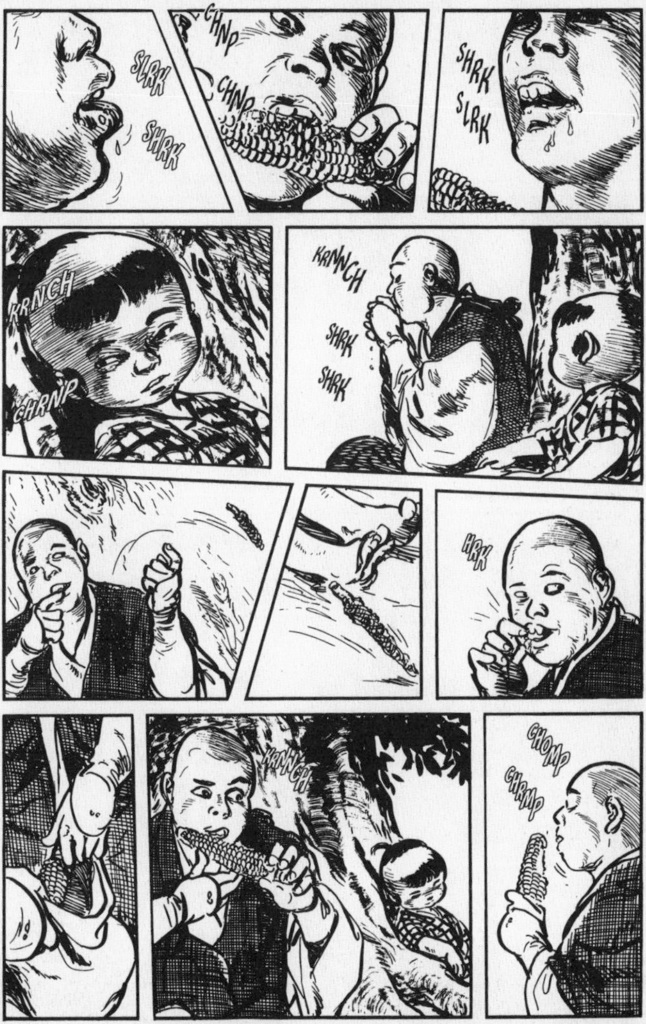
SLRK
SHRK
CHNP
CHNP
SHRK
SLRK
KRNCH
CHRNP
KRNNCH
SHRK
SHRK
HRK
KRNNCH
CHOMP
CHRMP

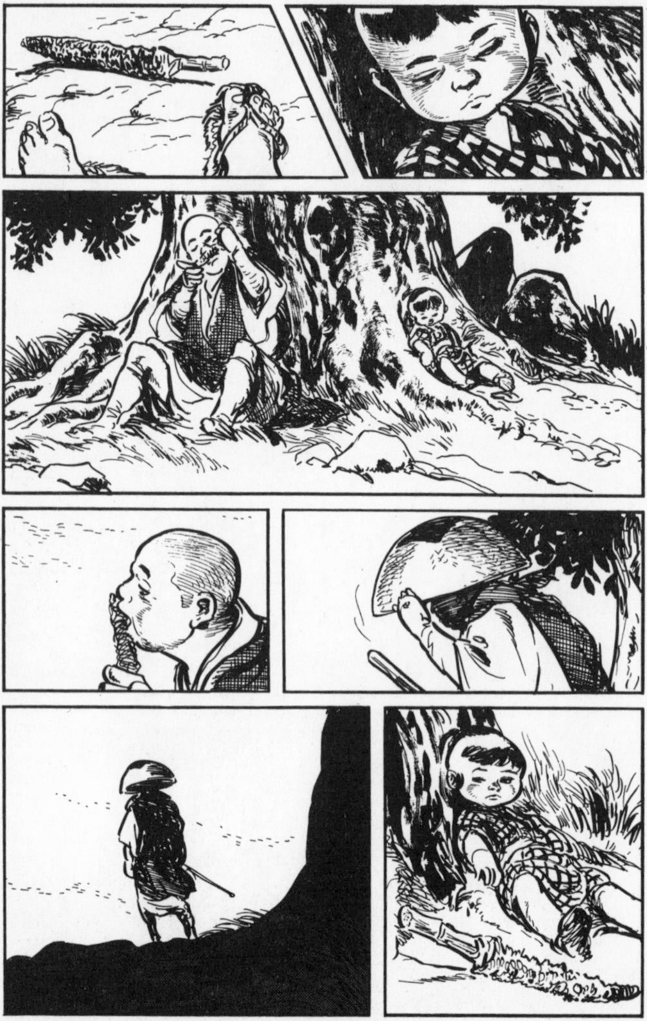

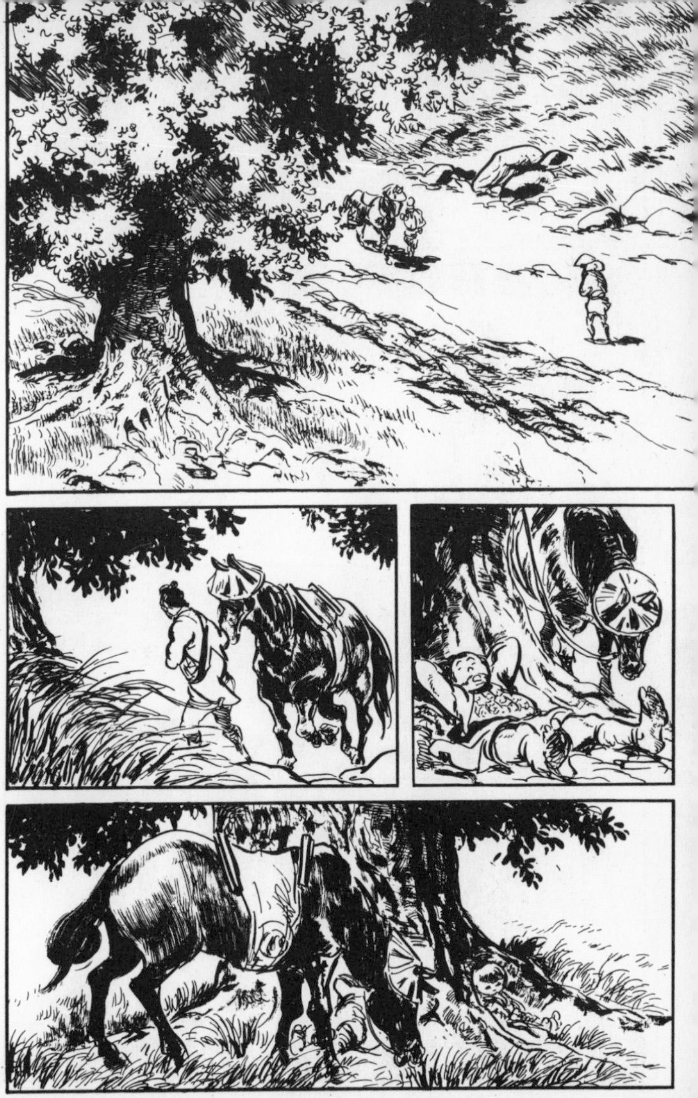

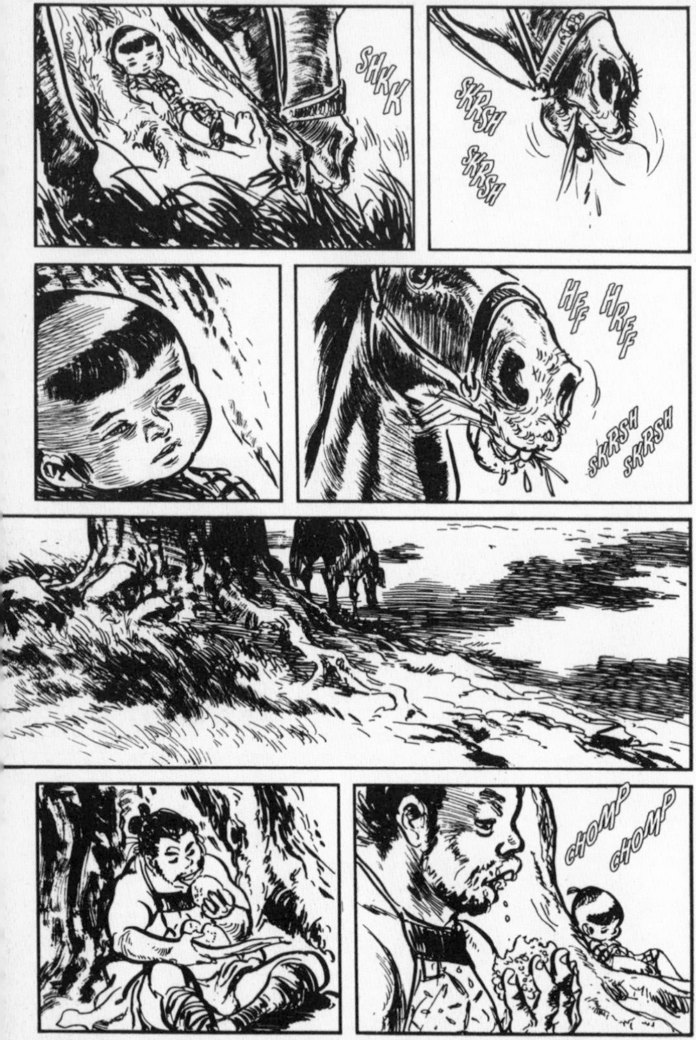
SHKK
SKRSH
SKRSH
HFF
HRFF
SKRSH
SKRSH
CHOMP
CHOMP

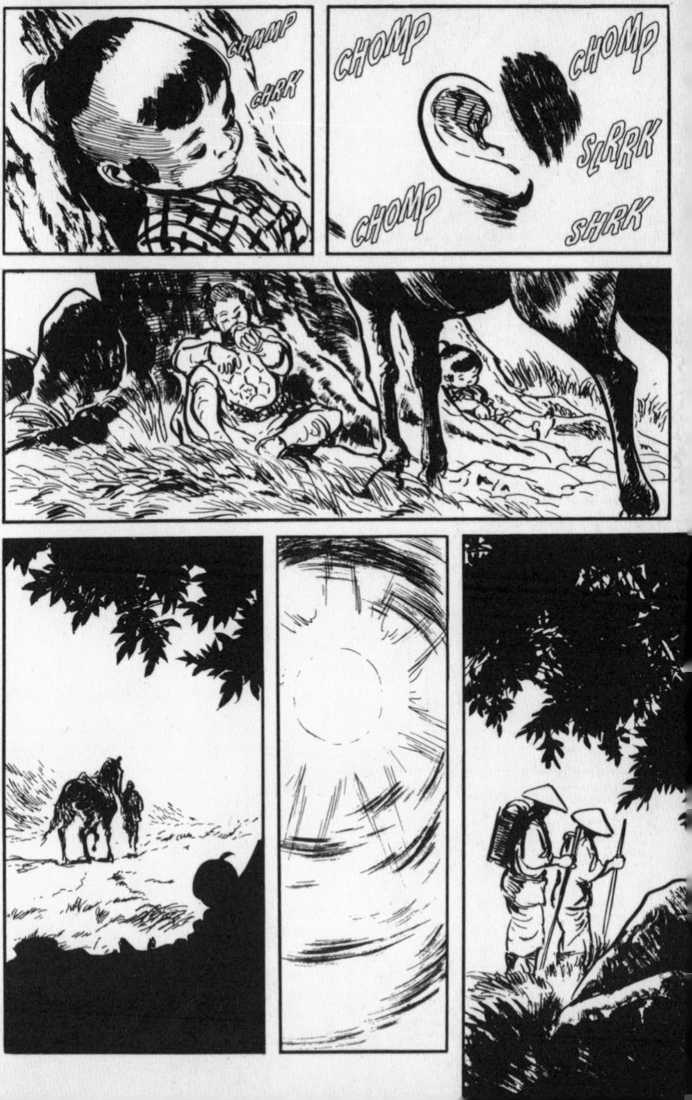
CHMMP
CHRK
CHOMP
CHOMP
SLRRK
CHOMP
SHRK

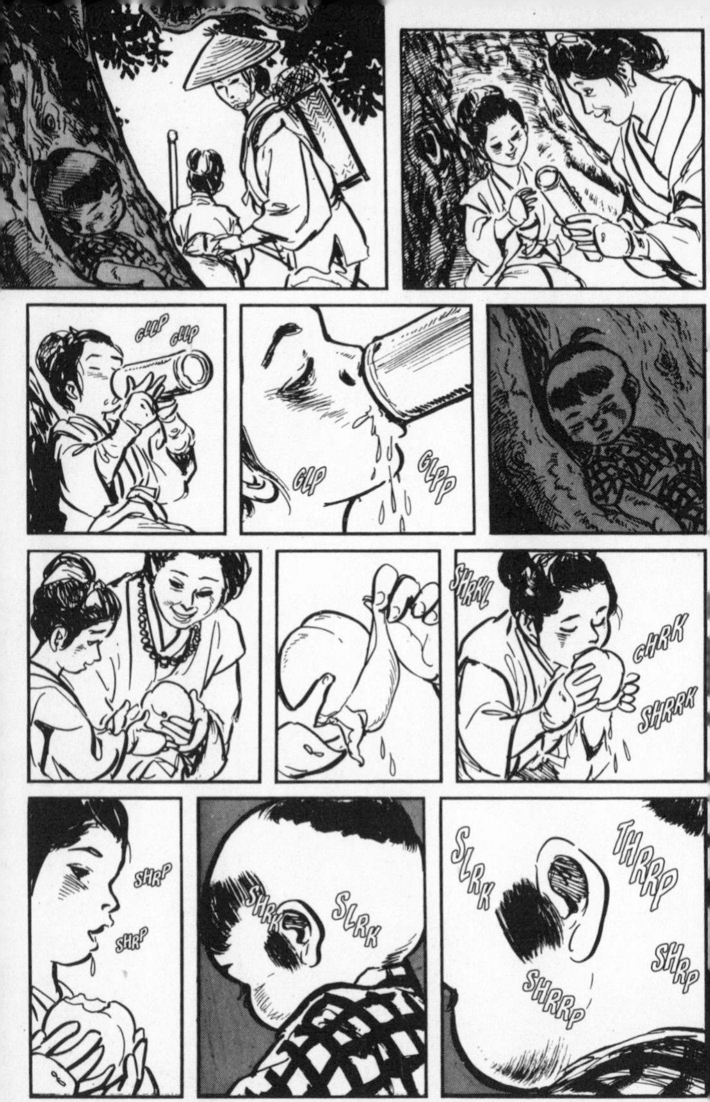
GLLP
GLLP
GLP
GLPP
SHRKL
CHRK
SHRRK
SHRP
SHRP
SHRK
SLRK
SLRK
THRRP
SHRRP
SHRP

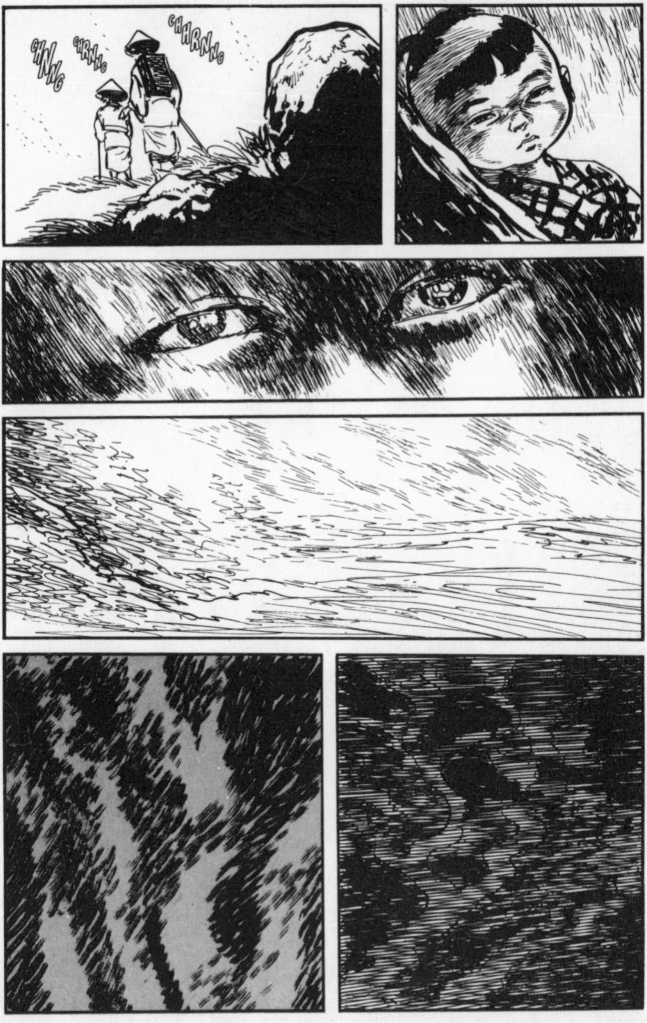
CHNNG
CHRNNG
CHHRNNG

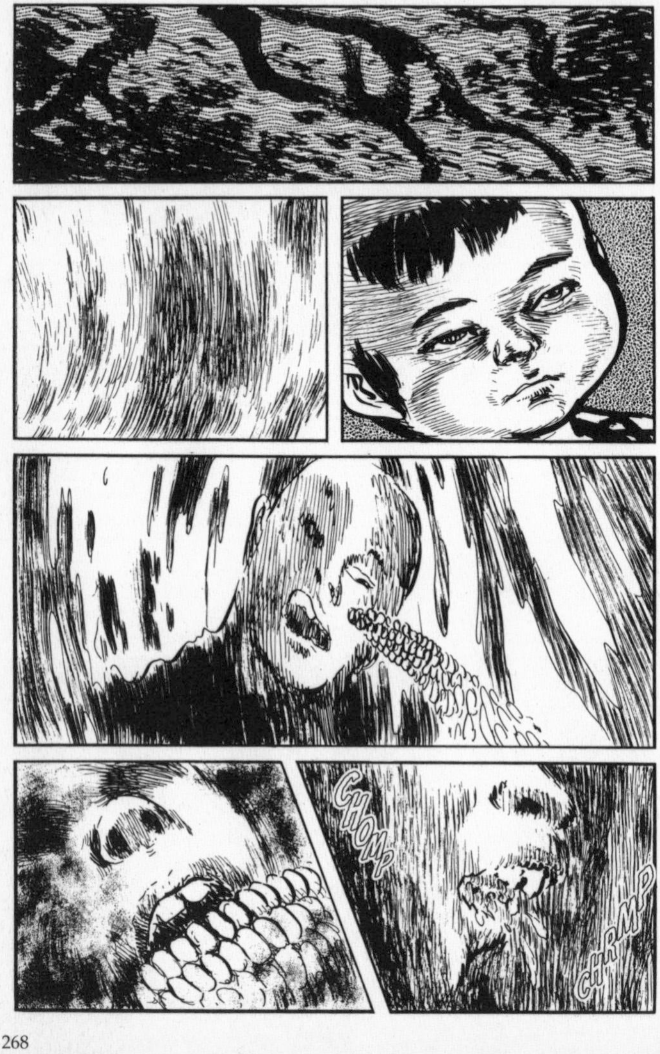
CHOMP
CHRMP

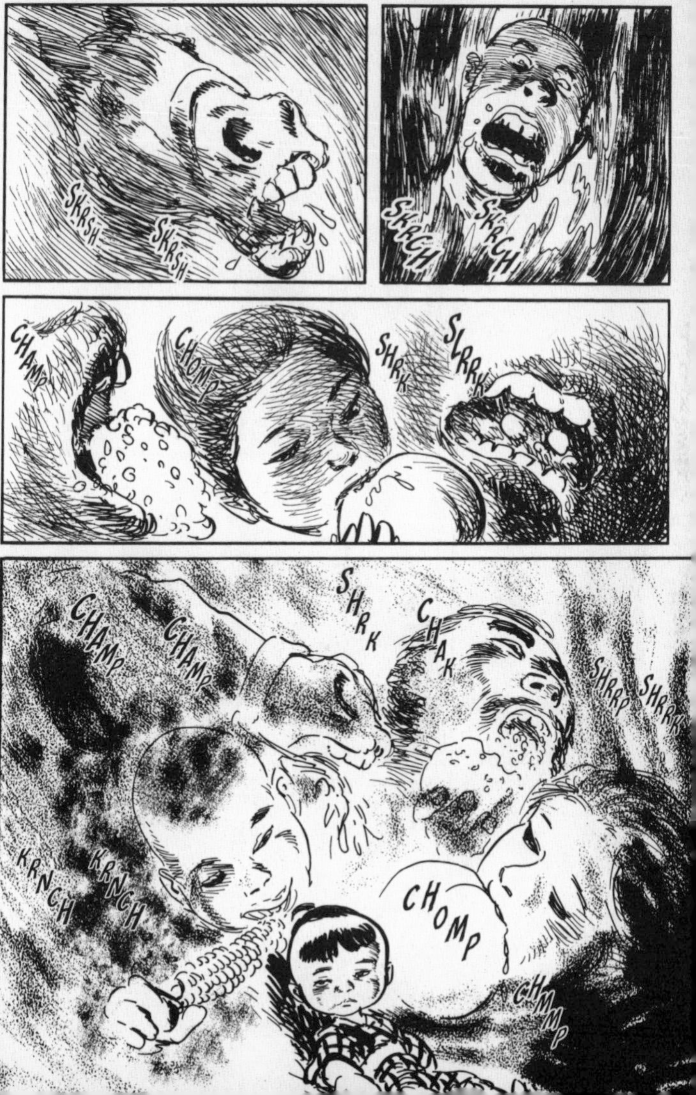
SKRSH
SKRSH
SKRCH
SKRCH
CHAMP
CHOMP
SHRK
SLRRK
CHAMP
CHAMP
SHRK
CHAK
SHRRP
SHRRK
KRNCH
KRNCH
CHOMP
CHMMP

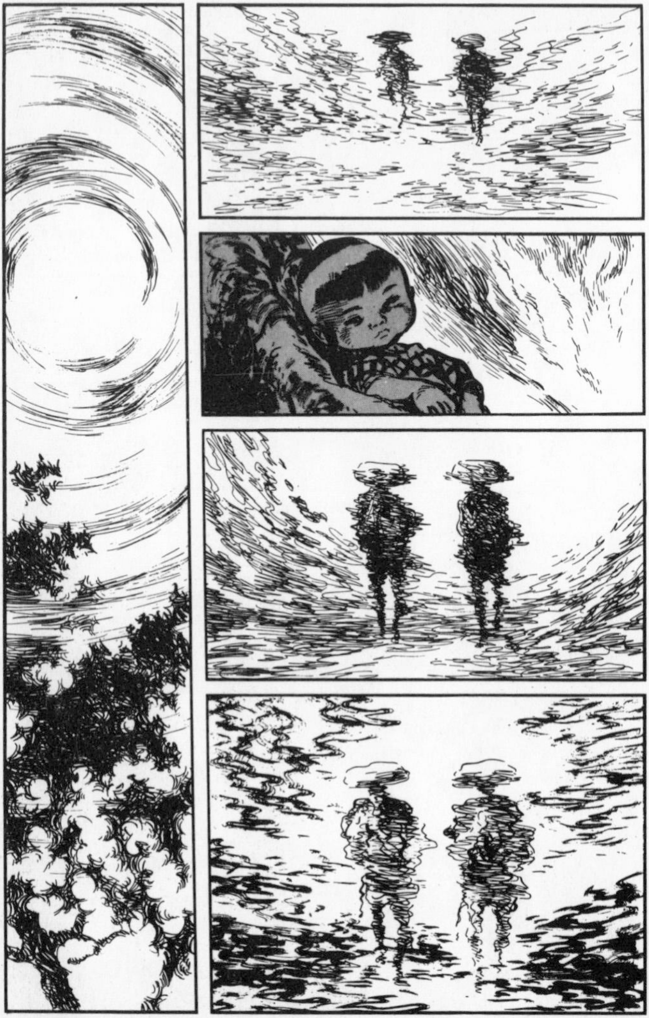

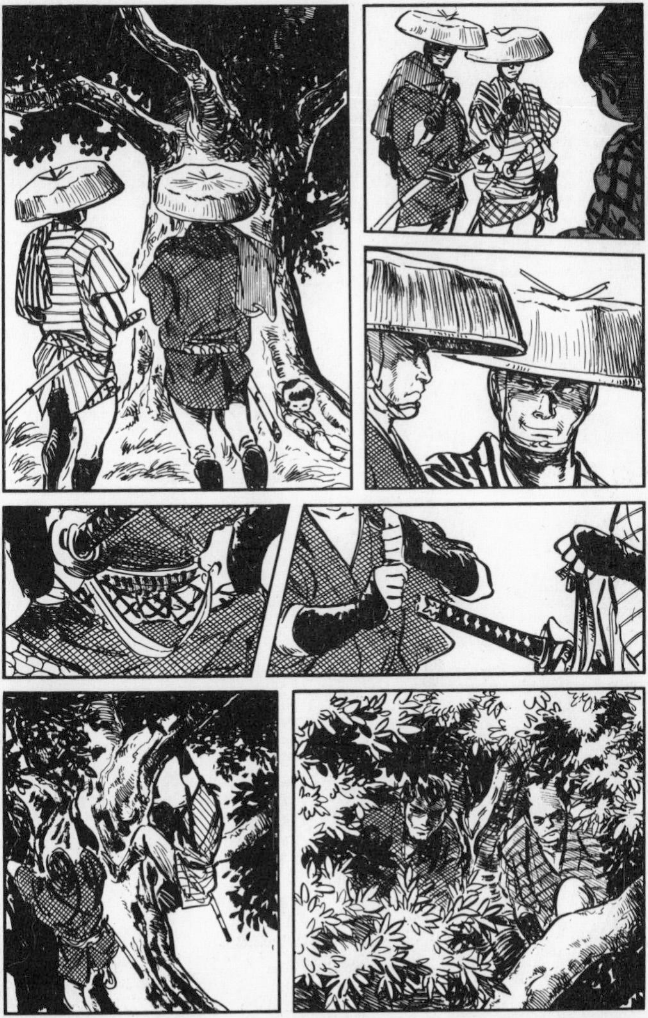

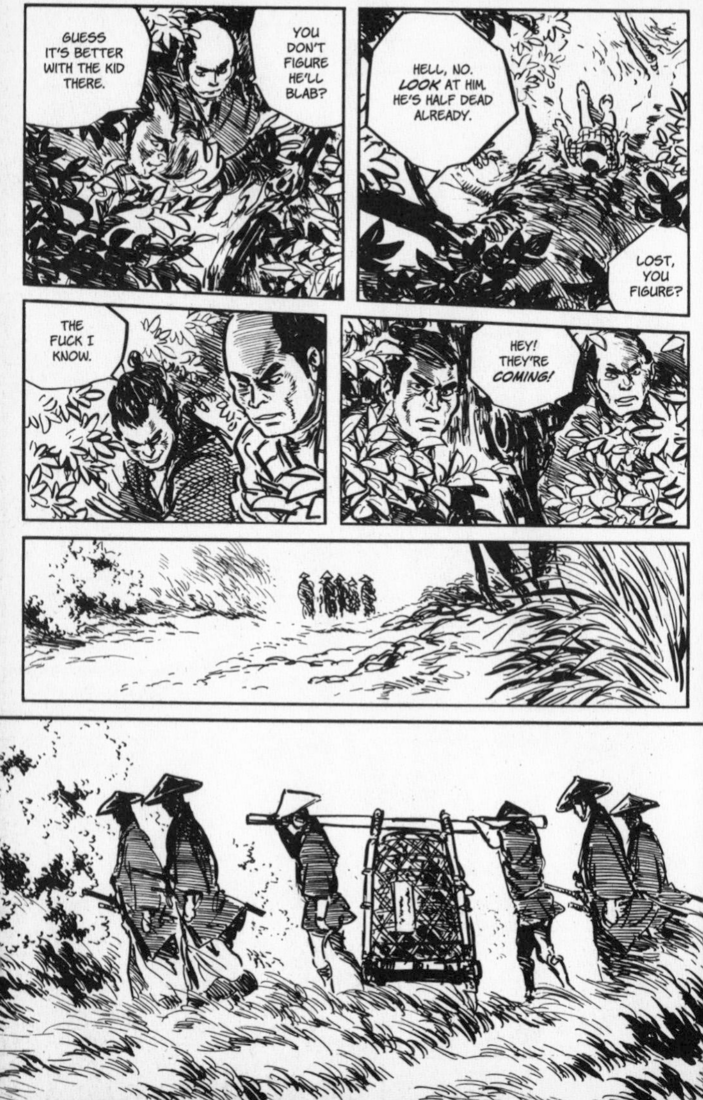
GUESS IT'S BETTER WITH THE KID THERE.
YOU DON'T FIGURE HE'LL BLAB?
HELL, NO. *LOOK* AT HIM. HE'S HALF DEAD ALREADY.
LOST, YOU FIGURE?
THE FUCK I KNOW.
HEY! THEY'RE *COMING!*

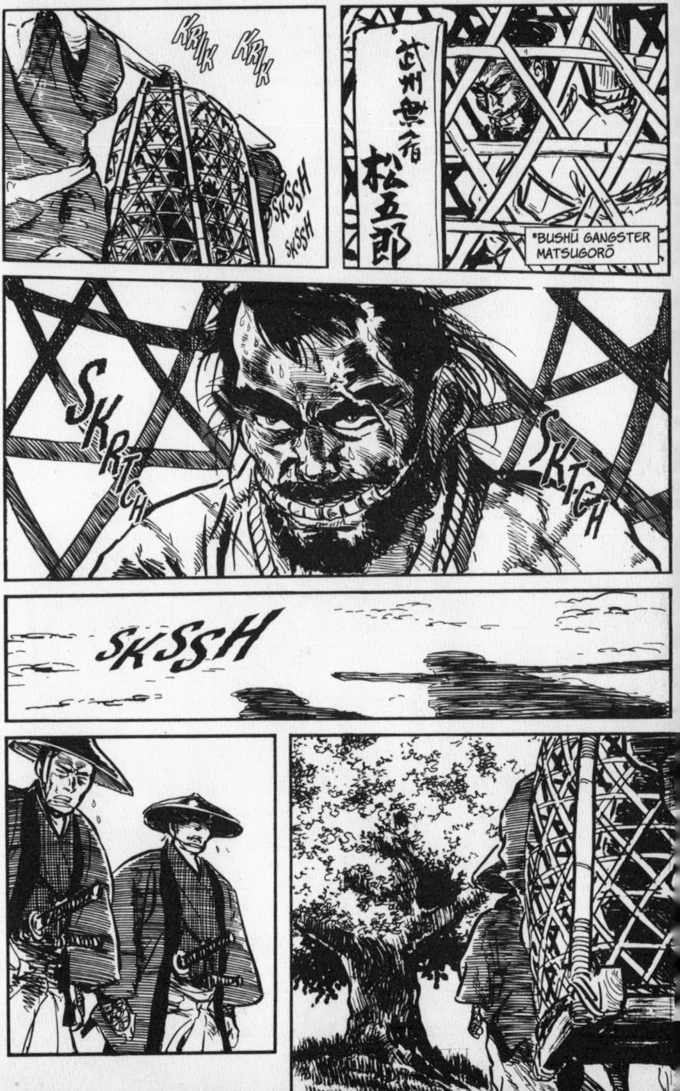
KRIK KRIK
SKSSH
SKSSH
武州無宿
松五郎
*BUSHŪ GANGSTER MATSUGORŌ
SKRTCH
SKTCH
SKSSH

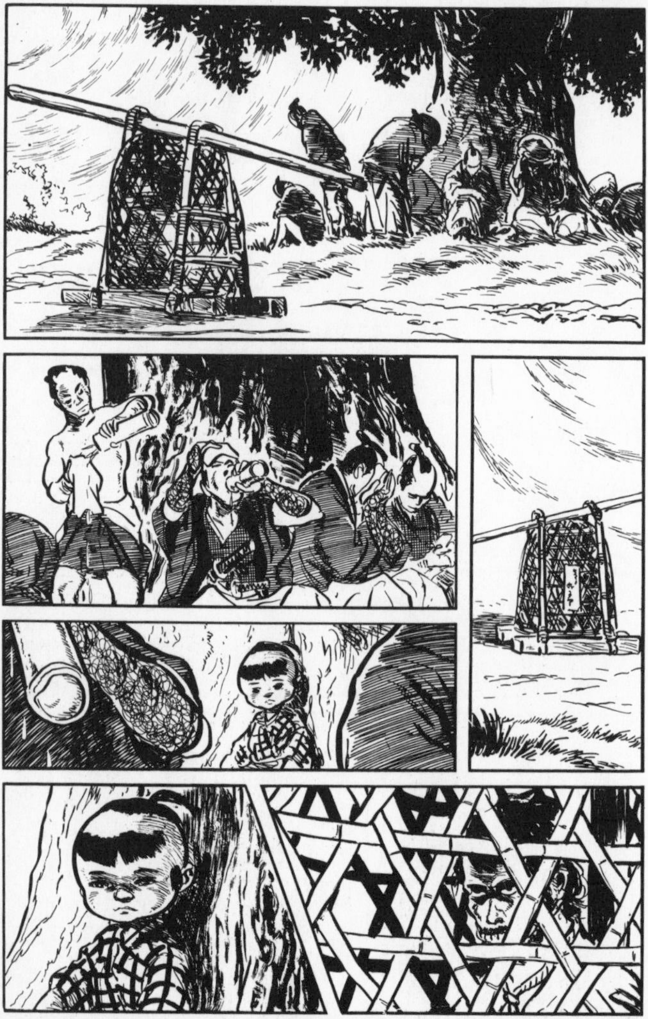

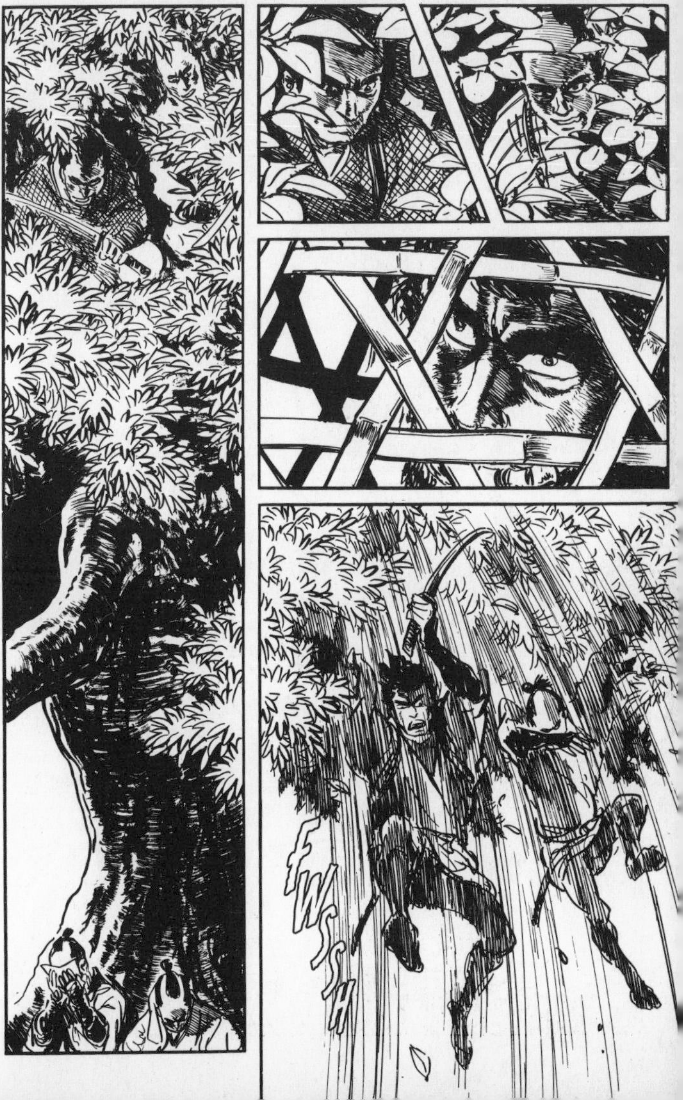
FWSSH

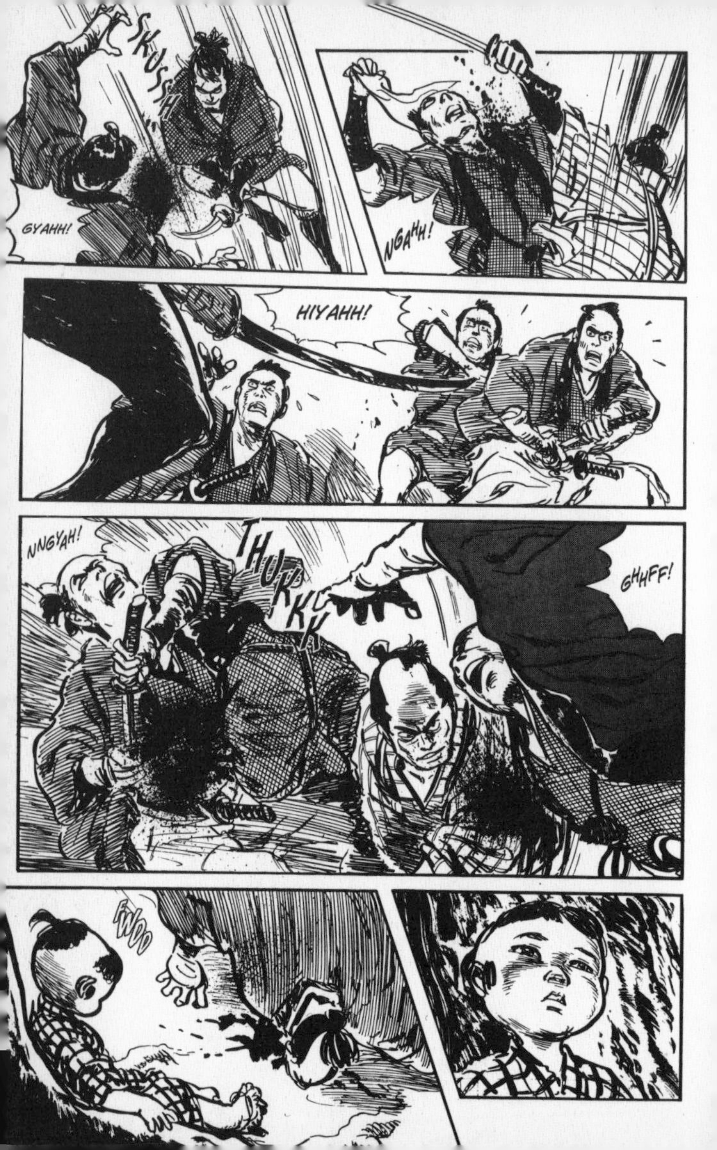
SKUSSH
GYAHH!
NGAHH!
HIYAHH!
NNGYAH!
THUKKK
GHHFF!
FWOO

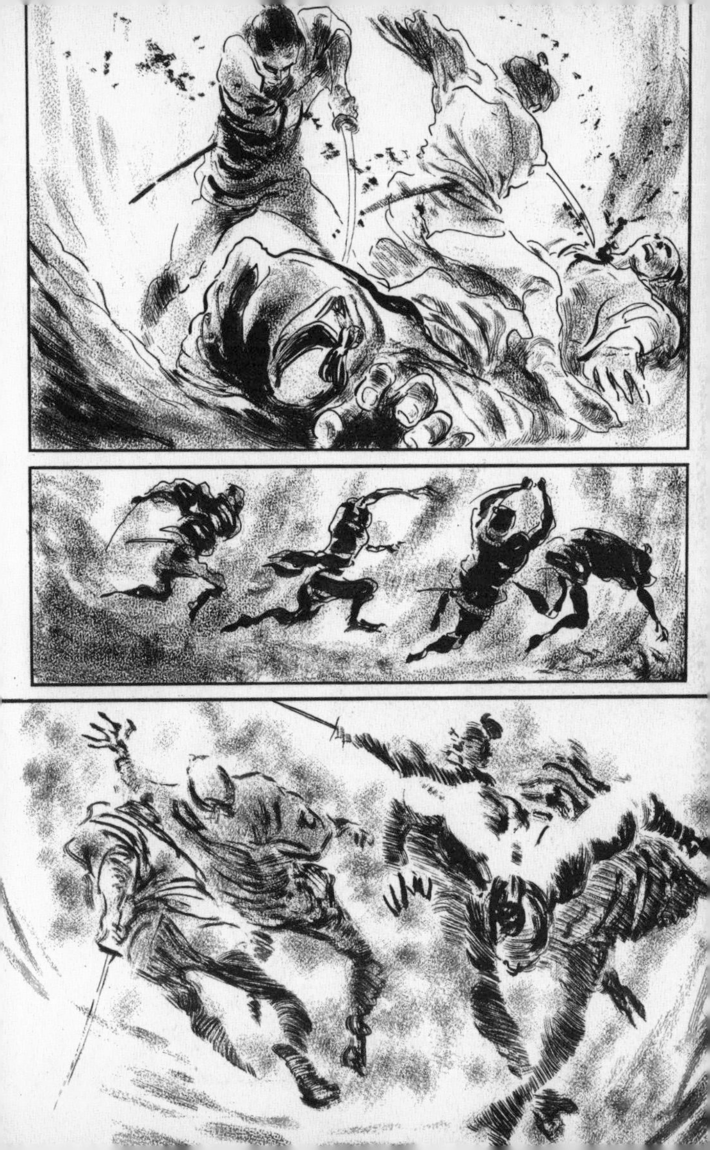

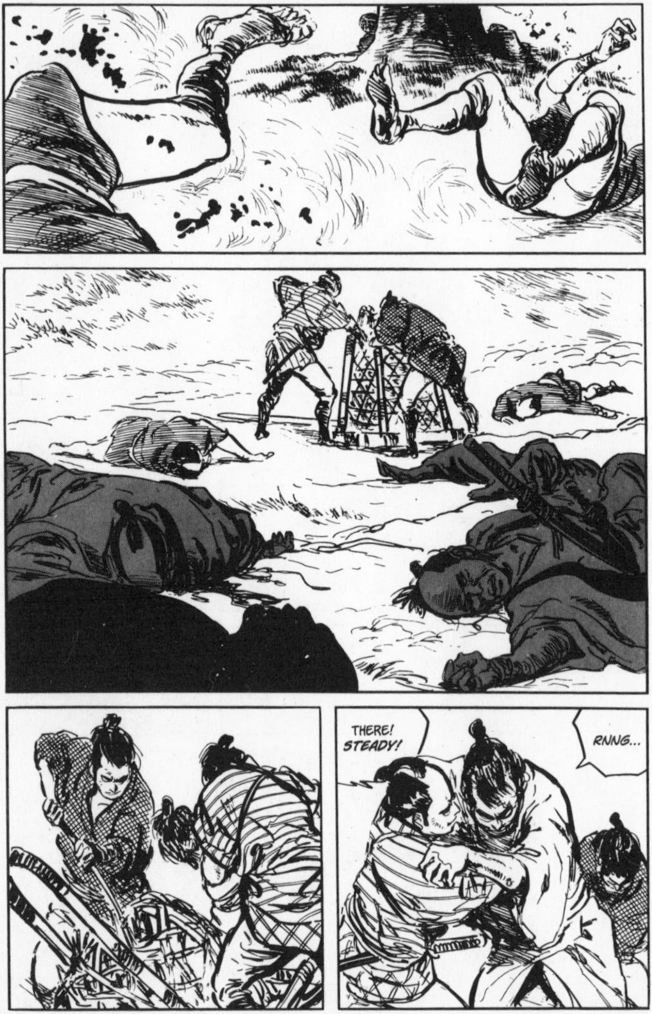
THERE! STEADY!
RNNG...

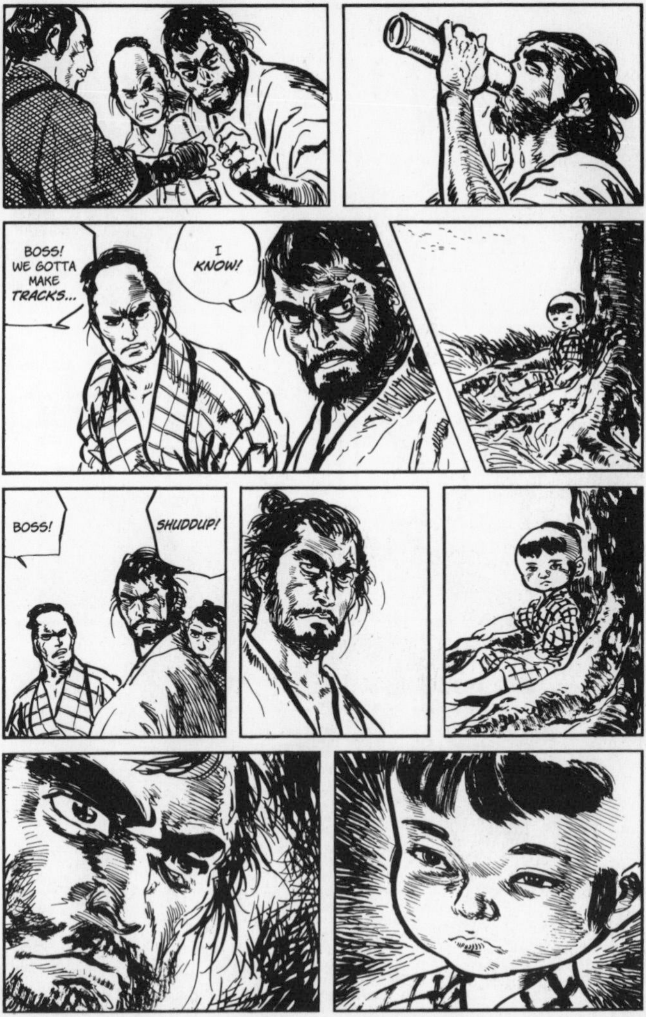
BOSS! WE GOTTA MAKE TRACKS...
I KNOW!
BOSS!
SHUDDUP!

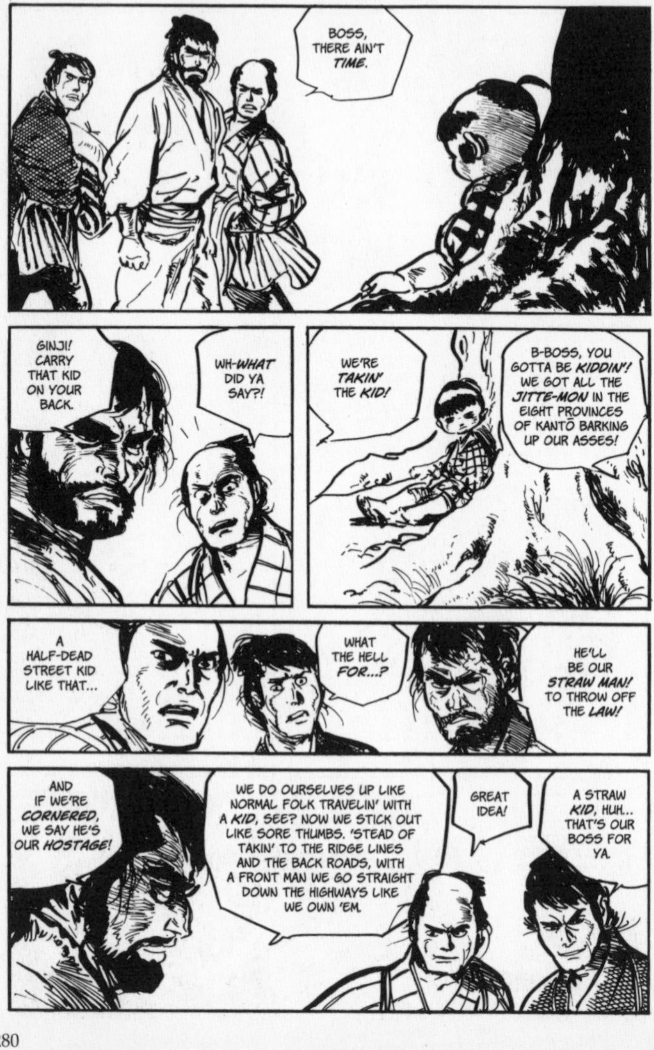
BOSS, THERE AIN'T TIME.
GINJI! CARRY THAT KID ON YOUR BACK.
WH-WHAT DID YA SAY?!
WE'RE TAKIN' THE KID!
B-BOSS, YOU GOTTA BE KIDDIN'! WE GOT ALL THE JITTE-MON IN THE EIGHT PROVINCES OF KANTŌ BARKING UP OUR ASSES!
A HALF-DEAD STREET KID LIKE THAT...
WHAT THE HELL FOR...?
HE'LL BE OUR STRAW MAN! TO THROW OFF THE LAW!
AND IF WE'RE CORNERED, WE SAY HE'S OUR HOSTAGE!
WE DO OURSELVES UP LIKE NORMAL FOLK TRAVELIN' WITH A KID, SEE? NOW WE STICK OUT LIKE SORE THUMBS. 'STEAD OF TAKIN' TO THE RIDGE LINES AND THE BACK ROADS, WITH A FRONT MAN WE GO STRAIGHT DOWN THE HIGHWAYS LIKE WE OWN 'EM.
GREAT IDEA!
A STRAW KID, HUH... THAT'S OUR BOSS FOR YA.

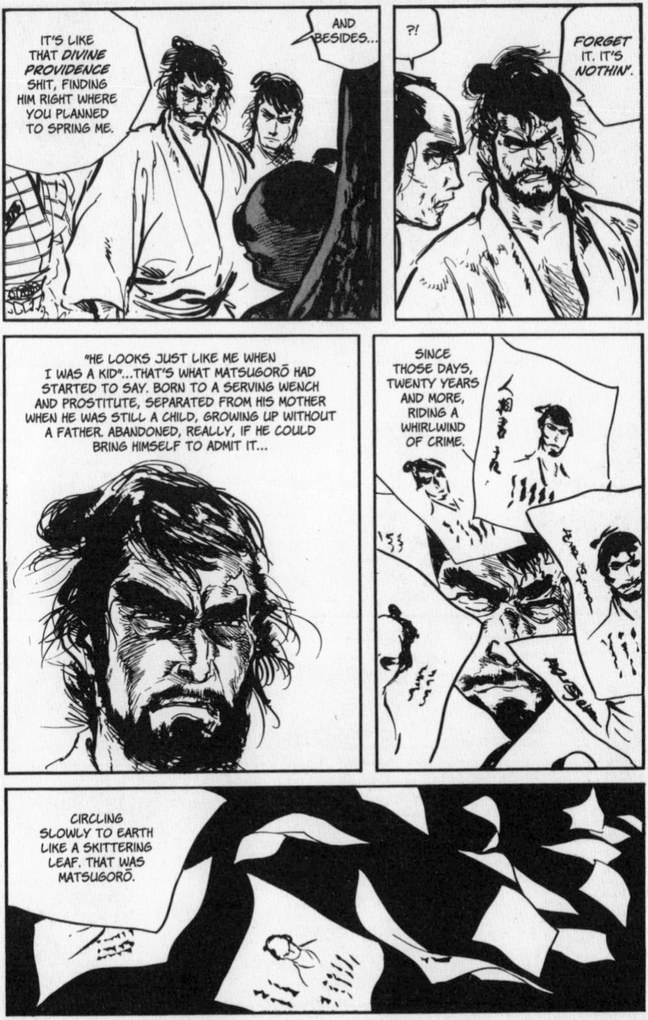
IT'S LIKE THAT *DIVINE PROVIDENCE* SHIT, FINDING HIM RIGHT WHERE YOU PLANNED TO SPRING ME.
AND BESIDES...
?!
FORGET IT. IT'S *NOTHIN'*.
"HE LOOKS JUST LIKE ME WHEN I WAS A KID"...THAT'S WHAT MATSUGORŌ HAD STARTED TO SAY. BORN TO A SERVING WENCH AND PROSTITUTE, SEPARATED FROM HIS MOTHER WHEN HE WAS STILL A CHILD, GROWING UP WITHOUT A FATHER. ABANDONED, REALLY, IF HE COULD BRING HIMSELF TO ADMIT IT...
SINCE THOSE DAYS, TWENTY YEARS AND MORE, RIDING A WHIRLWIND OF CRIME.
CIRCLING SLOWLY TO EARTH LIKE A SKITTERING LEAF. THAT WAS MATSUGORŌ.

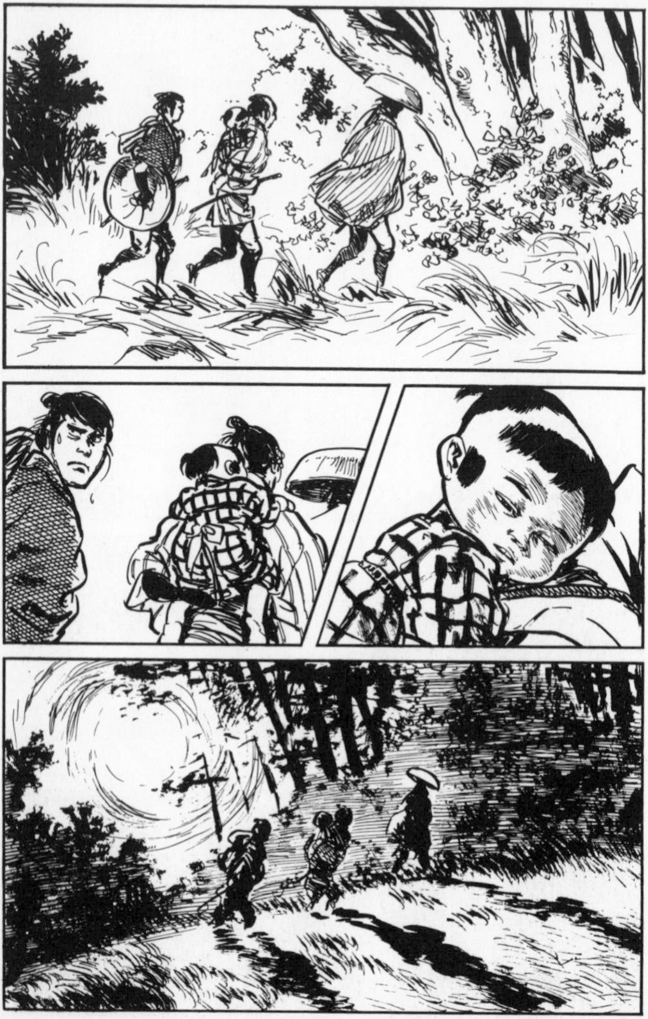

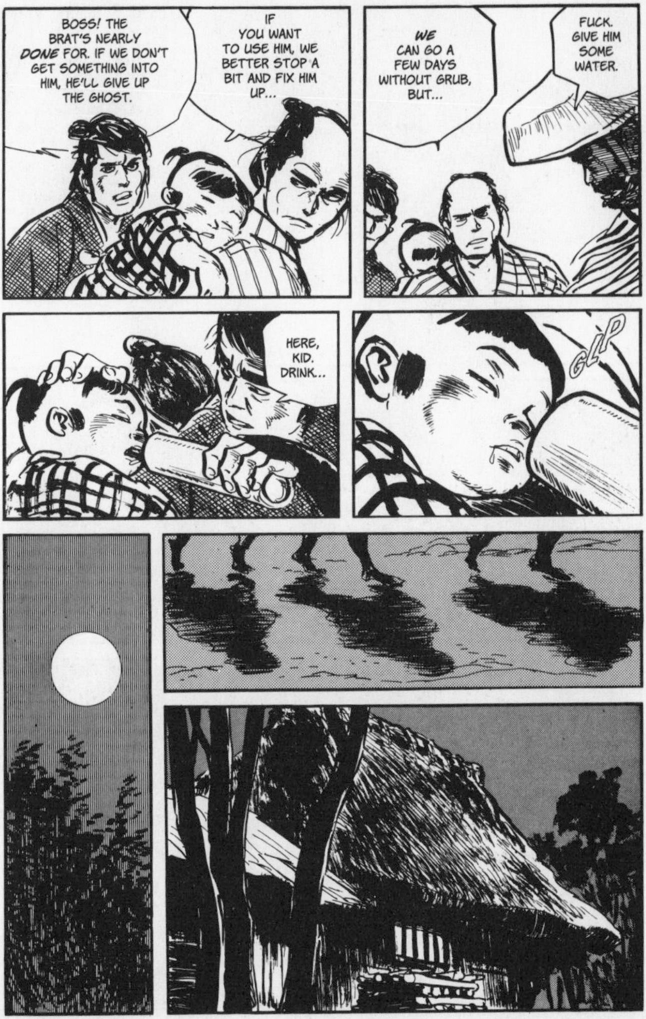
BOSS! THE BRAT'S NEARLY *DONE* FOR. IF WE DON'T GET SOMETHING INTO HIM, HE'LL GIVE UP THE GHOST.
IF YOU WANT TO USE HIM, WE BETTER STOP A BIT AND FIX HIM UP...
WE CAN GO A FEW DAYS WITHOUT GRUB, BUT...
FUCK. GIVE HIM SOME WATER.
HERE, KID. DRINK...
GLP

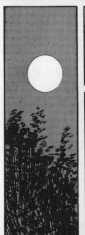

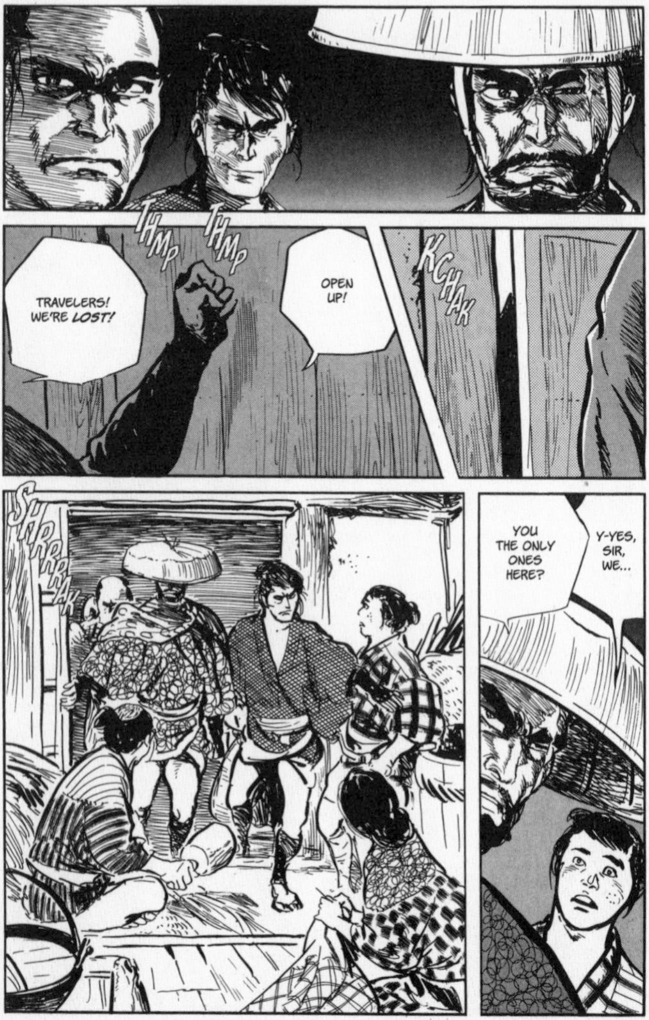
THMP
THMP
TRAVELERS! WE'RE LOST!
OPEN UP!
KCHAK
SHRRRAK
YOU THE ONLY ONES HERE?
Y-YES, SIR, WE...

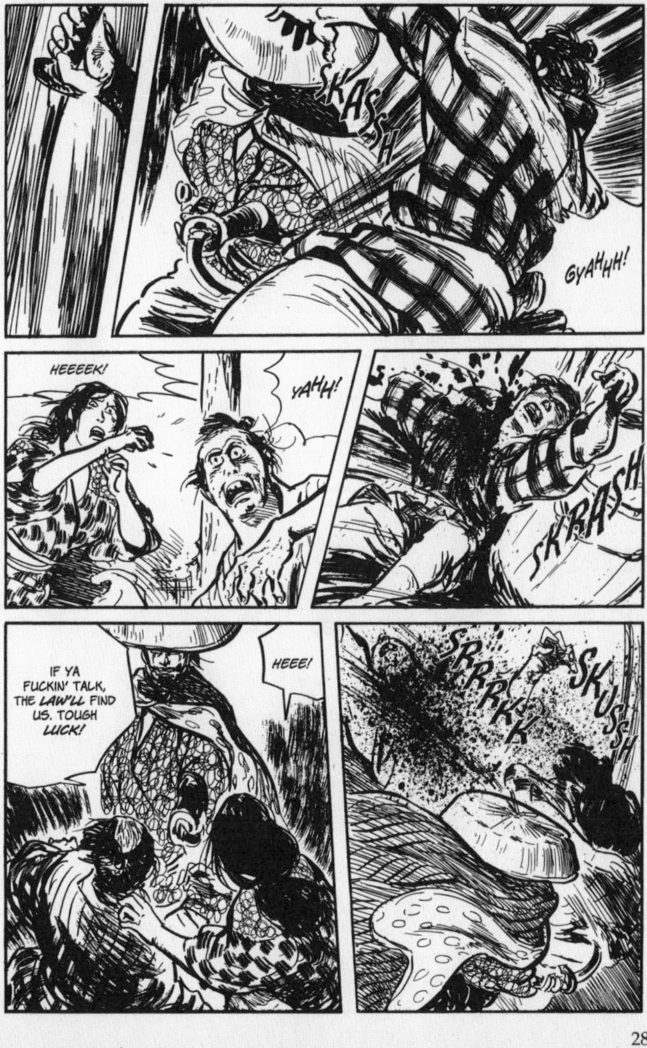
SKASSH
GYAHHH!
HEEEEK!
YAHH!
SKRASH
IF YA FUCKIN' TALK, THE *LAW'LL* FIND US. TOUGH *LUCK!*
HEEE!
SRRRKKK
SKUSSH

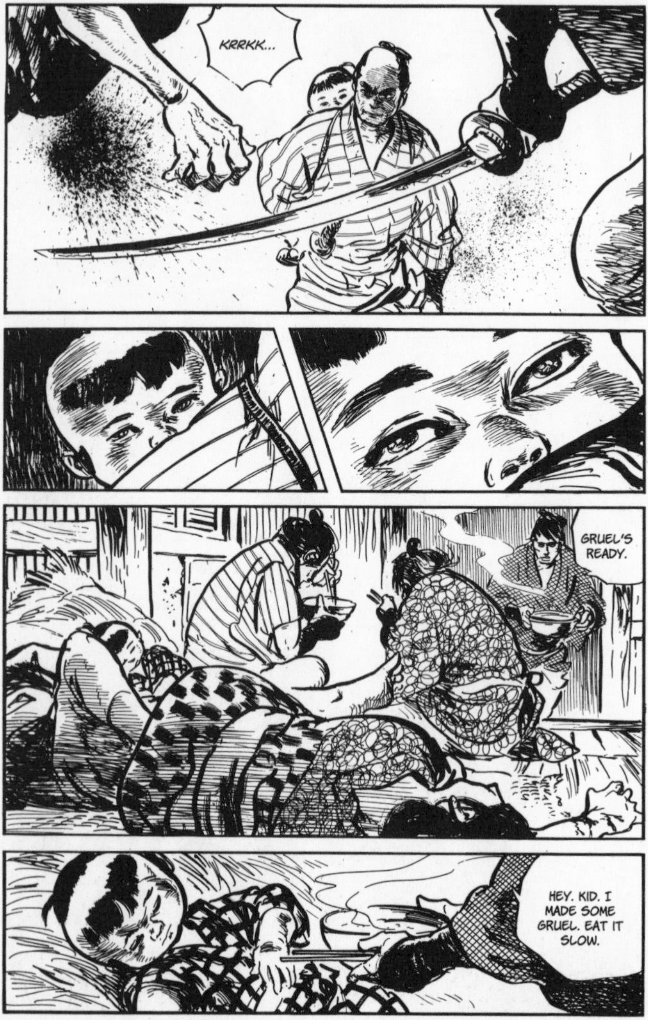
KRRKK...
GRUEL'S READY.
HEY. KID. I MADE SOME GRUEL. EAT IT SLOW.

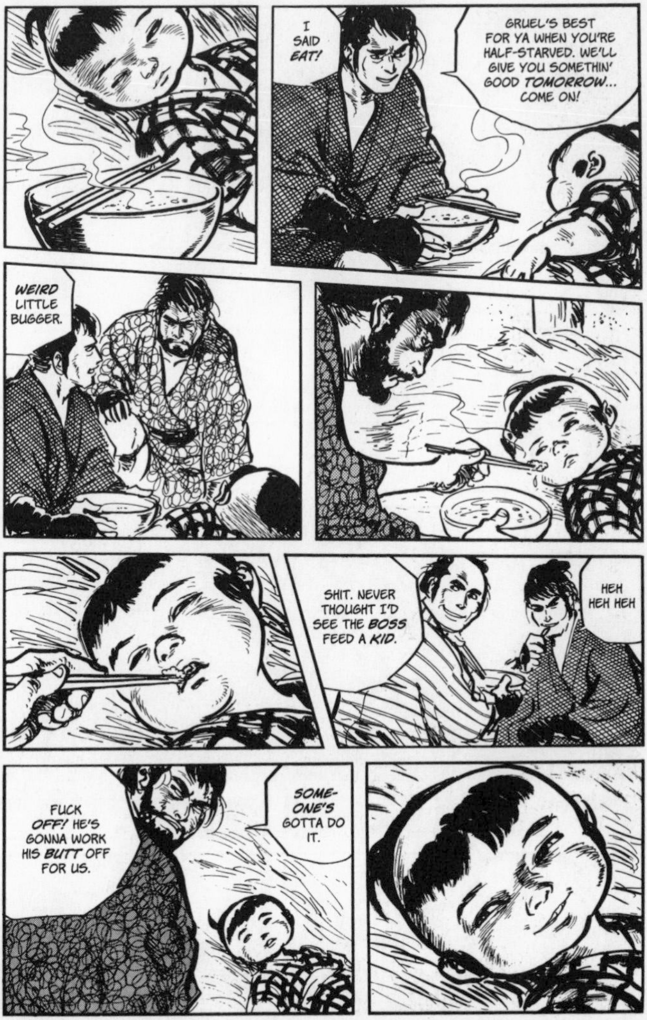
I SAID *EAT!*
GRUEL'S BEST FOR YA WHEN YOU'RE HALF-STARVED. WE'LL GIVE YOU SOMETHIN' GOOD *TOMORROW*... COME ON!
WEIRD LITTLE BUGGER.
SHIT. NEVER THOUGHT I'D SEE THE *BOSS* FEED A *KID*.
HEH HEH HEH
FUCK *OFF!* HE'S GONNA WORK HIS *BUTT* OFF FOR US.
SOME-ONE'S GOTTA DO IT.

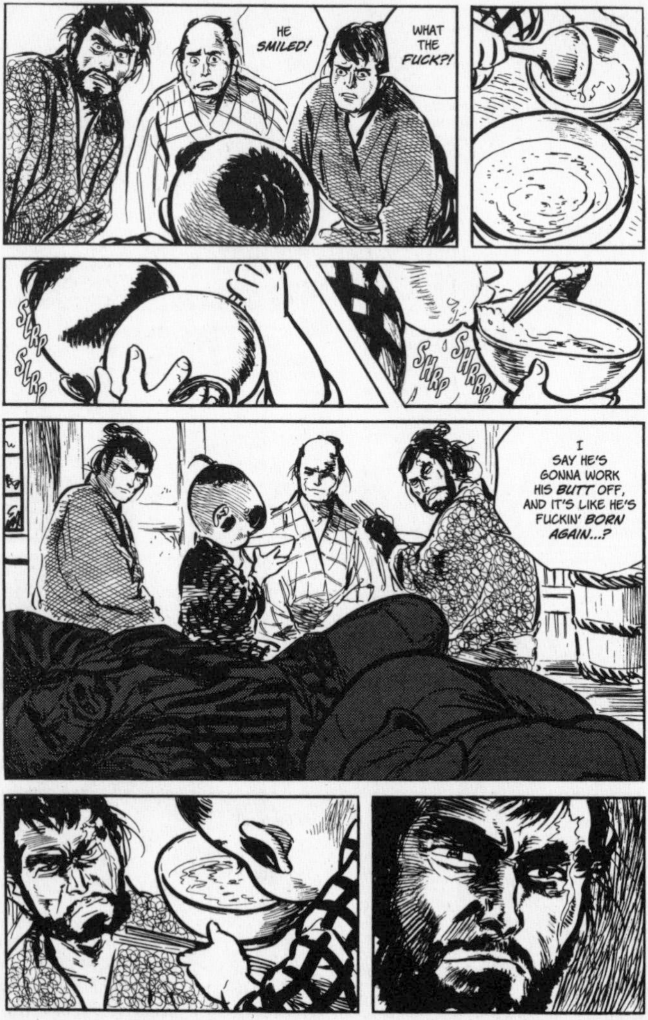
HE *SMILED!*
WHAT THE *FUCK?!*
SLRP SLRP
SHRP SHRRP
I SAY HE'S GONNA WORK HIS *BUTT* OFF, AND IT'S LIKE HE'S FUCKIN' *BORN AGAIN...?*

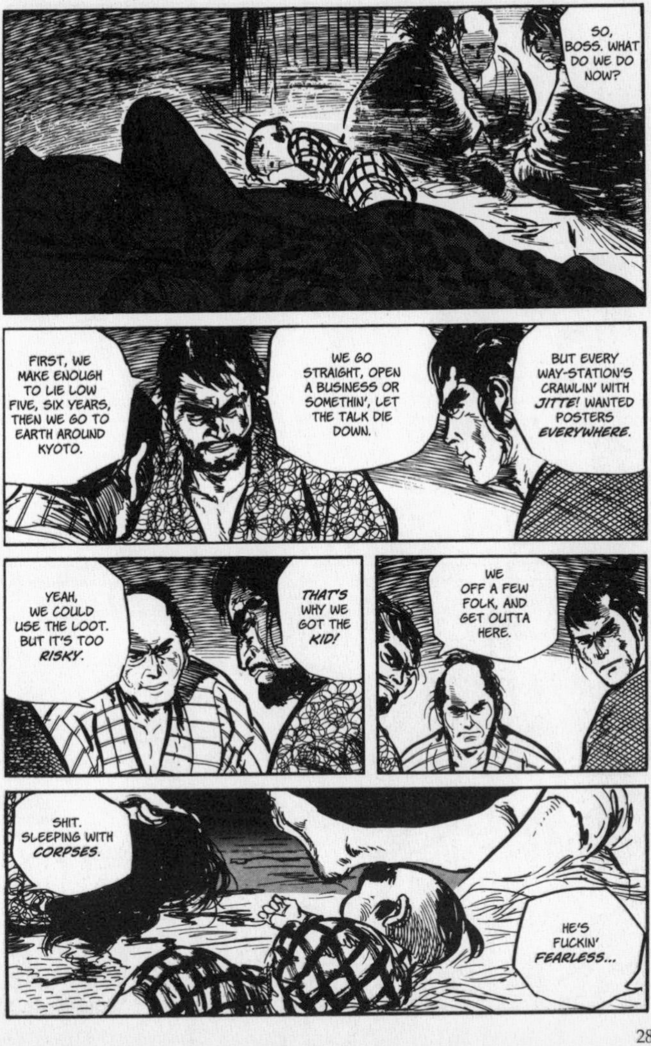
SO, BOSS. WHAT DO WE DO NOW?
FIRST, WE MAKE ENOUGH TO LIE LOW FIVE, SIX YEARS, THEN WE GO TO EARTH AROUND KYOTO.
WE GO STRAIGHT, OPEN A BUSINESS OR SOMETHIN', LET THE TALK DIE DOWN.
BUT EVERY WAY-STATION'S CRAWLIN' WITH JITTE! WANTED POSTERS EVERYWHERE.
YEAH, WE COULD USE THE LOOT. BUT IT'S TOO RISKY.
THAT'S WHY WE GOT THE KID!
WE OFF A FEW FOLK, AND GET OUTTA HERE.
SHIT. SLEEPING WITH CORPSES.
HE'S FUCKIN' FEARLESS...

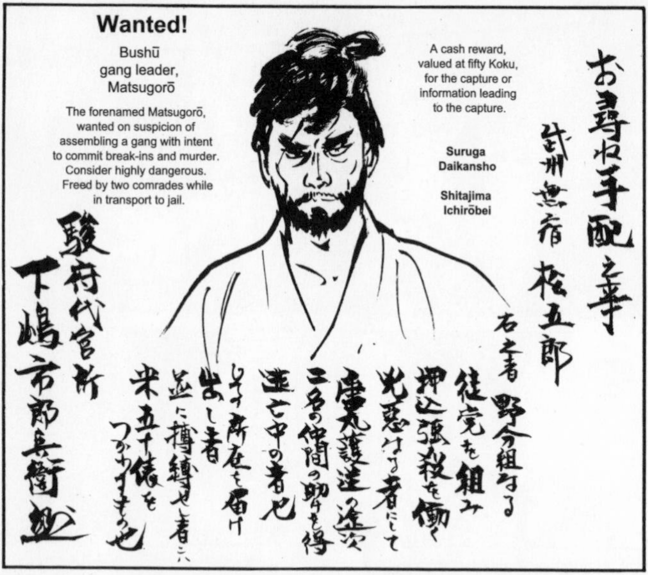
Wanted!
Bushū gang leader, Matsugorō
The forenamed Matsugorō, wanted on suspicion of assembling a gang with intent to commit break-ins and murder. Consider highly dangerous. Freed by two comrades while in transport to jail.
A cash reward, valued at fifty Koku, for the capture or information leading to the capture.
Suruga Daikansho
Shitajima Ichirōbei
お尋ね手配之事
武州無宿 松五郎
駿府代官所
下嶋市郎兵衛

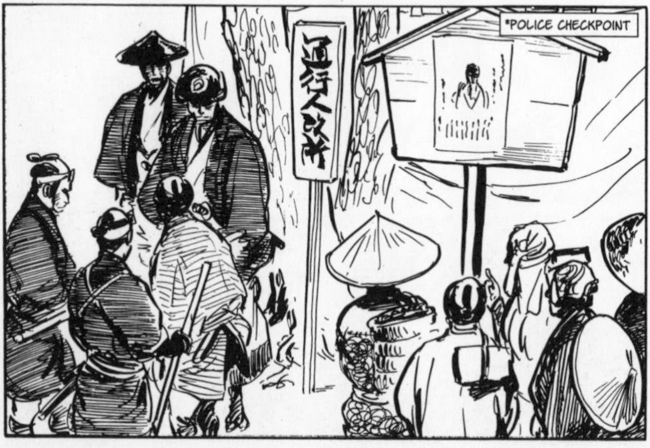
*POLICE CHECKPOINT
通行人改所

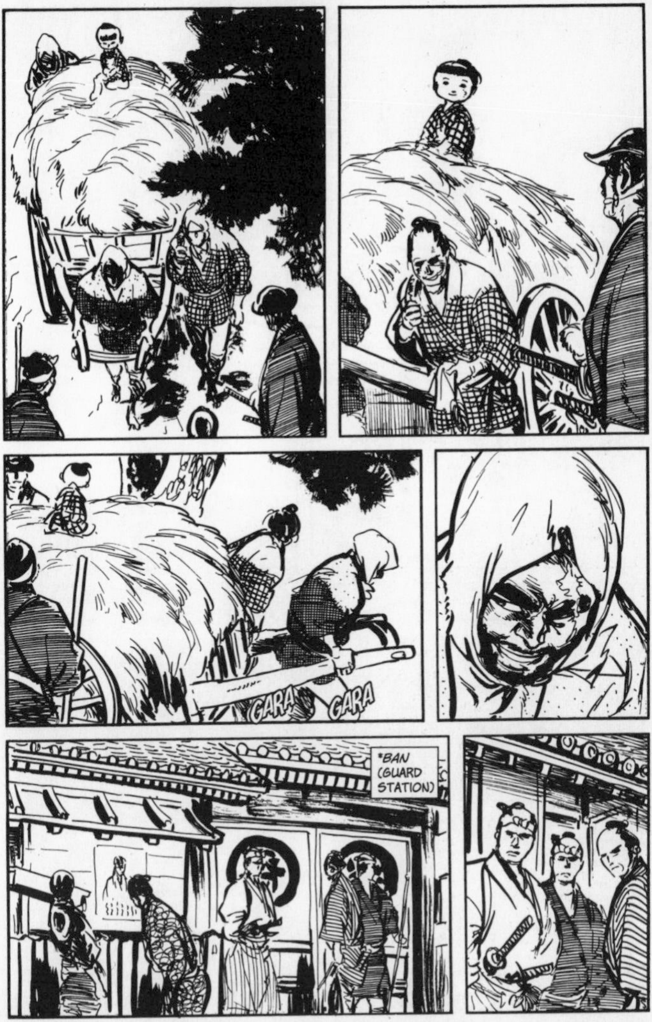
GARA GARA
*BAN (GUARD STATION)

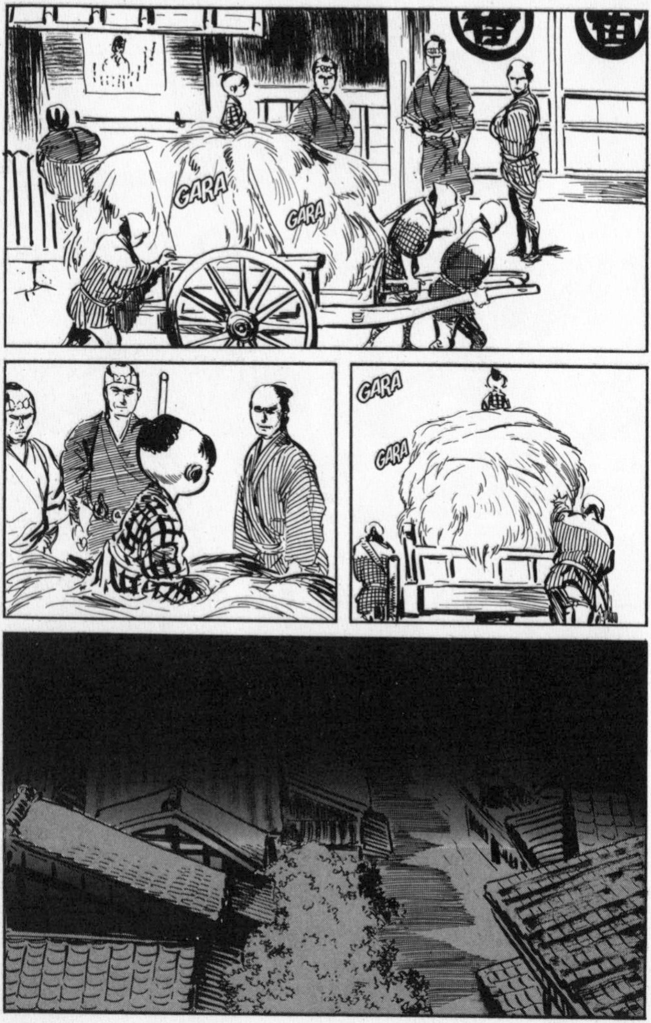
GARA
GARA
GARA
GARA

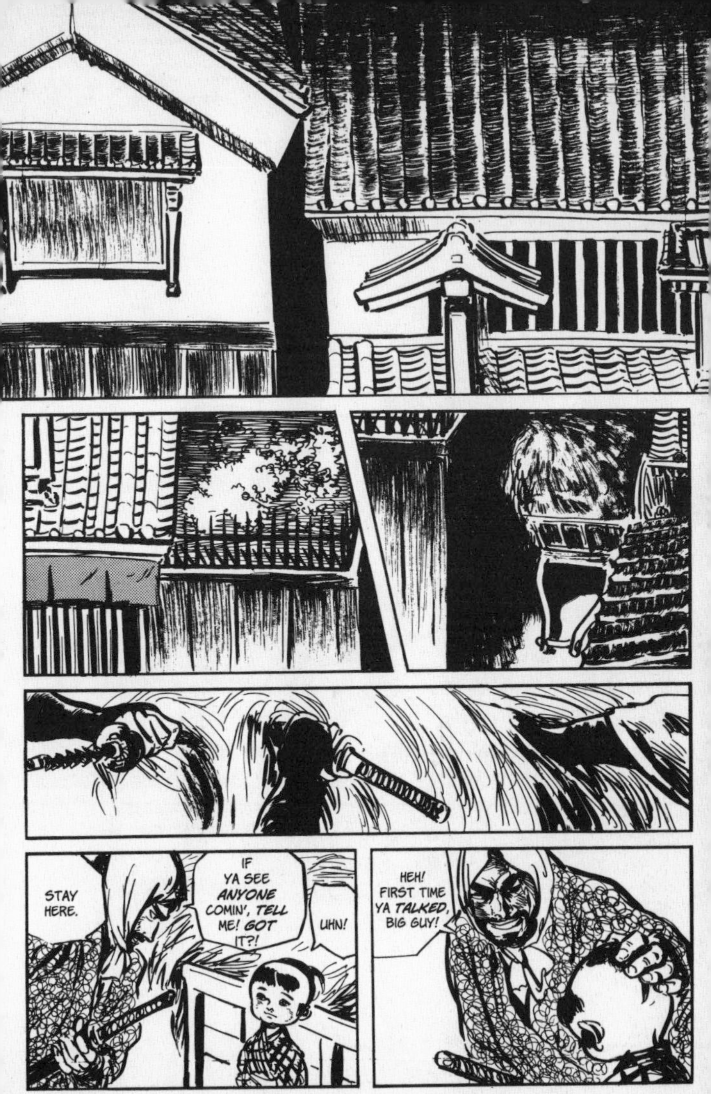
STAY HERE.
IF YA SEE ANYONE COMIN', TELL ME! GOT IT?!
UHN!
HEH! FIRST TIME YA TALKED, BIG GUY!

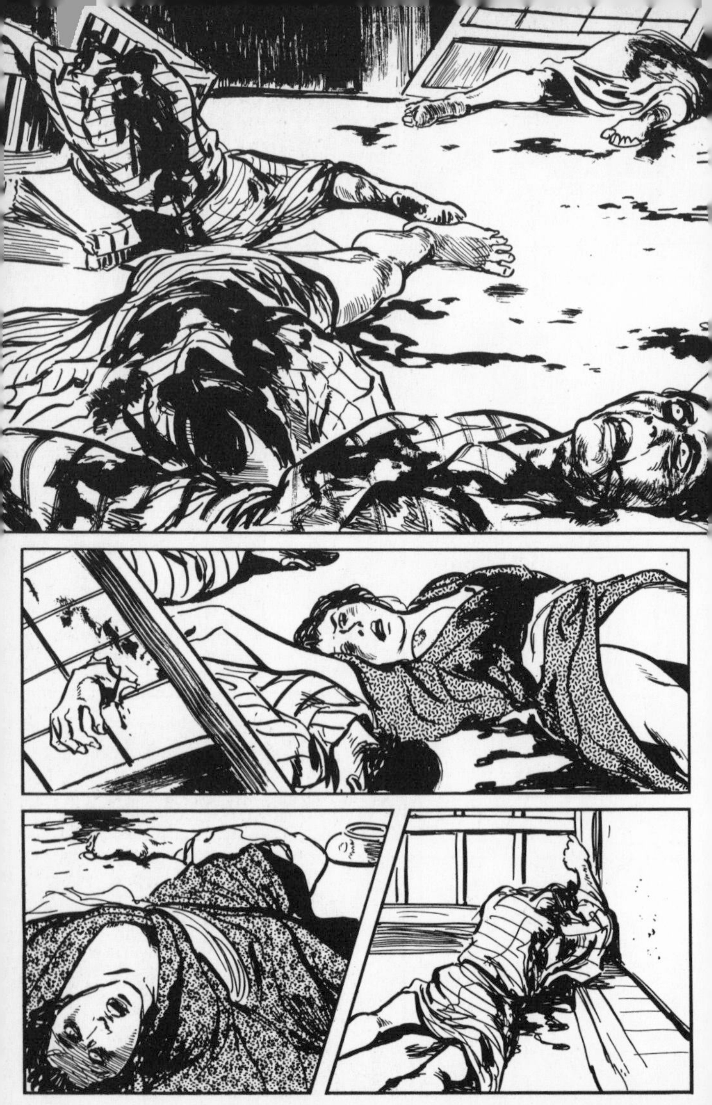

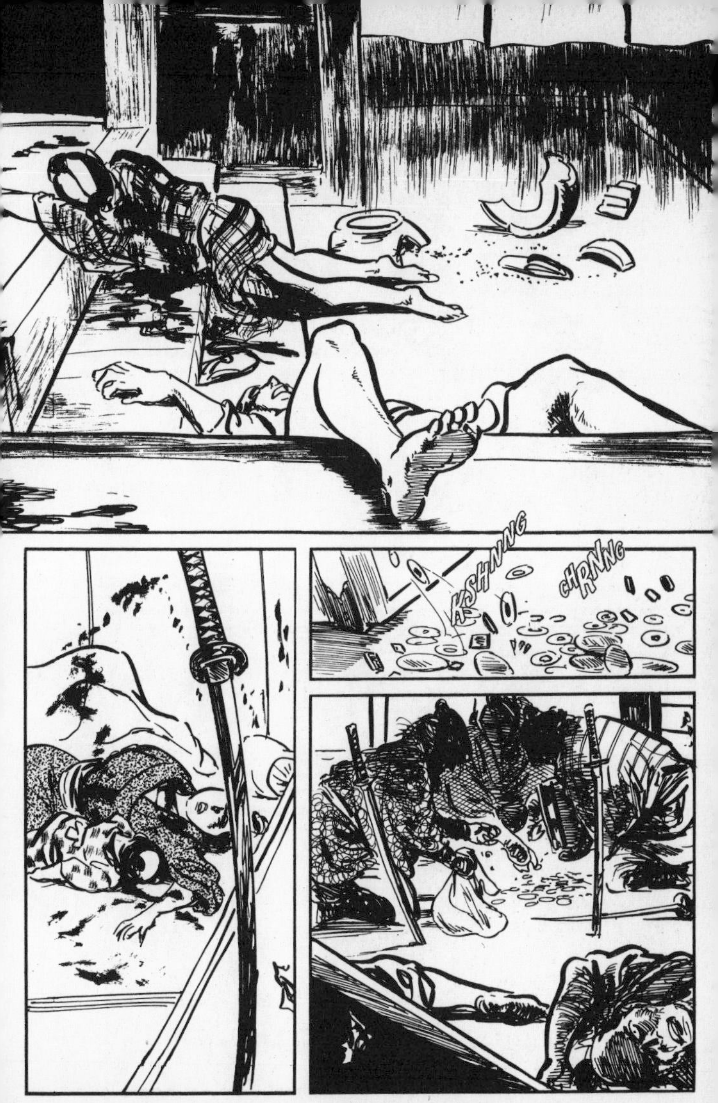
KSHNNG
CHRNNG

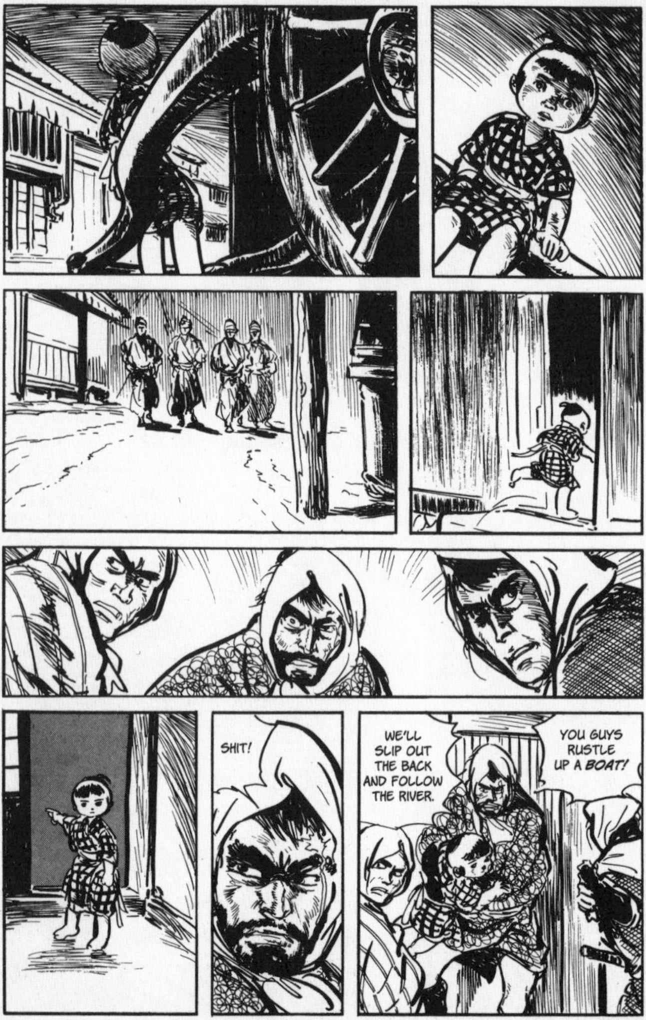
SHIT!
WE'LL SLIP OUT THE BACK AND FOLLOW THE RIVER.
YOU GUYS RUSTLE UP A *BOAT!*

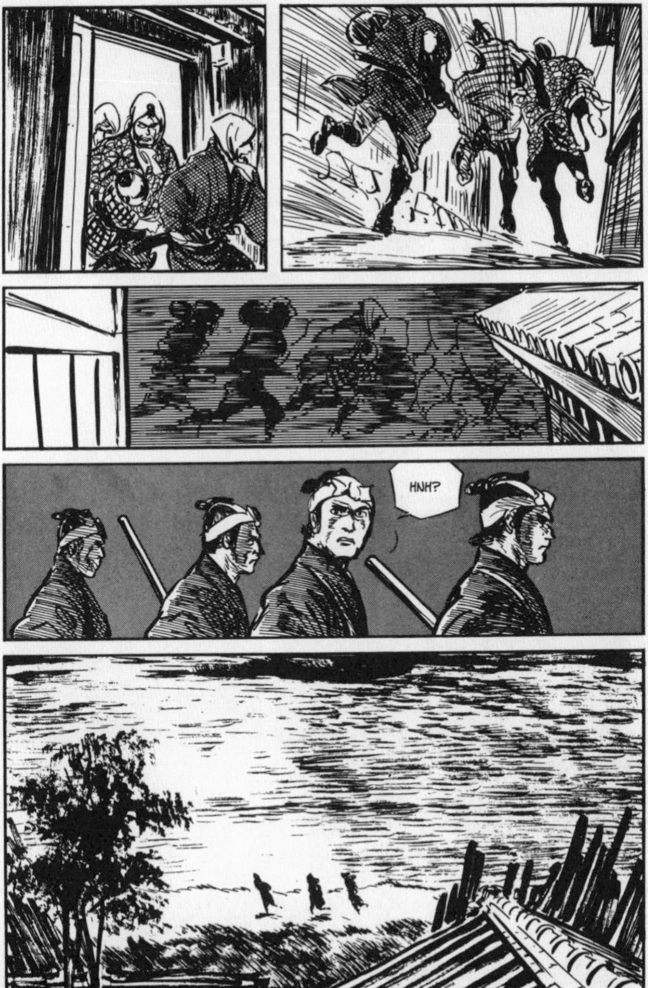
HNH?

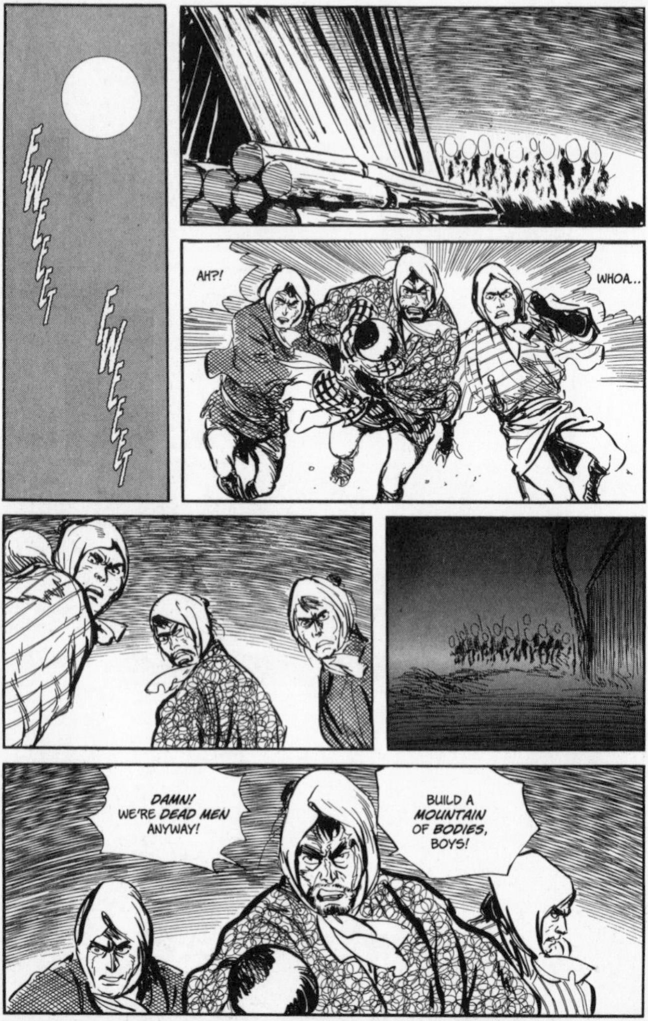
FWEEET
FWEEET
AH?!
WHOA...
DAMN! WE'RE DEAD MEN ANYWAY!
BUILD A MOUNTAIN OF BODIES, BOYS!

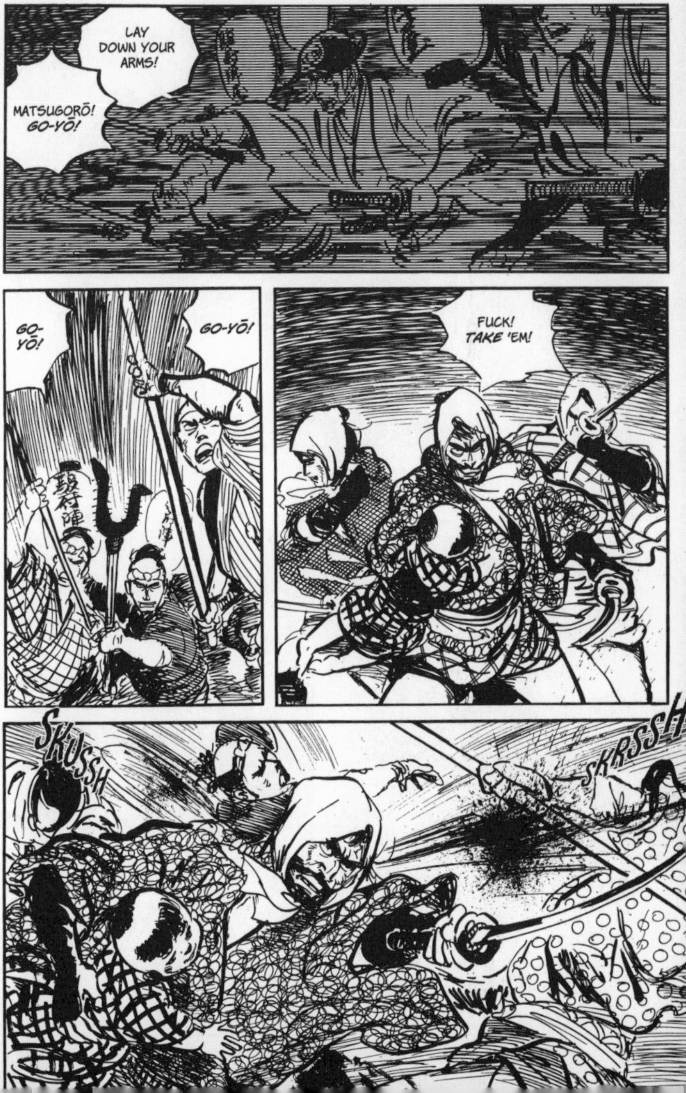
LAY DOWN YOUR ARMS!
MATSUGORŌ! GO-YŌ!
GO-YŌ!
GO-YŌ!
FUCK! TAKE 'EM!
SKUSSH
SKRSSH

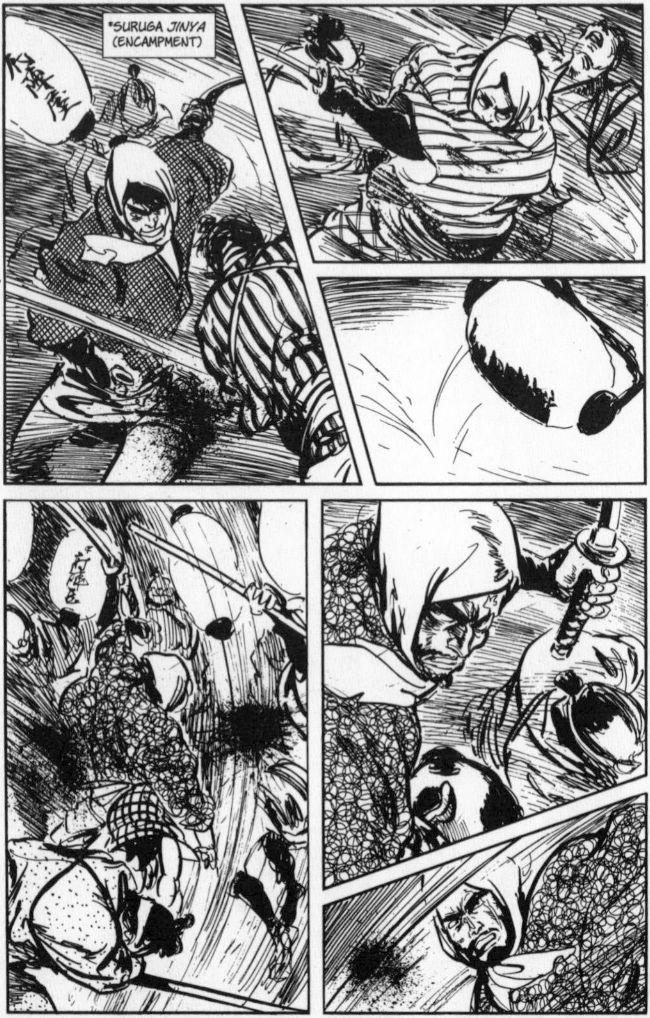
*SURUGA JINYA
(ENCAMPMENT)

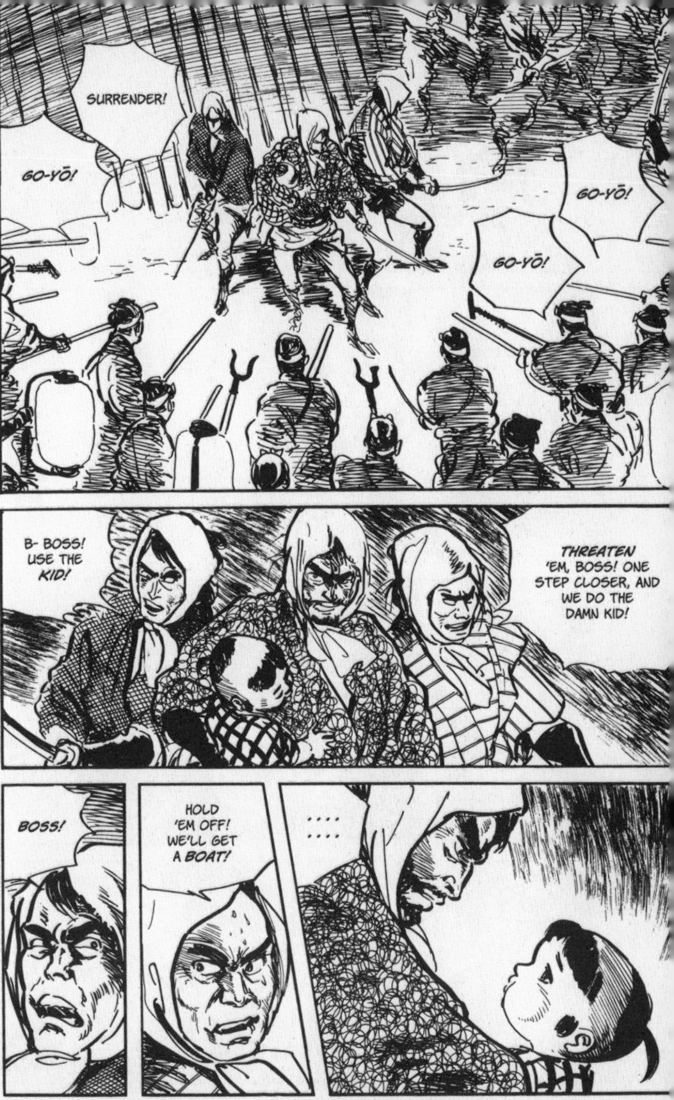
SURRENDER!
GO-YŌ!
GO-YŌ!
GO-YŌ!
B- BOSS! USE THE KID!
THREATEN 'EM, BOSS! ONE STEP CLOSER, AND WE DO THE DAMN KID!
BOSS!
HOLD 'EM OFF! WE'LL GET A BOAT!
....
....

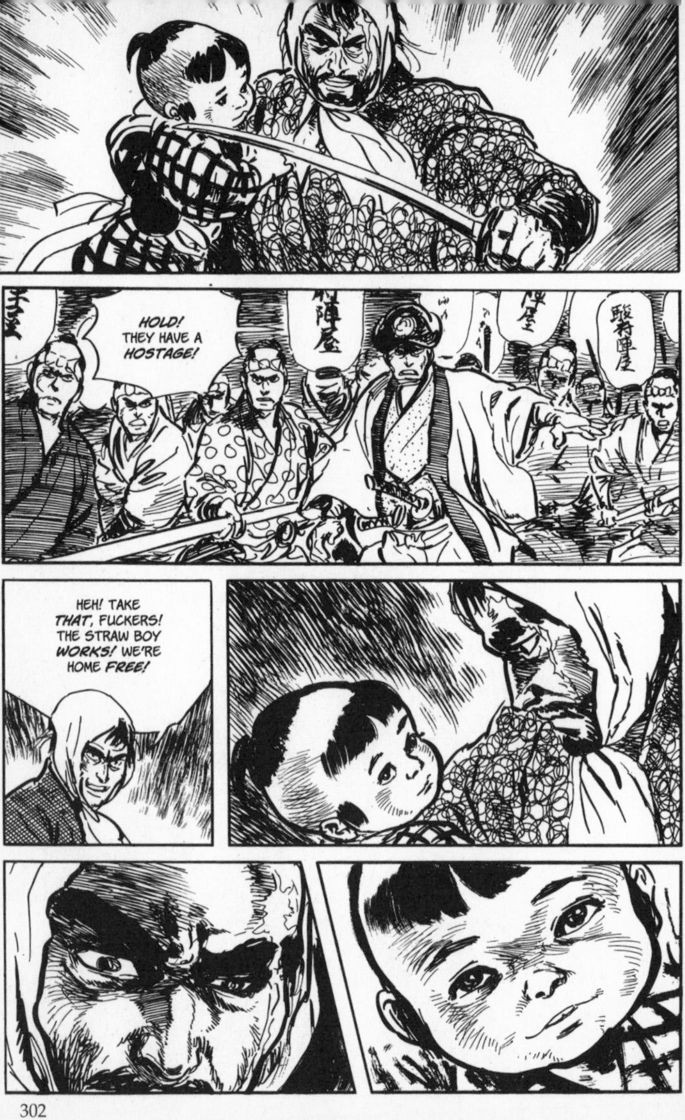
HOLD! THEY HAVE A HOSTAGE!
HEH! TAKE THAT, FUCKERS! THE STRAW BOY WORKS! WE'RE HOME FREE!

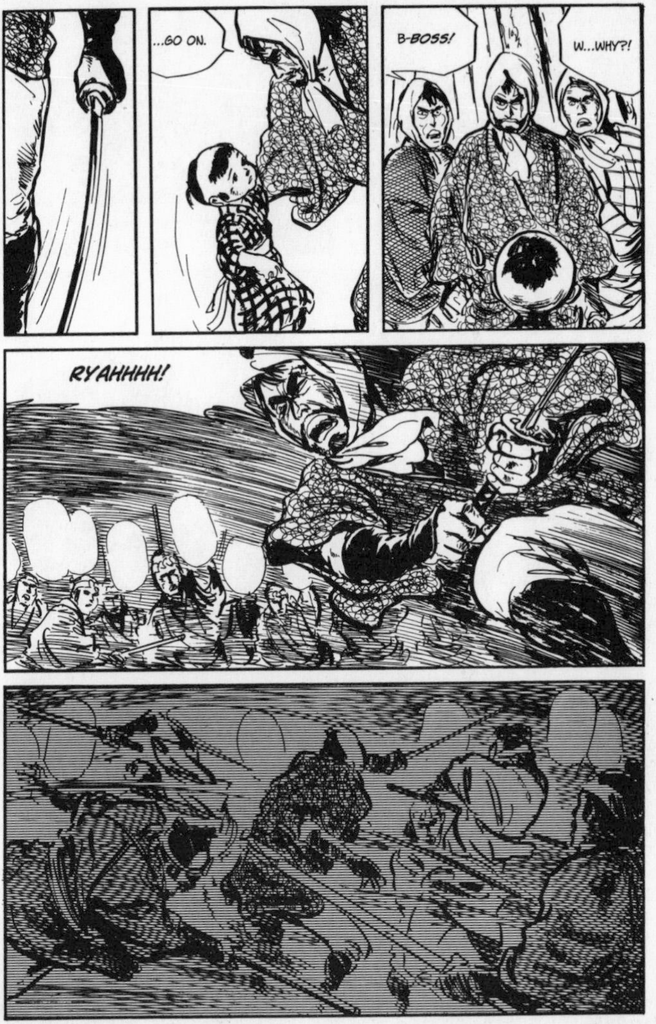
...GO ON.
B-BOSS!
W...WHY?!
RYAHHHH!

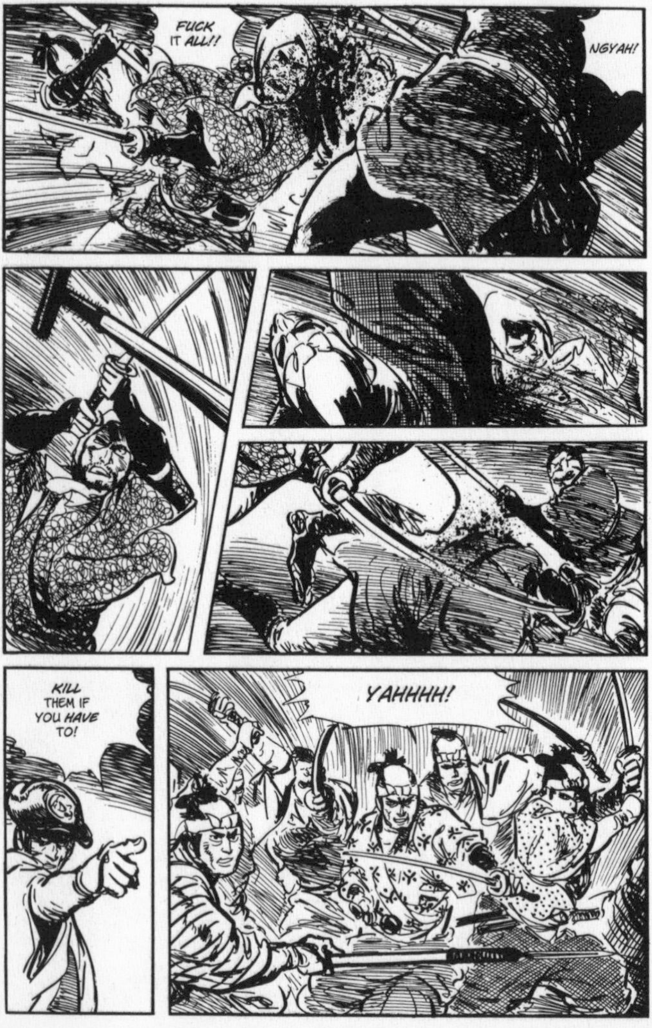
FUCK IT ALL!!
NGYAH!
KILL THEM IF YOU HAVE TO!
YAHHHH!

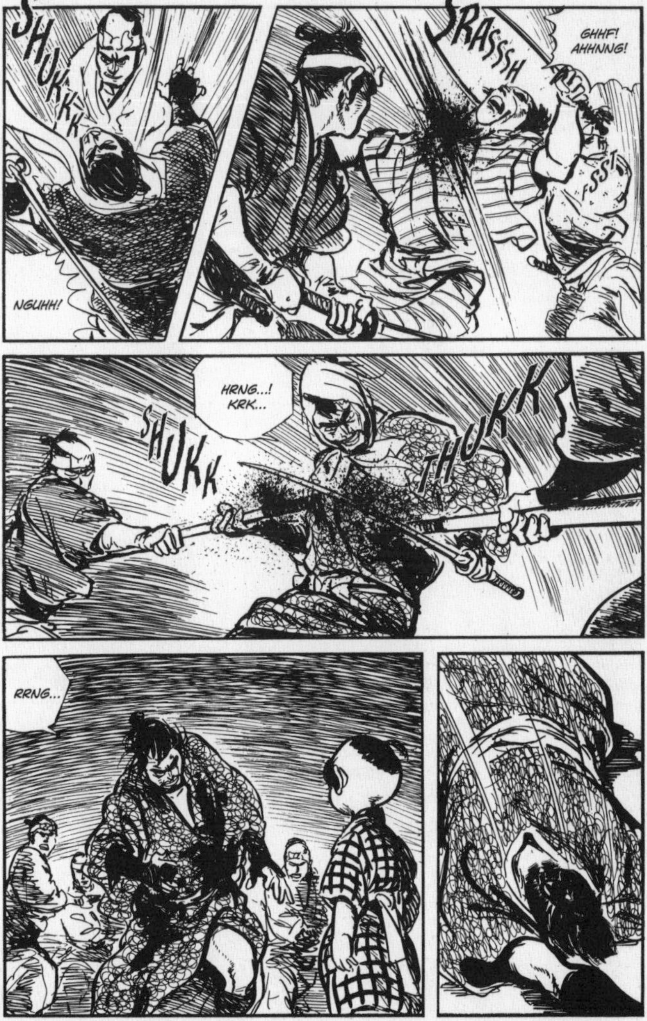
SHUKKK
NGUHH!
SRASSSH
GHHF! AHHNNG!
FSST
HRNG...! KRK...
SHUKK
THUKK
RRNG...

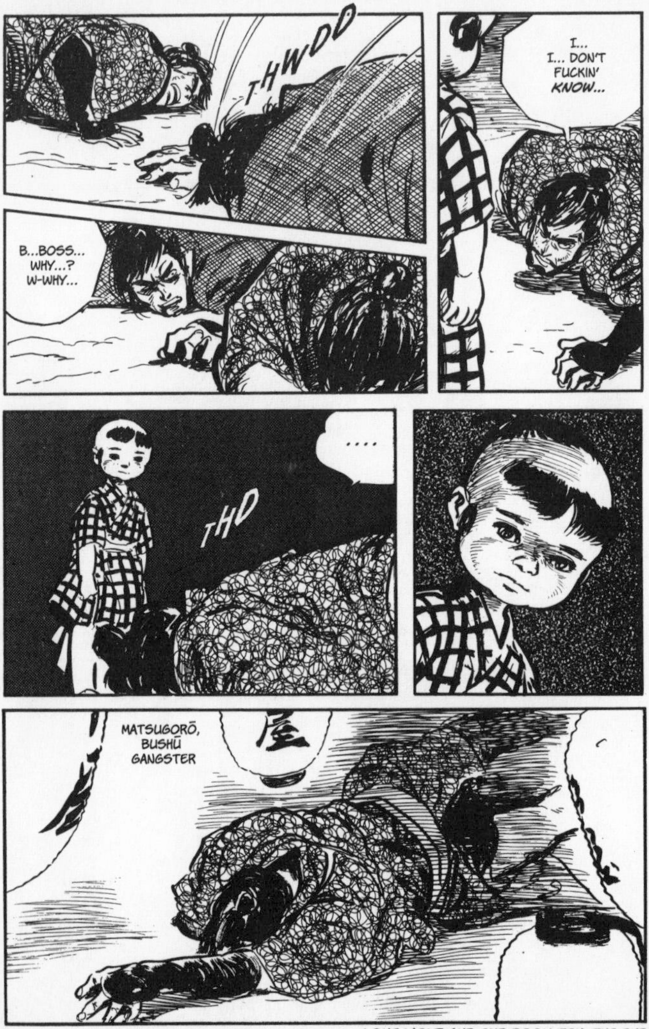
THWDD
I...
I... DON'T FUCKIN' KNOW...
B...BOSS... WHY...? W-WHY...
....
THD
MATSUGORŌ, BUSHŪ GANGSTER
屋

LONE WOLF AND CUB BOOK TEN: THE END
TO BE CONTINUED

GLOSSARY

bushū

Another term for Musashi, the area encompassing most of the Kantō Plain around modern-day Tokyo.

dōtanuki

A battle sword. Literally, "sword that cuts through torsos."

gojō-bako

Lacquered, waterproof box used to carry official correspondence between the shōgunate in Edo and its regional officials.

go-yō

Official business. As a lantern carried by the officers of the *daikan* magistrate, the equivalent of today's national police, or as the shout of the police apprehending a criminal, "*go-yō*" was one of the most dreaded words in the world of Edo Japan's criminal elements.

han

A feudal domain.

hanshi

Samurai in the service of a *han*.

honorifics

Japan is a class and status society, and proper forms of address are critical. Common markers of respect are the prefixes *o* and *go*, and a wide range of suffixes. Some of the suffixes you will encounter in *Lone Wolf and Cub*:

dono – archaic; used for higher-ranked or highly respected figures
sama – used for superiors

jitte-mon

A policeman. The street cops of the Edo period carried *jitte*, a specialized weapon about 18 inches long, with no cutting edge — just two prongs designed to catch and snap off an opponent's sword blade.

jizō

Local deities, represented by simple stone statues by the roadside. Often decorated with red cloth bibs.

Kantō

Literally, "east of the gate." Eastern Japan, north of the mountain chain around Mount Fuji, especially the region around Edo, present-day Tokyo.

kenkyaku

Swordsman, *kenshi*.

koku

A bale of rice. The traditional measure of a *han*'s wealth, a measure of its agricultural land and productivity.

Kyoto shoshidai

The shōgun's emissary to the Imperial Court in Kyoto. Although real power lay with the shōgun in Edo, the shōgunate maintained the fiction that the emperor was the ultimate authority in Japan. The *shoshidai* maintained contact with the imperial household and the aristocracy, and oversaw tax collection and other *shōgunate* business in the old capital.

meifumadō

The Buddhist Hell. The way of demons and damnation.

nagamaki

A two-handed weapon taller than a man, with a long, curved blade.

ri

Old unit of measurement. Approximately 4 kilometers (2.5 miles).

rōnin

A masterless samurai. Literally, "one adrift on the waves." Members of the samurai caste who have lost their masters through the dissolution of *han*, expulsion for misbehavior, or other reasons. Prohibited from working as farmers or merchants under the strict Confucian caste system imposed by the Tokugawa shōgunate, many impoverished *rōnin* became "hired guns" for whom the code of the samurai was nothing but empty words.

sakki

The palpable desire to kill, directed at another person. Sometimes called blood lust. Based on the concept of *ki*, or energy, found in spiritual practices and Japanese martial arts like Aikido. These body energies can be felt beyond the physical self by the trained and self-aware.

sekisho

Checkpoint regulating travel from Edo to other parts of the country. All travelers had to submit papers at official checkpoints along the main highways in and out of Edo.

shinobi

A generic term for ninja, meaning "one who moves in secrecy." Ninja had their heyday in the time of warring states before the rise of the Tokugawa clan. Originally mercenaries serving different warlords, by the Edo period they were in the service of the central government. The most famous *shinobi* were the ninja of Iga and Kaga, north of Kyoto. The Kurokuwa that appear in *Lone Wolf and Cub* were officially the laborers and manual workers in Edo Castle. Whether they truly served as a secret spy corps is lost in history.

yakuza

Japan's criminal syndicates. In the Edo period, *yakuza* were a common part of the landscape, running houses of gambling and prostitution. As long as they did not overstep their bounds, they were tolerated by the authorities, a tradition little changed in modern Japan.

zanbatō

The mythical horse-slicing stroke used by Ōgami Ittō.

KAZUO KOIKE

Though widely respected as a powerful writer of graphic fiction, Kazuo Koike has spent a lifetime reaching beyond the bounds of the comics medium. Aside from co-creating and writing the successful *Lone Wolf and Cub* and *Crying Freeman* manga, Koike has hosted television programs; founded a golf magazine; produced movies; written popular fiction, poetry, and screenplays; and mentored some of Japan's best manga talent.

Lone Wolf and Cub was first serialized in Japan in 1970 (under the title *Kozure Okami*) in *Manga Action* magazine and continued its hugely popular run for many years, being collected as the stories were published, and reprinted worldwide. Koike collected numerous awards for his work on the series throughout the next decade. Starting in 1972, Koike adapted the popular manga into a series of six films, the *Baby Cart Assassin* saga, garnering widespread commercial success and critical acclaim for his screenwriting.

This wasn't Koike's only foray into film and video. In 1996, *Crying Freeman*, the manga Koike created with artist Ryoichi Ikegami, was produced in Hollywood and released to commercial success in Europe and is currently awaiting release in America.

And to give something back to the medium that gave him so much, Koike started the *Gekiga Sonjuku*, a college course aimed at helping talented writers and artists — such as *Ranma 1/2* creator Rumiko Takahashi — break into the comics field.

The driving focus of Koike's narrative is character development, and his commitment to character is clear: "Comics are carried by characters. If a character is well created, the comic becomes a hit." Kazuo Koike's continued success in comics and literature has proven this philosophy true.

GOSEKI KOJIMA

Goseki Kojima was born on November 3, 1928, the very same day as the godfather of Japanese comics, Osamu Tezuka. While just out of junior high school, the self-taught Kojima began painting advertising posters for movie theaters to pay his bills.

In 1950, Kojima moved to Tokyo, where the postwar devastation had given rise to special manga forms for audiences too poor to buy the new manga magazines. Kojima created art for *kami-shibai*, or "paper-play" narrators, who would use manga story sheets to present narrated street plays. Kojima moved on to creating works for the *kashi-bon* market, bookstores that rented out books, magazines, and manga to mostly low-income readers. He soon became highly popular among *kashi-bon* readers.

In 1967, Kojima broke into the magazine market with his series *Dojinki*. As the manga magazine market grew and diversified, he turned out a steady stream of popular series.

In 1970, in collaboration with Kazuo Koike, Kojima began the work that would seal his reputation, *Kozure Okami (Lone Wolf and Cub)*. Before long the story had become a gigantic hit, eventually spinning off a television series, six motion pictures, and even theme-song records. Koike and Kojima were soon dubbed the "golden duo" and produced success after success on their way to the pinnacle of the manga world.

When *Manga Japan* magazine was launched in 1994, Kojima was asked to serve as consultant, and he helped train the next generation of manga artists.

In his final years, Kojima turned to creating original graphic novels based on the movies of his favorite director, Akira Kurosawa. Kojima passed away on January 5, 2000 at the age of 71.

THE RONIN REPORT

by Tim Ervin-Gore

Lone Wolf and Cub in Film, Part 1

Sword of Vengeance

Note: this is not a review, but a discussion piece. If you haven't seen this movie yet, read only the first two paragraphs. The rest might spoil your movie watching experience.

As *Lone Wolf and Cub* swept Japan in a wave of black-ink blood, a series of films and television programs followed closely in its tide. While the manga these were based on is indisputably a masterpiece, not all of the live-action adaptations were as great. Only two years after the manga began its serialization, the first of a six-movie set, known as the "Baby Cart" series, hit the screens in Japan. These films were the cream of the *Lone Wolf* crop, with screenplays by creator Kazuo Koike, graceful direction by Kenji Misumi, consistent acting by Wakayama Tomisaburo as Ogami Itto, and a well-cast Akihiro Tomikawa as Daigoro. Amazingly, the six films in the series were produced within a five-year time frame. Kojima's scripts, cut-and-pasted packages of important elements and pertinent scenes from the manga, form a condensed universe of Ogami's Japan. Visually, the comic book translates easily to the director's eye, owing to artist Goseki Kojima's cinematic style. *Lone Wolf and Cub* reads like a monument to film, with repeating frames, extremely graceful timing, and similar framing compositions and patterns.

Though comic books and film share many aesthetic similarities, it is difficult to successfully adapt a comic book to film, as it usually involves significant trimming and changing the plot to fit the short attention span of movie watchers, who expect to be engaged by an entire story within two hours. Conversely, comics readers often desire lengthy narratives to justify the cover price (or at least they should). That said, the film adaptations of the "Baby Cart" series were up against tough odds, but they turned out to be pretty darn good. This is at least partly attributed to the amount of film afforded by its serialization. But certainly, the films themselves stand on their own and hand-feed the viewer a serious dose of drama, honor, beauty, and profuse, squirting blood.

The first film in the series, *Sword of Vengeance* (the pre-translated Japanese title is closer to "Son for Hire, Sword for Hire"), starts in a very respectful manner, with the beheading of the young lord from the manga story "The White Path Between the Rivers." From the first moment, the avid reader will notice how well the movie was put together. The sets are lovingly recreated, the pace and emotion fits the original text, and many of the characters are faithfully depicted. However, in an abrupt departure, a retainer of the young lord, not Ogami, as in the original story, tenderly instructs him on the ceremonial placement of the fan against his abdomen. With one minor plot modification, the ironic juxtaposition of tenderness and violence that is central to Ogami's character is lost. The overall theme of Ogami's inner conflict, with everyone he respects questioning his path and being cut down in the process, is central to the book's story. This deletion affects the viewer's perception. Ogami comes across more as a heartless servant of an evil master. This sentiment continues throughout the movie as Wakayama

Tomisaburo, playing a scruffy and stoic Ogami, travels the byways of feudal Japan. In a short period of contextual narration, the shogunate takes the center stage to become the evil organization with Retsudo Yagyu at the helm. Then, in keeping with Koike's narrative style, the story breaks to the present, as Ogami and Daigoro wander the countryside together, pushing an excellent reconstruction of the infamous baby cart, complete with spring-loaded pole arms and "son for hire, sword for hire" flag. The countryside scenery is captivating, the music is emotionally moving, and a terribly rough samurai with his incredibly darling son are rolling across the lush landscape. Koike took the time to include a scene where Daigoro suckles at the breast of an unknown woman, but damn the limits of film for reducing the context of that breast to a crazy woman in the street. For some reason, having the breast belong to a fighting sister of a Yakuza clan

("Baby Cart on the River Styx," Vol. 1) made the scene in the comic book more resonant. Still, this is an important cue to Ogami's logical tenderness, and it's a good thing that Koike kept this detail in the film. The pace of the film is contemplative, maybe too much for American audiences, but fans of *Lone Wolf and Cub*'s somber gait might appreciate the breathing room. This slow movement shows respect for time, and the scattered sword battles in the film seem more urgent in comparison.

Like the comic book, the story flashes back periodically, but the only clues to the switch seem to be costume and set changes. For the non-reader, this could make it seem like Ogami is dressed as a bum during the day, then cleaning up and going home at night. This is due in part to another deviation from the original story. In the part of the movie that would encompass the story "The White Path Between the Rivers," Daigoro is an infant when his mother is cut down by the Ura-Yagyu. Though it's understandable that a director would accelerate Daigoro's age to bridge the book's time gap, it takes longer to perceive the flashback effect. Fortunately, this is easy to overlook. As for the rest of this important, contextual chunk of movie, the details are exquisite. The priest bells carried by the Yagyu ninja have a terrifying ring, the *ihai* set-up is arranged with precision, and the setting of the river duel is picture-perfect, as if that very location was the inspiration for Kojima's art.

Technically, the movie is superb. The atmosphere is airy and tense, and the camera movements lend generously to the tone of the story. The sword fights are brief and violent, with gallons of projectile blood squirting off in every direction, a fitting testimony to Kojima's intense storyboards. The bloodshed is ample, and some of the special effects are remarkable. At one point a man slowly separates into halves after a decisive stroke by Wakayama's Ogami. In some ways, the distracting gore makes up for a lack of sword skill by some of the actors; it would be difficult for all of the actors to wield swords and spears with the idealized grace of Kojima's panels. But after watching a gaggle of Hong Kong sword movies, you might feel slighted by the choreography in *Sword of Vengeance*. Another observable oddity occurs in the film's soundtrack. In a few scenes that take place during one hell of a rainstorm, the audio drops when the dialogue pauses, as if it's only raining when someone is speaking. This was likely done to reduce the overall noise, but the attenuation is very dramatic and comes off sounding absurd and unnatural.

As the backing plot for this film, Ogami is hired to infiltrate a gang of ronin and kill a corrupt lord. At this point, the story "Wings to the Bird, Fangs to the Beast" (Vol. 1) smoothly converges with the general plot. Again, the movie remains faithful to Kojima's art: the setting of the bath town is exquisite; the people cast as the prisoners to the gang of ruffians are perfectly attired and act their parts like they're reading from the book; the honorable, defiant, public sex scene is left intact, and provides the director with another of at least three opportunities to expose a woman's breasts. And, let's be blunt here for a moment, despite its wrappings of honor and skill and humanity and corruption, *Lone Wolf and Cub* also uses liberal amounts of violence and sexiness to drive interest in the story, and the film uses the same elements to entertain and engage.

In some ways, moving pictures can tease out new elements and angles, and bring a greater context to a preexisting story. When done right, comics-to-film adaptations (and vice versa) can turn out great. Unfortunately, often one medium can't afford to adapt fully to the other, but the "Baby Cart" series is a fine example of doing it right — well, at least so far. This is just the first film of the six-film series, and there are five more to watch. But since the films were all created in such a short period of time, there's a good chance they'll share similar production qualities. At any rate, for the dedicated *Lone Wolf and Cub* reader, it's simply a delight to see elements of these great stories depicted so well on film, and for those who study popular media in general, the "Baby Cart" series is both a successful comics-to-film transfer, and an exhibit of the similarities between the two.